Race and Gender in the Northern Colonies

edited by
Jan Noel

Canadian Scholars' Press Inc.　　　Toronto　　　2000

Race and Gender in the Northern Colonies

Race and Gender in the Northern Colonies
Edited by Jan Noel

First published in 2000 by
Canadian Scholars' Press Inc.
180 Bloor Street West, Suite 1202
Toronto, Ontario
M5S 2V6

Copyright © 2000 by Jan Noel, the contributing authors, and Canadian Scholars' Press. All rights reserved. No part of this publication may be reproduced in any form without written permission of the publisher, except for brief passages quoted for review purposes.

Every reasonable effort has been made to identify copyright holders. CSPI would be pleased to have errors or omissions brought to its attention.

We acknowledge the financial support of the Government of Canada through the Book Publishing Industry Development Program for our publishing activities.

Canadian Cataloguing in Publication Data

Main entry under title:

Race and gender in the northern colonies

Includes bibliographical references.
ISBN 1-55130-182-2

1. Canada — Social conditions — To 1763. 2. Canada — Social conditions — 1876–1867.* 3. New England — Social conditions. 4. Canada — History — To 1763 (New France). 5. Canada — History — 1763–1867. 6. New England — History — Colonial period, ca. 1600–1775. I. Noel, Janet.

FC161.R32 2000   971   C00-932251-5
F1032.R28 2000

Managing Editor: Ruth Bradley-St-Cyr
Marketing Manager: Susan Cuk
Production Editor: Katya Epstein
Proofreading: Trish O'Reilly, Katya Epstein
Page layout and cover design: Brad Horning
Cover Image: Detail from "Minuets of the Canadians" (from *Travels through the Canadas*, 1807) by George Heriot (1766–1844). See full image on the previous page. Reproduced by permission of the National Gallery of Canada, Ottawa.

00 01 02 03 04 05 06   6 5 4 3 2 1

Printed and bound in Canada by AGMV Marquis

Contents

Chapter One
 Introduction
  Jan Noel 1

Chapter Two
 Community to Individual: The Transformation
  of Manhood at the Turn of the Nineteenth Century
  E. Anthony Rotundo 21

Chapter Three
 Festivities, Fortitude, and Fraternalism:
  Fur Trade Masculinity and the Beaver Club, 1785–1827
  Carolyn Podruchny 53

Chapter Four
 Excerpt from *Astoria*
  Washington Irving 81

Chapter Five
 Women of New France
  Allan Greer 87

Chapter Six
　Women, Religion and Freedom in New France
　　　Terrence Crowley 101

Chapter Seven
　Tituba's Confession: The Multicultural
　Dimensions of the 1692 Salem Witch-Hunt
　　　Elaine G. Breslaw 119

Chapter Eight
　New England's Well-Ordered Society
　　　Carol Karlsen 147

Chapter Nine
　The Six Nations Indians in the Revolutionary War
　　　Barbara Graymont 177

Chapter Ten
　Political Dialogue and the Spring of Abigail's Discontent
　　　Elaine Forman Crane 191

Chapter Eleven
　The Black Population of Canada West on the
　Eve of the American Civil War: A Reassessment
　Based on the Manuscript Census of 1861
　　　Michael Wayne 209

Chapter Twelve
　Queen's Bush
　　　Benjamin Drew, ed. 231

Chapter Thirteen
　Black Parents Speak: Education in
　Mid-Nineteenth-Century Canada West
　　　Claudette Knight 257

Chapter Fourteen
American Mariners and the Rites of Manhood, 1830–1870
Margaret S. Creighton 277

Chapter Fifteen
The Sentimentalization of American Seafaring:
The Case of the New England Whalefishery, 1790–1870
Lisa Norling 303

Chapter Sixteen
'Better Than Diamonds': Sentimental Strategies
and Middle-Class Culture in Canada West
Cecilia Morgan 323

Chapter Seventeen
The Case of the Missing Midwives: A History of Midwifery
in Ontario from 1795–1900
C. Leslie Biggs 351

Chapter Eighteen
What If Mama is an Indian?
Sylvia M. Van Kirk 369

Appendix A
Thayendanegea
Barbara Graymont 383

Appendix B
Koñwatsiʔtsiaiéñni
Barbara Graymont 407

Appendix C
Distribution of the Black Population
of Canada West by Place of Residence, 1861
Michael Wayne 415

Acknowledgements

The author expresses appreciation to the editors and the manuscript assessors for their helpful suggestions; and to her students for their unfailing guidance on what works in a classroom.

Chp. 2. E. Anthony Rotundo, "Community to Individual: The Transformation of Manhood at the Turn of the Nineteenth Century," in *American Manhood*, ed. E. Anthony Rotundo (Basic Books, 1993), 10–30 and notes. Reprinted with permission from the publisher.

Chp. 3. Carolyn Podruchny, "Festivities, Fortitude, and Fraternalism: Fur Trade Masculinity and the Beaver Club, 1785–1827," in *New Faces of the Fur Trade: Selected Papers of the Seventh North American Fur Trade Conference*, ed. J. Fiske et al. (Carleton University Press, 1997), 21–42. Courtesy of Michigan State University Press.

Chp. 4. Washington Irving, "Excerpt from Astoria," in *Astoria* (Routledge and Kegan Paul, 1987), 28–33. Originally published in 1839 (now public domain).

Chp. 5. Allan Greer, "Women of New France," in *The People of New France* (University of Toronto Press, 1997), 60–75. Reprinted with permission of the publisher.

Chp. 6. Terrence Crowley, "Women, Religion and Freedom in New France," in *Women and Freedom in Early America*, ed. Larry Eldridge (New York University Press, 1997), 109–25. Reprinted with permission of the publisher.

Chp. 7. Elaine G. Breslaw, "Tituba's Confession: The Multicultural Dimensions of the 1692 Salem Witch Hunt," *Ethnohistory*, 44:3 (summer 1997), pp. 535–56. Copyright 1997, American Society for Ethnohistory. All rights reserved. Reprinted by permission of Duke University Press.

Chp. 8. Carol Karlsen, "New England's Well-Ordered Society" From *THE DEVIL IN THE SHAPE OF A WOMAN: Witchcraft in Colonial New England* by Carol F. Karlsen. Copyright © 1987 Carol F. Karlsen. Pages 190–8, 201–2, 206–11, 216–21, 246–51, 256–7, 326–8, 330, 332, 333–4, 341, 342. Used by permission of W. W. Norton & Company, Inc.

Chp. 9. Barbara Graymont, "The Six Nations Indians in the Revolutionary War," in *The Iroquois in the American Revolution: 1976 Conference Proceedings*. Rochester: Research Division of the The Rochester Museum and Science Center 1981.

Chp. 10. Elaine Forman Crane, "Political Dialogue and the Spring of Abigail's Discontent," *William and Mary Quarterly*, 3rd series, 56, no. 4 (October 1999): 744–60. Reprinted with permission from the Omohundro Institute of Early American History and Culture.

Chp. 11. Michael Wayne, "The Black Population of Canada West on the Eve of the American Civil War: A Reassessment Based on the Manuscript Census of 1861," *Histoire Sociale / Social History*, Vol. 28, no. 56 (November 1995), pp. 465–499. Reprinted with permission of the Department of History, University of Ottawa.

Chp. 12. Benjamin Drew, ed., "Queen's Bush," from *The Narratives of Fugitive Slaves in Canada* (coles Canadiana Collection, 1981), 189–205, 215–233. Public domain.

Chp. 13. Claudette Knight, "Black Parents Speak: Education in Mid-Nineteenth Century Canada West," *Ontario History* 59, no. 4 (December 1997): 269–284. Reprinted with permission from the publisher.

Chp. 14. Margaret Creighton, "American Mariners and the Rites of Manhood, 1830–1870" in *Jack Tar in History*, ed. C. Howell and R.

Twomey (Acadiensis Press, 1991), 143–163. Reprinted with permission from the University of New Brunswick.

Chp. 15. Lisa Norling, "The Sentimentalization of American Seafaring: The Case of the New England Whalefishery, 1790–1870," in *Jack Tar in History*, ed. C. Howell and R. Twomey (Acadiensis Press, 1991), 164–178. Reprinted with permission from the University of New Brunswick.

Chp. 16. Cecilia Morgan, "'Better than Diamonds': Sentimental Strategies and Middle-Class Culture in Canada West," *Journal of Canadian Studies* 32, no. 4 (winter 1998): 125–37, 140–8. Reprinted with permission from Trent University.

Chp. 17. Reprinted by permission of The Ontario Historical Society. C. Lesley Biggs, "'The Case of the Missing Midwives': A History of Midwifery in Ontario from 1795–1900" from *Ontario History*, vol. 75, no. 1 (March 1983), pp. 21–35.

Chp. 18. S. Van Kirk, "What If Mama Is an Indian?" in *The Developing West*, ed. John Foster (University of Alberta Press, 1983), 125–136. Reprinted with permission from Silvia Van Kirk, Department of History, University of Toronto.

App. A. B. Graymont, *s.v.* "Thayendanegea" in *Dictionary of Canadian Biography* (University of Toronto Press, 1966), 803–812. Reprinted with permission from the publisher.

App. B. B. Graymont, *s.v.* "Koñwatsi?tsiaiéñni" in *Dictionary of Canadian Biography* (University of Toronto Press, 1966), 416–418. Reprinted with permission from the publisher.

App. C. Michael Wayne, "The Black Population of Canada West on the Eve of the American Civil War: A Reassessment Based on the Manuscript Census of 1861," *Histoire Sociale / Social History*, Vol. 28, no. 56 (November 1995), pp. 465–499. Reprinted with permission from the publisher.

Chapter One
Introduction

Jan Noel

Even today there are areas of upstate New York and Vermont where wilderness takes over. One doesn't want to be looking for accommodation late at night while driving northward on the deserted stretch from Saratoga to Montreal. Yet, though the lonely traveller may not recognize it, the frontier between New York/New England and the territories north of the St. Lawrence and Great Lakes has always been highly permeable. Along those lakes, as Richard White so brilliantly demonstrated in his *The Middle Ground: Indians, Empires and Republics in the Great Lakes Region, 1650–1815*, natives, French, British, and American individuals and cultures met and merged though interchanges that could be profitable to all parties. In their efforts to communicate they sometimes devised bizarre mimicries or misconstructions of the other cultures that might, nonetheless, work well. There were interchanges among other groups too, such as the fires of New York's 'burnt over district' that set neighbouring Upper Canada ablaze with camp meetings, antislavery passion and preparations for the millennial Time of the End. Then, when time did not end, came the slaves themselves, to British territory when the Fugitive Slave Act meant runaways were no longer safe in the northern States. There they helped to form an Upper Canadian black population some twenty thousand strong.[1] So, firstly, we examine the border colonies because such interesting traffic passed that way. History is sadly truncated if national historians travel without passports and stop investigating when the subject reaches the 49th parallel.

The articles chosen for this collection deal for the most part with either the colonial period of American history, which began in 1607 and ended with the Revolution of 1775–1783; or with the colonial period north of the border, which spans a considerably longer period. Though Québec was established in the same decade Jamestown was, the British conquest of 1760 and then the American Revolution gave colonialism a new lease on life north of the border. British interests eventually controlled eight colonies north of the Republic (Newfoundland, New Brunswick, Nova Scotia, Prince Edward Island, Upper and Lower Canada,[2] Red River[3] and British Columbia).[4] Colonial status came to an end for most of these northerners when all but Newfoundland entered Confederation in 1867–73. Thus the book's focus is primarily on seventeenth and eighteenth century America, while consideration of French-then-British colonies to the north begins in the seventeenth century and stretches far into the nineteenth. Besides crossing boundaries, a number of the articles intertwine race and gender in complex ways. For that reason they are not placed in separate sections; they appear in an order that is roughly chronological.

Crossing national frontiers, this volume also concerns itself with theoretical frontiers. Despite the esoteric aspects of various kinds of postmodern analysis, they have nonetheless helped us see that much of what once seemed natural about the social order is more accurately seen as constructed and contingent. Below we shall look at a few examples of path-breaking analysis in the areas of race, women's history, and the history of masculinity. It is not new for Canadian historians to look southward for theoretical models to adopt or adapt. American colonial historians, possessing a plethora of university chairs and scholars as well as outstanding journals such as *The William and Mary Quarterly*, have understandably carried new forms of analysis of race and gender farther than the much smaller contingent of historians specializing in the British North American colonies north of the 49th parallel.

Even so, in the realm of historical understanding the cross-border traffic can travel two ways. If White's theory of the middle ground and American theories of masculinity offer models helpful to Canadian historians, Americans might consider the northernmost colonies as laboratories for different ways that more isolated societies could evolve with a pace and a pattern unlike anything seen in the great Republic. For example, when American newspaperman J. W. Bond visited Red River in the mid-nineteenth century, neither door locks nor land deeds were in common use. The unstinting hospitality reminded him of the customs of the American seaboard a half-century earlier.[5] The eighteenth century seaboard transposed onto nineteenth century prairie, just as though political, social, and economic revolutions had never occurred, is at the very least a tantalizing ghost, and perhaps an instructive body for study. Canadian studies of the Metis also supply numerous instances of creative cultural amalgams that extend the principles of White's *Middle Ground* far beyond the time and place he discusses.[6]

The influx of blacks after 1850 provides another case for comparison. Canadians have long prided themselves on the fact that since slavery was abolished in the British empire in 1833 (and Upper Canada had passed a bill for gradual abolition earlier, in 1793), slaves were able to find freedom "under the British lion's paw." However, rain plagues every patriotic parade sooner or later; and evidence has accumulated over the past decades that Canadian blacks — both eighteenth-century Loyalists and nineteenth-century fugitives — faced harsh discrimination. Still, several hundred Upper Canadian black men had white wives, and the majority of the black population integrated to various (and largely unknown)[7] degrees into white settlements. It seems, as the fugitive slave accounts reprinted in this book indicate, that black experiences in Canada varied. Certainly they provide rich ground for comparison with both slaves and free blacks in the States.

I

As noted above, much of what historians once considered natural about the social order is no longer viewed that way. This book addresses a period when the foundations of some enduring social constructions were laid. Valerie Babb in her book *Whiteness Visible: The Meaning of Whiteness in American Literature and Culture* argues, for example, that the desire for Amerindian land and a growing reliance on black slavery caused initial Christian/heathen distinctions to evolve into white/non-white distinctions. In the seventeenth century, white indentured servants were shipped as cargo, sold at auction, and bartered in a manner similar to slaves. However, colonial documents reveal the gradual development of the concept of whiteness as a superior category. A 1705 Virginia code, for example, forbade Negroes, mulattos, and Amerindians *even if they were Christians* from keeping white servants or slaves, signifying that the old heathen/Christian dichotomy was being superseded by one of colour. One of the purposes of emphasizing whiteness was to consolidate the very disparate European immigrants into a collectivity that defined itself by its skin. From the 1700s on, Babb writes,

> whiteness is a key to the maintenance of American nation-state identity. It replaced a cohesive Old World culture whose beliefs, traditions, and practices bound a people together over time.[8]

This created a false dualism that ignored the cultural blending and appropriation that was occurring. But it had its uses. Whiteness as a unifying device also helped mitigate class warfare between white elites and white labour as America became an economic power. It provided

> the defense of removals and a system of human enslavement at odds with American ideals; and the rationalization of "manifest destiny" and westward expansion as the United States sought to become a world power.[9]

In our own day, the very notion of race is questioned, because it uses the superficial category of colour to lump together peoples from quite disparate ethnicities, cultures, and regions of the world. While we may continue to use the conventional and well-understood term "race," it is increasingly clear that this notion, which has had so much social potency, is artificial and scientifically little more than skin deep. Its days may be numbered.

Racial concepts were certainly somewhat fluid during the lifetime of Joseph and Molly Brant. Three short pieces by Barbara Graymont in this collection introduce this leading eighteenth-century Mowhawk Valley family that enjoyed high status and intimate bonds with whites at a time when the colour bar was still relatively low. Wealthy upstate landowner and Indian Agent William Johnson was Irish, a "race" still often referred to as "black" by Englishmen of the day. Johnson saw honour and utility, not disgrace, in allying himself with an illustrious native line. He sent Joseph to private school in Connecticut. Regarding his relations with Joseph's older sister Molly, Graymont writes that this spirited woman first attracted Johnson's attention with her horsemanship. She went on to bear at least eight children by him. Graymont writes that:

> Although Johnson referred to her in his will as his "prudent and faithfull housekeeper" ... there is a persistent tradition that they were married according to Indian ceremony ... Johnson treated her with every respect, furnished her and the children with every comfort and luxury befitting an upper class family, and provided generously for them in his will.[10]

Molly also brought to the relationship the authority of an Iroquois matron, a position singled out by anthropologists as exemplifying high female status. After the alliance was sealed, Joseph distinguished himself as a Loyalist warrior, and Molly as a Loyalist agent among the New York tribes. In urging her people to support the British she was, according to agent Daniel Claus, so effective that "one word from her goes farther with them than a thousand from any white Man without Exception ... " Commander Alexander Fraser added that "Molly Brants [sic] influence over them [at Carleton Island]...is far superior to that of all their Chiefs put together."[11] The Brants' skin colour did not banish them to the political and social periphery, particularly during the Revolutionary period when (as Graymont shows in her article on the Iroquois) Six Nations allegiance was so hotly sought by two armies. Their case illustrates (as do so many of the articles in this volume) that race and gender are contingent categories, subject to mediation by class, ethnicity, place, and circumstance.

The middle ground was nonetheless shrinking rapidly. At war's end, Joseph Brant's dream of a native territory in America was shattered when the British government refused to back the aspirations of its native allies at the peace table. Loyal Iroquois had to settle for the lesser prize of territories in Upper Canada. Joseph, apparently recognizing how the ground had shifted towards European culture, made a controversial decision to allow white farmers to settle on the new Mohawk lands on the theory that they would instruct the natives in the appropriate new ways. Brant himself lived the life of a squire in Burlington. His sister saw the way ahead in becoming a lady of good works in the house the government granted her in Kingston, and in negotiating the delicate business of marrying her daughters to white gentlemen.

The position of natives deteriorated in the nineteenth century. While their support was essential to the British victories in the War of 1812 at Detroit and Michilimackinac, such strategic importance ended with that war. They also faced the insidious influence of heightened, "scientific" concepts about race and about the dangers of miscegenation. Along with their exposure to these hardening racial theories, Easterners grew up with the sight of demoralized and impoverished native groups living on the periphery of settler societies. The newcomers could not, A. S. Morton once explained, comprehend or accept the existence of a thriving mixed blood middle class when they stumbled upon it in the isolated Red River colony. University of Toronto historian Sylvia Van Kirk in her *Many Tender Ties': Women in Fur Trade Society in Western Canada, 1670–1830* gave concrete evidence of westerly 'middle ground' by demonstrating the numerous, often felicitous and enduring, unions of traders and natives in the Hudson Bay Company's domains. In her classic study of the Metis family of Scottish fur trader Alexander Ross, which is reprinted here, Van Kirk turned her attention to the progeny of one of these "country marriage," showing the dilemmas they faced as the Metis colony of Red River metamorphosed into the Canadian frontier town of Winnipeg.

Van Kirk shows that even Red River's most talented native son, who could garner degrees and honours at Eastern colleges and newspapers, could not surmount the insidious colour bar erected as the white immigration of the 1850s and deepening racial discrimination cast its pall on the remote outposts of the Northwest. James Ross retreated to a traditional form of male tavern camaraderie during the 1869 uprising. However, drinking patterns acceptable in leading Canadian politicians such as John A. Macdonald were condemned in Ross as "Indian drinking." Ross believed this was part of the reason he failed to receive the expected government appointment in the new province, sidelining this most distinguished native son as the new order emerged. Facing exclusion, many Metis left the colony and migrated westward.

Turning to another "race," blacks did not enjoy even the dubious benefits of European romanticism about "noble savages." "I should have suffered often the pain of being skinned alive could it make me white," one late nineteenth century Nova Scotia black declared.[12] The readings reprinted here deal with blacks in Canada West. Michael Wayne attempts, in his study of the 1861 manuscript census, to place the discussion on sound empirical footing. He challenges long-held notions about the group that sought safety in Canada after the passage of the Fugitive Slave Act in 1850. Estimates of this group's population have traditionally been about 40,000, but Wayne's revision cuts that number by up to a half.

The next reading moves from the census to the settlers themselves. The accounts of fugitives in the Queen's Bush (wild land east of Lake Huron) were collected by the Boston school principal and writer Benjamin Drew when he went from cabin to cabin in the area in 1855. While it is true Drew was trying to counter a recent defense of slavery by another Boston author, he was aware of concerns about the authenticity of fugitive accounts. He strove for accurate transcription of the narratives and claimed to make "less than a dozen verbal alterations" in editing, though he clearly did not resist the educator's passion to standardize grammar and syntax. There is only a small sampling here, for Drew interviewed 113 blacks in Windsor, Chatham, London, Dresden, and many other settlements. Drew's narratives have been called "the most comprehensive antebellum account of what slavery meant to the Negro. And...no less valuable in its depiction of fugitive life in the North and in Canada."[13] There are harrowing accounts of slavery and escape, and reactions to the new homeland that ranged from bitterness over land swindles to John Little's ringing call to blacks to abandon servile jobs and "Go into the backwoods of Queen Victoria's dominions, and you can secure an independent support."

Claudette Knight's 1997 study, "Black Parents Speak," shows that segregation persisted: white reformers were wary about alienating the first generation of white public school attendees by allowing blacks to sit in the same classrooms. Though conceding the justice of the blacks' cause, they bowed to local prejudices. Knight's article captures the palpable discomfort of officials who wanted to believe blacks found fair treatment in British realms but found the cost of delivering it too high. Her interpretation also lends support to the contention of James W. St. G. Walker that

> The Underground Railroad era was a positive moment in Upper Canada's past, for Canada did indeed offer a haven to American slaves ... [but it] also fostered a myth: that the North Star led not just out of slavery but into freedom, equality, and full participation in Canadian life ...[14]

Knight shows how persistent some black parents were in seeking the schooling that had been denied under slavery. The finding echoes those of other writers on the fugitives' determination to secure a range of services and institutions in Canada West.[15]

II

Turning now to the articles on gender in the collection, we begin with those on women's history. The astonishing outpouring of scholarship, initially inspired by feminist movements in the late twentieth century, continues to enlarge our view of the past. Feminist historians have taught us that gender roles were constructed and, in a patriarchal world, hierarchical. They have proved beyond doubt that history's battles, heroics, and ignominies, its progress, its diplomacy, its resistances, and its economic and intellectual breakthroughs occurred in parlours, sewing rooms, hospitals, church groups and convents as well as in the more public spaces of male-centred history. Historians of women have shown that daily life is 'political' too. They have (to paraphrase Alan Petersen) shown it possible to write non-patriarchal history that represents the world from the point of view of women and their interests.

One product of this rich scholarship has been vigorous international debate about precisely when, and indeed *whether*, early modern or *ancien régime* women began to face increasing restriction due to their sex. As long ago as 1919 Alice Clark was documenting in her *Working Life of Women in the Seventeenth Century* the decline of women's independence and occupational range as that century progressed. Leonore Davidoff and Catherine Hall's *Family Fortunes: Men and Women of the English Middle Class, 1780–1850* found women still active in family businesses in the eighteenth century but commonly displaced by all-male partnerships before 1850. Numerous studies of various settings suggest pre-Victorian or pre-industrial women sometimes had a wider occupational range and more equality with men, due to factors such as home-based production, aristocratic or religious status that overrode gender restrictions, or frontier conditions. This might take such humble form as "equality of the fields," where peasants of both sexes shared similar status and similarly heavy outdoor work; or such exalted form as ladies ruling courts and manors. English historians such as Amanda Vickery and Robert Shoemaker have recently challenged what Shoemaker calls "the prevailing view that women had significantly greater economic and political opportunities in pre-industrial England."[16] Historians of France continue to measure the efficacy of the seventeenth-century Querelle des Femmes and the eighteenth-century Revolution in silencing women of the courts, streets, convents and salons.

The debate extends to colonial history too. Elaine Forman Crane's 1998 *Ebb Tide in New England: Women, Seaports and Social Change 1630-1800* questions Laurel Thatcher Ulrich's portrayal of domestic and subordinate "Goodwives" who at most might temporarily assume broader responsibility in the capacity of "deputy husbands."[17] Given women's demographic preponderance in New England seaports, Crane questions the applicability of the "deputy husband" concept to the many who made their own way economically as spinsters and widows. Moreover, Crane observes mid-seventeenth century prominence of women in some New England congregations as voting members, at times outspoken ones. There were also frequent female transactions in mercantile account books at this time, but fewer thereafter.[18] It appears that New England women may have slid down from original high ground.

Similar debate enlivens the history of New France. My own work has made the case that legal protections, a shortage of women, the social contributions of convents, and the frequent absences of men for war or trade made women throughout the colony's history a favoured group, particularly in comparison to nineteenth century Canadian women, whose property rights and occupational range were narrower. Studies by Lilianne Plamondon, Kathryn Young, and Josette Brun document major commercial activity by colonial women. Turning to the lower, more numerous ranks, Yves Landry measures fertility and lifespans to show that immigrant filles du roi prospered relative to counterparts who remained in France.[19]

There is, however, a darker view. It looms large, for example, in discussion of writers such as Eleanor Leacock and Carol Devens of the power of seventeenth-century Jesuits to impose patriarchal practices on Montagnais-Naskapi and Huron women,[20] who were baffled by the strange notion that wives should submit to their husbands and men should direct the farming. It also emerges when one stresses the formal precedence of men in European political and legal frameworks, as do John Bosher[21] and Allan Greer. Greer's carefully measured overview of women in New France is reprinted here.

Terrence Crowley, for his part, believes the debate should revolve not around general assessments of the position of women in New France but around specific groups. His contribution to this collection examines the position of nuns. In contrast to male religious orders, they received many colonial recruits and served the populace through their hospitals and schools. Crowley asserts that the "prominent role played by Roman Catholic women in French colonial life contrasted sharply with the situation in British possessions to the south ... [and] allowed them to make a vital contribution to colonial development."[22] The depiction is consistent with the intelligent and forceful convent administrators discussed in the scholarship of Micheline D'Allaire and Marguerite Jean.[23]

The selections on New France are followed by several on women in New England. Even without the benefit of convents, the Puritans produced their own luminaries, Anne Hutchinson, the preacher, and Anne Bradstreet, the poet. The idea, seen in Crane's work, that second or third generations found patriarchal traditions reasserting themselves against women in churches, the economy, and before the law, is one that also shapes Carol Karlsen's influential analysis of Salem witchcraft. In the villages of rural Massachusetts where inheritance of land was a contentious issue, the growing numbers of widows and spinsters began to find their claims overridden. Our excerpt from *The Devil in the Shape of a Woman* gives a sample of Karlsen's skill in untangling the dense web of ecclesiastical and legal practice. The evidence leads her to conclude that the strange outbursts by young women at Salem were psychosocial reactions to their narrowing options. Karlsen's work has the additional merit, as Edmund S. Morgan wrote, of uncovering "the assumptions, explicit and implicit, that governed everyday relationships of men and women in early New England."[24]

Elaine Breslaw's suggestive article, "Tituba's Confession," is also included here because it adds a racial dimension to Karlsen's gendered interpretation of the happenings at Salem in 1692. Tituba was a Carib Indian servant whose stories set the witch hunt in motion. She may have used Amerindian religious figures, such as a devilish man from afar with powers of possession, to explain the strange behaviour of the Salem girls. Along with native influence, the author's other theme is female agency. Tituba accused a distant figure in order to protect herself and those around her. Unfortunately, this lifted the bizarre behaviour out of the realm of village gossip and precipitated a theological crisis in which Puritan divines felt they must intervene. This set the participants on their deadly path towards court and gallows.

In New England a century later, Abigail Adams was famous for three words she wrote to her husband John in the early days of the American Revolution. Mindful that the Republic would stand in need of a new code of laws, she implored him (and his fellow Patriots) to "Remember the ladies." Elaine Forman Crane's analysis in this collection reveals Abigail drawing on a veritable library of political theorists and philosophers. Lacking a feminist circle, being dependent on John, and governed by her own sense of the limits of well-bred wifely conduct, Adams acquiesced when John dismissed with a joke his own refusal to consider advancing the political rights of half the population. Crane's account explains why Adams was able to articulate such a plea but then quietly bear its rebuff. It brings home to the reader the futility of feminist consciousness without networks such as would coalesce a generation later around abolition and prohibition. It also contributes to the ongoing discussion of gender and the American Revolution.[25] The impotence of Adams contrasts sharply with the power of command enjoyed by her Revolutionary contemporary Molly Brant. But, as we have seen, the days when natives (male *or* female) could sway empires were numbered.

Studies of gender in Upper Canada (1791–1867) turn to characteristic nineteenth century concerns such as social and scientific reform. Cecilia Morgan in her article "'Better than Diamonds': Sentimental Strategies and Middle-Class Culture in Canada West," reprinted in this volume, sorts out numerous strands of gender to reveal how complex the codes were. Reformers of both sexes might undermine conservative notions of order by appealing to higher truths of the heart. "Sentimental appeals based on selfless maternity," Morgan writes, "evoked the highest moral values, possessing a rationality, logic and sincerity superseding the supposedly logical reasoning of courtrooms and juries." In causes such as temperance and antislavery, this language of feeling reached "beyond the individual to justify the mobilization of middle-class men and especially women, producing a consciousness that went beyond tears to the moral indignation underpinning social and moral reform movements … " Yet Morgan also shows that other reformers, such as crusading black journalist Mary Ann

Shadd, could take an alternative path, cutting through the rhetoric to lash out at conventions of gender *and* colour.

Another nuanced presentation of Upper Canadian gender is found in the work of Leslie Biggs, whose "Case of the Missing Midwives" is also found in this volume. Biggs shows the gradual elimination of midwifery when the business of delivering babies was turned over to educated male professionals (and women barred from acquiring such education). Biggs' findings are consistent with the influential work of Marjorie Griffin Cohen, whose book shows a male takeover of other skilled occupations of rural women as Upper Canada's staples economy developed.[26] Yet, as Biggs shows, this was not always a clearly drawn battle of the sexes, and midwives had their male defenders in the medical establishment and the press.

All the parallels we have sketched suggest that much can be gained by removing the national blinders from the study women's history. Davidoff and Hall's *Family Fortunes* has been a beacon in that regard. That book's impact on international gender history is reminiscent of the impact that E. P. Thompson's *Making of the English Working Class* once had on working class history. The period under review calls out for comparison of European, British, American, and colonial findings to illuminate (or question) the "renfermement des femmes" in various parts of the world between the reigns of Elizabeth I and Victoria. One hopes this collection, with its juxtaposition of articles on women of New France, New England, and Upper Canada, will be a useful step in that direction.[27]

III

This brings us to the book's third subject, emerging notions of masculinity in colonial times. Historical writing on masculinity builds on the feminist premise that gender is contingent, changing over time in relation to other aspects of the culture in which it is situated. Harry Brod, one of the leading theorists of the new "men's studies," observes that

> Like women's studies, men's studies aims at the emasculation of patriarchal ideology's masquerade as knowledge ... While *seemingly* about men, traditional scholarship's treatment of generic man as the human norm in fact systematically

excludes from consideration what is unique to men *qua* men ... [Men's] studies situate masculinities as objects of study on a par with femininities, instead of elevating them to universal norms.[28]

Many such writings incorporate "the fundamental feminist insight that gender is a system of power and not just a set of stereotypes or observable differences between men and women."[29] There has also been a general recognition that that term masculini*ties* is appropriate. Various kinds of 'hegemonic masculinity' conferred privileges on some, but inflicted anguish and punishment on other definable groups of men who did not share the dominant values.

British and Australian writers were particularly prominent as this field took shape in the 1980s. Among British scholars, Victor Seidler has traced modern ideas of masculinity back to the Protestant Reformation, appending the idea of repressed/repressive masculinity to Weber's theories of Protestantism and the rise of capitalism. Seidler also discusses ways the Scientific Revolution, the Enlightenment, and the philosopher Immanuel Kant associated rationality and a cerebral form of morality with masculinity, all helping to divorce masculine ideals from nature and the emotions.[30] Davidoff and Hall are joined by British historian John Tosh[31] in presenting some surprisingly domestic early nineteenth century fathers who, even if they *were* hard-driving entrepreneurs, fed their sick children by hand, and loved gardening and sentimental poetry. In America, Donald Yacovone[32] found abolitionists and firemen exchanging tender and evidently asexual male endearments. E. Anthony Rotundo, whose work is included in this book, was one of the first to synthesize the history of manhood in America from Puritan times to modern ones. His well written book has provided a general framework, allowing other writers to construct more specific histories — of fatherhood and fraternal organizations, for example. Rotundo's chapter "Community to Individual" is reprinted here because it characterizes the Puritan patriarch of colonial times, who felt called upon to give kindly counsel and mild correction to servants and family. He compares that figure with the aggressive nineteenth century middle-class male given over to work and the pursuit of wealth, whose wife assumed the mantle of virtuous guardian of the common good. In his book's introduction, Rotundo adds to the picture railway promoter

Henry Poor, who claimed work was the source of a man's self respect, and worked so hard his wife alleged he "shoot[s] around like a rocket."[33] Rotundo explains the economic changes that by 1800 called for less community-minded, more materialistic and individualistic males, better equipped than Puritan patriarchs to seize frontier opportunities to the west and commercial ones to the east.

Likewise, sailors and whalers, as the two articles by Margaret Creighton and Lisa Norling show, gradually adopted such standards, with some nautical variations. Creighton's study of seamen suggests the more a man's work resembled a woman's the lower its status. Thus, aboard ship, the black sailor was consigned to cooking, since there were no women. The men also developed rituals for recreating home life at sea. Whaling, Norling argues, was redefined from a family occupation in colonial times to a masculine one thereafter. So, at sea, women's participation tended to shrink to merely symbolic presence on mastheads and in songs. Given the international character of seafaring, these two innovative American studies may serve as models for gendered study of British North American mariners too.

While Canadian writing on pre-Confederation masculinity is a field still in its infancy, another article in this collection shows what a promising start has been made. Carolyn Podruchny captures Montréal's fur trade barons who aped aristocrats with their fine dining and ruffled attire. She argues that they were seeking respectability and exercising their masculinity by excluding women. Yet there was still a whiff of Canadian wilderness about these urban gentlemen. They nostalgically recalled — and after the wine flowed, re-enacted at their banquets — canoeing days of yore. As for the working class men who actually did the wilderness paddling, the excerpt from Washington Irving's *Astoria* captures the New York reaction to these figures when they journeyed south to work for John Jacob Astor in 1810. Their conviviality contrasted with the driven and acquisitive individualism identified by Rotundo as the wave of the future in post-Revolutionary America.

In the 1830s, the powerful presence of Hudson's Bay Company Governor George Simpson would begin to impose the masculine virtues of Anglo-America on the western trade, curtailing the use of alcohol and insisting on greater efficiency and longer work weeks even at the Company's isolated posts.[34] In the East, the voyageur had by then been reduced to a tourist attraction on the St. Lawrence River, who risked disappointing expectant passengers when he knew only smutty songs or French ones. Romantic tourists had to sing Thomas Moore's immortal Canadian Boat Song for themselves while the wilderness hero mutely paddled.[35]

Comparative studies of colonial societies north and south of the 49th parallel are all too rare. Because the past three decades have produced an unusually rich array of articles on colonial gender and race on both sides of the border, that seems a particularly useful place to start the discussion. We hope readers can use the collection to compare themes and regions as well as methodologies, which vary greatly even in the small sampling here. Apart from their comparative value the fifteen articles and the two nineteenth-century accounts offer insight into formative moments in the history of colonial villages, seaports, and frontiers. They reveal the northern colonies in an evolution nearly three centuries long, encompassing the human past on both sides of the famous line.

NOTES

1. See Michael Wayne's article reprinted in this volume, "The Black Population of Canada West on the Eve of the American Civil War: A Reassessment Based on the Manuscript Census of 1861." The author by various calculations estimates the census figure of 17,053 might be boosted as high as 23,000 to account for under-reporting. This revises the traditional estimate of forty thousand blacks sharply downward. Wayne also makes the case that fugitive slaves were a minority of Canada West's black population in 1861, and he indicates that only about twenty per cent returned to the States after the Civil War.
2. In 1841 these two colonies were officially renamed Canada West and Canada East (though the terms Upper and Lower Canada continued in common use). In 1841 the two were also formally united as the Province of Canada with a single Assembly, though they continued to pursue largely distinctive courses, and some important legislation continued to apply to only one or the other.
3. Red River was under the control of the Hudson's Bay Company rather than the British government per se, until its sale to Canada in 1869.

4. Created by the amalgamation of Vancouver Island colony and the mainland in 1866.
5. J. W. Bond, *Minnesota and Its Resources* (New York: 1853) 292. See also my *Canada Dry* (Toronto: University of Toronto Press, 1995), chap. 14.
6. See for example Sylvia Van Kirk, *Many Tender Ties: Women in Fur Trade Society, 1670–1870* (Winnipeg: Watson and Dwyer, 1980); and Gerhard Ens, *Homeland to Hinterland: The Changing Worlds of the Red River Métis in the Nineteenth Century* (Toronto: University of Toronto Press, 1996).
7. Wayne, "The Black Population of Canada West," (see note 1) 70, suggests that more study of the majority of blacks who coexisted in white communities might revise current views of the extent of discrimination: "...we cannot even say with certainty that most blacks shared the assumption of both nineteenth-century whites and present-day historians that race mattered more than class, gender, religious affiliation or nationality in defining who they were or in determining their place in Canadian society."
8. Valerie Babb, *Whiteness Visible* (New York: New York University Press, 1998), 37.
9. Babb (see note 7), 3. For another fascinating discussion of American concepts of blackness see Barbara E. Lacey, "Visual Images of Blacks in Early American Imprints," *William and Mary Quarterly* 3rd series, 53, no. 1 (January 1996).
10. "Koñwatsitsiaiéñni .... Mary Brant", *Dictionary of Canadian Biography* vol. 4 (Toronto: University of Toronto Press, 1966), 417, reprinted in this collection.
11. "Koñwatsitsiaiéñni," (see note 9), 417–18.
12. Cited in Robin W. Winks, *The Blacks in Canada, A History*, 2nd ed. (Montreal, McGill-Queen's University Press, 1997), 114.
13. Tilden G. Edelstein, "Introduction" to *The Refugee: A Northside View of Slavery* (Don Mills: Addison-Wesley, 1969), xxii.
14. James W. St. G. Walker, *Racial Discrimination in Canada: The Black Experience*, Canadian Historical Association Booklet No. 41 (Ottawa: Canadian Historical Association, 1985), 6.
15. See, for example, Shirley Yee, "Gender Ideology and Black Women as Community-Builders in Ontario, 1850–70" in *Rethinking Canada*, ed. V. Strong-Boag and A. C. Fellman (Toronto: Oxford, 1997), 136–48;

and the collection by Peggy Bristow et al., *"We're Rooted Here and They Can't Pull Us Up": Essays in African Canadian Women's History* (Toronto: University of Toronto Press, 1994).
16. Robert Shoemaker, *Gender in English Society 1650–1850* (London: Longman, 1998); Amanda Vickery, "Golden Age to Separate Spheres? A Review of the Categories and Chronology of English Women's History," *Historical Journal* 36 (1993).
17. Laurel T. Ulrich, *Good Wives: Image and Reality in the Lives of Women in Northern New England, 1650–1750* (New York: Knopf, 1982).
18. A similar interpretation emerges in a number of the articles in Laura McCall and Donald Yacovone, *A Shared Experience: Men, Women and the History of Gender* (New York: New York University Press, 1998). Fluid gender boundaries are there portrayed as extending into the first half of the nineteenth century, a period the editors characterize as "Before the Fall."
19. Yves Landry, *Orphelines en France, pionnières au Canada: les filles du roi au XVIIe siècle* (Montreal: 1992); Lilianne Plamondon, "Une femme d'affaires en Nouvelle-France: Marie-Anne Barbel, Veuve Fornel", *Revue d'histoire de l'Amerique francais* 31 (September 1977); Kathryn Young, *Kin, Commerce, Community: Merchants in the Port of Quebec, 1717–1745* (New York: Lang, 1995); Josette Brun, "Les femmes d'affaires en Nouvelle-France au 18e siècle: le cas de l'Ile Royale," *Acadiensis* 27, no. 1 (Autumn 1997).
20. Eleanor Leacock, "Montagnais Women and the Jesuit Program for Colonization," in *Women and Colonization: Anthropological Perspectives*, ed. Mona Etienne and Eleanor Leacock (N.Y.: Praeger, 1982); Carol Devens, "Separate Confrontations: Gender as a Factor in Indian Adaptation to European Colonization in New France," *American Quarterly* 38, no. 3.
21. John Bosher, "The Family in New France," in *In Search of the Visible Past*, ed. Barry Gough (Waterloo, Ont., Wilfrid Laurier University Press), 1976.
22. Terrence Crowley, "Women, Religion and Freedom in New France" in *Women and Freedom in Early America*, ed. Larry Eldridge (New York University Press: 1997), 110–11.
23. Micheline D'Allaire, *L'Hôpital-Général de Québec 1692–1764* (Montreal: Fides, 1977); Marguerite Jean, *Evolution des communautés religeuses des femmes au Canada de 1639 à nos jours* (Montreal: Fides, 1977).

24. This quote was included in the cover promotion for *The Devil in the Shape of a Woman* (New York: Norton, 1987).
25. A recent contribution that also summarizes the literature is Rosemarie Zagarri, "The Rights of Man and Woman in Post-Revolutionary America," *William and Mary Quarterly*, 3rd ser., 55, no. 2 (April 1998).
26. Marjorie Griffin Cohen, *Women's Work, Markets and Economic Development in Nineteenth Century Ontario* (University of Toronto Press, 1988). See especially chap. 5.
27. Larry Eldridge made an earlier contribution to comparative history by including two articles on New France (including the Crowley one reprinted here) in his edited collection *Women and Freedom in Early America* (New York University Press, 1997). See also Jacob Cooke, ed., *Encyclopedia of the North American Colonies*, 3 vols. (New York: Scribner's, 1993), with its entries on Gender for New France, New Spain and the American colonies. Another burgeoning approach to comparative race and gender history takes an imperial perspective. See, for example, Anne McClintock, *Imperial Leather: Race, Gender and Sexuality in the Colonial Contest* (New York: Routledge, 1995). Antoinette Burton, Nupur Chaudhuri, Catherine Hall, and Canadian historian Ruth Roach Pierson have also begun to mine this rich vein.
28. Harry Brod, "The Case for Men's Studies" in *The Making of Masculinities*, H. Brod (Boston: Allen and Unwin, 1987), 40.
29. Harry Brod and Michael Kaufman, "Introduction" in *Theorizing Masculinities*, ed.Brod Kaufman (Thousand Oaks, Calif.: Sage Publications, 1994), 2.
30. Victor Seidler, *Rediscovering Masculinity: Reason, Language, and Sexuality* (London: Routledge, 1989).
31. John Tosh, "Authority and Nurture in Middle-Class Fatherhood: The Case of Early and Mid-Victorian England," *Gender and History* 8, no. 1 (April 1996).
32. Donald Yacovone, "Abolitionists and the Language of Fraternal Love" in *Meanings for Manhood: Constructions of Masculinity in Victorian America*, ed. Mark Carnes and Clyde Griffen Chicago (University of Chicago Press, 1990). See also Yacovone's article in *A Shared Experience* (see note 17).
33. E. Anthony Rotundo, *American Manhood: Transformations in Masculinity from the Revolution to the Modern Era* (New York: Basic Books, 1993), 4.

34. See J. Noel, *Canada Dry* (Toronto: University of Toronto Press, 1995), chap. 13.
35. See Patricia Jasen, *Wild Things: Nature, Culture and Tourism in Ontario 1790–1914* (Toronto: University of Toronto Press, 1995), 64–66.

Chapter Two
Community to Individual: The Transformation of Manhood at the Turn of the Nineteenth Century

E. Anthony Rotundo

Anyone who tries to learn about manhood before 1800 encounters a world of meaning far different from that of the twentieth century. Early New Englanders rarely used words like *manhood* and *masculinity*. In fact, the significance of gender was not a topic of constant discussion, as it would be in later years. Still, the lack of an obsession with gender before 1800 did not mean an absence of ideas on the subject. People recorded their ideas of what it meant to be a good man, and they were influenced by their own religious texts and by new ideas pouring in from abroad. In their laws and in the enforcement of discipline, they revealed many assumptions about the meaning of manhood. Distinctions between men and women helped to order society in colonial New England, and played a notable part in the systems of belief that flourished before 1800.

COMMUNAL MANHOOD

If there was one position in society that expressed the essence of manhood for early New Englanders, it was man's role as head of the household. Every person — young or old, male or female — had to find a place within a family, but the family head could only be a male. In time, most men could head a household, and colonial New Englanders learned to associate males with authority through their constant contact with men in that role. The two other institutions at the heart of the society — church and state — were also governed solely by men, but those figures of authority might be distant. It was the man at the head of the family who embodied God's authority in the daily life of each person.[1]

Why did men hold this position? Why, in other words, was authority male and not female? The Puritans who shaped New England's institutions and customs built their society on their religious beliefs. Their God was a man, and when He created humankind, He made a man first and then made woman as a helpmeet. Puritans read in their scriptures that God said to Eve, "Thy desire shall be to thy husband, and he shall rule over thee."[2] And they knew as well that woman, not man, had started the fall from grace. Thus, the Puritans, who believed that God arranged all living things in rank order, placed man above woman and second only to God.[3]

When the men of early New England explained their superiority in earthly terms, they spoke of their greater strength of body and mind. In a world where all but a few people lived by the work of their hands, men's physical strength seemed to qualify them better than women to support the household. And since men were also credited with greater strength of mind, they seemed more fit than women to make wise decisions in governing a family.[4]

Eighteenth-century New Englanders elaborated these distinctions between the sexes. They divided human passions into those that were typically male and those that were quintessentially female. Ambition, assertiveness, and a lust for power and fame were thought to be "manly" passions. A taste for luxury, submissiveness, and a love of idle pleasures were considered "effeminate" passions. But whether a man was struggling with manly or effeminate passions, he was assumed to have greater reason than woman — and it was reason that helped a person to govern the passions. To New Englanders of the seventeenth and eighteenth centuries, men's powers of mind suited them better than women to head a household.[5] Because most males eventually occupied this role and few females ever could, governing a family meant participation in a division of power by gender. To head a household, for all intents and purposes, was to be a man.

To understand why this social trust — this male prerogative — was so important, one must understand the nature of the family in New England before 1800. The family, to start with, was the primary unit of production. Farms, shops, and great mercantile firms were all family enterprises. The family also served as the fundamental unit of society. Early Americans — and men in particular — reckoned their status in great measure by the family in which they were born. Even as a man's family helped to locate him within the ordered ranks of society, it placed him in historical time as well, for his family linked him to generations of ancestors and descendants.[6]

In the view of the community, the head of the household was the embodiment of all its members. The basic unit of the political system was the family, and the head of the family was its link to community governance. He was the household's voting representative in public councils, and public officers held him responsible for the behavior and welfare of those in his care. In addition, the family was viewed as "a little commonwealth," which meant not only that it was the government writ small but that the government was the family writ large. The head of the household set the standard of firmness and vigilant concern by which public rulers were measured.[7] He was also responsible for the godliness of his family, leading them in daily worship. To head a household, in sum, was to anchor the status system, preserve the political order, provide a model of government, sustain piety, ensure productive activity, and maintain the economic support of one's dependents.

Even with so much authority vested in one person, the household was not governed by tyranny. It was a patriarchy, the rule of a family by a father figure. Ideally, a father loved each member of his household, but even where such love did not exist, the head of the Puritan household was constrained in his actions by the duties he owed to each person in his charge. In particular, a man's wife — though not his equal — was his partner, and some of his power was readily delegated to her. But to all members — sons and daughters, servants, boarders, and aged kin — the head of the family owed benevolent rule, and he could expect to answer to his community if he failed badly in this or any other duty.[8]

Indeed, *duty* was a crucial word for manhood, as it was for New England society itself. Every social relationship was organized as a conjunction of roles (father-son, husband-wife, neighbor-neighbor, for example), and each role was governed by a set of duties owed to others.

The importance of these obligations showed through in everyday language. Even grown men signed letters to their parents, "Your dutiful son," and people wrote constantly of their "Duty, to God and Man."[9]

Sociologists tell us that any society is organized by roles, but some societies balance the importance of social roles by paying great attention to the distinctive qualities of each individual in ordering human relationships. Colonial New England was not such a place. There, people thought of their world as "an organic social order in which rights and responsibilities were reciprocal and in which terms like *individuality* or *self-reliance* had little place."[10] A person's identity was bound up in the performance of social roles, not in the expression of self.

Every colonial New Englander, regardless of sex, put a high premium on the fulfillment of duty; but in a place and time where men wielded the social authority, they especially were judged by their contribution to the larger community. Before 1800, New Englanders saw a close link between manhood and "social usefulness." A mother could boast that her little son's growing integrity and honor were "good foundations upon which one may reasonably build hopes of future usefulness." Likewise, a study of heroes in magazine articles of the late eighteenth century has shown that a man's "publick usefulness" was a crucial measure of his worth. Men who carried out their duties to family and community were men to admire.[11]

The performance of social obligation often required a man to act against his own will. To carry out such obligations, a man had to learn submission to superiors, to fate, to duty itself. The Christian faith of New Englanders was a stern, effective teacher of submission. It enabled acquiescence in the will of God and resignation to the "pleasure of the Sovereign of the Universe."[12] Submission was more than a Christian virtue, though. It was also a habit of thought well suited to life in a society of rank order. So young people deferred to old, sons yielded to fathers, women submitted to men, and men of all ages acquiesced in their social responsibilities. Moreover, society was arranged by class as well as age and gender. People of the upper orders expected their inferiors to defer to them, so a man bowed to his superiors just as he submitted to God's will.[13]

But no man, however well placed, could deal cruelly with his inferiors. Every man was expected to treat dependents with kindness and restraint.

Life in a New England community involved delicate balances, maintained at an intimate distance. People placed a high value on personal qualities that kept social relations smooth. A man was admired if he was gentle and amiable. This quality demanded self-restraint and placed a tremendous emotional burden on the details of social behavior, but the effort was considered worthy. If a man could cultivate a high regard among his fellows while minimizing conflict, he became a valuable asset in a close-knit society.[14]

The ideal man, then, was pleasant, mild-mannered, and devoted to the good of the community. He performed his duties faithfully, governed his passions rationally, submitted to his fate and to his place in society, and treated his dependents with firm but affectionate wisdom. Pious, dutiful, restrained — such a man seems almost too good to survive on this earth.

In fact, it is not clear that the men who conjured up his image expected him to exist in pure form. He was, after all, a composite of ideal traits, a collection of virtues that men yearned to bring to life. And, when one reads the descriptions of his character, one senses the lurking fear of a wholly different set of male traits. When the minister William Bentley sketched his vision of "the good man," he filled it with statements about what this paragon did *not* do: he was "without dissimulation," "pure from guile," "easily dissuaded from revenge." A physician named Alexander Anderson, reading a biography of Gustavus Vase, explained his deep respect for the man in this way: "I admire his resignation — a very useful virtue — I speak from the want of it myself."[15]

Behind the admiration for the virtuous, socially useful man, then, lay the fear of a different kind of person — a man who was contentious and willful, who stood up and fought for his own interests. This defiant behavior frightened men who wanted to believe in a corporate ideal. They were alarmed when selfish impulses were set loose around them, and they were even more alarmed to know that those same impulses were at work inside themselves.

From the earliest days of Puritan settlement, self-assertion played a crucial pail in the daily life of New England. The very duties that demanded submission to some people and some social expectations required action against others. Whether the head of a household was laying claim to a scarce resource on behalf of his family or chastising a child for idleness, self-assertion was needed for the performance of a man's social duties. Moreover, a new society on a different continent presented men with endless opportunities for personal gain. The man who was willing to vent his "manly passions" — ambition, avarice, assertiveness — the best chance of exploiting those opportunities. Some historians have described the operation of individual initiative from the moment of Puritan settlement. There were many acceptable outlets for this sort of initiative in the seventeenth century. The constant creation of new towns on the New England frontier — while in part a response to overcrowding in older settlements — could also represent an assertion of economic ambition or even a set of ideas at odds with the orthodoxies of earlier communities. Meanwhile, personal wealth was admitted, along with age, sex, and birth, as a determinant of social rank in the Puritan colonies. The development of a small but visible merchant class in coastal towns also testified to a certain tolerance for individual ambition. And the near constant state of warfare with the native peoples of the region enabled men to express their manly passions to the fullest — and often bloodiest — extent with the enthusiastic support of their society.[16]

It is worth noting that this tolerance of certain forms of self-assertion was extended to men more than to women. To be sure, women performed certain male duties as needed, they carried on their own informal networks of trade, and they were honored for moments of bravery in frontier warfare.[17] But these exceptions to the rule were far more limited in scope than those allowed to men. And the most dramatic acts of suppression in Puritan New England (the prosecutions of Anne Hutchinson and of numerous "witches") were directed against assertive women, not assertive men. In theory, any acts of individual ambition threatened social unity. In practice, a woman who refused to be submissive challenged a patriarchal society more profoundly than did a defiant man.

For men, the flexibility of the social code created an area of compromise between communal ideal and individual desire. Much economic ambition could be rationalized as a man's way of adding to the common wealth, and political self-advancement could always be explained as a desire to serve the community in some greater cause.

Most historians of early New England agree that assertive individualism was contained without being suppressed until the early 1700s. Throughout the eighteenth century, however, the manly passions were an increasingly divisive social force. In 1704, a Massachusetts minister named John Danforth denounced "The Vile Profanations of Prosperity," announcing with dread that "This Sheba, SELF, has blown the Trumpet of Rebellion." The rebellious claims of the self were most evident in seaports where merchant families lived in growing luxury and where artisans found the best opportunities for self-advancement. Meanwhile, the steady westward migration created many new towns in each generation and slowly weakened communal values. At the same time, new modes of thought supported individual action. In the second quarter of the eighteenth century, the Great Awakening advanced the idea of personal independence and undermined hierarchy as a social principle. By mid-century a new stream of ideas was flowing from England to North America. Critical of a static social order and patriarchal authority, these revolutionary ideas gained adherents quickly.[18]

By the 1770s, then, Americans had learned to feel more comfortable with the notion of self-assertion. By throwing off their belief in the virtue of submission, they prepared themselves for revolution. In turn, the uprising against British authority raised the idea of the independent self to a new level of reverence. The war for independence — and the change in attitudes toward individual initiative that came with it — were often framed in the language of manliness. The Declaration of Independence itself used the word *manly* to mean resolute courage in resisting tyranny: "[The King] has dissolved Representative Houses repeatedly, for opposing with manly firmness his invasions on the rights of the people." And when Royall Tyler wrote the first successful American comedy, *The Contrast*, in 1787, he created a character to embody American virtues and named him Colonel Manly. What were these Manly American virtues? The Colonel was brave, frank, independent in thought and feeling, and free from submission and luxury. The use of the language of manhood to suggest virtue continued throughout the period. Benjamin Goodhue, a staunch opponent of the French Revolution, wrote of relations with that country in 1798: "We shall be compelled shortly to either manfully oppose the injuries We endure ... , or submissively submit to the degrading terms those haughty Despots choose to impose."[19]

During the revolutionary crisis and the early decades of the new republic, the language of manliness was used more and more for positive social purposes. To some extent, this positive new usage represented an addition to old concepts of manhood. Benjamin Goodhue's pointed contrast of *manfully* with *submissively* indicates the changed meaning of manliness. A man was one who resisted arbitrary authority, who refused submission. This new addition to the old definition of manhood had subversive implications, for a social order based on rank could only exist where men were encouraged to submit.

In the late eighteenth century, as men were using *manliness* with new meanings, they were also creating a new society based on the free expression of the traditional manly passions: assertiveness, ambition, avarice, lust for power. These male drives would provide the motive force for political and economic systems of a novel sort. The new federal constitution, instead of suppressing self-interest, assumed its existence and built a system of government on the play of competing interests. Unfettered individualism was not yet honored in public discourse, but the individual citizen — with all his rights and interests — was now the source of power in the American republic. Likewise, a more dynamic form of commercial life was in the making. National leaders like Alexander Hamilton saw compelling reasons to turn loose the forces of individual enterprise. And the modern systems of banking and finance, which are fueled by personal profit and individual interest, have their roots in this era.[20]

The late eighteenth century, then, was a time of nascent individualism. The forces of community and tradition faltered in their struggle to contain personal ambition, and the claims of the individual self appeared in all realms of a man's life with growing legitimacy.

Since the settlement of New England, the aggressive passions that threatened social order had been associated with manhood and with selfish interest. When John Danforth had railed against "this Sheba, SELF," he was lamenting the presence of "manly" vices such as greed and assertiveness. Throughout the eighteenth century, the connection between male passion and individual interest had persisted. Thus, when influential thinkers of the late eighteenth century pondered the growing claims of the self, they thought only of the *male* self. From the start, individualism was a gendered issue.[21]

To gain full consideration as individuals, women had to follow a path very different from that of men. The first positive recognition of the female self — unique, separate from others, and transcendently important — came not in the public realm, but through romance. Though romantic love was not enshrined as a cultural ideal until the nineteenth century, it grew steadily in importance during the second half of the eighteenth. At that time, romantic love disentangled itself from family considerations in choosing a spouse. A couple, when "struck with love," experienced a reaction between unique selves. Romance was a profoundly individual experience. Although American men and women had certainly fallen in love before the late eighteenth century, their experience had not as a rule been glorified. As romantic love moved to a cultural position of honor and fascination, it brought the distinctive traits of the individual woman (and the individual man) into a favorable light.[22]

While romance exalted the unique female self in the private realm, the recognition of woman as an individual in the public arena never happened in the eighteenth century. In this dimension, individualism touched men and women differently. As American men erected a new political system in which power flowed upward from the individual man, however, women's attempts to create some legitimate political role for themselves helped to lay the basis for the new gender arrangements that would flourish in the nineteenth century.[23]

Women of the new republic, like the females of the colonies, could not vote or hold public office.[24] In constructing a place for themselves in politics, women turned to two common articles of social faith: that a woman's proper place was in the home; and that a republic could only last if its citizens — that is, its male participants — had a strong sense of public virtue. Men would have to learn this virtue somewhere, and where better than the home? Republican mothers would instill incorruptible honesty and a love of liberty in their boys.[25]

By creating this new role for themselves, women were filling a gap created by the nascent individualism of men. In the past, men had held the moral responsibility for the good of the community. Under the new constitution, political self-interest was assumed, and men began to create "an aggressive, egalitarian democracy of a modern sort."[26] With male self-assertion emerging as legitimate political behavior, women took men's place as the custodians of communal virtue.

This new role did not place male and female on equal footing; in fact, women were providing a service to men and society. By preserving the sense of common social virtue, women were freeing men to pursue self-interest. As historian Linda Kerber has written, "The learned woman, who might very well wish to make choices as well as to influence attitudes, was a visible threat to this arrangement."[27]

Viewed in one way, women's new political mission simply re-created the supportive, subordinate role women had always played in the colonies: the new, moral womanhood made the new, individualistic manhood possible. On the other hand, republican motherhood laid the foundation for a different and more effectual women's role in the nineteenth century. It gave women a clearly defined political function, something they had never had before. Republican motherhood, moreover, elevated the status of domesticity by giving it relevance and importance in relation to the public domain. And woman's new function as the custodian of virtue exalted her to a higher moral plane. No longer viewed primarily as the sinful daughter of Eve, she was now thought to exert an uplifting moral influence on men.[28]

These changes laid the basis for a new relationship between the sexes in the nineteenth century. Though still subordinate to men, women were increasingly seen as separate, too. Their high moral status made the domestic world a base of influence as well as a confinement. As the age of individualism began, the redefinitions of manhood and womanhood were part of the same process.

SELF-MADE MANHOOD

In 1802, an ambitious young man named Daniel Webster was setting out in the world to seek his fortune. Like so many other men of his era, Webster saw before him a wide-open, changing society that was full risk and possibility. In a metaphor of movement, he described what he saw:

> The world is nothing but a contra-dance, and everyone *volens, nolens,* has a part in it. Some are sinking, others rising, others balancing, some gradually ascending towards the top, others flamingly leading down. Some cast off from

Fame and Fortune, and some again in a comfortable allemande with both.[29]

Webster joined eagerly in this dance of social fortunes.

Nor was he alone. At the dawn of the nineteenth century, young men of the North faced a world of immense opportunity. The settlement of vast new areas inspired visions of great wealth. The Revolution had introduced a more dynamic view of the social order, and the new American governments had removed some of the old legal barriers to social advancement. Most of all, the spread of the market economy created new opportunities.[30]

As obstacles fell and opportunities grew, the reassessment of self-interest and individual initiative, which had begun in the late eighteenth century, gained momentum and spawned new ideas. One of these ideas gripped the popular imagination with special force in the early nineteenth century: the notion that free competition would reward the best man. People believed that a man could now advance as far as his own work and talents would take him. This belief in a free and open contest for success shared a common assumption with another new attitude that emerged at the turn of the nineteenth century: that the individual, not the community, was the fundamental unit of society.

This shift in thinking from community to person had profound implications for notions of manhood. Men rejected the idea that they had a fixed place in any hierarchy, be it cosmic or social. They no longer thought of themselves as part of an organic community from which they drew personal identity. And they ceased to see themselves as segments in an unbroken family line. The metaphors by which men had defined themselves were losing their power in the new century.

In their stead, a new image developed. Society was a collection of atoms — unranked humans without assigned positions of any sort — and found his proper place in the world through his own efforts. This man — this atom — was free of the cord of generations that had given his forefathers a place in historical time. The past did not weigh him down in his struggle to make himself whatever he dreamed of being. The individual was now the measure of things and men were engrossed with themselves as *selves*. The dominant concerns were the concerns of the self — self-improvement, self-control, self-interest, self-advancement. Passions like personal ambition and aggression — though not seen as virtues — were allowed free passage in society. And the important bonds between people were now fastened by *individual* preference more than birth or social duty.[31]

With assertiveness, greed, and rivalry set free in the marketplace and in the public councils, old dilemmas arose in new forms. The Puritans had viewed those passions as a threat to social order and had tried to control them through a code of communal beliefs and rules. That older system could not work in a society based on the individual. How, then, could the new order be saved from destruction by the very engines of male passion that drove it? How could the individual man be civilized?[32]

Of course, manhood was more than an abstract idea. It was also a standard of behavior for individual men. In this era of competition and self-advancement, men had to vent their aggressive, "manly" passions, but they needed to learn how to do it without being socially destructive. Two different strategies emerged to prevent liberated self-interest from laying waste to the social order. These tactical methods contradicted each other, and the conflict between them did much to define bourgeois manhood in the nineteenth century.

To understand the two main strategies that men used to control their aggressions, it helps to look at the ways of defining manhood by naming its opposite. If a man is not a man, then what is he? One answer is obvious in the context of this book about gender: if a man is not a man, he must be like a woman. But nineteenth-century men had a second answer: if a man is not a man, he must be like a boy.

What was the difference between a boy and a man? The "stigma of boyishness," as one man called it, had to do with frivolous behavior, the lack of worthy aims, and the want of self-control. Any action that was likened to "the play of boys" was contemptible, and a man was "juvenile" if he indulged in boys' sports. In James Fenimore Cooper's *Last of the Mohicans,* Natty Bumppo chides himself for using up his ammunition impulsively by shaking his head "at his own momentary weakness, ... [and] uttering his self-disapprobation aloud .... "Twas the act of a boy!' he said." In the same novel, the Mohican, Magua, vowed on the eve of battle that he and his warriors should "undertake our work like men," not like "eager boys." Boys had enthusiasm, not judgment, and aggression without control.

A sense of carefully guided passion marked the difference between boyhood and manhood. Henry David Thoreau revealed this assumption in *Walden* when he described the difference between oral and written language. The spoken word he associated with boyhood, "transitory, ... a dialect merely, almost brutish, and we learn it unconsciously like the brutes from our mothers." However, the written word "is the maturity and experience of that [spoken language]; if that is our mother tongue, this is our father tongue, a reserved and select expression, ... which we must be born again in order to hear." Thoreau scornfully heaps mother and son together, connecting the woman and the boy to what is unconscious, spontaneous, "almost brutish." Manhood, by contrast, is a "reserved and select expression," mature, consciously learned, under the careful control of reason.[33]

What lies beneath this contrast between boyhood and manhood is a set of assumptions about how to control the aggressive passions that were considered a male birthright. As the thinking went, a boy was driven by his passions, by his eager, impulsive, "almost brutish" nature. Yet he needed to become a purposeful man. How would he make this transition? To suppress his aggressions — or even to moderate them — would deprive him of the assertive energies that he needed to make his place in the competitive arena of middle-class work in the nineteenth century. But without a clear focus, those energies would be wasted. They might even become destructive.

With little conscious articulation, men devised experiences that helped transform the impulsive passions of the boy into the purposeful energies of the man. Academies, colleges, and apprenticeships in commerce and the professions served some of these purposes. Probably more effective were the ubiquitous debating clubs, literary societies, and young men's associations that sprang up inside and outside the formal institutions of learning. True to their era of individualism, these groups did not rely on elder authorities to shape their manhood. Rather, their youthful members socialized each other.[34] In the absence of women and older men, they trained each other in the harnessing of passions and the habits of self-command. Aside from these self created institutions, some young men turned to demanding life experiences — as sailors, cowboys, boatmen, forty-niners, wandering laborers, and (most dramatically) Civil War soldiers — to teach them the self-discipline needed for the active life of the marketplace.

The training in manhood that these schools of experience provided was not based on a conscious philosophy, nor did it grow from articulated plans or procedures. Men happened upon these arrangements and they did not describe — or prescribe — them in any systematic fashion. In an era of voluntary associations and ungoverned competition, this informal system of turning boys into men made a kind of spontaneous sense.

But this was a haphazard way to channel energies and limit impulse. In fact, this system looked dangerous to men and women raised in an earlier society where passion was governed by deep-seated ideals of order and the eager vigilance of the community. To many, this new system looked like no system at all. Individual desire threatened social ties, unchecked competition raised the specter of destructive personal conflict, and self-assertion without social control posed a real possibility of anarchy. As the public world of the individual emerged, a new set of social arrangements arose alongside of it to provide moral order. In the process, a second system for governing manly passion was born.

Through most of the nineteenth century, manhood was a matter of age *and* gender. Many of the traits that marked a man were found wanting in both women and boys. Reason and emotional control played little part in womanhood or boyhood, according to conventional wisdom.

But the contrasts based on age and gender differed in crucial ways. Boys shared a common male nature with men. They did need help in cultivating qualities like self-control and reason (which were regarded as "potential" in males, requiring development), but boys were "inherently" like men. Women, on the other hand, diverged sharply from men in their "intrinsic" nature. And, unlike boys, women were scorned if they cultivated manly qualities. The definition of manhood based on gender difference was a bit more sharply etched than the one based on age.

In fact, the assumed differences between women and men provided a foundation for the doctrine of separate spheres. This elaborate cultural construction evolved in the early nineteenth century. It was a system of symbols that middle-class men and women used to order their social world and understand their mutual relations. Historians have recently come to appreciate the profound impact of the idea of separate spheres on politics, personal relationships, and American culture at large. According to this view, the social realm was divided into two spheres — home and the world. Home was the woman's domain, so it was filled with the piety and purity that were "natural" to the female sex. This atmosphere of virtue made home the logical place to raise children, and woman the fit and proper person to do the job. The female sex extended its moral influence over men as well. In the good and godly environment of the home, women supplied the other sex with moral nurture and spiritual renewal.[35]

Men needed to be strengthened in conscience and spirit because they spent so much time in "the world." The world, according to this moral geography, was the realm of business and public life. It was the emerging marketplace of competitive trade and democratic politics, the arena of individualism. And, just as women's domesticity fitted them for the duties of the home, so men's presumed aggression suited them for this rough public life. Indeed, the world was viewed as the locus of sin and evil. It demanded greed and selfishness of a man, tempted him with power and sensual enjoyment, and set him against other men.[36] An article that appeared in an 1830 issue of *Ladies Magazine* described the world by way of contrast with the values of home:

> We go forth into the world, amidst the scenes of business and pleasure ... and the heart is sensible to a desolation of feeling; we behold every principle of justice and of honor, and even the dictates of common honesty disregarded, and the delicacy of our moral sense is wounded; we see the general good sacrificed to the advancement of personal interest.

Still, virtue had its own sphere, "the sanctuary of the home," where a man could fortify himself against the evil influences of the world: "There sympathy, honor, virtue, are assembled; there the eye may kindle with intelligence, and receive an answering glance; there disinterested love, is ready to sacrifice everything at the altar of affection."[37] From this point of view, the social fabric was torn every day in the world and mended every night at home. Men's sphere depleted virtue, women's sphere renewed it.

This view of the social world had its own historical roots. It built upon the idea of republican motherhood and tapped the growing cultural belief that women were the virtuous sex. As many Northern communities were shaken by evangelical tremors at the start of the nineteenth century, the doctrine of the spheres drew upon the evangelical perception of the world as a sinful place.[38]

Most of all, this new ideology was a response to emerging changes in the workplace. As commercial markets spread at a growing pace, the tempo of middle-class work quickened, and men in business, law, and finance needed increasingly to spend time in each other's presence, both in the office and out. In the second quarter of the nineteenth century, the commercial and professional offices themselves were moved out of homes and into specialized districts. Thus, men were working longer hours and spending more of those hours farther from home. First by time and then by space, men's work limited their presence at home. As many middle-class women were freed by their husbands' prosperity from the necessity of paid labor, they focused more than ever on their domestic duties. Increasingly, women seemed creatures of the home; increasingly, men did not.[39]

The doctrine of separate spheres responded to changes in the workplace, and it may also have affected those changes in their later stages. The changes themselves were physical, however, and the ideology of the spheres gave them a different dimension by attributing a moral meaning to them. The ideology was at once a critique of the new commercial world and a blueprint for adapting to it. This elaborate metaphor identified the new world of individualism and self-interest as evil. Then, rather than question this evil, the doctrine of the spheres offered women as a mechanism to temper it.[40]

The idea of the separate spheres was the climax to some of the cultural changes that began in the eighteenth century. While men of the colonial era had struggled to reconcile ideals of public virtue and personal interest, those ideals realigned themselves along a male-female axis in the nineteenth century.[41] In other words, the doctrine of separate spheres entrusted women with the care and nurture of communal values — of personal morality, social bonds, and, ultimately, the level of virtue in the community. Men were left free to pursue their own interests, to clash and compete, to behave — from an eighteenth-century point of view — selfishly. Women now stood for traditional social values, men for dynamic individualism.

Because bourgeois women were expected to sustain the morality of the men, they acquired the basis for a female political role. Building on the concepts of republican motherhood and the republican wife, the doctrine of separate spheres further empowered nineteenth-century women to cultivate virtue in their sons and husbands. This gave them an indirect means to change behavior in the public arena, but they soon seized more direct forms of influence. After all, it would be difficult to take responsibility for a man's personal virtue and ignore his behavior in public. And it would be hard to watch over personal morality and social bonds without tending social morality as well. When the line between private and public virtue was so hard to draw, woman's role as the custodian of moral goodness inevitably pulled her into the public arena. The metaphor of separate spheres implied a political role for women, even if it denied one explicitly.[42]

The feminine custody of virtue had a second crucial implication: it put women at odds with expected male behavior. After all, if the doctrine of separate spheres was a critique of "the world" and the world was man's realm, then the doctrine was also a critique of manhood. Looked at in these gendered terms, the ideology of the spheres was a plan for the female government of male passions. It gave men the freedom to be aggressive, greedy, ambitious, competitive, and self-interested, then it left women with the duty of curbing this behaviour.

Here, then, was a second idea of how to control male passion. While one concept of control assumed that male groups would focus assertive energies and diffuse their potential for social destruction, the second one directed women to bridle the aggressive drives — the engines of individualism — that were associated with men and their sphere. These two philosophies of control were more than merely that; they were really opposing conceptions of manhood. Although they shared basic assumptions about men's intrinsic nature and social purpose, the two conceptions made sharply different judgments of value about manliness and the male sphere. One trusted the unchecked operation of men's nature to be self-correcting and to create the greatest social good. The other envisioned ungoverned manhood as a socially destructive force.

These two strategies for the control of male passion balanced against each other neatly; one meant learning at home, the other meant learning in the world; one meant lessons from females, the other meant lessons from males. But the most obvious piece of symmetry was missing: one strategy involved mothers, while the other involved peers. Where were fathers? In the new society that developed early in the nineteenth century, fathers declined in their importance to sons, and their place was taken by mothers. This change had great significance for the lives of middle-class men and boys; it also had great significance for the way in which middle-class boys learned the strategies to control "male" passion.

PARENTS AND SONS

When Francis J. Grund visited the United States in the 1830s, the Englishman noted that among Boston businessmen a man might "become the father of a large family and even die without finding out his mistake."[43] With allowance for hyperbole, this is still an astonishing change. Throughout the colonial period, the father had been the dominant figure in the family, yet by the 1830s he was secondary in the household. How had this happened so quickly?

In truth, the foundations of the patriarchal style had been eroding throughout the second half of the 1700s, as ideas and social conditions began to change. By the middle of the eighteenth century, a growing population in the old farming towns of New England had led to a decline in the amount of land available to each man. Thus, fathers could no longer control their sons by promising the gift of a farm later in life. The father lost power and authority.[44] This gradual change in the middle years of the 1700s paved the way for acceptance of a new concept of parenting, one that reached America from England in the 1760s and 1770s. In the emerging view, parents were no longer to act as stringent authorities, but were to increase their roles as moral teachers.[45] In this context, the new notion developed that woman was the embodiment of virtue.[46] Thus, the female sex was viewed as inherently suited to the new concept of parenthood, while males appeared less fit for a primary role. By the early nineteenth century, when the work of middle-class men began to pull fathers away from home, fathers readily yielded their traditional role in shaping the character of their sons.[47] Indeed, the change was probably underway in many families even before the father began spending his time elsewhere.

What was left for a father to do in the nineteenth century? The role he now played was reduced, yet still important. He remained as head of the household, which meant that decisions about the running of a bourgeois family were ultimately a man's.[48] Furthermore, it was his work that supported the household financially. He also served in roles that involved him more directly with his children, especially his sons.[49] One of these was his function as chief disciplinarian. Any major infraction of family rules meant that a boy would have to confront his father. Of course, the mother handled the moment-to-moment punishment, since the father was gone for so much of the day. This undoubtedly made the father's ultimate role in discipline more fearsome, and it must have served to underline his authority and his distance.[50]

A father did have other important duties that asserted his authority in less awesome fashion. He was expected to prepare his son in a practical sense for entry into the world. A father, for instance, was in charge of his son's education. In an era before age-graded universal schooling, this involved far more decision making than it does in the twentieth century. And the decisions about education led directly toward a most important choice — the choice of a calling.[51] Fathers were expected to advise their sons on this matter, and they used whatever influence they had to get their young men started.[52] In some cases, fathers themselves tried to select a son's career. Many of the most dramatic clashes between fathers and sons came over the issue of career choice.[53]

A bourgeois father prepared his son for the world in another way — he supplemented his wife's work in the teaching of virtue. Few moments of major discipline were complete without a lecture from the father; and, as the head of family religious devotions and the chief tutor to his sons, the father had many other opportunities to offer moral instruction. While much of this moral education simply reinforced his wife's teaching, a man held sway over certain areas of ethics. These were values governing work, achievement, and property. Fathers taught their sons the importance of perseverance and thrift, of diligence and punctuality, of industry and ambition. This more than any other was a task that fathers seemed to relish.[54]

Yet a man's obligations to his sons were not only instrumental and worldly; he was also encouraged to love and cherish them. Given the lofty formal expectations held up for a father, and given his growing absence from the household, this love was not always offered with great personal warmth or informal ease. But there are, scattered through the middle-class family documents of the nineteenth century, instances of tenderness or relaxed fun between father and son.[55] Once a son was grown and established in his own life, a warm, friendly relationship often emerged.[56]

As the nineteenth century passed, the trend toward absence of the father grew. Longer work hours and lengthy commutes from the new middle-class suburbs removed men even more from the presence of their sons.[57] Yet, in the final decades of the century, a quiet countertrend emerged. Some men were becoming more involved with their sons. They sought closer emotional ties, expressed affection with growing ease, enjoyed playful times with their boys.[58] In these relationships at the end of the century, there was a glimpse of a different sort of future and a new set of expectations for fathers and sons. At the time, though, this newer style remained a countertrend, quietly visible in relation to the dominant theme of formal authority and father absence.

Father-son relationships in the nineteenth century presented a complex picture. Fathers still had a place of emotional importance in the lives of their sons. A father was the first man a boy knew, was the ultimate source of material comforts, made decisions that controlled a boy's life, and was a boy's predominant role model as a man. Yet he was still a diminished figure, frequently absent from the house, and for most middle-class boys, not the primary parent.

The reduction of fathers' status had partly to do with changes inside the father's life and role. But the reduction was also due to a dramatic enlargement of the other parenting role. For the first time in American history, the mother had become the primary parent.

Of course, women had played a vital role in the lives of their sons and daughters throughout the colonial period. They had always been responsible for the physical care of the children, and they were expected to nurture their young ones emotionally during the early years of childhood. But there were new expectations of motherhood that emerged at the turn of the nineteenth century — expectations that helped to start a revolution in the relations between mothers and sons.[59]

We know that in the late eighteenth century, the cultural assessment of women's moral character shifted from negative to positive. This change brought another change in its wake: mothers were now expected to mold the character of their sons, a task that in previous generations had always belonged to fathers. Encouraged by ministers and social critics who told them that the fate of the republic hung in the balance, middle-class women tried to give their sons a sense of virtue that would suit them to face the new, impersonal world of commerce and competition.[60]

Closely related to this moral expectation was a more personal one: a mother was expected to build strong and lasting bonds with her son. This marked a dramatic change from earlier conceptions. Colonists had believed that a woman's love was uncritical and indulgent. That was fine for nurturing a small child, but unconditional love, the colonists thought, would ruin older children, especially boys.[61] Thus, after the age of five or six, most colonial boys passed to the influence — if not always the physical care — of their fathers.[62]

In the late eighteenth century, Americans reassessed the mother's role. With affection now viewed as a vital part of child-rearing, a woman's unstinting warmth and tenderness suddenly became an asset. It was, in itself, good for children, and it could help as well in the crucial task of character development.[63]

Circumstances conspired to encourage women in fulfilling this mission. With family size declining, a mother could devote more attention to each child.[64] Now that the father was gone from home most of the day, a woman could focus her energy more directly on her children. In addition, sons now remained at home for much longer. During the seventeenth and eighteenth centuries, they were often apprenticed or bound out as servants before their midteens; by the end of the nineteenth century, young men were sometimes staying with their families until their late twenties.[65]

Most mothers took on these new challenges of nurture and uplift with energy and a great sense of purpose. There was a sense not just of stewardship, but of companionship in women's relations with their sons. A New York City woman named Sarah Gilbert described life with her son as a series of shared activities: "He was my companion wherever I went, we ... [knelt] in prayer together, we ... went to the house of God together, in the pleasurable promenade was my companion[,] in a business walk he was with me." Henry Poor remembered a similar experience in the hardscrabble Maine frontier town where he grew up. His mother "was almost the only friend and companion of my boyhood and youth." He added: "I felt myself on such terms of familiarity and sympathy with her, that I could pour out my whole heart without reserve."[66]

Meanwhile, nineteenth-century mothers were devoting themselves faithfully to their other major task, the development of moral character. A woman could cultivate virtue through stories, conversation, shared prayer, or simple exhortation, and her intimate familiarity with her sons helped her to use these different techniques of moral instruction for the greatest effect.[67]

But a boy needed to do more than learn his mother's lessons. He needed to internalize them and carry them out into the world. In short, he needed to make them part of his conscience. This "tyrannical monitor" — as one youth called his conscience — was not easily developed, but many mothers found a method (unconsciously, it seems) for helping it along. By linking her own happiness to her son's good behavior, a woman could pull her child's deepest feelings into her moral world and keep them fastened there. As one mother wrote to her son: "O! think how it would break my heart if you were not a *Good boy*, if you are not even exemplary."[68]

Through this combination of love and moral suasion, many boys developed strong consciences. A letter written by John Kirk, a salesman and abolitionist, suggests the staying power of maternal efforts. Kirk was a grown man with children of his own when he wrote to his mother:

> How often have I been admonished by your godly prayers and your pious exhortations, when far from home and friends, how often when none but God could see or hear [me, your] monitions followed me, and caused the tears of penitential sorrows and affection to flow from my weeping eyes.[69]

After a full life, Kirk still heard his mother's prayers: she had a power over him which transcended time and space. When the conscience of a nineteenth-century man spoke, it generally spoke in feminine tones.

The content of a mother's message of virtue was what one might expect. It was a warning against drink, gambling, and sex. But more persistently, it was an injunction against those vices that came easily in a world engulfed by commerce — selfishness, greed, envy.[70]

A woman's lessons to her sons contained worldly messages, too. A young man would not survive long in the world if he were not industrious, persevering, and wise in his use of time. But the fundamental lessons were lessons of self-restraint. Above all, a boy learned from his mother to hold back his aggressions and control his own "male" energies.[71]

It was in this new environment that middle-class boys of the nineteenth century were shaped for manhood. With the father no longer dominant and with the mother a powerful and effective tutor in virtue, a boy learned early in life to bridle "male" impulse and approach the world with wary caution. But before he reached the world of men, he entered the world of boys. There he learned another, very different idea of how to cope with his drives and ambitions.

NOTES

1. Edmund S. Morgan, *The Puritan Family: Religion and Domestic Relations in Seventeenth-Century New England,* rev. ed. (New York, 1966), 19–20, 133, 136, 142–50.
2. Genesis 3:16.
3. Morgan, *Puritan Family* (see note 1), 12–13.
4. Morgan, *Puritan Family* (see note 1), 43–44; David Hackett Fischer, *Albion's Seed: Four British Folkways in America* (New York, 1989), 83; John Demos, *A Little Commonwealth: Family Life in Plymouth Colony* (New York, 1970), 83–84.
5. Philip Greven, Jr., *The Protestant Temperament: Patterns of Child-Rearing, Religious Experience, and Self in Early America* (New York, 1977), 211, 243–51; Phyllis Vine, "The Social Function of Eighteenth-Century Higher Education," *History of Education Quarterly,* 16 (1976): 412.
6. Steven Mintz and Susan Kellogg, *Domestic Revolutions: A Social History of American Life* (New York, 1988), 5–6.
7. Mintz and Kellogg, *Domestic Revolutions* (see note 6), 6; Melvin Yazawa, *From Colonies to Commonwealth: Familial Ideology and the Beginnings of the American Republic* (Baltimore, 1985), 19–27.
8. Morgan, *Puritan Family* (see note 1), 45–46, 115, 147–50; Laurel Thatcher Ulrich, *Good Wives: Image and Reality in the Lives of Women in Northern New England 1650–1750* (New York, 1982), 35–50.
9. See, for example, Samuel Gay to Martin Gay, Jan. 18 and Feb. 22, 1776, and Jotham Gay to Martin Gay, Apr. 21, 1760, Gay-Otis Manuscript

Collection, CUL. On the importance of a man's performance of his duties, see also Benjamin Greene to Samuel and Stephen Salisbury, Sept. 9, 1781, Salisbury Family Papers, Box 4, AAS; William Bentley, *The Diary of William Bentley, D.D.* (Gloucester, Mass., 1962), 1:19; Joseph Jenkins to Rebekah Jenkins, n.d. (1803), Joseph Jenkins Letters, EI; Ernestus Plummer to Caroline Plummer, Mar. 9, 1808, Bowditch Family Papers, Box 12, EI.

10. Ulrich, *Good Wives* (see note 8), 8.
11. "Good foundations" quoted in Greven, *Protestant Temperament* (see note 5), 177; Theodore P. Greene, *America's Heroes: The Changing Models of Success in American Magazines* (New York, 1970), 45–46. Usefulness was a central theme of Timothy Pickering's letters to his son John, Nov. 15, 1786, Aug. 4, 1788, Oct. 14, 1793, Jan. 2 and Jan. 17, 1794, Apr. 28 and June 15, 1798, Pickering Family Papers, EI; William Bentley also stressed usefulness as a male virtue. See Bentley, *Diary* (see note 9), 1:53; 3:223.
12. Alexander Anderson diary, June 18, 1795, NYHS; Benjamin Goodhue to Stephen Goodhue, Mar. 26, 1796, Goodhue Family Papers, EI. See also Benjamin Goodhue to Stephen Goodhue, Apr. 16, 1796; Nathan Mitchell diary, Sept. 27, 1786, MHGS; Joseph Jenkins to Rebekah Jenkins, n.d. [1803], Joseph Jenkins Letters, EI; Philip Schuyler to Angelica Church, July 17, 1804, Schuyler Family Papers, NYSLA; Bentley, *Diary* (see note 9), 4:588; Ernestus Plummer to Caroline Plummer, Aug. 10, 1810, Bowditch Papers, Box 12, EI; Edmund Quincy to Samuel Salisbury, June 20, 1780, Salisbury Papers, Box 4, AAS; Ezra Stiles, *The Literary Diary of Ezra Stiles,* ed. F. B. Dexter (New York, 1901), 418.
13. Timothy Pickering to George Williams, Mar. 21, 1786, Pickering Papers, EI; Bentley, *Diary* (see note 9), 1:41, 199; John Pierce memoirs, vol. 1, July 2, 1806, Pierce Collection, MHS.
14. Philip Schuyler to Catherine Schuyler, Jan. 26, 1800, Schuyler Papers, NYSLA; Timothy Pickering to George Williams, Mar. 21, 1786, Pickering Papers, EI; James R. McGovern, *Yankee Family* (New Orleans, 1975), 271; Yazawa, *From Colonies* (see note 7), 33–45.
15. Bentley quoted in Joseph Waters, "Biographical Sketch," in Bentley, *Diary* (see note 9), 1:xiv–xv; Alexander Anderson diary, Oct. 7, 1795, NYHS.
16. Darret Rutman, *Winthrop's Boston* (Chapel Hill, N.C., 1965); Bernard Bailyn, "The Apologia of Robert Keayne," *William and Mary Quarterly,*

3rd ser., 7 (1950); Bernard Bailyn, *The New England Merchants in the Seventeenth Century* (Cambridge, Mass., 1955).
17. Ulrich, *Good Wives* (see note 8), esp. chaps. 2, 3, 9.
18. Danforth quoted in J. E. Crowley, *This Sheba, Self: The Conceptualization of Economic Life in Eighteenth-Century America* (Baltimore, 1974), xiv. See also John Demos, *Entertaining Satan: Witchcraft and the Culture of Early New England* (New York, 1982), esp. 394–400; Kenneth Lockridge, *A New England Town: The First Hundred Years, Dedham, Massachusetts, 1636–1736* (New York, 1970), 91–164; Philip Greven, Jr., *Four Generations: Population, Land, and Family in Colonial Andover, Massachusetts* (Ithaca, N.Y., 1970); Richard L. Bushman, *From Puritan to Yankee: Character and Social Order in Connecticut, 1690–1765* (Cambridge, Mass., 1967); Jay Fliegelman, *Prodigals and Pilgrims: The American Revolution against Patriarchal Authority, 1750–1800* (Cambridge, Mass., 1982); Yazawa, *From Colonies* (see note 7), 83–194.
19. Declaration of Independence, in Daniel Boorstin, ed., *An American Primer* (Chicago, 1966), 69; Royall Tyler, *The Contrast: A Comedy in Five Acts* (New York, 1970); Benjamin Goodhue to Stephen Goodhue, Mar. 24, 1798, Goodhue Papers, EI.
20. See Joseph Ellis, *After the Revolution: Profiles of Early American Culture* (New York, 1979), on the reluctance of the younger generation of revolutionaries to believe in individual economic enterprise as a social good.
21. On political individualism as a gendered issue, see Linda Kerber, *Women of the Republic: Intellect and Ideology in Revolutionary America* (Chapel Hill, N.C., 1980), 15–27, 284–85.
22. Jesse Appleton to Ebenezer Adams, Feb. 10, 1797, Jesse Appleton Letters, AAS; Fliegelman, *Prodigals and Pilgrims* (see note 18), chaps. 2, 5, 6; Herman Lantz et al., "Pre-Industrial Patterns in the Colonial Family in America: A Content Analysis," *American Sociological Review*, 33 (June 1968), 413–26; Herman Lantz, Raymond Schmitt, and Richard Herman, "The Pre-Industrial Family in America: A Further Examination of Magazines," *American Journal of Sociology*, 79 (Nov. 1973), 577–78, 581; Ellen Rothman, Hands and Hearts: A History of Courtship in America (New York, 1984), 30–31, 35.
23. The following account of women's creation of a political role for themselves in the new republic is based especially on Kerber, *Women of*

the Republic (see note 21), and also on Mary Beth Norton, *Liberty's Daughters: The Revolutionary Experience of American Women, 1750–1800* (Boston, 1980), 228–99.

24. Through an apparent loophole in the New Jersey constitution, women in that state were able to vote from the 1780s until 1807. See Norton, *Liberty's Daughters* (see note 23), 191–93.
25. New ideas about child-rearing that became popular in the late eighteenth century stressed the importance of affectionate nurture (see Fliegelman, *Prodigals and Pilgrims*; see note 18). Since this quality had traditionally been — and still was — associated with women, it was natural that men should accept women's assertion that they were the sex fit to teach republican virtue.
26. Kerber, *Women of the Republic* (see note 21), 285.
27. Ibid.
28. Ruth Bloch, "The Gendered Meanings of Virtue in Revolutionary America," *Signs*, 13 (1987).
29. Daniel Webster to Habijah Fuller, Aug. 29, 1802, *The Writings and Speeches of Daniel Webster*, vol. 17 (Boston, 1903).
30. The broad changes described here and in the paragraphs that follow are explored in David Hackett Fischer, "America; A Social History, Vol 1, The Main Lines of the Subject, 1650–1975," unpub. MS, and *Growing Old in America,* expanded ed. (New York, 1978), 77–78, 99–112; in Richard Brown, *Modernization: The Transformation of American Life* (New York, 1976), and "Modernization and the Modern Personality in Early America, 1600–1865: A Sketch of a Synthesis," *Journal of Interdisciplinary History*, 2 (1972); and, in microcosm, in Daniel Scott Smith, "Population, Family, and Society in Hingham, Massachusetts" (Ph.D. diss., University of California, Berkeley, 1973).
31. The best description of the new individualism and its implications is still Alexis de Tocqueville's *Democracy in America.* On the social and cultural conditions, see esp. vol. 2. The version used here is the Henry Reeve text, rev. Francis Bowen, ed. Phillips Bradley (New York, 1945).
32. Generations of historians have explored the attempts of early nineteenth-century Americans to answer these questions. A classic formulation is Marvin Meyers, *The Jacksonian Persuasion: Politics and Belief* (New York, 1957). A recent, compelling exploration is Paula Baker, "The Domestication of American Politics: Women and American Political

Society, 1780–1920," *American Historical Review*, 89 (1984), 620–35.
33. James Fenimore Cooper, *The Last of the Mohicans* (New York, 1968 [1826]), 127, 324–35; Henry David Thoreau, *Walden*, ed. Sherman Paul (Boston, 1960), 70.
34. Not all debating clubs and literary societies were segregated by age. Some of them, especially in small towns, mixed adult men with male youths. But even in those settings, young men learned the purposeful channeling of energy incidentally — through competition and emulation — rather than through formal instruction. See, for instance, Samuel Howard to James C. Howard, Jan. 28, 1828, James C. Howard Papers, SHSW.
35. Linda Kerber has reviewed the historical literature on separate spheres insightfully in "Separate Spheres, Female Worlds, Women's Place: The Rhetoric of Women's History," *Journal of American History*, 75 (1988). The single most important interpretation is Nancy F. Cott, *The Bonds of Womanhood: "Woman's Sphere" in New England, 1780–1835* (New Haven, Conn., 1977).
36. Cott, *Bonds of Womanhood* (see note 35), 63–74; Mary Ryan, *The Empire of the Mother: American Writing about Domesticity, 1830–1860* (New York, 1982).
37. L. E., "Home," *Ladies Magazine*, 3 (1830), 217–18.
38. Bloch, "Gendered Meanings" (see note 28), 37–58. On the evangelical roots of the doctrine of the spheres, see Cott, *Bonds of Womanhood* (see note 35), 65.
39. On the creation of specialized commercial districts, see Stuart Blumin, *The Emergence of the Middle Class: Social Experience in the American City, 1760–1900* (New York, 1989), 83–87; on women's increasing focus on domestic duties in prosperous households, see Cott, *Bonds of Womanhood* (see note 35), 43–45, 57–62.
40. Cott, in *Bonds of Womanhood* (see note 35, 69–71), discusses the way in which the doctrine of the spheres proposed accommodations to the changes which it deplored.
41. Bloch, "Gendered Meanings" (see note 28)53–58.
42. A large and rich historical literature that discusses the political implications of women's moral role has emerged in recent years. Important statements within this literature include Cott, *Bonds of Womanhood* (see note 35), 197–206; Baker, "Domestication" (see note 32), 620–47; Mary Ryan,

The Cradle of the Middle Class: The Family in Oneida County, New York, 1790–1865 (New York, 1981), esp. chap. 5; Barbara Leslie Epstein, *The Politics of Domesticity: Women, Evangelism, and Temperance in Nineteenth-Century America* (Middletown, Conn., 1981); Carl N. Degler, *At Odds: Women and the Family in America from the Revolution to the Present* (New York, 1980), chap. 13.

43. Quoted in McGovern, *Yankee Family* (see note 14), 85.
44. E. Anthony Rotundo, "American Fatherhood: A Historical Perspective," *American Behavioral Scientist*, 29 (1985), 9–10. This article appears in revised form as "Patriarchs and Participants: A Historical Perspective on Fatherhood," in Michael Kaufman, ed., *Beyond Patriarchy: Essays by Men on Pleasure, Power, and Change* (New York, 1987).
45. Fliegelman, *Prodigals and Pilgrims* (see note 18).
46. Bloch, "Gendered Meanings" (see note 28).
47. The role of shaping a daughter's character already belonged in great measure to the woman. See Norton, *Liberty's Daughters* (see note 23), 97.
48. To be sure, a woman had great — sometimes overwhelming — influence on family decisions. But by cultural agreement, the decisions were the man's to make.
49. Fathers served as breadwinners, heads of household, and chief disciplinarians to daughters as well, but the focus here is on fathers and sons.
50. See E. Anthony Rotundo, "Fathers and Sons: Roles and Relationships," unpub. MS, 189–92.
51. On educational decisions, see Theodore Russell to Charles Russell, Dec. 18, 1831, and Nov. 6, 1832, Charles Russell Papers, MHS; Dean S. Howard to James Howard, Nov. 30, 1831, Howard Papers, SHSW; William H. Olmstead to Aaron Olmstead, June 7 and Nov. 8, 1838, Aaron Barlow Olmstead Papers, NYHS.
52. Often, the most useful thing a father could do was to offer a home and financial support to a young man through extended years of education and early career struggles. See Ryan, *Cradle* (see note 42), 168–72; Ebenezer Gay to Arthur Gay, May 13, 1838, and May 9, 1839, Gay-Otis Collection, CUL.
53. Howard Doughty, *Francis Parkman* (Cambridge, Mass., 1983 [1962]), 87; Robert Abzug, *Passionate Liberator: Theodore Dwight Weld and*

the Dilemma of Reform (New York, 1980), 22–27; Char Miller, *Fathers and Sons: The Bingham Family and the American Mission* (Philadelphia, 1982), 73–77, 121–28.

54. Rotundo, "Fathers and Sons" (see note 50), 194–95; Rotundo, "American Fatherhood" (see note 44), 11–12.
55. For instance, Charles Russell to Theodore Russell, Sept. 27, 1834, Russell Papers, MHS; Othman Abbott, *Recollections of a Pioneer Lawyer* (Lincoln, Neb., 1929), 82. On changing expectations in this regard, see Kirk Jeffrey, "Family History: The Middle Class Family in the Urban Context, 1830–1870" (Ph.D. diss., Stanford University, 1972), 207–8, and Rachel Deborah Cramer, "Images of the American Father, 1790–1860," unpub. MS, 51–52.
56. Rotundo, "Fathers and Sons" (see note 50), 271–72.
57. Sam Bass Warner, Jr., *Streetcar Suburbs: The Process of Growth in Boston, 1870–1900* (Cambridge, Mass., 1962); Kenneth Jackson, *The Crabgrass Frontier: The Suburbanization of the United States* (New York, 1985), 41–44; Blumin (see note 39), 275–81.
58. Edward Everett Hale to Harriet Freeman, June 26 and Aug. 22, 1885, Papers of the Hale Family, Special Correspondence of Edward Everett Hale, LC; B. Franklin Kendall to Elizabeth Kendall, July 26, 1882, Kendall Papers, NYHS; Edward Wagenknecht, *The Seven Worlds of Theodore Roosevelt* (New York, 1958), 172–73.
59. Ulrich, *Good Wives* (see note 8), 154–58; Norton, *Liberty's Daughters* (see note 23), 85–94.
60. Ruth Bloch, "American Feminine Ideals in Transition: The Rise of the Moral Mother, 1785–1815," *Feminist Studies*, 4 (1978); Cott, *Bonds of Womanhood* (see note 35), 84–87; James Barnard Blake diary, Aug. 3, 1851, AAS; William G. McLoughlin, *The Meaning of Henry Ward Beecher: An Essay on the Shifting Values of Mid-Victorian America, 1840–1870* (New York, 1970), 88.
61. Vine, "Social Function" (see note 5), 411–12; Greven, *Protestant Temperament* (see note 5), 246–47; Ulrich, *Good Wives* (see note 8), 154.
62. Norton, *Liberty's Daughters* (see note 23), 92–94.
63. Jan Lewis, "Mother's Love: The Construction of an Emotion in Nineteenth-Century America," in *Social History and Issues in Human Consciousness: Some Interdisciplinary Connections*, ed. Andrew E.

Barnes and Peter N. Steams, (New York, 1989). As represented in Lewis' article, the ideology of maternal nurture did not exist in its full-blown form until at least the 1820s. But as Cott has noted in (*Bonds of Womanhood,* see note 35, 85–87), mothers and ministers were articulating some of its principles in the very earliest years of the century. For two examples of women who raised their children according to these precepts in the 1800s and 1810s, see the letters of Betsy Salisbury (Salisbury Papers, AAS) and Mary A. O. Gay (Gay-Otis Collection, CUL).

64. People were conscious of this connection, and the advantages of family limitation for good mothering became an argument for birth control during the nineteenth century. See Degler, *At Odds* (see note 42), 201.

65. Fischer, *Albion's Seed* (see note 4), 101–2, on "sending out." On the late nineteenth century, see Ryan, *Cradle* (see note 42), 167–68.

66. Sarah Gilbert to Charles Russell, June 26, 1837, Russell Papers, MHS; Poor quoted in McGovern, *Yankee Family* (see note 14), 11. Not all mother-son relationships yielded affection or companionship, but such relations tended to be hidden from view by the importance attached to that bond. For an example of a more distant mother-son relation, see Charles Milton Baldwin diary, June 4, 1870, NYSLA.

67. McGovern, *Yankee Family* (see note 14), 9; Abzug, *Passionate Liberator* (see note 53), 16; Mary A. O. Gay to W. Allan Gay, Feb. 15, Dec. 12, and Dec. 31, 1840, Sept. 2, 1847, and Feb. 17, 1850, Gay-Otis Collection, CUL.

68. Henry Dwight Sedgwick, *Memoirs of an Epicurean* (New York, 1942), 21; Betsy Salisbury to Stephen Salisbury, Jr., Sept. 16, 1809, Salisbury Papers, AAS. See also letters of Apr. 11 and June 20, 1814.

69. John Kirk to his mother, Dec. 18, 1852, Kirk Letterbooks, vol. 1, CHS. See also Sedgwick, *Memoirs* (see note 68), 23; Lewis Wallace, *Lew Wallace: An Autobiography* (New York, 1906), 27; James Barnard Blake diary, Nov. 9, 1851, AAS.

70. See, for example, Betsy Salisbury to Stephen Salisbury, Jr., Sept. 16, 1809, Salisbury Papers, AAS.

71. Betsy Salisbury to Stephen Salisbury, Jr., Apr. 11, June 20, July 5, and Aug. 9, 1814, Salisbury Papers, AAS; Polly Whittlesey to William Whittlesey, Apr. 30, 1832, William W. Whittlesey Papers, WRNS. The simultaneous training offered by mothers in ambition and pious morality is described well in Ronald P. Byars, "The Making of the Self-made Man:

The Development of Masculine Roles and Images in Ante-bellum America" (Ph.D. diss., Michigan State Univ., 1979). Byars is perceptive generally about the swirling crosscurrents of male-female relations before the Civil War.

Chapter Three
Festivities, Fortutide, and Fraternalism: Fur Trade Masculinity and the Beaver Club, 1785–1827

Carolyn Podruchny

In 1785, wealthy fur trade merchants in Montreal founded the Beaver Club, an elite dining club restricted to men who had wintered in the North American interior, often referred to as "Indian Country." Although the Beaver Club existed alongside other dining and entertainment clubs in Montreal, it was unique in its membership, raison d'être, and rituals. The club was initiated to provide a forum for retired merchants in which to reminisce about the risky and adventurous days of fur trading, and a forum for young fur traders to enter Montreal's bourgeois society.[1] The initial membership of nineteen expanded to a peak of fifty-five, as the club met regularly until 1804. Following a three-year suspension, dinners were then resumed. It probably began to decline after the merger between the North West Company and Hudson's Bay Company in 1821, when the business center of the fur trade moved from Montreal to Hudson Bay. Evidence shows that members continued to meet until 1824, when the club ended. Efforts to resurrect the club in 1827 were unsuccessful.

The Beaver Club is the best-known institution of the Montreal fur trade. Many scholars have glorified the exclusive fraternity and the extravagant style of the dinners, and idealized the strength of the men who wintered in "Indian Country." Although mention of the Beaver Club is widespread, details are few, and its treatment is uncritical, romantic, celebratory, and lacking in historical context.[2] This chapter explores the social meaning of the Beaver Club for its members and for wider Montreal society. The club should be seen as a variant of men's clubs typical of the North Atlantic world in the late eighteenth and early nineteenth century.

Fraternal association provided a forum for men to establish business connections, share ideas, and construct and cement a common culture of shared values and social ideals. One of the most important of these ideals was the respectable man. Club rules and rituals defined the substance and boundaries of respectable behavior. The Beaver Club was distinct from many fraternal associations because it embodied a fascination with the "wild" and "savage." Men who had braved the unknown, encountering what they thought were strange, exotic, and potentially menacing natives, and surviving the rigors and dangers of travel by canoe, came together in Montreal to remember and honor their rugged adventures in the North American interior. In some ways fur trade merchants appropriated the "rugged" and "wild." Although they did not actually share the physical experiences of their laborers or the natives with whom they traded, they pretended to have done so in their reminiscences. At the same time members forged a bourgeois civility, which excluded women and the working class. In the privacy of the club, the fur traders could enjoy acting in a rough manner while upholding their respectable reputations to the outside world. In some ways the divergent ideals of respectability and rowdiness reflected a transition from an earlier fur trade society dominated by rough and ready traders, whose claims to status and power came solely from their success in the trade, to a later society dominated by a professional, mostly English and Anglican, elite, who brought urban middle class ideals to their management of the fur trade.

I. BOURGEOIS MEN'S CLUBS

Montreal was a mercantile city that relied on the fur trade and international import-exports for its economic survival until 1821. It served as the financial heart for a large part of the fur trade in North America. After 1770 its local economy became more vigorous, with a growing population and diversification of economic interests.[3] Although Montreal and Quebec City constituted the major urban centers of the Canadian colonies, their populations in the mid-eighteenth century reached only five thousand, less than half the size of New York, Philadelphia, and Boston, the largest cities in the Thirteen Colonies.[4] Montreal's middle class, which included businessmen, liberal professionals, and colonial officials, were the beneficiaries of the post-Conquest economic growth. Within this group the merchant bourgeoisie increased in number, diversity, and power. Fur trade merchants' prestige and influence were especially strong. This group of more than one hundred men made fast fortunes in the fur trade, bought property, gained political power, and became a part of the governing class of the colony. Partners in Montreal fur trade firms were commonly referred to as bourgeois. The dozen or so large companies began to pool resources in the early 1770s and eventually merged into the North West Company in 1784.[5]

As Montreal flourished, clubs became important institutions for urban sociability. Increasing affluence and leisure time among merchants led to the growth and popularity of clubs that provided organized forums for social entertainment, fellowship, and business networking. Similar patterns existed in eighteenth-century England, where voluntary organizations fostered a new sense of social order in towns, promoted urban advancement, were committed to intellectual innovation and social improvement, transmitted new ideas, and contributed to public vitality. Clubs played significant social and cultural roles in the transition from a pre-industrial order to a modernizing industrial society by promoting social division based on class and wealth rather than rank and status, and by stressing harmony and order within the middle class.[6] In eighteenth century America, fraternities, such as the Freemasons, accompanied the growth of market relations and towns. Clubs forged patronage relationships, which formed the primary means of survival and advancement in the eighteenth-century business world. Merchants relied heavily upon the reputation and ties of trust provided by clubs.[7] In Montreal, sodalities, such as the Beaver Club, helped to cement the bonds between members of the bourgeois class, provided vehicles for business and social bonding, and instilled values that helped shape their attitudes and behavior.

The Beaver Club dinners were part of a large continuum of vigorous socializing among fur traders and Montreal's bourgeoisie. Men and women entertained regularly, and one of the most popular activities was dining. In December 1797, Colonel George Landmann had not been in Montreal for more than twenty-four hours before receiving invitations to dine for the next ten days from army officers, government officials, and merchants. His descriptions of feasting and hard drinking extended to parties held by fur traders before spring fur brigades set out.[8] Montreal businessman and fur trader Joseph Frobisher's dining diary from 1806 to 1810 illustrates his participation in the broad circuit of dining and parties among Montreal's social elite. Even though Frobisher was not in the best health, he frequently dined out or entertained in his home every night of the week.[9]

Although men and women frequently dined together, fraternization among men was formalized in clubs and associations, such as the Beaver Club. Other men's dining clubs in Montreal that formed part of the pattern of socializing among Montreal's bourgeoisie included the Brothers in Law Club, which, like the Beaver Club, allowed members of the same occupation to meet in a convivial setting. This exclusive group of Montreal lawyers met several times a year to dine, between 1827 and 1833.[10] Others included the Bachelor's Club, the Montreal Hunt Club, and the exclusive Montreal Fire Club, to which many Beaver Club members belonged.[11]

Several Beaver Club members and many of their guests became members of the Masonic order, one of the most prestigious and well-connected fraternal associations in the North Atlantic world. Although it drew men from many backgrounds, its character was bourgeois, and like the Beaver Club, it helped its membership forge a bourgeois identity. Sir John Johnson, an Indian department official and member of the legislative council of Lower Canada, was a regular guest at Beaver Club dinners. He was appointed the Masonic Provincial Grand Master for Canada in 1788. His father, Sir William Johnson, a prominent merchant and superintendent of Indian affairs for northern British North America, founded one of the first Masonic lodges in New York in 1766. Beaver Club member William McGillivray became Provincial Grand Master of the District of Montreal. His younger brother, Simon McGillivray, also a Beaver Club member, became a Freemason in 1807 and was appointed Provincial Grand Master of Upper Canada in 1822.[12] Many lodges were founded at fur trade and military posts in the late eighteenth century, such as Michilimackinac, Niagara, Cataraqui, and Mackinaw. As well, colonial military regiments, whose officers regularly attended Beaver Club dinners, were closely tied to early Masonic lodges.[13] The last meeting of the Beaver Club was held at the Masonic Hall Hotel.[14] These ties with Freemasonry aided the fur traders in business and politics. Fur trade scholar Heather Devine has found that the rapid success of Scottish Nor'Westers as merchants was due to their entry into Sir William Johnson's political, social, and economic networks. Through patronage, Johnson established close ties with some Scottish émigrés, particularly Simon McTavish.[15] These ties seemed to persist into the nineteenth century in Montreal, as Sir John Johnson was a regular guest at the Beaver Club.

The club was comprised mainly of men who either worked for or were sympathetic to the North West Company. Members included the most powerful men in the fur trade business, such as Charles-Jean-Baptiste Chaboillez, Maurice Blondeau, Benjamin Frobisher, Joseph Frobisher, Thomas Frobisher, James McGill, John McGill, William McGillivray, Duncan McGillivray, and Roderick McKenzie, as well as some of the most famous explorers of the North American interior, such as Alexander Henry, the younger, Alexander McKenzie, and Simon Fraser.[16] Some members were less socially prominent, and a few had dubious backgrounds, such as interpreter and trader Joseph-Louis Ainsse, who was accused of plundering at Michilimackinac, who betrayed a commandant, and who embezzled from the Indian Department. American trader Peter Pond, described as violent and unprincipled, was suspected of being involved in the murders of at least three fur traders.[17] However, in the context of the Beaver Club, these social differences were often flattened, and suspect backgrounds were ignored in the interests of maintaining a respectable appearance. Fur traders who worked in rival companies, such as the XY Company, were not welcome, even if they had been members previously. For example, Alexander McKenzie was elected to the Club in 1795, disappeared from its records while he was a partner of the XY Company, but was reelected in 1808, four years after the XY Company's dissolution. At the same meeting former XY partner A. N. McLeod was also elected. Another XY Company partner, John Gregory, was initially elected in 1791, but does not reappear in the club minutes until 1809.[18] Some well-known fur traders, such as David Thompson and Daniel Williams Harmon, never became members, probably because they spent most of their lives in the Northwest.[19]

Beaver Club folklore extolled the political and economic power of its members. Member James Hughes recalled the club as the "acme of social attainment and the pinnacle of commercial success in Lower Canada," proudly reported distinguished visitors to the club, and hinted that the fur traders controlled affairs of state.[20] Guests included militia officers, government officials, businessmen, and professionals, such as judges, lawyers, and doctors, as well as distinguished visitors to Montreal, including John Jacob Astor, Washington Irving, and Thomas Moore. The political and economic networks formed between fur trade businessmen, colonial officials, Indian Department administrators, and military officers were encouraged by their regular socializing. Members and guests were often connected through family as well as through business. For example, the frequent guest Alexander Auldjo was a leader among Montreal businessmen, supporter of the English Party, and member of the Scotch Presbyterian Church. David David, a fur trader, businessman and militia officer who became a Beaver Club member in 1817, was appointed director of the Bank of Montreal in 1818. Another frequent visitor was John Forsyth, a successful merchant actively involved in improving Montreal's financial infrastructure, a militia officer, and a member of the legislative council.[21]

Meetings were held in the off-season of the trade once a fortnight from the first week in December until the second week in April. Beginning at four in the afternoon, dinners often lasted until four in the morning.[22] Dinners were held in various Montreal hotels and taverns, such as City Tavern, Richard Dillion's Montreal Hotel, Palmer's Hummums, and Tesseyman's, as was common for private parties, business and political meetings, and gatherings of male friends in the eighteenth century.[23] The passing around of a calumet, or peace pipe, marked the beginning of the Club's formal rituals, continuing with a speech, or "harangue," made by the evening's president, and formal toasts.[24] Dinner fare included country food, such as braised venison, bread sauce, "Chevreuil des Guides" (stew), venison sausages, wild rice, quail, and partridge "du Vieux Trappeur," served in crested glass and silverware.[25] After dinner, the club became more informal, as men began to drink more heavily, sing voyageur songs, and reminisce about the good old fur-trading days. Festivities continued until the early morning, with men dancing on the tables, reenacting canoeing adventures, and breaking numerous bottles and glasses. The approbation of rough and rowdy behavior, at odds with the urbane civility of other Montreal dining clubs, especially those where women were included, allowed fur traders a private space in which to embrace rugged masculine ideals.

II. Gender, Class, and Fraternalism

The Beaver Club was instrumental in developing the gender and class identities of its members. It brought bourgeois men together in an insulated setting and promoted representations of idealized masculinity. Gender formation and class formation were closely associated in the late eighteenth- and early nineteenth-century North Atlantic world. Some scholars, such as British middle class historians Leonore Davidoff and Catherine Hall, argue that class and gender always operate together, and that class always takes a gendered form.[26] As bourgeois men came together in business and fraternal orders, they began to limit the boundaries of their collective identity. The increasing marginalization of women from the world of public commerce after the Conquest extended to their exclusion from fraternal associations, which were often seen as extensions of men's business interests. Bourgeois men also sought to distinguish themselves from other classes. They generally considered the lower orders as their social and economic inferiors and, despite their aspirations to gentry, they often called the higher orders their moral inferiors.[27] Through fraternal associations, the bourgeois were able to consolidate their class and forge bourgeois harmony.

Women were excluded from most fraternal associations for various reasons. One of the key components to middle-class constructions of femininity and masculinity was the division between the public sphere, the realm of rational activity, market forces, and production, and the private sphere, the realm of morality, emotion, and reproduction. Although men and women moved in both these spheres, men appropriated the former, while women dominated the latter.[28] The subsequent marginalization of women in the public sphere contributed to the exclusion of women from club meetings, as fraternal associations were frequently associated with men's trade and business. Like many other men's clubs, Beaver Club meetings were held in taverns, where few middle-class women ventured. Hall argues that taverns were increasingly defined as inappropriate settings for women who wished to maintain their gentility, as temperance movements became an important component of the evangelical project to raise the moral tone of society.[29] Other scholars suggest that the absence of women was important to the process of forging masculinity. Mark Carnes' study of fraternal associations in Victorian America argues that their rituals provided solace and psychological guidance, away from women, for a young man's passage from the maternal affection of childhood to manhood.[30] In the all-male atmosphere men could practice distinctive social behaviors, such as smoking, swearing, gambling, and drinking, with little interruption. In her work on American mariners, Margaret Creighton asserts that these masculine activities were not meant to make the men more appealing to women; rather, they made them more acceptable to other men.[31] Men were subject to gender expectations generated by both sexes. Away from women, men could focus on themselves, cultivate their own desires and identities, and escape the pressures of women's expectations. In the Beaver Club, fur traders were able to revere their lives in the North American interior, where, away from their Euro-American wives and mothers, they pursued their aspirations for rugged adventure.

Fur-trade laborers, such as voyageurs, interpreters, and guides, were almost never included in Beaver Club festivities. The social organization of the Montreal fur trade firmly divided partners from low-ranked workers.[32] In the mid-eighteenth century, some men were able to rise from the rank of worker to manager, but by the time of the emergence of the North West Company in the 1780s, the hierarchy was firmly in place. Older fur traders counseled young clerks to be obedient and polite to superiors, to be self-important when out in the field, and to hold themselves apart from their laborers to command respect and submission.[33] However, bourgeois attitudes to lower orders could be complex and contradictory, especially for fur traders who had lived and worked alongside their labor force in an isolated and dangerous setting. Many fur-trade bourgeois admired voyageurs for their strength and skill, and established relationships with them built on trust and interdependence. At the same time most fur-trade bourgeois considered voyageurs to be thoughtless, irrational, and rude.[34] Club rituals imitating voyageurs helped the bourgeois to distance themselves from their workers. The romanticization of voyageurs' activities cast them as exotic curiosities. At the same time, bourgeois men appropriated voyageurs' experiences in the fur trade. They reminisced about paddling canoes and running through rapids, even though this was the work of the voyageurs. The bourgeois did not risk their lives in rapids and portages, carry backbreaking packs, paddle at outrageous speeds, nor survive on minimal food, as did the voyageurs. Rather, they directed crews, managed accounts, distributed food, and had better rations than their voyageurs. Both the distancing from and the imitation of voyageurs reflected a code of ethics that applauded rugged behavior of the bourgeois in the right settings.

Most eighteenth- and nineteenth-century bourgeois admired upper orders, and cherished noble values such as courage, loyalty, prowess in combat, and gallantry in love.[35] This admiration was not unproblematic, as the bourgeois found aristocratic behavior often at odds with many of their notions of respectability and honor. Nonetheless, members of higher social orders were not excluded from the Beaver Club. The desire to achieve the status of a gentleman inspired in the fur trade bourgeois a fascination for nobility and aristocracy. Although many merchants were hostile to the old seigneurial order, they were nonetheless influenced by it. Military service, purchasing noble titles, and acquiring property were common ways that the bourgeoisie could associate themselves with nobility and aspire to gentry.[36] Fur trade bourgeois usually procured their own crest and motto, which were important signifiers of membership in the gentry.

Aristocratic association was a common theme in club folklore. Members honored nobility, such as the Duke of Kent, Lord Selkirk, and Lord Dalhousie, the Governor General of Canada, by inviting them to club dinners.[37] For example, at an 1894 auction Brian Hughes was delighted to buy his grandfather's snuffbox bearing the inscription: "The Earl of Dalhousie to James Hughes, Esq., in remembrance of the Beaver Club, May 24, 1824."[38] Club members also tried to imitate nobles through lavish spending and material accoutrements. Hughes relates his grandfather's memories of members richly adorned with their medals, ruffles, gold lace, gold-clasped garters, and silver-buckled shoes. Members often displayed their wealth through hospitality to their peers and to visitors.[39] When traveling through Montreal in the early nineteenth century, John Lambert describes how the "Nor'Westers'" lavish displays of hospitality inspired both jealous resentment and "interested deference" in non-members.[40]

Status anxiety may have been behind the merchants' desire to cultivate a strong noble demeanor. One British visitor in 1820, Edward Talbot, cautioned his readers about the vanity and lack of refinement of the newly rich merchants in Montreal, originally servants or mechanics "of low origin and scanty acquirements" who made fortunes in the fur trade. Talbot was appalled by the aristocratic pretensions of this group, but grudgingly admitted that some members of the North West Company belonged to the highest class in Montreal society.[41]

Despite their affinity for the aristocracy, bourgeois values also reflected the struggles of a vigorous urban elite to establish independent claims to power and status. Davidoff and Hall assert that the British middle-class challenge to aristocratic hegemony was based on their claim to moral superiority.[42] Robert Nye has found that the French bourgeois were preoccupied with moral discipline, inner values, and control of reproduction and sex to carefully regulate inheritance strategies.[43] Many similarities can be found with the fur-trade bourgeois, who earned their position through hard work, careful planning, and merit. One of the club's medals was inscribed with the motto "Industry and Perseverance," which emphasized the efforts of men rather than their birthright.[44] Loyalty and commitment were also important ideals to club fraternity, as members were expected to attend the meetings if in town, and were forbidden from hosting parties or accepting other invitations on club days.[45] Like other bourgeois, the fur traders were encouraged to marry within their social group. For example, John Forsyth married the daughter of prominent Quebec merchant Charles Grant; Joseph Frobisher married the daughter of Jean-Baptiste Jobert and niece of Charles-Jean-Baptiste Chaboillez, founding members of the Beaver Club; Simon McTavish married the daughter of Chaboillez; and William McGillivray married the daughter of Beaver Club member Sir John McDonald of Garth.[46] However, many of the Northwest Company bourgeois married native or mixed blood women, especially after spending many years in the interior. These marriages were often strategies for building trading alliances and surviving in the bush.[47] Some, such as McGillivray, abandoned their country wives when they left the interior to become merchants in Montreal.[48]

In the Beaver Club gender and class divisions came into sharp relief, as membership was explicitly restricted to bourgeois men. However, the club was less selective of ethnicity and religion. Of the nineteen initial

Beaver Club members, eight were French-Canadian, six were Scottish, three were English, and two were American.[49] Although Scots came to dominate the Montreal fur trade and the Beaver Club, a French-Canadian presence persisted.[50] The inclusion of a variety of ethnicities and religious affiliations reflected the composition of people involved in the Montreal business and fur-trade world. The fraternal rituals of the club helped to smooth over tension arising from ethnic and religious difference. Hall suggests that clubs and voluntary associations in late eighteenth- and early nineteenth-century Britain gave their members a sense of collective identity, which helped unite men of different religious backgrounds, trades, and classes.[51] The same was probably true of the Beaver Club, which helped smooth ethnic and religious differences between its members.

The club was characterized by an odd tension between its efforts to promote harmony and a collective bourgeois identity, and its hierarchical nature. The ideal of egalitarianism was manifested in the club's organizational structure. Each member had an equal vote in electing new members, deciding on fines for those who had broken club rules, and in other club affairs. Also, members took turns rotating as president, vice president, and cork of the club, enforcing general equality without challenging the structure of hierarchy.[52] The privacy of the club probably contributed to the spirit of egalitarianism. Members felt the privilege of belonging, being set apart from the rest of society, and sharing in secrets from the outside world.[53]

Exclusivity expressed in numerical limits helped to maintain social hierarchy. Initially the Beaver Club began with nineteen men, but was expanded to forty with eight honorary members by 1807, to fifty and ten honorary members in 1815, and by 1816 the limit was fifty-five members and ten honorary members.[54] Only men who received a unanimous vote and met the club requirements could join. Bourgeois respectability required wealth and leisure, as the men were expected to dedicate time and money to club. Members had to purchase a gold medal recording the date of their first winter spent in the interior. They were fined for breaking club rules, such as failing to attend a dinner if they were in Montreal, not wearing their medals to the dinners, and forgetting to notify the secretary of guests they intended to bring to dinner.[55] Members were required to pay for their dinners even if they did not attend club meetings, and were only excused from the fee if they were ill.[56] Social pressure to drink large amounts of alcohol at the meetings was high, and men had to pay for their drinks.[57]

The club also served to distinguish fur traders from other bourgeoisie. The condition that men had to winter in the interior to join the club verified the candidate's strength and fortitude. Members were differentiated from guests by their medals, which served as a common marker to identify the members as a group. Private dinners that excluded guests were held at the beginning of every year to plan the year's events.[58] Only members had voting privileges, and each was provided with a printed book of the club's mandate, the rules and regulations, and membership list.[59]

The club's five formal toasts reflected the tension between the ideals of an emerging urban bourgeoisie, and those of an older rough and ready fur-trade society. The first toast, "the mother of all the saints," paid respect to the church, while toasts to the king and the fur trade honored the state and commerce. The rules and regulations did not indicate allegiance to any specific church, and members ranged from Roman Catholics to Presbyterians to Anglicans. The toast to "the mother of all the saints," probably the Virgin Mary, may have been a convenient way to acknowledge the importance of religion without restricting devotion to a single church. At the same time, the toast may have paid homage to an earlier fur-trade world dominated by Roman Catholicism. In the toast to "voyageurs, wives, and children," the fur traders venerated themselves and the institution of the family. It is unclear whether the toast to "voyageurs, wives, and children" referred to the fur traders themselves and their families, or to those the fur traders considered their dependents, that is, their workers, wives, and children. Finally, the last toast, to absent members, could be seen as a tribute to fraternity and brotherly love. By acknowledging these values through ritual toasts, fur traders reinforced bourgeois standards of virtue among themselves and taught them to young clerks, as the club served to initiate young fur traders and bring those who had spent years in the North American interior back into respectable society.[60] Formal toasting was a way to draw the group together to participate in a unified activity, sharing similar sentiments about religion, occupation, and masculinity that were different from that of the larger society. Perhaps the jovial and convivial atmosphere allowed these men to reassert older values while recognizing their contradiction within a changing world.

Two Beaver Club members, Simon Fraser and John McDonald of Garth, wrote a memorandum in 1859, near the end of their lives, which captured the spirit of fur traders' masculine ideals:

> We are the last of the old N[orth]. W[est]. Partners. We have known one another for many years. Which of the two survives the other we know not. We are both aged, we have lived in mutual esteem and fellowship, we have done our duty in the stations allotted us without fear, or reproach. We have braved many dangers, we have run many risks. We cannot accuse one another of any thing mean & dirty through life, nor done any disagreeable actions, nor wrong to others. We have been feared, loved & respected by natives. We have kept our men under subordination. We have thus lived long lives. We have both crossed this continent, we have explored many new points, we have met many new Tribes, we have run our Race, & as this is probably the last time we meet on earth, we part as we have lived in sincere friendship & mutual good will.[61]

III. THE GENTLEMAN AND THE WILD MAN

The fur trade bourgeois differed from other North Atlantic bourgeoisie in their masculine ideals and in their struggles to attain respectable status. As merchants, the fur traders often worked independently of social hierarchies and were open to a wide variety of cultures.[62] Merchants have been described as adventurers, gamblers who took risks for which they expected a high return.[63] The fur trade brought them into the midst of the wild, where they experienced firsthand the wonders of exotic people and places. Fur traders struggled to manage their fascination with the wild and savage while operating within an urban context of respectability. They cultivated respectability and patriotism in order to secure business contacts, and also were subject to the exigencies of their class. Yet, the rough skills learned by the fur traders in their perilous adventures were a source of pride, and they helped to create a distinction between "refined" women and "rough" men in an urban context.

The traders thus constructed their own particular type of masculinity, combining bourgeois ideals of respectability with their rugged and wondrous fur trade experiences. These two impulses were not dichotomous nor necessarily in conflict, as strength was important to respectability and honor. The Beaver Club became a safe and private forum for honoring coarse and rude behavior, such as excessive drinking and carousing, not acceptable for bourgeois men in public settings. At the same time, gentility was represented in the club's stately settings, formal rituals, and illustrious assembly. Visitors, such as Landmann, commented on the wild feasting and hard drinking that went on during club dinners, and yet gratefully recalled the "greatest civilities" received from club members.[64] While the club helped fur traders to reconcile their desires to be both rough and gentle, however, it also served to emphasize boundaries between civilized bourgeois society on the one hand, and on the other the rough bush society of voyageurs, country wives, and natives.

Some of the most interesting aspects of the Beaver Club were the formal and informal ceremonies of the meetings. The solemn rituals instilled meaning in the club's ideals, while the revelry provided a place and time in which to cement fraternal bonds. Rituals and ceremonial occasions can be seen as sites of struggles between competing representations, serving as markers for collective identity.[65] The dominant impulse in the rituals was a romanticization of the fur trade, which emphasized its importance in the men's lives, but also eased anxiety about the lack of fit between fur-trade life and urban bourgeois society.

The tension between the fur traders' desire to be refined and to be rash found expression in the structure of club meetings. The dinners began formally, following specified rituals, but then developed into wild and reckless parties. The fixed scheduling of club dinners contributed to the formal atmosphere. Formality was also expressed in codes of dress. At club functions members were obliged to wear their medals on blue ribbons or on black ribbons to honor a member's death.[66] The dinner itself reflected a tension between the savage and the civil. Country food, such as wild rice and venison, was served in crested glass and silverware in stately settings.[67] After the formal rituals of club dinners, informal socializing and frolicking could begin. A defined social space was an important part of the fraternal process because it was a time to solidify bonds and express brotherly love and harmony. Conversations must have often turned to business, with deals discussed and strategies developed.[68] However, the time for play at the dinners was also a time to turn tables, reverse meanings, and poke at the social order expressed in the rituals and rules of the club. Frequent amusements were the singing of voyageur songs, such as *La claire Fontaine* and *En roulant ma boule*.[69] James Hughes' stories include an account of the men arranging themselves on the floor, then imitating the vigorous paddling of a canoe, and mounting wine kegs to "shoot the rapids" from the table to the floor.[70] Rules ensured that every member could drink as he pleased after the toasts had gone around, firmly dividing the formal ritual from informal play.[71] In winter 1797 Landmann described in detail a wild club party: initially all men consumed a bottle of wine during the dinner, but after the married men retired, leaving the bachelors to "drink to their health," the party really began in "right earnest and true highland style," which involved war whoops, singing, heavy drinking, breaking plates and glasses, and dancing on the tables. Landmann estimated that 120 bottles of wine had been consumed at the dinner by about twenty men.[72]

In the eighteenth century, consumption of alcohol was considered a gratifying and convivial activity and accompanied almost every social occasion. In the Beaver Club it contributed to the building of trust and friendships.[73] Lambert felt that the wild abandon of the fur traders' spending and celebrating was well deserved considering the rigors and risks of fur trading.[74] Perhaps many of the members considered the wild revelry a necessary release from the tension and discomfort of their experiences in the bush. Hughes also recounted that retired fur traders tried to recreate the "untrammeled license" that they enjoyed in the wilderness.[75] Club dinners provided a safe social space for licensed wildness and drinking closely associated with release. Holding one's liquor was a source of pride. At one party Landmann admired Alexander Mackenzie and William McGillivray for being the only two men remaining in their seats when everyone else had passed out.[76] Excessive drinking could have been a demonstration of wealth. Lambent hints that the North West Company bourgeois aroused the jealousy and resentment of Montreal society for their lavish spending and incredible hospitality, which was meant to display wealth.[77]

However, disapproval of excessive drunkenness in public, and especially alcoholism, led the bourgeois to confine heavy drinking and wild abandon to an appropriate context. In a letter to John Askin, Alexander Henry inquired if he enjoyed his visit to the Beaver Club, where he no doubt joined in the merriment of drink, and a few paragraphs later criticized a late colleague for excessive drinking.[78] In the late eighteenth century public drunkenness and swearing were increasingly condemned.[79] Serious drinking was recognized as a social ill, and associated with poverty, misery, disease, and death.[80] Beaver Club members may have been especially cautious to define a framed time and place for their wild abandon.

Some rituals especially captured the tension in fur traders' attitudes toward their bush experiences. Passing the calumet,[81] common to many native cultures, often marked the beginning of conferences or treaties, and paid tribute to spirits.[82] Although the fur traders probably appreciated the solemn and sacred nature of the calumet, a greater appeal must have lain in the exotic aspects of adopting native traditions. Traveler John Palmer noted that Indian manners, customs, and language, especially war whoops, were closely imitated at club dinners.[83] The attitude of the fur traders toward natives was complex and often contradictory. Fur traders lived with natives, often married them, depended on them for survival, and traded with them. Respect and common understanding existed in the relationship. Yet, to the fur traders, natives were a savage people, both appealing and dangerous. The tradition of bourgeois traders marrying native women created a particular anxiety for the bourgeois to distance themselves from native influences in a respectable urban environment. Fur traders were fascinated with the savage, and the safe and constricted atmosphere of the club allowed them a place and time to explore and revel in savagery, while maintaining a respectable distance. Ritualizing native customs may have provided a way for the bourgeois to both dissociate from and honor them. Also, exotic rituals instilled romance in fraternal orders, and spoke to the desire for spiritualism. Passing the peace pipe around must have underscored the values of brotherly love and fraternity, as Club rules refer to the calumet as the "usual emblem of Peace."[84]

A significant aspect of fraternal bonding was reminiscing about fur-trade experiences, an activity that was so highly valued it was part of the mandate published in the members' club rules.[85] In retelling his own adventures, each member asserted claims to valor and strength, while also renewing links of friendship and camaraderie.[86] Reminiscing allowed members to recast their fur-trade memories by highlighting acceptable aspects of that life, such as the manly honor of completing difficult journeys, while silencing other memories, such as abandoned country wives and families. Yet at the same time, retelling their experiences may have allowed many to mourn their country families and friends, and their lost youth. Reminiscing was an essential method in teaching and revering the masculine values of strength, courage, fortitude, and perseverance gained in fur-trade experience. A poem presented to the club by John Johnston on 19 November 1814 described the pleasure of meeting together with the wanderers of Canada's wide domain, "to recount the toils and perils past." While urging members to participate in the War of 1812 to protect the fur trade, the poem complimented traders for their force, skill, and "manly heart," and lauded their brave suffering in difficult situations.[87] Military service was valued because it provided evidence of a man's courage and honor. Fur traders reminded each other to protect their honor, to avoid imposition, and to always defend themselves when attacked. Not only was strength in action highly valued, but also strength in rhetoric. One clerk congratulated another for his force and elegance with words and manly roughness with his argument in his letters.[88] The motto of the Club, "fortitude in distress," clearly indicated the primacy of the masculine ideals of ruggedness, might, and courage. The mandate of the Club proudly asserted that all initial members had been fur traders from an early age, referring to them as "voyageurs."[89] Members even considered changing the name to the "Voyageur Club."[90]

There was no clear definition of the term *voyageur*. It was used for all hardy travelers, and yet often the term referred only to French-Canadian fur trade laborers. Regardless of the bourgeois' use of language, their attitudes toward fur-trade workers were no less ambiguous than their attitudes toward natives. The Beaver Club toast to "voyageurs, wives and children" may have been another example of the bourgeois trying to mimic their workers by calling themselves voyageurs. By singing voyageurs' songs, and by reenacting canoeing, fur traders could identify with voyageur toughness and rugged risk-taking masculinity, while they distanced themselves from their men in the everyday world. At the same time, the bourgeois appropriated the voyageurs' experiences and culture, as they revered the activities and adventures of their workers, in which the bourgeois did not participate.

IV. Conclusions

Fur traders were different from other elite men in Montreal. Their experience in the fur trade was foreign to respectable urban society but was not easily forgotten by its participants. Their rough ways formed in bush society were both a source of anxiety and a source of pride. The Beaver Club provided them with a forum in which to make sense of their past experiences, cast them in a positive light, and assert their particular brand of the ideal man. At the same time, the Beaver Club was primarily a respectable men's dining club, where Montreal's bourgeois society met to forge business alliances, exchange information, share ideas, and cement social ties. Although the club allowed members to indulge in idealization of the savage and an older rough and ready fur-trade world, the respectable man remained the dominant ideal.

At club meetings, secluded from women, the lower orders, and native people, Montreal's bourgeois men could focus on themselves, cultivate their own desires and identities, and affirm their values. Men could honor strength, courage, and perseverance, all acceptable aspects of bourgeois masculinity, but they could also venerate risk taking, the spirit of adventure, and a taste for the exotic, qualities that boarded on the rough and uncouth. The privacy of the Club allowed the traders to indulge in rough behavior, while protecting their respectable reputations. These masculine ideals also brought the distinction between rough men and refined women into greater relief. The secluded fraternal setting, where men shared their memories and emotions, could not be confused with the domestic sphere, which was the domain of women.

Notes

1. I use the term *bourgeois* in this chapter sometimes to refer to the emerging middle class. However, in the Montreal fur trade merchants and managers were referred to as "bourgeois." Although most of the fur trade bourgeois were part of Montreal's bourgeoisie, the terms have distinct meanings.
2. For examples see Lynn Hetherington, "Canada's First Social Club," *The University Magazine* 9 (April 1910): 296–305, esp. 297, and Robert Watson, "The First Beaver Club," *The Beaver* Outfit 262, no. 3

(December 1931): 334–37, esp. 335. Many works on fur-trade and Montreal history cite frequently George Bryce, *The Remarkable History of the Hudson's Bay Company including that of the French Traders of the North-West, XY, and Astor Fur Companies* (Toronto: William Briggs, 1900) and *Mackenzie, Selkirk, Simpson: The Makers of Canada* (Toronto: Morang & Co., Ltd., 1910); Clifford P. Wilson, "The Beaver Club," *The Beaver*, Outfit 266, no. 4 (March 1936): 19–24, 64; Donald Creighton, *The Empire of the St. Lawrence* (Toronto: MacMillan Co., 1956), 27; Marjorie Wilkins Campbell, *The North West Company* (New York: St. Martin's Press, 1957) and *McGillivray: Lord of the Northwest* (Toronto and Vancouver: Clarke, Irwin & Co. Ltd., 1962). An exception is provided by Lawrence J. Burpee, who does not cite his evidence, but discusses primary and secondary sources within the text. Lawrence J. Burpee, "The Beaver Club," *Canadian Historical Association Annual Report* (1924): 73–91. Another exception is Jennifer Brown, whose brief mention of the Beaver Club describes its role of easing the transition of fur traders back into community life after long absences in the interior. Jennifer S. H. Brown, *Strangers in Blood: Fur Trade Company Families in Indian Country* (Vancouver: University of British Columbia Press, 1980), 44.

3. Louise Dechêne, "La Croissance de Montréal au XVIIIe Siècle," *Revue d'histoire de l'Amérique française* 27, no. 2 (September 1973): 163–79, esp. 167; Jean-Paul Bernard, Paul-André Linteau, and Jean-Claude Robert, "La Structure professionnelle de Montréal en 1825," *Revue d'histoire de l'Amérique française* 34, no. 3 (December 1976): 383–415, esp. 390–91. Fernand Ouellet argues that the Montreal fur trade began to decline as early as 1803, but admits that "even in decline, the famous fur trade would continue to exert a considerable influence on certain elements of society." Fernand Ouellet, *Economic and Social History of Quebec, 1760–1850* (Ottawa: Institute of Canadian Studies, Carleton University, 1980), 181–82, 186.

4. David T. Ruddel, *Québec City, 1765–1831* (Ottawa: Canadian Museum of Civilization, 1987), 23.

5. Fernand Ouellet, *Lower Canada 1791–1840, Social Change and Nationalism,* trans. Patricia Claxton (Toronto: McClelland and Stewart, 1980), 38–39, 63, and *Economy, Class, and Nation in Quebec: Interpretive Essays,* ed. and trans. Jacques A. Barbier (Toronto: Copp,

Clark, Pitman, 1991), 79–80; and Brown, *Strangers in Blood* (see note 2), 35–36. See also Creighton, who describes the political program of the Montreal merchants in *Empire of the St. Lawrence* (see note 2), 23, 35–55.

6. Peter Clark, "Sociability and Urbanity: Clubs and Societies in the Eighteenth Century City," The Eighth H. J. Dyos Memorial Lecture (Leicester: University of Leicester, Victoria Studies Centre, 1986), 17–19, 23.

7. Steven Conrad Bullock, "The Ancient and Honorable Society: Freemasonry in America, 1730–1830," (Ph.D. diss., Brown University, 1986), 5, 78, 84.

8. George Landmann, "Notes By Roderick McKenzie on books read by him ... ," Part One, in *Adventures and Recollections of Colonel Landmann, Late of the Corps of Royal Engineers* (London: Colburn and Co., 1852), 232–33, 295–96. Ottawa, National Archives of Canada, Masson Collection, Miscellaneous Papers, MG19 C1, vol. 44, microfilm reel #C–15639, n.d. pages 11–19; Charles Bert Reed also describes the parties at Fort William in *Masters of the Wilderness* (Chicago: University of Chicago Press, 1914), 70–71. Reed's article on the Beaver Club is almost entirely a quotation of Brian Hughes' describing the stories he was told by his grandfather, James Hughes, who was a Beaver Club member. Burpee is skeptical about much of the information provided by Hughes because many of the particulars are inconsistent with other historical sources. Burpee, "The Beaver Club" (see note 2), 89–90.

9. Journal of Joseph Frobisher, 1806–10, Ottawa, National Archives of Canada, McTavish, Frobisher & Company Collection, MG19 A5, vol. 4.

10. Brothers in Law Society of Montreal Minute Book, 1821–33, Montreal, McCord Museum of Canadian History Archives, M21413.

11. The Bachelor's Club was listed frequently in the Journal of Joseph Frobisher and mentioned in a letter from James Caldwell, Montreal, to Simon McTavish, New York Coffee House in London, 5 December 1792. Montreal, McGill Rare Books, MS 43111, Simon McTavish Correspondence, 1792–1800. The Montreal Hunt Club was formed in 1826, with Beaver Club member John Forsyth as its first president. Marcel Caya, ed., *Guide to Archival Resources at McGill University* (Montreal: McGill University Archives, 1985), 3:294. Many Beaver Club

members belonged to the Montreal Fire Club, which operated between 1786 and 1814, with a membership limit of fourteen. It was formed to provide mutual assistance in case of fire, as well as convivial association. Montreal, McGill Rare Books, MS 437, Montreal Fire Club Minute Book, 1786–1814. Some of the clubs seemed to be class based, and not exclusive to men. In the late 1790s, Isaac Weld describes a club of Montreal's "principal inhabitants," both men and women, which met once a week or fortnight to dine. Isaac Weld, Jr., *Travels Through the States of North America, and the Provinces of Upper and Lower Canada, During the Years 1795, 1796, and 1797*, 4th ed., 2 vols. (London: John Stockdale, 1807), 1:315.

12. A. J. B. Milborne, *Freemasonry in the Province of Quebec, 1759–1959* (Knowlton, QC: P.D.D.G.M, G.L.Q., 1960), 40, 61–68; J. Lawrence Runnalls, "Simon McGillivray 1783–1840," *The Papers of the Canadian Masonic Research Association* (Hamilton: 44th Meeting of the Association of The Heritage Lodge, No. 73, A.F. & A.M., G.R.C., 1966), 3:1487–89.

13. John E. Taylor, "Freemasonry in Old Canada and the War of 1812–15," *The Papers of the Canadian Masonic Research Association* (Toronto: 23rd Meeting of the Association, A.F. & A.M., G.R.C., 1958), 2:783, 787; A. J. B. Milborne, "The Murals in the Memorial Hall, Montreal Masonic Memorial Temple," *The Papers of the Canadian Masonic Research Association* (Montreal: 8th Meeting of the Association, A.F. & A.M., G.R.C., 1953), 1:255–57.

14. Beaver Club Minute Book, 1807–27, Original, 3 February 1827, Montreal, McCord Museum of Canadian History Archives, M14449, 120. Photostats and typescript can also be obtained at McGill Rare Books and the National Archives of Canada.

15. Heather Devine, "Roots in the Mohawk Valley: Sir William Johnson's Legacy in the North West Company," in *The Fur Trade Revisited: Selected Papers of the Sixth North American Fur Trade Conference, Mackinac Island, Michigan, 1991*, ed. Jennifer S. H. Brown, W. J. Eccles, and Donald P. Heldman (East Lansing, Michigan State University Press, 1994), 217–42, esp. 228–30. Also see Brown, *Strangers in Blood* (see note 2), 36–38.

16. It is difficult to determine whether Simon McTavish, general director of the North West Company, was a member of the Beaver Club. His name

does not appear in the Minute Book, but he is listed as a member since 1792 in the 1819 issue of the *Rules and Regulations of the Beaver Club: Instituted in 1785* (Montreal: W. Gray 1819), McCord Museum of Canadian History Archives, M1444S0, 10 (the name "De Rocheblave" is written on the front cover). Some scholars assert that fur traders disliked McTavish so much that they never invited him to join, or that "the Marquis" himself refused to meet his colleagues on an equal footing in the Club. Burpee, "The Beaver Club" (see note 2), 74–75.

17. David A. Armour, "Ainsse (Ainse, Hains, Hins), Joseph–Louis (Louis–Joseph)," in *Dictionary of Canadian Biography* (hereafter *DCB*) (Toronto: University of Toronto Press, 1983), 5:7–9; Barry M. Gough, "Pond, Peter," in *DCB*, 5:681–86.
18. Beaver Club Minute Book (see note 14), 4, 26, 47.
19. This is suggested by Burpee, "The Beaver Club" (see note 2), 75.
20. Reed, *Masters of the Wilderness* (see note 8), 75, 77, 79, 80.
21. Gerald J. J. Tulchinsky, "Auldjo, Alexander," in *DCB* (see note 17), 6:18–20; Elinor Kyte Senior, "David, David," in *DCB* (see note 17), 6:179–81; Gerald J. J. Tulchinsky, "Forsyth, John," *DCB* (see note 17), 7:309–11; Bruce G. Wilson, *The Enterprises of Robert Hamilton: A Study of Wealth and Influence in Early Upper Canada, 1776–1812* (Ottawa: Carleton University Press, 1983), 12–13.
22. Reed, *Masters of the Wilderness* (see note 8), 69.
23. Thomas Brennan, *Public Drinking and Popular Culture in Eighteenth-Century Paris* (Princeton, N.J.: Princeton University Press, 1988), 8; Kym Rice, *Early American Taverns: For the Entertainment of Friends and Strangers* (Chicago: Regnery Gateway, 1983), 88.
24. *Rules and Regulations* (see note 16), 3; Beaver Club Minute Book (see note 14), 2.
25. For an example of a Beaver Club menu, see Jehane Benoît, "Wintering Dishes," *Canadian Collector* 20, no. 3 (May/June 1985): 25–27. For mention of Beaver Club glass and silverware, see Watson, "The First Beaver Club" (see note 2), 337.
26. Leonore Davidoff and Catherine Hall, *Family Fortunes: Men and Women of the English Middle Class, 1780–1850* (Chicago: University of Chicago Press, 1987), 13, 30.
27. Ibid., 18–23. Also see Robert A. Nye, *Masculinity and Male Codes of Honor in Modern France* (New York: Oxford University Press, 1993), 8, 31–33.

28. Davidoff and Hall, *Family Fortunes* (see note 26), 13, 25, 29.
29. Catherine Hall, *White, Male and Middle Class: Explorations in Feminism and History* (New York: Routledge, 1992), 158.
30. Mark C. Carnes, *Secret Ritual and Manhood in Victorian America* (New Haven, Conn. and London: Yale University Press, 1989), 14.
31. Margaret S. Creighton, "American Mariners and the Rites of Manhood, 1830–1870," in *Jack Tar in History: Essays in the History of Maritime Life and Labour,* ed. Colin Howell and Richard J. Twomey (Fredericton, N.B.: Acadiensis Press, 1991), 132–63, esp. 147.
32. Brown, *Strangers in Blood* (see note 2), 35, 47–48.
33. G. Moffatt, Fort William, to George Gordon, Monontagué 25 July 1809, Toronto, Archives of Ontario, George Gordon Papers, MU 1146.
34. For example, see W. Kaye Lamb, ed., *Sixteen Years in Indian Country: The Journal of Daniel Williams Harmon, 1800–1816,* (Toronto: MacMillan Company of Canada Ltd., 1957), 197–98.
35. Davidoff and Hall, *Family Fortunes* (see note 26), 18; Nye, *Masculinity and Male Codes of Honor* (see note 27), 32.
36. Ouellet, *Economy, Class, and Nation* (see note 5), 62, 80, 94–95, 109.
37. Campbell, *The North West Company,* 130, 140; "Incidents, Deaths, & c." *Canadian Magazine* 2, no. 11 (14 May 1824): 473.
38. Reed, *Masters of the Wilderness* (see note 8), 57–58.
39. Ibid., 68, 75.
40. John Lambent, *Travels Through Canada, and the United States of North America, in the years 1806, 1807, & 1808. To Which are Added, Biographical Notices and Anecdotes of Some of the Leading Characters in the United States,* 2 vols. 2nd ed. (1813; London: C. Cradock and W. Joy, 1814), 295–96, 524.
41. Edward Allen Talbot, *Five Years' Residence in the Canadas: Including a Tour through Part of the United States of America in the Year 1823,* 2 vols. (London: Longman, Hurst, Rees, Orme, Brown and Green, 1824), 2:282–84. John Duncan also criticizes the Montreal bourgeoisie for their deficiency in enterprise and public spirit. John M. Duncan, *Travels Through Part of the United Slates and Canada in 1818 and 1819,* 2 vols. (Glasgow: Wardlaw and Cunninghame, 1823), 2:156–57
42. Davidoff and Hall, *Family Fortunes* (see note 26), 18–20, 30.
43. Nye, *Masculinity and Male Codes of Honor* (see note 27), 32–34.
44. Hetherington, "Canada's First Social Club" (see note 2), 298.

45. Beaver Club Minute Book (see note 14), 2; *Rules and Regulations* (see note 16), 5.
46. Tulchinsky, "Forsyth" (see note 21), 311; Fernand Ouellet, "Frobisher, Joseph," in *DCB* (see note 17), 5:331–34, esp. 333 and "McTavish, Simon," in *DCB* (see note 17), 5:560–67, esp. 566; Campbell, *McGillivray* (see note 2), 111.
47. Brown, *Strangers in Blood* (see note 2), 81–110; Van Kirk, *"Many Tender Ties": Women in Fur Trade Society in Western Canada, 1670–1870* (Winnipeg, Manitoba: Watson and Dwyer Publishing, Ltd., 1980), 28–52
48. Campbell, *McGillivray* (see note 2), 68; Brown, *Strangers in Blood* (see note 2), 90; Van Kirk, *Many Tender Ties* (see note 47), 50.
49. Beaver Club Minute Book (see note 14), 3.
50. For example, F. A. Larocque and J. M. Lamothe were elected in 1815 and Dominique Ducharme attended the last meeting in 1827. Beaver Club Minute Book (see note 14), 94, 112, 121.
51. Hall, *White, Male and Middle Class* (see note 29), 157.
52. Beaver Club Minute Book (see note 14), 1–2; *Rules and Regulations* (see note 16), 5–6.
53. Bullock found the same with the Freemasons. Although the organization kept its work and rituals secret, they participated visibly in public life and believed they were working toward a public, rather than a private, good, and they demanded public honor. Bullock, "The Ancient and Honorable Society" (see note 7), 4–5.
54. Beaver Club Minute Book (see note 14), 1, 90, 113; *Rules and Regulations* (see note 16), 5.
55. *Rules and Regulations* (see note 16), 3–6. Hetherington discusses three surviving medals at the Chateau de Ramezay in Montreal and at the Library of the Parliament Buildings in Ottawa, as well as some privately owned plates and snuff boxes. Hetherington, "Canada's First Social Club" (see note 2), 298. Watson mentions that cups and silver plates bearing the mark of the Beaver Club were put up at auctions throughout the country. Watson, "The First Beaver Club" (see note 2), 337. Also, a picture of a gold brooch of a beaver, said to be worn by wives of Beaver Club members, appears in "The HBC Packet," *The Beaver*, Outfit 264, no. 3 (December 1933): 5–6.
56. For an example of a member charged for a dinner he did not attend, see Beaver Club Minute Book (see note 14), 21 January 1809, 32. For an

example of a member excused from dinner fees because of illness, see Beaver Club Minute Book (see note 14), 53, 82.
57. See the accounts listed at the end of every dinner in the Minute Book (see note 14).
58. For example, see the first meeting of the years 1815–16 and 1816–17, Beaver Club Minute Book (see note 14), 97–98, 113.
59. *Rules and Regulations* (see note 16), 4.
60. Ibid., 3.
61. W. Kaye Lamb, ed., *The Letters and Journals of Simon Fraser, 1806–1808* (Toronto: MacMillan Company of Canada, 1960), 271, Montreal, McCord Museum of Canadian History Archives, M18638, Memorandum recording the meeting of Simon Fraser and John McDonald of Garth, the last two surviving partners of the North West Company, 1 August 1859, Original.
62. Brown, *Strangers in Blood* (see note 2), 2–3.
63. Wilson, *The Enterprises of Robert Hamilton* (see note 21), 12, 20–21.
64. Landmann, *Adventures and Recollections* (see note 8), 233–34.
65. Nye, *Masculinity and Male Codes of Honor* (see note 27), 10–11.
66. Beaver Club Minute Book (see note 14), 1–2; *Rules and Regulations* (see note 16), 5.
67. Benoit, "Wintering Dishes" (see note 25), 25–27; Watson, "The First Beaver Club" (see note 2), 337.
68. Reed, *Masters of the Wilderness* (see note 8), 68.
69. *Rules and Regulations* (see note 16), 3; Reed, *Masters of the Wilderness* (see note 8), 68.
70. Reed, *Masters of the Wilderness* (see note 8), 68.
71. Beaver Club Minute Book (see note 14), 1; *Rules and Regulations* (see note 16), 6.
72. Landmann, *Adventures and Recollections* (see note 8), 234, 238.
73. Rice, *Early American Taverns* (see note 23), 98. Bullock found that for Masons convivial drinking and conversation were very important for specific expressions of brotherly love and fraternity. Bullock, "The Ancient and Honorable Society" (see note 7), 62.
74. Lambert, *Travels Through Canada* (see note 40), 295.
75. Reed, *Masters of the Wilderness* (see note 8), 65.
76. Landmann, *Adventures and Recollections* (see note 8), 296; Rice, *Early American Taverns* (see note 23), 98.

78   *Race and Gender in the Northern Colonies*

77. Lambert, *Travels Through Canada* (see note 40), 295–96; 524. Clark found that in eighteenth-century English clubs conspicuous consumption and excess were an essential ingredient of club sociability, Clark, "Sociability and Urbanity" (see note 6), 20.
78. Alexander Henry, Montreal, to John Askin, Strathbane, 9 May 1815, *The John Askin Papers, Vol. 2, 1796–1820*, ed. Milo M. Quaife (Detroit: Detroit Library Commission, 1928–31), 781–83.
79. Clark, "Sociability and Urbanity" (see note 6), 21.
80. Rice, *Early American Taverns* (see note 23), 101.
81. *Rules and Regulations* (see note 16), 3.
82. Basil Johnston, *Ojibwa Ceremonies* (Toronto: McClelland and Stewart, 1982), 33, 160.
83. John Palmer, *Journal of Travels in the United States of America and in Lower Canada, Performed in the Year 1817; Containing Particulars Relating to the Prices of Land and Provisions, Remarks on the Country and the People, Interesting Anecdotes, and an Account of the Commerce, Trade, and Present State of Washington, New York, Philadelphia, Boston, Baltimore, Albany, Cincinnati, Pittsburg, Lexington, Quebec, Montreal, &c.* (London: Sherwood, Neely, and Jones, 1818), 216–17.
84. Other bourgeois fraternities also imitated native culture, the most obvious being the Improved Order of the Red Men, established in the United States in 1834. Carnes describes in detail the order's rituals and language, inspired by native culture, such as sachems invoking the "Great Spirit of the Universe" and paleface warriors fearlessly facing death. Unfortunately Carnes's only explanation for why native culture was chosen as a model for the fraternity is that the men who were transforming America into an urban, industrial society desired to recreate a primitive past. Mark C. Carnes, "Middle-Class Men and the Solace of Fraternal Ritual," in *Meanings for Manhood: Constructions of Masculinity in Victorian America*, ed. Mark C. Carnes and Clyde Griffen (Chicago: University of Chicago Press, 1990), 37–52, esp. 39–45.
85. *Rules and Regulations* (see note 16), 3.
86. Reed, *Masters of the Wilderness* (see note 8), 69.
87. Beaver Club Minute Book (see note 14), 83.
88. Frederick Goedike, Aguiwang, to George Gordon, Michipicoten, 29 October 1811, George Gordon Papers.

89. *Rules and Regulations* (see note 16), 1.
90. Beaver Club Minute Book (see note 14), 28 September 1807, 6–7.

Chapter Four
Excerpt from *Astoria*

Washington Irving

>Two expeditions set on foot — The Tonquin and her crew — Captain Thorn, his character — The partners and clerks — Canadian voyageurs, their habits, employments, dress, character, songs — Expedition of a Canadian boat and its crew by land and water — Arrival at New York — Preparation for a sea voyage — North west braggarts — Underhand precautions.

In prosecuting his great scheme of commerce and colonization, two expeditions were devised by Mr. Astor, one by sea, the other by land. The former was to carry out the people, stores, ammunition, and merchandize, requisite for establishing a fortified trading post at the mouth of Columbia river. The latter, conducted by Mr. Hunt, was to proceed up the Missouri, and across the Rocky mountains, to the same point; exploring a line of communication across the continent, and noting the places where interior trading posts might be established. The expedition by sea is the one which comes first under consideration.

A fine ship was provided called the Tonquin, of two hundred and ninety tons burthen, mounting ten guns, with a crew of twenty men. She carried an assortment of merchandise for trading with the natives of the sea board and of the interior, together with the frame of a schooner, to be employed in the coasting trade. Seeds also were provided for the cultivation of the soil, and nothing was neglected for the necessary supply of the establishment. The command of the ship was intrusted to Jonathan Thorn, of New York, a lieutenant in the United States navy, on leave of absence. He was a man of courage and firmness, who had distinguished himself in our Tripolitan war, and, from being accustomed to naval discipline, was considered by Mr. Astor as well fitted to take charge of an expedition of the kind. Four of the partners were to embark in the ship, namely, Messrs. M'Kay, M'Dougal, David Stuart, and his nephew, Robert Stuart. Mr. M'Dougal was empowered by Mr. Astor to act as his proxy in the absence of Mr. Hunt, to vote for him and in his name, on any question that might come before any meeting of the persons interested in the voyage.

Besides the partners, there were twelve clerks to go out in the ship, several of them natives of Canada, who had some experience in Indian trade. They were bound to the service of the company for five years, at the rate of one hundred dollars a year, payable at the expiration of the term, and an annual equipment of clothing to the amount of forty dollars. In case of ill conduct they were liable to forfeit their wages and be dismissed; but, should they acquit themselves well, the confident expectation was held out to them of promotion and partnership. Their interests were thus, to some extent, identified with those of the company.

Several artisans were likewise to sail in the ship, for the supply of the colony; but the most peculiar and characteristic part of this motley embarkation consisted of thirteen Canadian "voyageurs," who had enlisted for five years. As this class of functionaries will continually recur in the course of the following narrations, and as they form one of those distinct and strongly marked castes or orders of people, springing up in this vast continent out of geographical circumstances, or the varied pursuits, habitudes, and origins of its population, we shall sketch a few of their characteristics for the information of the reader.

The "voyageurs" form a kind of confraternity in the Canadas, like arrieros, or carriers of Spain, and, like them, are employed in long internal expeditions of travel and traffic: with this difference, that the arrieros travel by land, the voyageurs by water; the former with mules and horses, the latter with batteaux and canoes. The voyageurs may be said to have sprung up out of the fur trade, having originally been employed by the early French merchants in their trading expeditions through the labyrinth of rivers and lakes of the boundless interior. They were coeval with the *coureurs des bois,* or rangers of the woods, already noticed, and, like them, in the intervals of their long, arduous, and laborious expeditions, were prone to pass their time in idleness and revelry about the trading posts or settlements; squandering their hard earnings in heedless conviviality, and rivalling their neighbours, the Indians, in indolent indulgence, and an impudent disregard of the morrow.

When Canada passed under British domination, and the old French trading houses were broken up, the voyageurs, like the *coureurs des bois,* were for a time disheartened and disconsolate, and with difficulty could reconcile themselves to the service of the new comers, so different in habits, manners, and language, from their former employers. By degrees, however, they became accustomed to the change, and at length came to consider the British fur traders, and especially the members of the North-west Company, as the legitimate lords of creation.

The dress of these people is generally half civilized, half savage. They wear a capot or surtout, made of a blanket, a striped cotton shirt, cloth trousers, or leathern legging moccasins of deer skin, and a belt of variegated worsted, from which are suspended the knife, tobacco pouch, and other implements. Their language is of the same piebald character, being a French patois, embroidered with Indian and English words and phrases.

The lives of the voyageurs are passed in wild and extensive rovings, in the service of individuals, but more especially of the fur traders. They are generally of French descent, and inherit much of the gaiety and lightness of heart of their ancestors, being full of anecdote and song, and ever ready for the dance. They inherit, too, a fund of civility and complaisance; and, instead of that hardness and grossness which men in laborious life are apt to indulge towards each other, they are mutually obliging and accommodating; interchanging find offices, yielding each other assistance and comfort in every emergency, and using the familiar appellations of "cousin" and "brother," when there is in fact no relationship. Their natural good will is probably heightened by a community of adventure and hardship in their precarious and wandering life.

No men are more submissive to their leaders and employers, more capable of enduring hardship, or more good humoured under privations.

Never are they so happy as when on long and rough expeditions, toiling up rivers or coasting lakes; encamping at night on the boarders, gossiping round their fires, and bivouacking in the open air. They are dexterous boatmen, vigorous and adroit with the oar and paddle, and will row from morning unto night without a murmur. The steersman often sings an old traditionary French song, with some regular burden in which they all join, keeping time with their oars: if at any time they flag in spirits or relax in exertion, it is but necessary to strike up a song of the kind to put them all in fresh spirits and activity. The Canadian waters are vocal with these little French chansons, that have been echoed from mouth to mouth and transmitted from father to son, from the earliest days of the colony; and it has a pleasing effect, in a still golden summer evening, to see a batteau gliding across the bosom of a lake and dipping its oars to the cadence of these quaint old ditties, or sweeping along, in full chorus, on a bright sunny morning, down the transparent current of one of the Canadian rivers.

But we are talking of things that are fast fading away! The march of mechanical invention is driving every thing poetical before it. The steam-boats, which are fast dispelling the wildness and romance of our lakes and rivers, and aiding to subdue the world into common-place, are proving as fatal to the race of the Canadian voyageurs as they have been to that of the boatmen on the Mississippi. Their glory is departed. They are no longer the lords of our internal seas, and the great navigators of the wilderness. Some of them may still occasionally be seen coasting the lower lakes with their frail barks, and pitching their camps and lighting their fires upon the shores; but their range is fast contracting to those remote waters and shallow and obstructed rivers unvisited by the steam-boat. In the course of years they will gradually disappear; their songs will die away like the echoes they once awakened, and the Canadian voyageurs will become a forgotten race, or remembered, like their associates, the Indians, among the poetical images of past times, and as themes for local and romantic associations.

An instance of the buoyant temperament and the professional pride of these people was furnished in the gay and braggart style in which they arrived at New York to join the enterprise. They were determined to regale and astonish the people of the "States" with the sight of a Canadian boat and a Canadian crew. They accordingly fitted up a large but light bark canoe, such as is used in the fur trade; transported it in a waggon from the banks of the St. Lawrence to the shores of lake Champlain: traversed the lake in it, from end to end; hoisted it again in a waggon and wheeled it off to Lansingburgh, and there launched it upon the waters of the Hudson. Down this river they plied their course merrily on a fine summer's day, making its banks resound for the first time with their old French boat songs; passing by the villages with whoop and halloo, so as to make the honest Dutch farmers mistake them for a crew of savages. In this way they swept, in full song, and with regular flourish of the paddle, round New York, in a still summer evening, to the wonder and admiration of its inhabitants, who had never before witnessed on their waters, a nautical apparition of the kind.

Such was the variegated band of adventurers about to embark in the Tonquin on this arduous and doubtful enterprise. While yet in port and on dry land, in the bustle of preparation and the excitement of novelty, all was sunshine and promise. The Canadians especially, who with their constitutional vivacity, have a considerable dash of the gascon, were buoyant and boastful, and great braggarts as to the future; while all those who had been in the service of the North-west Company, and engaged in the Indian trade, plumed themselves upon their hardihood and their capacity to endure privations. If Mr. Astor ventured to hint at the difficulties they might have to encounter, they treated them with scorn. They were "north-westers;" men seasoned to hardships, who cared for neither wind nor weather. They could live hard, lie hard, sleep hard, eat dogs! — in a word they were ready to do and suffer any thing for the good of the enterprise. With all this profession of zeal and devotion, Mr. Actor vas not over confident of the stability and firm faith of these mercurial beings. He had received information, also, that an armed brig from Halifax, probably at the instigation of the North-west Company, was hovering on the coast, watching for the Tonquin, with the purpose of impressing the Canadians on board of her, as British subjects, and thus interrupting the voyage. It was a time of doubt and anxiety, when the relations between the United States and Great Britain were daily assuming a more precarious aspect, and verging towards that war which shortly ensued. As a precautionary measure, therefore, he required the voyageurs, as they were about to enter into the service of an American association, and to reside within the limits of the United States, should take the oaths of naturalization as

American citizens. To this they readily agreed, and shortly afterwards assured him that they had actually done so. It was not until after they had sailed that he discovered that they had entirely deceived him in the matter.

Chapter Five
Women of New France

Allan Greer

Men from Europe who visited New France almost always had something to say about the women of the colony, and their comments were mostly complimentary. Here is a representative example: "They are witty, which affords them superiority over men in almost all circumstances." Peter Kalm's journals are chock full of remarks about the ladies: how they "dress and powder their hair every day, and put their locks in papers every night," the way they tease Swedish gentlemen about their awkward use of French, the songs they sing, and so on. By and large, passages such as these from the travel literature are little more than superficial observations on the manners of the upper classes, often spiced with a playful inversion of the "natural" sexual hierarchy. Bacqueville de La Potherie took some of the shine off his gallantry by revealing his expectations about Canadian women: "Although they are, in a certain sense, part of a New World, their manners are not as bizarre or as savage as one would imagine. On the contrary, the sex there is as polite as anywhere in the kingdom." Interesting, though it may be, from a number of points of view, source material of this sort tells us nothing straightforward about the "position of women" in New France or about how well the realities of that period measured up to modern standards of sexual equality.

French-Canadian women and the men who wrote of their charming "superiority" all inhabited an early modern world in which it was assumed that woman, because of her nature, needed to be governed by man. Some of our writers were too polite to insist on masculine power in a heavy-handed way, but the ideologues of the period could be startlingly frank when they got down to the fundamental principles of patriarchy. Likening the family to a kingdom, the French political philosopher Jean Bodin wrote of "the authoritie, power, and commaund that the husband hath over his wife, by the lawes both of God and man: as also the subjection, reverence, and obedience which the woman oweth unto her husband..." The bishop of Québec took this same, basically patriarchal, model for granted when he issued advice to colonial wives. A woman owed her husband, not only "a sincere and cordial love," but also "respect, obedience and the sweetness and patience to bear with his faults and his bad moods." Like other collectivities, the family should operate on the basis of authority and, in this case, it was the paterfamilias who provided that authority, guiding and, if necessary, punishing wife, children, and servants alike. Patriarchy was not a program or a policy consciously devised by power-hungry men; in normal circumstances, it was not a subject for debate and discussion; we should recognize patriarchy as something more profound — a pattern of thinking and acting that had, over the centuries, entered into the customs and into the very languages of Europe, structuring relationships and shaping personal identities.

Most societies build elaborate cultural edifices around the basic male-female polarity, and the Iroquoian peoples who shared the St. Lawrence valley with the French had their own construction of gender. There were enough superficial similarities with European ways that the French could recognize some Iroquois practices as "normal." Women worked hard taking care of hearth, home, and food, whereas men roamed far and wide; only males could aspire to the prestige attached to success in war; public speaking, a key to political influence, was a male monopoly; and civil chiefs and war chiefs were always men. Yet, in spite of all these shared elements, the Iroquois gender regime stands in basic contrast with that of the French, for it was not patriarchal. Women shouldered the burdens of the domestic economy, but they also enjoyed full control over the household, and a man who did not make himself acceptable to some female-dominated family group would soon go hungry. Descent went through the female line, and therefore only women could bestow the names that men needed when they were elevated to chieftain status. This gave women a preponderant voice in the selection of chiefs. The male monopoly over "public office" was further offset by the fact that chiefs exercised only very limited powers; among the non-authoritarian Iroquois, command and obedience had nothing to do with the running of villages, tribes, or families. Leaders never made decisions without consulting the wishes of the community and, as members of the community, women made their views known. The Jesuit Joseph-François Lafitau, an astute observer of the Christian Iroquois community of Kahnawaké, was struck by the power of Amerindian women:

> Nothing, however, is more real than this superiority of the women. It is of them that the nation really consists; and it is through them that the nobility of the blood, the genealogical tree and the families are perpetuated. All real authority is vested in them. The land, the fields and their harvest all belong to them. They are the souls of the Councils, the arbiters of peace and of war. They have charge of the public treasury. To them are given the slaves. They arrange marriages. The children are their domain, and it is through their blood that the order of succession is transmitted. The men, on the other hand, are entirely isolated ...

With the phrase "all real authority," Lafitau shows himself to be the captive of his time and his culture, unable to find terms to describe a society in which no group ruled over another. Others have followed his lead, labelling the Iroquois "matriarchal," but the term is misleading, for, although women possessed important powers, they did not rule the community in a general sense. Neither matriarchal nor patriarchal, the Iroquois had pronounced gender *difference* without a gender *hierarchy*.

Christianity had surprisingly little effect on Iroquois sexual equality. In some of their earliest missionary efforts in Canada, the Jesuits did their best to enforce patriarchal norms, encouraging parents to beat their children, humiliating "rebellious" wives, and trying to get men to dominate their families. These early attempts to re-engineer Amerindian society met with limited success, however, and the missionaries soon adopted a gentler approach. Among the Iroquois, the most numerous of the Native converts living on the reserves of Canada, the Jesuits found the women more receptive to their religious message than the men, and so they were all the less inclined to promote male rule. To the aboriginal institutions of civic life, the Church added a new set of positions of influence (such as "dogiques," or teachers of religion), which, in Kahnawaké at least, were mostly occupied by women. As a consequence, women seem to have enjoyed even greater powers in this Catholic settlement than they did in the old Iroquois homeland.

And what about the white women of French Canada? In their colonial world, as mentioned above, roles were assigned, identities shaped, and conduct judged according to the norms of patriarchy. Recognizing this basic cultural fact takes us only so far in coming to terms with women's actual experience in New France, however. After all, studies in women's history generally indicate that ideals of feminine submissiveness and domesticity tend to leave room for all sorts of divergent behaviour and, even when they mount no overt challenge to male rule, women are often able to carve out female-controlled zones and to fashion for themselves lives of considerable autonomy and dignity. What, then, was the actual condition of women in New France? Were colonial women really in a favoured situation, either as compared with their European counterparts or in relation to Canadian women of later centuries? It depends in part on what is meant by "favoured" and also on which classes within that enormously diverse category "women" that one considers.

Our fictional habitant, Marie, had a range of rights, duties, and chores around the house and farm that kept her endlessly busy, but largely autonomous. As a point of contrast, we might consider the leisured existence of Elisabeth Bégon, a lady of the Canadian nobility whose letters are filled with parties, visiting, and political gossip; in the intervals between festivities, boredom was her main enemy. The cooking, the cleaning, and most of the child care in her household would have been done by servants who had precious little of Marie's independence or of Elisabeth's leisure. Servant girls in the city (slaves excepted) were mostly daughters of farm families who were contracted to work at no salary beyond room, board, and a small trousseau, remaining subject to the employer's authority until such time as they married. These three cases illustrate the diversity which makes the concept of a "position of women" rather elusive. Nevertheless, we can at least examine some of the legal, moral, and physical frameworks that conditioned female existence in the colony and consider the various lives women were able to construct for themselves.

We might begin with a look at marriage, since, for women even more than for men, the marital relationship was of crucial importance. Arranged marriages were almost unheard of and, although upper-class parents sometimes tried to veto a child's choice, young people were normally free to marry whom they pleased. By European standards, women married young, and widows remarried promptly, so that, in early Canada, to be an adult woman was, in the overwhelming majority of cases, to be a wife. Ease in finding a husband and setting up a household might be considered a "benefit," given the difficulties attached in this society to the single life, but it was hardly an unmixed blessing. With marriage began a relentless succession of pregnancies and children; for all but the rich, there were also domestic duties to do with preparing meals, sewing, mending and washing garments, cleaning house, tending the garden, and on and on. Then there were those bad moods of the husband which had to be cheerfully endured. Of course, there is no reason to think that complex human relations, like those of a husband and wife, ever conformed exactly to the bishop's simple formula; no doubt many women were forceful in defending their interests within the family. But if a husband dealt violently with a disobedient wife, the law was basically on his side; he was required only to confine himself to "reasonable correction."

Giving birth approximately every two years until menopause was the common experience of married women of all classes in the colony. Physicians were not normally involved in parturition unless a serious medical complication arose. Instead, women in labour depended on the assistance of female neighbours and/or a local midwife. In emergencies, a husband or male relative might even officiate. Midwives were usually middle-aged matrons who, through experience and the right sort of reassuring personality, had earned the confidence of their neighbours. In addition to helping the mother, they were also called upon to administer the sacrament of baptism to newborns who seemed in danger of dying (they might even stretch a point and baptize a stillborn), and this religious function made midwives an object of concern for the Church. Local *curés* were supposed to involve themselves in the selection of a parish midwife of unimpeachable moral standing and require her to take a Church-administered oath of office. However, all indications are that it was the women of each rural community who chose a midwife from among their number. The State also involved itself in a small way: towards the end of the French regime, a professionalized corps of trained and licensed midwives was established, though only in the cities of New France. Male doctors began delivering babies after the British conquest and, over the course of a century-long campaign against midwifery, they eventually succeeded in establishing a virtual monopoly in this area. During the French regime, however, childbirth was still almost entirely under the control of women.

Most Canadian mothers breast-fed their babies, though some urban women relied on wet nurses. Danielle Gauvreau estimates that about 15% of the babies born in Quebec City in the early eighteenth century were confided to habitant women, mostly in the nearby parish of Charlebourg, to be cared for until age two or three. This practice, later denounced by Rousseau as heartless and unnatural, was quite common in France at the time. There, mothers of the urban elite had recourse to wet-nursing — in part to maintain their social life free from the burdens of infant care and in part because they considered the rural environment healthier — but poor working women also shipped off their babies and, in their case, it was simply because no other child care was available. There was no real equivalent in New France to the impoverished female weavers of Lyon, and so wet-nursing in the colony tended to be for the wives of government officials, military officers, and merchants only; an elite practice, it involved only comparatively small numbers.

Mothers had primary responsibility for the education of young children. After her daughter died, Madame Bégon reverted to the teacher's role in raising her orphaned granddaughter. "I show her anything she wants to learn: sometimes history of France, sometimes Roman history, geography, rudiments of reading in French and Latin, writing, poetry, stories, any way she likes in order to give her a taste for writing and learning." Few Canadian mothers would have had the time or the knowledge to offer such an extensive education; the majority would have confined themselves to the catechism, and perhaps a bit of reading. Girls of elite families were schooled in the decorative branches of learning (art, music, foreign languages) by the Ursulines, while more basic instruction was also available in some communities from the Sisters of the Congrégation de Notre-Dame. It is often said that the women of New France were "better educated" than the men, and it may well be that the mother's duty to impart religious instruction to her children encouraged a larger proportion of women to develop their reading skills. Yet research in the parish registers of the French regime reveals that grooms were always more likely than brides to sign their names. Why the discrepancy? Reading and writing were quite separate skills in this period, reading associated more with religion, writing more with business, and therefore with the male sphere. It would be misleading flatly to assert that women were *more* educated than men, though it is certainly true to say that they were *differently* educated.

Women made an incalculable contribution to the early Canadian economy, "incalculable" if only because it cannot be measured. While the colonial records make it possible at least to estimate the production of wheat, furs, and other commodities handled mainly by men, we have no idea how much butter, wool, or eggs New France produced. The lack of documentation reflects the fact that activities that were viewed as "feminine" tended to be seen as subsidiary. Though there was a pronounced gender division of labour at the time, male and female spheres were not yet as radically severed as they would be in later centuries. With the advent of industrial capitalism came the model of the "breadwinner economy" in which a husband normally worked outside the home and earned a salary, while a wife looked after "his" home and children and (according to the ideal) remained in the "unproductive" domestic economy. The split between "productive" and "domestic" functions was much less pronounced in pre-industrial societies such as French-regime Canada, where the main economic unit was the family rather than the individual. Since the majority of the population lived in self-sufficient farming households, no one "brought home the bacon": the bacon (and the bread) were already home. Comparatively few men earned salaries, and most men — from habitants to merchants and high officials — worked, in some sense, "at home." Thus, although women's work was devalued, it was not ignored; nor was it viewed as utterly different from the "real" productive activity performed by men.

The family, rather than the individual, was the main economic actor during the centuries when France ruled Canada, and the family was a team, albeit with unequal members. In addition to taking care of all the usual female areas of responsibility, women frequently contributed directly to the husband's enterprises. It was not considered shocking for a woman to perform tasks identified as male, though men doing "women's work" risked ridicule. Habitant wives would lend a hand with field work, especially in the harvest season. Urban women married to craftsmen were often a vital part of the operation, at least where retail sales were involved, but even in the actual production. The wives of officers and government officials tended to take an active role in the political manoeuvring that was necessary to a successful career. Some occupations, such as innkeeping, were regarded as proper for either sex.

It was only natural that a widow who had long been involved in the family enterprise might try to continue it after her husband's death. This was particularly the case with commercial operations, so difficult to liquidate, even if one wished to do so. After her husband died, Marie-Anne Barbel ("Veuve Fornel") emerged as one of the colony's foremost traders, with interests in the fur business, brick-making, and real estate. One could list several other female entrepreneurs from the French regime, not all of them widows, and the fact that sex was not a barrier to business success should be noted. However, we should not lose sight of the fact that women entrepreneurs were the exception, not the rule. Nor were they unique to Canada: business women could also be found at this time in Europe and in the British colonies. Laurel Thatcher Ulrich coined the term "deputy husband" to describe an aspect of the married woman's role in colonial New England. It was considered normal in the seventeenth century for a wife to assume the position of head of household in an emergency or when the man was absent or dead. Were the men of New France more frequently away from home, and the women consequently more likely to take full charge of business, than was the case in other countries? On this point, we really have no solid evidence to go on. It is true that Canadian men were often off on fur-trade expeditions and military operations, but in other countries as well duty called men far from home and hearth.

In one important respect, the economic situation of women in French Canada differed from that in the colonial United States. Marital-property law under the Custom of Paris worked on principles quite dissimilar to those prevalent in places governed by English law. Both the English and the French legal traditions tended to amalgamate the identities of husband and wife when it came to buying, selling, owning, or renting property, but under English law (if we leave aside exceptions and qualifications, for the sake of simplicity), the consolidated identity was that of the husband. William Blackstone, writing about the time of the Conquest of Canada, explained his country's marital regime in these terms: "By marriage, the husband and wife are one person in law; that is, the very being or legal existence of the woman is suspended during the marriage, or at least is incorporated and consolidated into that of the husband; under whose wing, protection, and cover, she performs everything." In French Canada, as in the northern half of France, the marital merger did not require a woman to subsume her economic identity under her husband's name. Instead, the couple formed a sort of two-person corporation, the "marital community" (*communauté de biens*), owned equally by both. Pierre and Marie, our fictional habitant couple, could be thought of as possessing, each of them, a fifty percent share in a legal entity called Pierre-and-Marie, and it was this "person" which owned their land and all their other goods; it could buy or sell, sue or be sued, something neither of them could do as isolated individuals. Consequently, contracts under the civil law of French Canada normally required the signatures of both husband and wife.

This all looks very egalitarian, which it was in a sense, but the marital-community system was not as modern as it sounds. The Custom of Paris states unequivocally that "the husband is master of the community," and, when a married woman signed a contract along with her spouse, the notary always recorded the fact that she did so "with the permission of the said husband." We should therefore see the *communauté de biens* as conferring on women equal property rights within marriage, but not equal managerial powers. Thus, the day-to-day business affairs of the family were probably run in New France much as they were in, for example, colonial New England: wives were consulted, but men tended to take the lead. It was when one of the spouses died that the special characteristics of French law really came into play. Before the widow or widower could remarry, the old marital community had to be dissolved, and this required an inventory of all the couple's possessions (more wonderful source material for social historians), and a fifty-fifty division of both debts and assets; the survivor retained half, and the rest went to the heirs. If the debts outweighed the assets, a woman could "renounce the community," which means that she took away a few personal possessions, then left the rest to the creditors without being required to pay the remaining debts. (A widower had no such privilege; as "master of the community," he could not escape responsibility.) In practice, the results obtained after a man died may not have been very different from what occurred in the parts of North America subject to English law, for there men often provided in their wills for a "widow's portion" to support their wives and for bequests to help their children to get launched in life. In French Canada, however, the outcome did not depend on the man's will (in either sense of the term); married women had an inherent right to a full share of family property, just as daughters could not be deprived of an inheritance equal to that of their brothers.

This legal system survived the Conquest, much to the consternation of British visitors to Canada in the early nineteenth century. "The wife being by marriage invested with a right to half the husband's property," one of them wrote, "and, in being rendered independent of him, is perhaps the remote cause that the fair sex have such influence in France; and in Canada, it is well known, that a great deal of consequence, and even an air of superiority to the husband, is assumed by them." It was an intolerable infringement on a man's liberty to dispose of his property, the English protested, when he always needed to secure his wife's signature and, since wills had virtually no place in French-Canadian inheritance, a man was not even allowed to decide how his wealth would be distributed after his death. Of course, the indignation stemmed from the unshakable conviction that family property was, or should be, a man's property. Unlike the domestic tyrants found in so many early English novels, a French-Canadian father could not threaten a daughter who fell in love with the wrong man with being "cut off without a penny," and he did not have much economic leverage in relation to his wife either. The mechanisms of patriarchy were located elsewhere under the French system.

Although single women were much rarer in New France than in Europe, not every woman became a wife and mother. The religious life did offer one alternative to marriage, an alternative embraced by a small but substantial proportion of the female population — those who entered an order of nuns (about 3.7 per cent of women, according to one estimate). There were no contemplative orders in the colony; instead, they all concentrated on some useful task: the Ursulines had girls' schools, the Augustines de la Miséricorde de Jésus ran the *hôtels-Dieu* of Montréal and Québec, and the Sisters of Charity of the Hôpital-Général of Québec administered a general-purpose asylum for the destitute, crippled, and insane. And yet, religious devotion was the central focus of all nuns' lives. A typical day for members of the Hôpital-Général began at 4:30, with an hour's meditation before the holy sacrament; later there was a little time to look after inmates, but at 7:30 the nuns assembled in the chapel to recite the *tierce, sexte,* and *none,* followed by mass at 8:00 ... And so the day passed, with individual and collective devotions occupying as much time as tending to the unfortunate. This was as it should be, for nuns were supposed to be women who experienced a special divine calling to take vows of chastity, poverty, and obedience, consecrating their lives to God.

As it happens, they also made a valuable contribution to colonial society with their medical, educational, and social efforts, something which the government recognized and rewarded with annual subsidies. Moreover, they also served other mundane purposes by virtue of their irrevocable commitment to opt out of the processes of biological and economic reproduction. A disproportionate number of nuns came from noble or wealthy families, in part because parents of these classes often found it convenient to place some of their daughters outside the inheritance game. The other reason for the upper-class bias in convent recruitment is that each novice had to pay a substantial "dowry," a capital sum intended to ensure the maintenance of the sister, so that the order would not be an economic drain upon the community.

Patriarchal Europe had never been entirely comfortable with the religious communities of women which it harboured. Detached from a family setting and from the authority of husband or father, they lived together in autonomous female collectivities. To contain this potential challenge to gender norms, and equally to ensure the protection of that most precious, but also most fragile of nuns' possessions, their chastity, the Church insisted on *clausura,* the strict confinement of religious women within the cloisters of their convent. The most idealistic women of the Counter-Reformation, among them Marguerite Bourgeoys of Montréal, chafed at this restriction, for they longed to go out into the world and do God's work wherever they were needed. Marguerite, and the Sisters of the Congrégation de Notre-Dame who followed her, objected to all the trappings of a regular religious order, including dowries and solemn and perpetual vows. Avoiding the former kept the Congrégation open to poor women, while shunning irrevocable vows ensured that only the fully committed stayed with the group. The Sisters did all sorts of pious work in the Montréal area, assisting the clergy, succouring the afflicted, and instructing the children. However, they were not unique. Sisterhoods such as the Congrégation, doing good in defiance of prevailing restrictions on women's religious life, were quite common in seventeenth-century Europe. The Ursulines, for example, began in Italy as just such a loose organization before they were forced to make themselves into something more like a conventional order of nuns. What made New France special was the fact that, as a newly founded Catholic society, it displayed the latest tendencies in Counter-Reformation idealism without the counterweight of older, entrenched customs and institutions. Consequently, restrictions such as *clausura* were less rigidly enforced. Still, even in Canada, the (male) Church hierarchy was unceasing in its efforts to bring the energies of religious women under control, and eventually it managed to transform even the Sisters of the Congrégation de Notre-Dame into something like a conventional order.

Nuns and quasi-nuns may have constituted only a small portion of the population, but even for women who married, religion could be an important part of life, one which opened vistas not otherwise considered part of the feminine sphere. Devotional confraternities gathered together lay people for collective prayer and many of them, notably the most popular, the Confrérie de la Sainte-Famille, came to be entirely female. These were always under the authority of the bishop and the parish priest, and the manual distributed to members stressed the duty of the Christian wife to care for her family and obey her husband. In some respects the Confrérie de la Sainte-Famille can be seen as a manifestation of the Catholic Church's tendency, in the wake of the Reformation, to portray feminine virtue in purely domestic terms. Yet there was still a notion that duty to God came before duty to family, even for a mother. The story was told of Marie Hallé, who left three children under the age of four at home asleep while she went to an early-morning meeting of the Sainte-Famille. She returned home to find them awake, nicely dressed, and waiting patiently; a mysterious lady in white (the Virgin Mary, no doubt) had taken care of them. Now, whereas modern experts in regulating motherhood would have seen this incident as a case of child neglect, the seventeenth-century Church presented it as a miraculous reward for exceptional piety. Clearly the Catholic clergy was somewhat ambivalent, on the one hand telling married women to concentrate on maternal and domestic duties and, on the other, holding up feminine ideals of a very different sort.

And what did the Confrérie de la Sainte-Famille mean to its women members themselves? It is difficult to know for sure, but there are indications that, in addition to its strictly religious purposes, the organization functioned, to some extent, as a women's mutual-aid society. A charitable bequest from Marie Leroy gave the Québec City Sainte-Famille chapter "one mattress, one bed frame, two pairs of sheets and six towels ... to be lent to poor women giving birth, asking them to take care of them and return them for the use of others." Officially dominated by male priests, but operated to a significant degree by women, the Confrérie seems to epitomize the larger situation of women under the patriarchal regime of the period.

In a general sense, men ruled in New France, just as they did in old France. Outside the Iroquois enclaves, where Native women bore heavy burdens but submitted to no one's authority, a basic early modern patriarchy prevailed. Male power was deeply rooted in the colony's European culture, though not specifically tied to the control of family property, as was the case in the British world. Nor was it as closely connected as it would be in later centuries to a monopoly over professional functions and the breadwinner's income. It was a more diffuse, and at the same time more overt, insistence that women and girls ought to obey husbands and fathers. In Canada and throughout the European world at the time, however, this basic principle of patriarchy left room for all sorts of complexity, diversity, and contradiction in the real-world relations of males and females. There were some particular circumstances of colonial existence — a looseness in the gender division of labour on pioneer farms, the relative importance of uncloistered nuns, and so on — which worked to the advantage of women. Yet, New France was hardly an early modern oasis of equality between the sexes.

Select Bibliography

Bégon, Elizabeth. *Lettres au cher fils. Correspondance d'Elisabeth Bégon avec son gendre (1748–1753)*. Montréal: Hurtubise HMH, 1972.

Choquette, Leslie. "'Ces Amazones du Grand Dieu': Women and Mission in Seventeenth-Century Canada." *French Historical Studies* 17 (Spring 1992): 627–55.

Cliche, Marie-Aimée. *Les Pratiques de dévotion en Nouvelle-France: Comportements populaires et encadrement ecclésial dans le gouvernement de Québec.* Québec City: Les Presses de l'Université Laval, 1988.

Gauvreau, Danielle. *Québec, une ville et sa population au temps de la Nouvelle-France.* Sillery: Les Presses de l'Université du Québec, 1991.

Noel, Jan. "New France: Les femmes favorisées." In *Rethinking Canada: The Promise of Women's History*, edited by V. Strong-Boag and A. Fellman, 23–44. Toronto: Copp Clark, 1986.

Rapley, Elizabeth. *The Dévotes: Women and Church in Seventeenth-Century France.* Montréal: McGill-Queen's University Press, 1990.

Spittal, W. G., ed. *Iroquois Women: An Anthology.* Ohoweken, Ont.: Iroqrafts, 1990.

Ulrich, Laurel Thatcher. *Good Wives: Image and Reality in the Lives of Women in Northern New England, 1650–1750.* New York: Knopf, 1982.

Chapter Six
Women, Religion and Freedom in New France

Terrence Crowley

Because corporate rather than individual rights were acknowledged in French North America before 1760, in historical writing New France has compared unfavorably with the English colonies. Monarchical sovereignty brooked no opposition in the French possessions overseas. State authority flowed into the undivided hands of governors, responsible for military affairs, and intendants or commissaries charged with overseeing finance, justice, and public order. Petitions were prohibited, public assemblies were illegal without government approval, and habeas corpus was not part of judicial criminal proceedings, although merchants in Quebec and Montreal were allowed to elect syndics to represent their position before the authorities. There was no printing press in Canada, and publications arriving from France had been subject to government censorship before printing.

New France therefore struck nineteenth-century American historian Francis Parkman as a repressive, tyrannical environment that stood in marked contrast to British America, where greater freedom prevailed. Writing about the British victory of 1760, Parkman concluded that "England imposed by the sword on reluctant Canada the boon of rational and ordered liberty .... A happier calamity never befell a people than the conquest of Canada by British arms."[1] Since most English-speaking historians of New France have been men who share similar liberal values, variations on this critique remained prominent. Recent historical inquiries concerning the end of the French regime have reinforced this unflattering portrait by exposing the political machinations of the French government attending the defeat by British arms in the Seven Years' War.[2]

Women's historians have come to different conclusions because they have based their assessments on criteria other than those of the liberal tradition. Women's history has been more positive in its portrayal of New France because its primary concern has been the examination of private lives within the comparative framework of women elsewhere. Oblivious to the liberal critique of *ancien régime* institutions, one historian has written that "with respect to their education, their range and freedom of action, women in New France seem in many ways to compare favorably with their contemporaries in France and New England."[3] But such an approach is too general. It does not sufficiently take into account the different conditions of women's lives. While most women in New France lived in families on farms along the riverways, or in the towns, others found a measure of freedom in collective institutions.

The prominent role played by Roman Catholic women in French colonial life contrasted sharply with the situation in British possessions to the south. Roman Catholicism constituted the state church in the French colonies. Although Protestants lived in New France, they were subject to various disabilities and were not permitted to conduct religious services. Counter-Reformation revivalism in France early in the seventeenth century, during the period when New France and Acadia were established, brought larger numbers of women into the Roman Catholic church. Expanded missionary efforts were integral to a reinvigorated sense of evangelism. Beginning in 1639, Roman Catholic nuns arrived in Canada to convert the country's indigenous peoples. As the colonies grew, the number of women's religious communities increased from two to seven. More religious orders were founded for women than for men in New France. A higher proportion of Canadian women assumed a religious life, and the female religious orders recruited more native-born people than their male counterparts did. The number of women in religious life surpassed the combined totals of priests and members of the male religious communities during the 1680s and continued to grow. By 1725 there were more than 260 nuns in a colony whose population totaled only some 25,000 people, a high proportion of whom were young.[4] Religious life afforded these women the opportunity to serve humanity and to attain a measure of independence in regulating their individual and collective lives largely away from male control. Such freedoms were primarily collective and involved the sublimation of individual desires in the interests of community, but they were hard won and required constant vigilance to maintain. The freedoms that religious life afforded women in New France allowed them to make a vital contribution to colonial development.

THE EARLY WOMEN'S RELIGIOUS ORDERS

The first female missionary efforts in New France were sponsored by wealthy French noblewomen. Marie-Madeleine de Chauvigny de la Peltrie read in the Jesuits' published report for 1635, the *Relation,* of the need for women to evangelize native children. A young widow stricken with a serious illness that had brought her close to death, la Peltrie made a vow that if her health was restored, she would build a house in New France and dedicate her life to teaching Indian children. When she recovered, she journeyed to Tours, where she interested Marie Guyart in her plan. Guyart was also a widow and was her own age; following the death of her husband she had entrusted the care of her son to a sister and entered the Ursuline order. Assuming the name Marie de l'Incarnation, she became assistant mistress of novices and instructor in Christian doctrine. Deeply mystical in her religious practices, Marie de l'Incarnation's mind was consumed by thoughts of the personal sacrifices that such a venture required. She arrived at Quebec in 1639 in the company of two other Ursulines, Madame de la Peltrie, and a young companion, and the Ursulines threw themselves into their mission with joyful enthusiasm. Within a few months they were teaching eighteen Indian girls and a few French offspring. They set upon learning Indian languages. Because the Ursulines had been drawn from two different areas of France, there were internal disputes that were finally settled when the nuns from Tours accepted an additional vow to teach children and those from Paris adopted the habit warn by the nuns from the Bordeaux region. In 1646 the Ursulines opened a novitiate, although they initially remained dependent on France for recruitment. When fire destroyed their convent in 1650, they rebuilt it.

Three Augustinian nursing nuns from Dieppe arrived in Canada in the same year as the Ursulines. Although they also belonged to a cloistered order, a smallpox epidemic raging when they landed called for immediate attention. Supported by Marie-Madeleine Vignerot (duchesse d'Aiguillon), the hospitalers constructed a two-story stone building at Sillery, outside Quebec, where the Jesuits in 1637 had begun the first reserve for native converts to Christianity. The "women in white," as the Indians called the nursing sisters, cared for some three hundred people in 1642, but they also opened a small school to provide religious instruction to young girls. Iroquois incursions forced them to seek refuge in Quebec in 1644. Two years later they constructed a hospital designated as Hôtel-Dieu because their constitution noted that they served "Jesus Christ in the person of those afflicted with illness. For this reason the House where they render these divine services of charity is called *Hôtel-Dieu*." They received Marie-Françoise Giffard as their initial postulate in 1646, and Giffard became the first Canadian-born nun.

The first hospital in the mission of Ville-Marie at Montreal was begun in 1644 by a woman who also had a powerful patroness in France. Jeanne Mance was not a nun, but before departing France she had secured an endowment of forty-two thousand livres from Angélique de Faure, the widow of Claude de Bullion, a former superintendent of finance. To carry on her work, she made arrangements with the Hospitallers of Saint Joseph. This nursing community had begun in 1634 with Jérôme Le Royer de la Dauversière, who had participated in the establishment of the original Montreal mission, as its co-founder. In 1659 three nursing sisters, Judith Moreau de Brésoles, Catherine Macé, and Marie Maillet, accompanied Jeanne Mance from France to assume responsibility for the hospital that she had begun.

Contending with Religious Patriarchy

Although Christianity preached the spiritual equality of men and women, as well as of all peoples, women labored under particular liabilities within the Roman Catholic church in the early modern era.[6] A papal constitution of 1566 required that female religious orders be cloistered and that nuns take solemn, rather than simple, vows.[7] Unlike male communities, which might be grouped together under a superior general drawn from among their number, the Council of Trent (1545–63) had ruled that women's orders be placed under a bishop. Constitutions for women's communities had to receive episcopal approval. Within these confines, nuns directed their own daily lives and collective interests when they assembled in a body known as the chapter. It was in the chapter that the orders elected the priests who served as spiritual directors.

Although sometimes rent by internal divisions, the female communities closed ranks in contending with religious patriarchy. The struggles of the Ursulines and the Hospitallers of Saint Joseph are illustrative. The first constitution of the Quebec Ursulines had been written by Jérôme Lalemant, the Jesuit superior at Quebec, after careful consultation with the members of the order and their final approval through secret ballot. After François de Laval became bishop in 1659, he visited the monastery and found that some of the nuns wanted a more simplified rule. When he proposed changes, Superior Marie de l'Incarnation headed a campaign to stop him. She disliked episcopal authority over religious communities and argued for a more centralized system involving the Holy See to excise local variations. "We are subject to bishops," Marie de l'Incarnation wrote, "and that is troublesome."[8] She interpreted the changes that Laval proposed as having the potential to turn the Ursulines into a contemplative order such as the Carmelites. The concerted opposition she mounted against the bishop's plans led Laval to delay a year and then to abandon his proposals by approving their original constitution in 1662. Later, in 1681, Laval did secure the agreement of the Quebec community to bring their practices in line with those observed by the order in Paris.

The Quebec Ursulines were successful in defending themselves against unwelcome episcopal intrusions, but the Hospitallers of Saint Joseph were forced into a compromise. Clerical authorities were unhappy with their presence in Montreal. Bishop Laval, the town's parish priests, and the Jesuits wanted the Augustinian nuns of the Quebec Hôtel-Dieu to extend their services into Montreal in order to merge the two communities. Like the Ursulines, the Augustinians conformed more closely to church regulations because they were a cloistered order, unlike the Hospitallers when they had departed France. Strictly opposed to losing their separate identity, the Montreal sisters engaged in a decade-long battle with male church officials to insure their survival. To end years of acrimony, they finally yielded to episcopal insistence that they accept solemn vows and be cloistered, as their mother house in France had become since their arrival in Canada. The continuity of their community was secured at a considerable price.

SECULAR SISTERS AND THE INTRICATE INTERPLAY OF CHURCH AND STATE

After royal government superseded company rule at Quebec in 1663, the state became a larger player in colonial religious life. The king claimed temporal powers over the church. Courts such as the Conseil souverain at Quebec or the king's council in France might, upon appeal, overturn ecclesiastical decisions considered contrary to laws and customs of the kingdom. Further, the government employed church resources to provide educational, medical, and social services for colonists. In return for the subsidies that they received from the state, the various components of the institutional church needed to secure the monarchy's approval, most often through royal letters patent. Because the government also served as arbiter when wings of the church conflicted, women learned to use to their advantage the internal divisions within the church and the state.

The beginnings in Montreal of the Congregation of Our Lady revealed the ways in which religious women were able to circumvent ecclesiastical restraints by carefully navigating the dual lanes of church and state. This order had been established in France in 1598 as a noncloistered teaching community, but after 1632 when *clausura* had been accepted, the Congregation of Our Lady resorted to a device that would not restrict its activities. Within their convent the nuns created a so-called external congregation of laywomen who received religious instruction and pedagogical training. Under the pretext that they were secular sisters rather than cloistered nuns, these women were able to teach in parish schools.

Marguerite Bourgeoys was an external member of the Congregation of Our Lady at Troyes, France, where the sister of the governor of Montreal, Paul de Chomedey (sieur de Maisonneuve) was also part of the community. Maisonneuve was opposed to sending cloistered nuns to the Montreal mission, but because Bourgeoys did not labor under such constraints, she joined the immigrants who headed for the St. Lawrence River island in 1653. At first she assisted with nursing, but in 1658 she was given a stone stable where she began teaching young children. The following year Bourgeoys recruited three more young laywomen in France to assist her. As their numbers grew to more than a dozen, Marguerite Bourgeoys contemplated the creation of a community of secular sisters free to move about for instructional purposes. From her spiritual director in France, she picked up the idea that the Gospels provided a variety of examples for religious women to follow. Bourgeoys was particularly taken with the idea that the Virgin Mary had herself traveled about. François de Laval did not agree; church policies were more important than biblical precedents to the prelate. He therefore advocated that all orders of religious women be cloistered, take solemn vows, assume a veil upon becoming nuns, and wear the wimple to hide part of their heads. For this reason the bishop preferred that the Ursulines extend their instructional work to Montreal rather than relying on the secular sisters gathered around Marguerite Bourgeoys. The Sulpicians, who were the town's parish priests as well as seigneurs after 1663, sided with Bourgeoys because they saw benefits from having nuns capable of teaching in outlying areas. Governor Remy de Courcelles and Intendant Jean Talon concurred that the Congregation of Our Lady served Montreal very well. Talon permitted the town's residents to assemble to petition the king to grant the sisters official recognition. Bourgeoys traveled to the French court in 1670, and the following year royal letters patent recognizing her community were issued. Laval waited another five years, until 1676, to acknowledge the order according to canon law. When he did so, the community was acknowledged as one of secular sisters rather than of nuns.

Laval's successor as bishop, Jean-Baptiste La Croix de Chevrières de Saint-Vallier, attempted to achieve uniformity among the women's religious orders by imparting a rule to the Congregation of Our Lady akin to that of the Ursulines. Solidly opposed, the sisters managed to get Saint-Vallier to put off the matter for a year while they discussed the new constitution. Delay was what the sisters needed. Particularly contentious was the question of dowries. In cloistered orders, women's families paid a dowry for young women upon admission, in the same manner that the middle and upper classes did for their offspring at the time of marriage. The secular communities tried to avoid this practice because it reinforced class differences between those who could pay and those who could not. Although the church hierarchy and state officials wanted dowries as a means of regulating entry into religious communities, they were generally ineffective in controlling admissions. The orders often found benefactors to assume the charge on behalf of young women, or they simply circumvented official decrees by requiring less money.

The sisters of the congregation were nevertheless opposed to the imposition of this cumbersome system that was part of all cloistered communities. They made their opposition known to the superior general of the Sulpicians in Paris, who altered the bishop's text to conform more exactly to their wishes, although a system of dowries was retained because it could be circumvented in various ways. Bishop Saint-Vallier agreed to the revisions even though they did not conform to his original idea. The new rule was accepted by the Congregation of Our Lady in 1698. Like the Ursulines, the Montreal group had managed to play various male authorities against each other in order to make their views prevail, even though they paid a price by accepting the dowry system, albeit at a lower monetary level than obtained in the cloistered orders.

Because the Congregation of Our Lady allowed women greater freedom and because its dowries for admission were lower, the order grew to be the largest community of women in New France, counting 70 of the 204 religious women in the colony by 1759.[9] Initially they served in the Montreal region, including the Sulpician-sponsored Indian settlement at La Montaigne, where, in 1685, they taught forty native children in cabins made of bark. In that year one sister traveled to Port-Royal to undertake the instruction of young girls in Acadia. Marguerite Bourgeoys insisted on moral rigor and training in pedagogy. Members of the community were told that they were to perform their duties "with purity of intention, without distinction of poor or rich, relatives or friends, pretty or deformed."[10] Instruction was provided free to the young girls, but fees might be charged for books, supplies, and firewood. The sisters followed the Ursulines in opening a boarding school that catered to wealthier colonists, but the congregation also began a House of Providence for poor adolescent girls age twelve to eighteen on the farm they began in 1668 at Point St. Charles outside the town.[11] By 1685 the House of Providence offered twenty young women instruction in religion and domestic skills. Although this work was extended temporarily to the town of Quebec in 1686, both enterprises closed within a few years because of lack of money. The sisters nevertheless fanned out into the smaller communities of the St. Lawrence Valley, opened a school in Quebec's lower town in 1691, and moved in 1727 to Louisbourg, the walled city that France had constructed on Cape Breton Island as the bulwark of its North American possessions. The Sisters of the Congregation of Our Lady helped to erode the near monopoly of men over the written word. In addition to religion, they taught reading, spelling, writing, and domestic skills. Wherever they went, there were beneficial results for female literacy.[12]

CONSTRAINT: THE FOUNDING OF QUEBEC'S HOSPICE

Events leading up to the creation of a new cloistered community of nuns to run Quebec's hospice (Hôpital Général) in 1701 revealed how the women's religious orders might score occasional triumphs without achieving ultimate victory when the forces of church and state combined. The idea for an asylum in the colonial capital originated with Bishop Saint-Vallier. He purchased a house outside the town and secured royal approval for a governing board in 1692. Although the Augustinian Hospitallers entertained reservations about departing from a strictly medical role, they accepted the administration of the hospice for the aged, the destitute, and the insane. Reluctance turned into outright opposition in 1699, when the bishop announced that he wanted the Augustinians to supply twelve of their members and an annual annuity to the hospice. Fearing depletion of their human and material resources, the nuns refused the bishop's request. Saint-Vallier then manipulated elections within the order to deny office to its superior, Jeanne-Françoise Juchereau de la Ferté.[13] In the following month, when he formally separated the two orders, the nuns mounted a dual-pronged attack. They got government officials to annul his decision and secured François de Laval to serve as mediator. When word arrived from France in 1700 that the monarchy confirmed the decision of its local officials, the bishop was mortified. Saint-Vallier sought out the nuns of the Hotel-Dieu, where "he cried with such profusion" that the nuns "were unable to hold back their tears."[14] Despite this display, neither side softened. Saint-Vallier departed for France. At the royal court he was able to use his powers of persuasion and the money that he personally contributed to the hospice as levers to secure a new decision in his favor. In 1701 the Council of State created a new cloistered religious order specifically for the Quebec hospice. The bishop provided financial guarantees, and the order was limited to twelve members.

Although the Augustinian hospitalers were forced to comply in the face of episcopal and royal resolution, the circumstances surrounding the founding of the Quebec hospice were exceptional. Having established such an asylum in France early in his career, Bishop Saint-Vallier identified emotionally with the project. He accorded a sixth of his large personal givings to the Hôpital Général, and late in life he lived there prior to his death.[15] Relations with the other women's religious communities were more dispassionate. Saint-Vallier secured the agreement of the Ursulines in 1697 to extend their teaching activities into Trois-Rivières, but because the settlement was too small to support an instructional order alone, they agreed to add a nursing role. The house in Trois-Rivières became independent of the Quebec mother house in 1732. The Ursuline convent established in New Orleans, Louisiana, was begun in 1727 with nuns from France rather than Quebec.

WHY WOMEN JOINED RELIGIOUS ORDERS

What attracted women to this expanding network of religious communities? In examining this question, it is important to remember that the family, rather than the individual, constituted the basic social unit in the West during the early modern era. In Canada during the French regime, children remained legally dependent until the age of twenty-five, and they needed parental consent to marry.[16] Because women entering a religious order exchanged the protection and support of one family for a larger one governed by a written constitution, dowries were involved in admission to most religious orders. While patriarchy prevailed in society and in the Roman Catholic church as a whole, nuns led largely self-directed lives: women were in charge on a daily basis, although the structures of the cloistered communities mirrored the hierarchy apparent in all walks of life. Choir nuns formed the elite. They came from families with more prestige, and they brought larger dowries into the community. Choir nuns were allowed to sing during the Mass, but they did not have to bother with the menial tasks accorded to the nuns called lay sisters. These women were from humbler social backgrounds, seldom knew how to read or write, and brought smaller amounts as dowries or none at all. Although their numbers constituted approximately a third of cloistered nuns by the eighteenth century, the lay sisters labored under other disabilities. In the chapter of the Quebec hospice, for instance, they had no vote except in the matter of choosing a priest to be spiritual director.[17] The Congregation of Our Lady did not observe such distinctions; there, both nuns and lay sisters voted on all matters.

Religious life offered women a variety of opportunities to employ personal talents. Despite their goal of service, business affairs figured prominently in the women's religious communities. Revenue flowing into the Hôtel-Dieu in Quebec, for instance, was so diverse that it can be divided into twelve categories.[18] The orders received gifts and endowments from private benefactors that were invested both in the mother country and in Canada. Fees, such as those that pensioners paid at the Quebec hospice, provided additional income. So did state subsidies. Dowries, whose amounts varied according to the orders' circumstances, produced 9% of revenue.[19] Some communities owned seigneuries, farms, or grist mills that had to be operated as well as managed; others raised livestock and ran market gardens. Craft work such as needlepoint and making brocades constituted an important part of revenue for several of the communities. Such a wide variety of economic activity provided religious women with various prospects for employment, not the least of which was the supervision of domestic servants and workers employed by the orders. Finances remained precarious, however. The Quebec hospital showed operating deficits in fifty-four of the years between 1663 and 1763, as did the town's hospice for forty-two years between 1701 and 1759. Similarly, the Sisters of the Congregation of Our Lady at Louisbourg eked out a bare existence for many years because of a poor investment made when they moved there.[20]

Noblewomen and women drawn from what might be loosely called the middle classes were attracted disproportionately into the religious life. Only a third of the nuns in the cloistered orders emanated from the farmers, laborers, and artisans, who constituted three-quarters of the colony's population, although communities of secular sisters such as the Congregation of Our Lady appealed more broadly.[21] A life of service dedicated to the poor and disabled clearly attracted women to enter the Quebec hospice, the most aristocratic of the orders. Although the Quebec hospital relied less on noble families, caring for the sick made life expectancy shorter, and the community came to draw more heavily on rural parishes to augment their ranks in the eighteenth century.[22] Both the Montreal hospital and the Sisters of the Congregation of Our Lady relied more fully on the merchant class in that town. Teaching careers would have been impossible for many women without the training and support provided by the religious communities.

Girls entered the religious life as postulates at the age of fourteen or fifteen. On average they took their vows four or five years later, at an age that was only slightly earlier than that when women married in the colony. Attrition was not high: less than a quarter of the women accepted left their orders. Those remaining in the cloistered communities lived the religious life for thirty-five years on average.[23] No aboriginal men were accepted as clerics in New France, but the women's religious orders were more receptive to the native born. Geneviève-Agnes Skanudaroua, a Huron, took vows as an Augustinian nun at Quebec in 1657, and Marie-Thérèse Gannensagouas (an Algonquin) and Marie-Barbe Atontinon (an Iroquois) were accepted as sisters of the Congregation of Our Lady. Similarly, British colonials captured in war occasionally joined the women's orders. Esther Wheelwright, whose father and grandfather had been Congregational ministers in Massachusetts, chose to remain in Quebec following her capture by Abenakis in 1703 despite concerted efforts by her family to secure her return. As Soeur de l'Enfant-Jésus, she joined the Ursulines and became superior of the order in 1760.

Many more Canadian women than men were attracted to a religious life in New France. Because the numbers entering such communities was highest during the episcopacies of Saint-Vallier (1688–1727) and of Debreil de Pontbriand (1741–60), there was a strong correlation between the disruptive influences accompanying the Anglo-French wars (1689–98, 1702–13, 1744–48, 1754–63) and the decisions by women to seek a religious life. By 1700 there were 140 nuns in New France. Montreal, a town of 1,500 people in 1715, was home to 100 sisters, although some were dispersed in the countryside attending to schools. While religious devotion began to wane in New France during the first quarter of the eighteenth century, women in religious orders nearly doubled.[24] In order to arrest this rapid expansion, the Crown raised the dowries required for entry to the cloistered orders from 3,000 to 5,000 livres in 1722, but when the effects of this measure proved too drastic, they were reduced to the former sum ten years later.[25] By the end of the French regime, the women's communities were composed almost entirely of Canadians while the majority of the male clergy remained French.

WOMEN AND RELIGIOUS ADHERENCE IN NEW FRANCE

The attractiveness of the women's religious communities in New France was paralleled in the larger society by greater devotion to institutional religion on the part of women than of men. Pious religious associations, called confraternities, made their first appearance in the colony in 1652 and continued to be formed until early in the eighteenth century. Most were open to both sexes, but some, including the Confraternity of the Holy Family, restricted their memberships to women alone. Under the watchful eye of parish priests at the local level, the confraternities encouraged regular observance of the sacraments, participation in religious services, private prayer, the upkeep of chapels, and visiting the sick or those in prison.[26] While overzealous priests who sometimes enrolled entire parishes make membership rolls suspect, women clearly predominated in the confraternities. Their lives were more sedentary than those of men, many of whom left farms to roam farther afield as fur traders and fishers. Men were thus more likely to make declarations about miraculous interventions, but women provided stronger continuing support for local churches.

Although neither of the two male religious orders founded in the Quebec colony during the seventeenth century survived the French regime, a new community of secular sisters emerged in Montreal and remains active even today. In 1737 Marguerite Dufrost de Lajemmerais, the wealthy widow of François-Madeleine d'Youville, joined with three companions to begin the Sisters of Charity. "We the undersigned," their agreement read, "to the greater glory of God, for the salvation of our souls and the relief of the poor, sincerely desire to quit the world and to renounce all that we own, in order to consecrate ourselves to the poor."[27] Popular opinion considered the women to be so foolish as to be *grises* — tipsy — and in time they adopted a gray habit in direct reference to the sobriquet, becoming known as *Soeurs grises*, or "Grey Nuns." In 1747 they assumed responsibility for Montreal's hospice, which had been established by François Charon, even though the bishop, the governor, and the intendant wanted the institution joined to its counterpart in Quebec. Marguerite d'Youville maneuvered adroitly through complicated proceedings to secure royal recognition of her order in 1753.[28]

Conclusion

The continuing growth of women's religious orders in New France suggests that freedom in community remained a viable option for at least one segment of the female population. The active participation of women in church life during the French regime served as the basis for the prominence that such organizations achieved. A religious life afforded not only protection and service to others; it also provided an ordered existence where daily lives were self-directed. Written constitutions served as a rudder to direct the course, while deliberations in the chapters of the communities provided direction to collective life. Although the decision to enter a religious community represented an act of individual liberty, the advantages of communal life were derived ultimately through the sublimation of self in the interests of the group. Obedience was one of the vows that all nuns were required to take. A constant mediation between individual will and collective interest was integral to the way the women's religious orders operated. Attrition from the communities, although admittedly low, was probably related to this issue, but the records are silent. Nevertheless, freedom within this context came to assume a different meaning from that predicated on the individual will alone.

The women's religious orders interpreted their freedoms more in terms of the collectivity than on an individual basis. The Ursulines and the Sisters of the Congregation of Our Lady successfully thwarted plans by bishops to alter their rules in a manner that they opposed. The Sisters of Saint Joseph and the Augustinian nuns of Quebec's hospital fought but were forced to capitulate, the latter in unusual circumstances and the former in order to bring their practices in line with their community in France. Circumventing ecclesiastical decrees through the creation of communities of secular sisters represented a major achievement since communities such as the Sisters of the Congregation and the Grey Nuns were able to work outside the confines of the cloister demanded by clerical authorities.

Religious orders flourished in New France partially because the monarchy chose to subsidize the Roman Catholic church rather than create secular institutions to provide educational, medical, and social services.[29] Women who wanted to be teachers, nurses, or social workers had few alternatives to exercising their ambitions through joining religious communities. Although this situation suggests obvious constraints, it should not detract from the positive achievements of religious women in this period of history.

The experience of the New World expanded women's evangelical role beyond that acknowledged in Europe. Because the first nuns in New France were missionaries, they received religious instruction in order to convert native peoples. Even nursing sisters ministered to the soul as well as to the body. Religious services for the sick were held daily with all the nuns in attendance. As the presence of these women was felt, public virtue was no longer conceived of as a male preserve, even though men monopolized positions of authority within the Roman Catholic church. The women's religious orders also developed a form of pedagogy that differed from that of their male colleagues by de-emphasizing physical punishments in favor of the promotion of learning.[30] Although freedoms in New France were constrained by law and patriarchy, the religious orders provided a means for women to make a contribution to human development. Freedom not only assumes different forms; it is also relative to time and place.

Notes

1. Francis Parkman, *The Old Regime in Canada,* 2 vols. (Toronto: Morang, 1900), 2:204.
2. John F. Bosher, "The French Government's Motives in the Affaire du Canada, 1761–1763," *English Historical Review* 96 (1981): 59–78; J.

F. Bosher and Jean-Claude Dube, *Dictionary of Canadian Biography,* s.v. "François Bigot."

3. Jan Noel, "New France: Les femmes favorisées," in *The Neglected Majority,* edited by Alison Prentice and Susan M. Trofimenkoff (Toronto: McClelland and Stewart, 1985), 2:18–40. See also Naomi Elizabeth Saunders Griffiths, *Penelope's Web: Some Perceptions of Women in European and Canadian Society* (Toronto: Oxford University Press, 1976), 31–51; and Leslie Choquette, "'Ces Amazones du Grand Dieu': Women and Mission in Seventeenth-Century Canada," *French Historical Studies* 17 (1992): 627–55. See also Micheline Dumont, "Une perspective féministe dans l'histoire des congrégations des femmes," in *Sessions d'études, 1990,* ed. La Société canadienne d'histoire de l'Église catholique (SCHEC) (Ottawa, 1990), 29–35.

4. Louis Pelletier, *Le clergé en Nouvelle-France: Étude démographique et repertoire biographique* (Montreal: Presses de l'Université de Montréal, 1993), 28. Marcel Trudel, *L'Église canadienne sous le régime militaire, 1759–1764* (Quebec: Presses de l'Université Laval, 1957), 1:89, 109, 2:222.

5. Quoted in François Rousseau, *La croix et le scalpel: Histoire des Augustines de l'Hôtel-Dieu de Québec (1639–1989), vol. 1, 1639–1892* (Sillery, Quebec: Septentrion, 1989), 125.

6. Outside of spiritual equality, the scriptures chosen by the early Christian church were sometimes explicit in advocating the subordination of women to men. See, for example, 1 Corinthians 14:34 and 1 Timothy 2:11–12. The gnostic gospels rejected by the ancient church had sometimes accorded women a prominent role. See Elaine Pagels, *The Gnostic Gospels* (New York: Random House, 1979).

7. Elizabeth Rapley, *The Dévotes: Women and Church in Seventeenth-Century France* (Montreal: McGill-Queen's Press, 1990), 56. Solemn vows entailed cloistering, while simple vows allowed involvement with the larger community.

8. Marie de l'Incarnation to her son, 3 October 1645, in *Marie de l'Incarnation: Écrits spirituels et historiques,* ed. Albert Jamet, 4 vols. (Paris: Desclée de Brouwer, 1929), 4:57

9. Trudel, *L'Église canadienne* (see note 4), 2:222.

10. [Marguerite Bourgeoys], *Les écrits de Mère Bourgeoys* (Montreal: Congrégation de Notre-Dame, 1964), 284.

11. See Emilia Chicoine, Le *métairie de Marguerite Bourgeoys à la Pointe-Saint-Charles* (Montreal: Fides, 1986).
12. Roger Magnuson, *Education in New France* (Montreal: McGill-Queen's Press, 1992), 134–38. Louise Dechêne, *Habitants et marchands de Montréal au 17e siècle* (Paris: Plon, 1974), 467–68. A. J. B. Johnston, *Religion and Life at Louisbourg, 1713–1758* (Montreal: McGill-Queen's Press, 1984), 86–108.
13. Cornelius J. Jaenen, *Dictionary of Canadian Biography*, s.v. "Jeanne-Françoise Juchereau de la Ferte."
14. Albert Jamet, ed., *Les annales de l'Hôtel-Dieu de Québec, 1636–1716* (Quebec: Hôtel-Dieu, 1939), 296–97
15. Henri Têtu, *Les Evêques de Québec: Notices biographiques* (Quebec: N. S. Hardy, 1889), 149.
16. See John F. Bosher, "The Family in New France," *In Search of the Visible Past*, ed. Barry Gough (Waterloo, Ont.: Wilfrid Laurier University Press, 1975), 1–13.
17. Micheline D'Allaire, *Les dots des religieuses au Canada français, 1639–1800* (Montreal: Hurtubise HMH, 1986), 43; Micheline D'Allaire, *L'Hôpital Général de Québec, 1692–1764* (Montreal: Fides, 1986).
18. Trudel, *L'Église canadienne* (see note 4), provides the most complete inventory of church property and income. For the women's religions orders, see 2:231–39, 274–79, 302–7, 322–27, 339–43, 356–61. See also Jacques Ducharme, "Les revenus des Hospitalières de Montréal au 18e siècle," in *L'Hôtel-Dieu de Montréal (1642–1973)* (Montreal: Hurtubise HMH, 1973), 209–44.
19. D'Allaire, *Les dots* (see note 17), 98.
20. D'Allaire, *L'Hôpital Général* (see note 17), 231–32; Rousseau, *La croix et le scalpel* (see note 5), 117; Johnston, *Religion and Life at Louisbourg* (see note 12), 86–108.
21. D'Allaire, *Les dots* (see note 17), 181–82; Trudel, *L'Église canadienne* (see note 4), 2:339. Pierre Hurtubise "Origine sociale des vocations canadiennes en Nouvelle-France," in *Sessions d'études 1978*, ed. La Société canadienne d'histoire de l'Église catholique (Ottawa, 1978), 41–56.
22. Rousseau, *La croix et le scalpel* (see note 5), 139.
23. D'Allaire, *Les dots* (see note 17), 57–59; D'Allaire, *L'Hôpital Général* (see note 17), 131–38.

24. Pelletier, *Le clergé en Nouvelle-France* (see note 4), 28; Dechêne, *Habitants et marchands de Montréal* (see note 12), 467, 478.
25. Province of Canada, *Edits, ordonnances royaux, déclarations et arrêts du conseil d'État du roi concernant le Canada* (Quebec: Assemblée legislative, 1854), 1:464, 529–30.
26. See Marie-Aimée Cliche, *Les Pratiques de dévotion en Nouvelle-France: Comportements populaires et encadrement ecclésial dans le gourvernement de Québec* (Quebec: Presses de l'Université Laval, 1988), 182–232; and Brigette Caulier, "Les confréries de dévotion à Montréal du 17e au 19e siècle," (Ph.D diss., University of Montreal, 1986).
27. Quoted in *L'Evolution des communautés religieuses de femmes au Canada de 1639 à nos jours*, by Marguerite Jean (Montreal: Fides, 1977), 54.
28. Canada, *Edits, ordonnances royaux* (see note 25), 616.
29. On church finances, see Guy Frégault, *Le 18e siècle canadien: Etudes* (Montreal: Hurtubise HMH, 1968), 104–11.
30. See Rapley, *The Dévotes* (see note 7), 150.

Chapter Seven
Tituba's Confession:
The Multicultural Dimensions of the 1692 Salem Witch-Hunt

Elaine G. Breslaw

The events of 1692 at Salem, Massachusetts, continue to attract scholarly and popular attention. Contemporary historians classify the witch scare as an episode in either social-political development or gender conflict. Such a focus permits a fuller discussion of economic development in Massachusetts (viewed as a conflict between a new mercantile order and an older agricultural society), of the political and legal instability resulting from the Glorious Revolution in England (1688–89), or of fears engendered by the rising incidence of Indian attacks.[1] Other works clarify our understanding of the relationship between gender boundaries and the dynamics of social, economic, and political change that ushered in the modern era.[2] Often lost in these scholarly analyses, however, are the ethnic-cultural factors that shaped the belief systems of the people involved. Of particular interest are the contributions of the slave woman Tituba: her character, her behavior, and the story she cold as the first to confess to the practice of witchcraft.[3]

Tituba was a pivotal character whose ethnic background and behavior merit deeper examination than they have received. Her confession, blending elements from English, African, and American Indian notions of the occult, was of key significance in the shaping of the bizarre events at Salem. It subsequently became a model for others desperate to save their lives.[4] Although many details in their stories were embellished and transformed by Puritan fantasies, fears, and cultural biases, the inspiration for and framework of their accounts of witchcraft stemmed from Tituba's story. By bridging the gap between her syncretic notions and the Puritan concept of evil, these reformulations, in turn, heightened the sense of impending doom surrounding the witch hunt and propelled it into new channels.

In her confession, Tituba, "an Indian Woman Servant to Mr. Samuel Parris of Salem village," convinced the Salem authorities that the devil had invaded their society.[5] Her importance for the ensuing events lies not in the occult activities that she supposedly inspired before 1692 but in the content and impact of her confession in March of that year.[6] She not only confirmed their fears of a conspiracy of Satan's followers but was the first to implicate others outside the Salem community and to suggest that men and members of the elite were part of the conspiracy. Of even greater significance, Tituba supplied the evidence of a satanic presence legally necessary to launch a witch hunt. Had she remained silent, the trials might not have occurred or, at the least, would have followed a different course.

Tituba's credibility to her Salem audience was enhanced by her identification as an American Indian whose culture had long been associated with demonic power.[7] Her story thus acquired verisimilitude not just from fantastic details that could be integrated into the Puritan belief system but from their assumed evil source. Although the content of her testimony and its relationship to Puritan perceptions of American Indians are seldom mentioned in the literature of Salem, the substance of Tituba's story, combined with the local fear of Indians, alerted the Puritan worthies to the dangers lurking in their community.

Most writers have assumed that Tituba was either African or of mixed American Indian and African descent, but nothing in the records indicates that she was anything but Indian. In 1974 Chadwick Hansen pointed out that all extant contemporary references to Tituba call her an Indian.[8] Tituba the half Indian, half African was the invention of Henry Wadsworth Longfellow in his 1868 verse drama *Giles Corey of the Salem Farms*, and unfortunately that fiction entered the historical literature.[9] In the century following she was gradually transformed into an African. Deodat Lawson, John Hale, and Robert Calef, all contemporaries of the events, repeat the terminology of the official documents and refer to Tituba and her husband, John, only as Indians.[10]

If Tituba and John had been of mixed Indian-African parentage, they would have been identified as "Negro" and not Indian in the Salem records. Whites assumed that anyone with any African features was a Negro.[11] During the Salem investigation two African-Americans were clearly identified as such: Mary Black, a slave in Benjamin Putnam's household, and Candy, Margaret Hawkes's servant from Barbados.[12] Tituba, unlike Mary or Candy, was called an Indian for reasons that apparently were visible and obvious to their contemporaries.

Little is known about Tituba's background beyond the fact that she and another slave, John Indian, who became her husband, were brought from Barbados by Samuel Parris, a merchant who later became a clergyman.[13] Whether Tituba and John were born in Barbados is not known, nor are their ages evident in the Salem records. Barbadian sources indicate that the most probable place of origin for Indian slaves in Barbados was the northeastern coast of South America, where settlements of Dutch-allied Arawaks were likely prey for England's slave traders.[14] A reference to the name Tattuba on a 1676 deed supports the Barbadian connection.[15] This Tattuba, a child at the time, is most likely the Tituba whom Parris brought to Massachusetts. Thus Tituba was between thirteen and eighteen years old when she arrived in Boston in 1680 and was no more than thirty during the witch trials.

On Barbados, Tituba had been exposed to the African influences omnipresent there. She was a product of an emergent Creole culture, marked by planter indifference to the religious and cultural lives of the slaves.[16] As a result, non-Christian and occult practices flourished on the island. The slaves' "idolatrous ceremonies and customs in honor of their God who is mainly the devil" appalled Felix Sporri, a Calvinist visitor of the 1660s.[17] Thomas Walduck, another observer, said that the slaves' activities were led by the "obia" (traditionally an African healer), who was known to torment others and cause "lameness, madness, loss of speech, loss of the use of all their limbs." The planters, he thought, occasionally participated in these ceremonies.[18]

Slaves, whether of American Indian or African ancestry, easily integrated and reformulated the ideas and techniques of English witchcraft and other religious practices without violating their essential worldview.

Conversely, as Walduck demonstrates, they introduced their white masters to new magical practices without altering the substance of English folklore or theology. In the seventeenth century supernatural omens and techniques associated with witchcraft were accepted and adapted by Europeans, Africans, and Indians regardless of their origin. The functions of the practices varied, but the borrowed forms provided a non-verbal language understood by both slaves and masters.[19]

Although familiar with various African and European magicoreligious practices, Tituba had not necessarily lost all sense of her Indian culture. Seventeenth-century planters depended on American Indian methods of food preparation and possibly of healing.[20] Arawaks and other South American Indians feared malevolent spirits that lived in the bush, could change shape at will, and had the power to kill or to cause excruciating pain, and whites in Barbados noted the rituals, trances, herbs, and poisons thought to provide protection against these spirits.[21] Even if the few Indians on the island could not remember a time spent among their own people, Indian "Magick and ways of Divination" persisted.[22] Tituba's familiarity with practices derived from three cultures can be deduced from the events of 1692.

In late December 1691 or early January 1692 Parris' daughter Betty and Abigail Williams, a niece living in his house, began to exhibit strange physical symptoms. The girls, aged nine and eleven, complained of painful pinching, crept under chairs, tried to crawl into holes, fell into fits, and babbled. Dr. William Griggs diagnosed the "evil hand," the work of the devil, and because the responsibility for spiritual cures lay with the church, the Reverend Parris initiated a series of prayers and a fast day and called on other ministers to assist him.[23]

Unbeknownst to Parris, Mary Sibley, a neighbor, appealed to the two Indians in his household to use countermagic to help the girls. On 25 February 1692, after several weeks of watching them suffer, Tituba and John, under Sibley's supervision, prepared a "witchcake," a concoction of rye meal and the girls' urine baked in ashes, and fed it to a dog. Supposedly, the dog was a "familiar," the animal companion of a witch. According to English folklore, the dog, bewitched by the cake, would reveal the name of the witch who was afflicting the girls.[24]

The ritual use of bodily substances such as hair, nail parings, and urine was common in folk and tribal cultures, including that of the English "cunning people."[25] The cooking of human excretions with other substances, such as ashes or even Indian corn or European wheat, was typical of South American Indian sympathetic magic. Bodily fluids were occasionally boiled to divine the identity of an evildoer, as in English folklore, but they were mixed and cooked with other substances to provide protection against witchcraft.[26] Tituba may have thought that the witchcake would cure Betty and Abigail or at least protect them against further injury. She willingly complied with Sibley's suggestion that she prepare it.

It was logical for Sibley to approach Tituba and John instead of making the witchcake herself. Because Tituba lived in the Parris household, she could readily collect samples of Betty's and Abigail's urine. In addition, Sibley may have perceived the two Indians as more familiar with occult powers than she was. It was a common perception.[27] Cotton Mather was hardly alone in describing Indians as Satan's "most devoted ... children," who evoked evil spirits in their wigwams.[28] Such fears had been revived in New England when violent conflict with Indians resumed in 1690, at the outset of King William's War (1689–98). Young Mercy Short of Salem, recently released from captivity, contributed to a growing panic with stories of Indian cannibalism and devil worship.[29] Mary Toothaker testified in July 1692 that the devil had appeared to her "in the shape of a Tawny man," a common descriptor for American Indians.[30]

It is unlikely that Tituba or John were known for their skill in magic before 1692.[31] There is no documentary or trial evidence that Tituba participated in occult rituals before that year. On the contrary, there is every indication that she lived an unremarkable life until the last week of February 1692. Had she been a "cunning person," the close-knit Puritans would have known —and told — about it. Yet no one accused her of wronging her neighbors or the Parrises before Abigail Williams and Parris himself denounced her at the end of February, after the preparation of the witchcake.

Various writers since the nineteenth century would have us believe that Tituba introduced the girls to some forbidden magical practices.[12] The allegation is groundless. Betty and Abigail had been dabbling in the occult and admitted having tried to tell their fortunes by using an egg and a glass (much like reading tea leaves). But they implicated no adult, nor did Parris accuse Tituba of introducing his daughter to the occult. He concurred with others that "when this witchcraft came upon the stage there was no suspicion of Tituba."[33]

Only one witness blamed Tituba for acts of witchcraft that took place before the witchcake incident of 25 February. Most of Tituba's accusers traced their tortures at her hands to that day. In early depositions Elizabeth Hubbard claimed that Tituba's specter had first come to her then, and the younger Ann Putnam cited the same day. Only Abigail Williams, who mentioned the possibility of several visitations in February, was less precise.[34] No earlier date was suggested. Many others accused of witchcraft in 1692 faced complaints of malefice or divination dating months or years earlier, but Tituba did not.[35]

The attempt at countermagic brought disaster. Betty and Abigail were frightened by their inadvertent involvement in the appeal to satanic power. After the witchcake episode, their symptoms became more extreme: they felt tortured by invisible hands and began to see the ghosts of murder victims. Moreover, two teenagers, Ann Putnam and Elizabeth Hubbard (Dr. Grigg's niece), began to complain of seeing similar apparitions. According to John Hale, only in March did adults begin to behave oddly and to blame their torments on "specters."[36] The first two women to claim that apparitions were pinching them, within two weeks of the witchcake incident, were Thomas Putnam's wife, Ann, and their servant Mercy Lewis.[37]

Parris apparently believed in the efficacy of the witchcake, because only when he had found out about it, probably a day or two afterward, did he abandon his cautious campaign to exorcise the afflicted girls through prayer and demand that they reveal their tormentors.[38] Abigail, the younger Ann Putnam, and Elizabeth Hubbard pointed to Sarah Good and Sarah Osborne, two quarrelsome and disagreeable women who fit the popular image of a witch, and Tituba.

Weeks later, on 27 March, Parris would publicly chastise Mary Sibley for her part in raising the devil in Massachusetts. In light of the girls' accusations, he ignored her complicity for the moment.[39] Instead of persecuting her, a church member and white woman, Parris turned to Tituba, a credible devil worshiper only by virtue of her ethnicity, for evidence of a diabolical plot. When questioned privately by Parris and some visiting ministers, Tituba denied being a witch. Subsequently she was either beaten by Parris or severely pressured to confess, and to avoid further punishment, she finally did.[40] On 29 February she was arrested on suspicion of having practiced witchcraft. The full import of her confession would not be revealed until after she was questioned by the magistrates.

Examined in the makeshift court in the meeting house from 1 to 5 March, Tituba at first disavowed "familiarity" with any "evil spirit" and denied that she had hurt the children, even though the devil had come to her and commanded her service. Instead, she implicated the two Salem women who had been arrested with her, as well as two Boston women whose names were unknown to her and one "tall man of Boston."[41] "They hurt the children and then lay all upon me," she protested. In the next breath she admitted hurting the children herself but charged that the four women and the man had forced her to do so by threatening her life and "worse" if she refused. She humbly apologized for her behavior: "I was Sorry & ... would doe Soe noe more, but ... would feare God."

Under close questioning by Judge John Hathorne, Tituba told of reluctantly pinching Elizabeth Hubbard, Betty Parris, and Abigail Williams and of threatening the younger Ann Putnam with a knife; the women "would have had me kill Thomas Putnam's Child last night." She reported meeting a hog (sometimes a black dog), a red rat, and a black one (one transcript has instead a red and a black cat), who told her to "serve" them. She described the Salem goodwives' familiars. Good had a yellow bird, a wolf, and a cat. Osborne "had a thing with a head like a woman with 2 leggs and wings," which Abigail Williams had seen turn "into the shape of goodie osburn" herself; she also had "a thing all over hairy, all the face hayry & a long nose & I don't know how to tell how the face looks with two Leggs, itt goeth upright & is about two or three foot high & goeth upright like a man and last night itt stood before the fire in Mr. parris's hall." The pair of witch women, Tituba said, were "very strong & pull me & make me goe w'th them"; sometimes all three rode on a stick or pole, with Tituba in front.

Further questioning brought out more details about these witches' appearance. The man had "white hayr" and wore black clothes but "some times Searge Coat of other Couler." One of the strange women wore "a black Silk hood w'th a White Silk hood under itt"; the other, shorter woman, dressed not as finely, wore a "Searge Coat w'th a White Cap." Suddenly, after listening quietly to Tituba's imaginative descriptions of these diabolical creatures, the children began to have "fits," and Tituba was asked who was hurting them. Three girls blamed Good's specter, and Tituba agreed. But Elizabeth Hubbard was so overcome that she denied knowing her tormentors; "they blinded hir." Tituba too seemed to fall into a trance and could no longer be questioned. The session abruptly and dramatically ended.

On the second day Tituba confessed to signing her mark in blood in a little book offered her by the "tall man of Boston." In the book she saw nine marks already made in red or yellow. One she knew belonged to Good, who she claimed had told her so in person on "the same day I came hither to prison." Another she took to be Osborne's, though Osborne would not admit it. The man had not told Tituba who had made the other seven. She herself had not signed the book immediately, because they were interrupted when "mistris [Elizabeth Parris] Called me into the other roome." Promising to return, the man had left her with a "pin tyed in a stick to doe it with." "And what," the examiner asked, "did he say to you when you made your mark?" Echoing a dominant theme of her confession, Tituba answered, "He sayd, Serve mee & always Serve mee."

Tituba's testimony was not merely the frightened response of a slave woman but, arguably, a sophisticated manipulation of her interrogators' deepest fears. She was sufficiently familiar with Puritan customs to know which questions required positive responses and what form they should take. When asked if she ever saw the devil, for instance, Tituba replied that he "came to me and bid me serve him." When more suspects were required, she indicated the four women and the man and then, probably sensing that a wider conspiracy would divert attention from herself, enlarged the group of evil ones to include seven more people.

Who were they? Tituba did not identify them definitely. The mystery of the seven, an effective diversion, also had a personal meaning for her. Among South American Indians, the Arawaks in particular, evil conflicted with social norms that deplored violence within the tribe; one did not curse members of one's own community. Thus evil beings were always identified with strangers or distant villagers.[42] It was no accident that Tituba placed the Massachusetts evil beings in a faraway town and claimed not to know them.

The details she provided regarding the clothing and physical appearance of the various specters not only increased Tituba's credibility as a witness but also distracted her questioners. The tall man with white hair and black clothes that signaled a dignified status fit the description of many respectable, elderly men in Salem. In the imaginations of others the man would become a black man or an Indian, the personified devil to many Puritans, but he was not so in Tituba's testimony.[43] A white man, quite possibly he represented her attempt to deflect attention from her Indian appearance and to direct it toward other whites. He may also have been meant as an indirect attack on Parris, a black-clothed white man who, significantly, had come from Boston.

During the second day of her hearing, Tituba, responding to her inquisitors' leading questions, told them about the devil's book that the man had wanted her to sign. After suggestive questions about a covenant, her story became more elaborate: the unidentified white man in black had said that he was God and that he wanted her to serve him for six years and to hurt the children. In return, she would be protected from harm and would receive "many fine things." With growing awareness of her power to create fear, and probably with malice, Tituba confessed to seeing the other names in the book. She had now supplied legal evidence of a satanic presence. Aroused to the magnitude of the conspiracy, the magistrates finally stopped tormenting her and commenced to search our the other malefactors. The witch hunt had begun.

Witch hunts in Puritan New England had been frustrated by a disjunction between folk and elite concepts of evil.[44] Magical practices, both evil and benign, were essential to non-Christian belief systems, whether African, Indian, or European. These systems assumed that persons with occult powers could use their knowledge for good or evil. The evil power could be as pervasive as the good, but the good could be used to overcome evil sorcerers.[45] To most people witchcraft was a practical method of protecting against an evil neighbor. It was usually free of satanic influence and likewise was practiced with little regard for Christian tenets. Thus Mary Sibley's collaboration with Tituba and John in preparing the witchcake was consistent with folk tradition carried on without concern for orthodox theology.

Christian theologians and the more learned members of the community identified magic with satanic evil. They denied that ordinary people could manipulate occult forces without assistance from the devil or that such forces could be benign.[46] Therefore the questioning of suspected witches concentrated on what they knew of a diabolical presence. Puritan divines, and the courts following their lead, needed evidence not of malefice but of satanic influence to convict people of practicing witchcraft. The Massachusetts legal system failed to secure convictions because few persons mentioned the devil in testimony or used his presence as a defense. Most of them spoke only of their misfortunes and personal injuries, not of a diabolical conspiracy.[47] Tituba, however, linked folk practices to the elite concept of evil that included the required satanic presence. She not only told the magistrates what they wanted to hear about the devil's pact but embellished her story with ideas so strange and new as to convince them of a satanic invasion.

Some of Tituba's testimony was readily derived from English folklore — night riding, marks in blood, specters — but much of it bespoke Indian or African practices, or alluded to qualities common to all three cultures. The book was an artifact of literate societies and the devil a feature of Christian theology. They would not be found in the pre-colonial American Indian or African cultures.[48] The association of witchcraft with Satanism, with its promise of power over others, was surprisingly rare in the English folk tradition and in New England.[49]

In responding to questions regarding Satan, Tituba included notions characteristic of American Indian beliefs about the source of evil. In those traditions magical power derived from an individual's inherent ability to manipulate the mystical elements of the universe; it did not imply an impersonal, supernatural energy.[50] Among the Arawaks, for instance, evil was believed to reside in individuals and to require no intermediate spiritual force. Nevertheless, it could exist in different degrees of strength. The most potent evil spirit, the kenaima, was a real person of flesh and blood, unlike the Christian devil.[51] Thus Tituba gave the evil presence substance as a persona, identifiable in her testimony as a white man in distant Boston.

Those confessing to the practice of witchcraft gradually modified Tituba's description of this devil to forms more consistent with their own conceptions. The white man then became a tawny or black specter. But at first, under Tituba's sway, the accusing girls talked about a white man presiding over a witches' sabbat, with women serving as his deacons.[52] As the confessions became embellished with more elements from European traditions, the black devil shared the blame with the white one and the witch took on a new form.

Tituba's suggestion about an evil man left men more vulnerable to accusation than in earlier years. Others sought to identify the male leader of the conspiracy from among their own. The first man to be investigated, toward the end of March, was tavern keeper John Proctor.[53] He was followed by at least thirty-nine men during the witch hunt. Giles Corey was accused by the younger Ann Putnam, Mercy Lewis, Abigail Williams, Mary Walcott, and Elizabeth Hubbard and arrested on 18 April.[54] Two days later William Hobbs of Topsfield was accused and questioned.

Tituba's story made it possible for the magistrates to believe that a man like George Burroughs, a minister, could be responsible for the satanic presence in their community when he was accused by Hobbs' daughter Abigail and the younger Ann Putnam. A warrant for his arrest was issued on the last day of April.[55] Burroughs was brought to Salem on 4 May, and by that time several more men were under arrest. Philip English, a prosperous Salem merchant, managed to escape the authorities, only to he captured in Boston.[56] On 10 May the two George Jacobses, father and son, and John Willard, all of Salem, were arrested. A few days later Roger Toothaker of Billerica was taken into custody.

A much higher proportion of men were accused of practicing witchcraft during the Salem crisis than during previous witch scares. In his study of pre-1692 incidents John Demos finds four women accused to every man.[57] On the other hand, of the identifiable accused in 1692, the ratio was fewer than 3:1 (104 women and 40 men). Moreover, the men accused at Salem faced greater danger to their lives. Only 1 of 22 accused men had been executed in all of New England before 1692.[58] In 1692, 5 of the 40 accused men were hanged. The statistics regarding women are comparable. Of the 104 women arrested in 1692, 14 were executed.[59]

As the crisis abated after October, a more conventional attitude prevailed. During 1693 a much smaller proportion of accused men were even tried by the courts. Indeed, "it was only at the height of the Salem outbreak that the secular authorities relinquished to any significant degree their assumption that witches were women."[60] But for a while Tituba's words shook their basic understanding of the servants of Satan. Her influential confession nor only widened the witch hunt to include a greater proportion of men but extended it beyond Salem. Abigail Hobbs was brought from Topsfield on 18 April on suspicion of having practiced witchcraft; on the strength of the "afflicted" girls' complaints her mother,

Deborah, two other women, and another man from Topsfield were also arrested. The list of accused outsiders included Mary Easty (sister of Rebecca Nurse, one of the more respectable, elderly church members in the town), Sarah Wild, and Nehemiah Abbott Jr.[61] By the end of May complaints had been heard about men and women in several Massachusetts communities — Andover, Rumney Marsh, Malden, Marblehead, Lynn, and Beverly — and had begun to spread to Boston. Thus Tituba's suggestion about an evil force from a distant community in the form of a member of the upper class had sent the Salem magistrates far afield to find the coconspirators. Neither social status nor geographic location provided immunity from persecution, any more than gender did.[62] A new conception of the witch, based partly on Indian belief, emerged following Tituba's confession.

The Indian woman had sketched the portrait of a witch who could fly through the air, take animal or human form, and submit to oaths and ordeals involving other spirits. These characteristics were all common to witches from Africa to Asia and throughout America.[63] Thus Tituba described the metamorphosis of Sarah Good's spirit into a hog and a dog. She had also seen animals change into the tall man and then back into animals, sometimes a hog and sometimes "a great black dogge," in a manner typical of the European witch and of the South American kenaima, who could put his spirit into the body of any animal he wished, even a mythical one.

The supposed ability of witches to fly on a stick or pole was almost universal. Both European and African traditions told of witches riding on sticks at night to attend secret meetings and to take part in misanthropic rituals.[64] Although the witches' meeting was another universal phenomenon, the details varied from culture to culture. Tituba's testimony contained some significant deviations from Puritan concepts.

Tituba drew on the common traditions when she told the magistrates of riding on a "poal" to Boston, with Osborne and Good behind her, to meet the other witches she could not name. But she denied knowing the way to their destination; she had seen neither "trees nor path, but was presently there."[65] In her account, it was as though her spirit had left her body and been transported instantaneously, unlike the Anglo-African witch sailing over the clouds on a stick. She may well have been recalling some vestige of the folklore of her background.

Many Indians of the Americas believed in a dream soul that could leave the body during sleep and visit faraway places. Indeed, every animate object was thought to have a spiritual quality that could leave it during sleep (as well as death) but could return to it only during sleep. Events that occurred during that dream state were considered tangible experiences of the spirit.[66] Thus Tituba's story of a witches' meeting may well have reenacted a dream state during which her spirit went to a distant city. Oddly, during her examination on 2 March she stated that she "was never att Boston," contradicting otherwise consistent testimony. Did she mean that her physical presence had not been there, only her dream soul? Or did the danger of admitting to such a meeting induce her to detach herself from the conspirators? For only the evil ones conspired in Boston. Hers was a reluctant collaboration.

Tituba alluded to other apparent dream states. She stated that the tall man had first visited her some two months before, just as she was about to fall asleep.[67] She may actually have had such a nightmare when Betty Parris became ill in December. In her account of this dream, evil took the shape of a man similar to the minister Samuel Parris. Thus Tituba, primed to believe that evil was at work in Salem, may have conceived that he had arrived from Boston to threaten her periodically in the lean-to of Parris's house.

More important, Tituba placed the evil one in Boston — outside the Salem community. By doing so, she evoked the Guianese concept of the malevolent persona who inhabits a different village from its victim. On the other hand, the Puritans, obsessed with the intrusion of evil into their own community, transformed Tituba's suggestion about a distant meeting into one held within their village. From the beginning of April through the trial of George Burroughs in August, every accuser claimed that the witches met nearby. Abigail Hobbs described a meeting in a field near the Parris house, and Abigail Williams said that she had seen many people assembled in the village to mock the Christian sacraments.[68]

These confessions conformed more closely to Puritan concepts in two ways: they set contact with the devil in Salem itself, and they pictured the meetings as mockeries of sacred rites. Their purpose was to destroy the Christian commonwealth. The Puritans gradually reshaped Tituba's vision of an evil stranger to fit their own vision of a satanic presence. But the origins of the conspiracy initiated by outsiders still lay in a distant place.

Many of those said to attend the meetings came from other towns or were newcomers to Salem.[69] Tituba's testimony, although modified and distorted in the retelling, continued to inspire confessions and accusations.

A significant Caribbean feature of Tituba's testimony was the hairy imp: "A thing all over hairy, all the face hayry & a long nose ... w'th two leggs, itt goeth upright & is about two or three foot high."[70] This creature was most likely based on the Guianese kenaimas, often described as little people who lived deep in the forest and came out at night to attack other people. Similarly, the evil spirit of the Ashanti of West Africa was supposedly covered with long hair, with bloodshot eyes, and was known to sit on the branches of a tree, dangling his legs.[71] The Jamaican Creole spirit came to be known as a duppy, "a malicious vindictive, imp-like spirit that haunts forests and burying grounds, a figure very likely derived from a combination of African and Amerindian beliefs."[72] The mention of these foreign creatures heightened the villagers' fear and motivated subsequent accusers to describe strange imps that attended their mocking of the sacraments.

The Indian and English concepts of magic and evil resembled each other closely enough that the details of Tituba's story were reinterpreted and incorporated into the English framework of belief.[73] That Tituba's commitment to the tall man was written in her blood evoked the cannibalism and bloodsucking associated with European witchcraft lore. In her mind that blood oath may have been a remnant of the memory of West Indian practices, of the sealing of compacts with blood among Africans or of the holding of the color red as a talisman against sickness and disease among Indians.[74]

Tituba also added details not implied in the questions posed to her. She spoke of a yellow bird and later of a green and white bird, of the black dog, of the two rats (or cats, as a second version of her testimony has it),[75] and of the hog. The dog appeared in many other testimonies and hallucinations, as did the yellow bird, which probably had special significance for Tituba. The Arawaks of Guiana took birds to be magical messengers. The goatsucker or nightjar, the supernatural ancestor of the Tetebetana clan that uttered a weird piercing call at night, was held in awe by many Guiana Indians.[76] Were the birds of Tituba's fantasy memories of her earlier existence? Did they represent an appeal to her guardian spirit for assistance? Certainly, others found these allusions useful. There was abundant material in Tituba's story for accused witches to draw on, and much of it appeared, with variations, in subsequent confessions.

Tituba's behavior at the end of her first day of testimony, when she claimed to be blind and went into a trance, would have been unusual for an English witch. Since the Reformation, in English and continental European belief, victims of witchcraft exhibited strange symptoms, but witches themselves did not go into trances, any more than priests did in the exercise of their offices.[77] In the African and Indian rituals of 1670s Barbados, however, the shaman or obeah did undergo possession of the spirit, with a resulting trance, while uncovering witchcraft.[78] For the peoples of the Caribbean, therefore, the trance was a familiar part of magicoreligious ceremonies, but the Puritans associated it with conjuring and devil worship.[79] Tituba's sudden blindness was taken as a sign that she herself was bewitched by the others, even though she did not immediately claim to be victim.

To protect herself Tituba now reverted to remembered concepts and practices and cunningly confessed to promoting an evil conspiracy that had merely been suspected. Cultural differences in the use of language made her confession that much easier. Whereas in Puritan society deception for personal gain or for self-preservation was equated with satanic practices, in Indian cultures a reluctance to contradict others and the use of metaphorical language were cultivated as diplomatic arts.[80] Thus Tituba's confession was a ploy to confirm Puritan anxieties, to shift blame to outsiders, and to distract her tormentors with the fear of evil. By locating the evil forces not only in Boston strangers but also in the two Salem women arrested with her, Tituba supported the allegations of the Parris and Putnam families. By appearing to collaborate with her own accusers, she demonstrated the correct deference to her betters.

By 5 March, the last day of Tituba's testimony, the magistrates had most of the pieces to the satanic plot: the devil's book, a cabal of nightriding witches, malefice. The few elements they lacked were not yet forthcoming, however, for Tituba offered no information about sexual orgies and suggested no relation between her witches' coven and Christian ceremony. Either such ideas were too distant from Tituba's Indian worldview[81] or, if she had learned them during her Puritan indoctrination, she forgot them under the stress of questioning.

The idea of the "black mass" or witches' sabbat was integral to European witch hunts of the fifteenth and sixteenth centuries. Zealous religious reformers and inquisitors imagined the witches' sabbat as the site of wild dancing and revels, a secret nocturnal assembly "presided over by Satan, where sexual orgies were performed and babies wasted and eaten."[82] The stories that unfolded in Salem were no less fantastic. Abigail Williams claimed to see the witches on the day set aside for a public fast. In a special ceremony held "at an house in the Village," she said, they parodied the Lord's Supper by taking "Red Bread and Red Drink." The next day Mercy Lewis confirmed Abigail's report.[83] Contradicting the conventional description of the devil as a black man, the girls, cued by Tituba's story, portrayed him as a white man who presided over a congregation at prayer.

What began early in March 1692 as the story of a nocturnal meeting of nine witches, some of whom had flown to Boston on a pole, had by the summer of that year given rise to the stereotype of a devil-worshiping witch who mocked the most sacred features of Christianity.[84] Stories spread about the inversion of church services, complete with baptisms, into a satanic cult and the transubstantiation of bread and wine into flesh and blood under a new malevolent leader, a white man. Cotton Mather noted this transformation: "The Witches do say, that they form themselves much after the manner of Congregational Churches; and that they have a Baptism and a Supper, and Officers among them, abominably Resembling those of our Lord."[85]

In outline that witches' sabbat followed Tituba's fantasy, but its details represented a Puritan reformulation. The story told by the girls was elaborated by the accused, who, for a variety of reasons, confessed to practicing witchcraft and participating in a diabolical alliance. The multiethnic dimensions of Tituba's confession had fueled a satanic plot that grew increasingly sinister in the retelling.

The Massachusetts magistrates, captives of their cultural milieu, did not consciously note the alien quality of Tituba's story. Her extraordinary fantasy about a satanic presence, based partly on Indian concepts of evil, partly on Creolized Caribbean beliefs, and partly on English witchcraft, was sufficiently familiar to be accepted by them. Creatively integrated into their framework of belief, it allowed the Puritans (and most historians since) to see Tituba as a simple slave trapped by forces beyond her control, a passive victim.[86] Her confession, evidence to the Puritans of a diabolical conspiracy, thus saved her life even as it simultaneously elevated the level of fear.

NOTES

1. On these themes see Paul Boyer and Stephen Nissenbaum, *Salem Possessed: The Social Origins of Witchcraft* (Cambridge, Mass., 1974); Alan Krohn, *Hysteria: The Elusive Neurosis* (New York, 1978), 163–66; James E. Kenses, "Some Unexplored Relationships of Essex County Witchcraft to the Indian Wars of 1675 and 1689," *Essex Institute Historical Collections* 120 (1984): 179–212; David Thomas Konig, *Law and Society in Puritan Massachusetts: Essex County, 1629–1692* (Chapel Hill, N.C., 1979); and Richard Slotkin, *Regeneration through Violence: The Mythology of the American Frontier, 1600–1860* (Middletown, Conn., 1973), chap. 5. See also Wallace Notestein, *A History of Witchcraft in England from 1558 to 1718* (New York, 1911), 280; and Keith Thomas, *Religion and the Decline of Magic* (New York, 1971, 526–34. For a review of the literature on Salem witchcraft see David D. Hall, "Witchcraft and the Limits of Interpretation," *New England Quarterly* 58 (1985): 253–81. A few studies put more emphasis on intellectual analysis: Richard Godbeer, *The Devil's Dominion: Magic and Religion in Early New England* (New York, 1992); Larry D. Gragg, *The Salem Witch Crisis* (New York, 1992); David D. Hall, *Worlds of Wonder, Days of Judgment: Popular Religious Beliefs in Early New England* (New York, 1989); and Bernard Rosenthal, *Salem Story: Reading the Witch Trials of 1692* (Cambridge, Mass., 1993).
2. See especially Jane Kamensky, "Words, Witches, and Women Trouble: Witchcraft, Disorderly Speech, and Gender Boundaries in Puritan New England," *Essex Institute Historical Collections* 128 (1992): 286–307; Carol F. Karlsen, *The Devil in the Shape of a Woman: Witchcraft in Colonial New England* (New York, 1987); and Lyle Koehler, *A Search for Power: The 'Weaker' Sex in Seventeenth-Century New England* (Chicago, 1980). On European women see especially Allison P. Coudert, "The Myth of the Improved Status of Protestant Women: The Case of the Witchcraze," in *The Politics of Gender in Early Modern Europe*,

ed. Jean R. Brink, Allison P. Coudert, and Maryanne C. Horowitz (Kirksville, Mo., 1989), 62–65; and Christina Larner, *Enemies of God: The Witchunt in Scotland* (Baltimore, Md., 1981), 64.

3. A few scholars have ventured to focus on Tituba and the effect of her testimony, but they offer little analysis of its content. See, for example, Chadwick Hansen, *Witchcraft at Salem* (New York, 1969), 37–38; Richard P. Gildrie, *The Profane, the Civil, and the Godly: The Reformation of Manners in Orthodox New England, 1679–1749* (University Park, Pa., 1994), 169–70; Gragg, *Salem Witch Crisis* (see note 1), 52–54; and Rosenthal, *Salem Story* (see note 1), 21–31. An earlier, more pointed attempt to evaluate the details of Tituba's confession is George Chever, "Prosecution of Philip English and His Wife for Witchcraft," *Historical Collections of the Essex Institute* 2 (1860): 71–78; 244–45.

4. The question of why the other accused persons confessed has received a great deal of attention, but little credit has been given to Tituba's behavior as a model. See Chadwick Hansen, "Andover Witchcraft and the Causes of the Salem Witchcraft Trials," in *The Occult in America: New Historical Perspectives*, ed. Howard Kerr and Charles L. Crow (Urbana, Ill., 1983), 50; Karlsen, *Devil in the Shape* (see note 2), 39–42, 50–52; Koehler, *Search for Power* (see note 2), 398; Herbert Leventhal, *In the Shadow of the Enlightenment: Occultism and Renaissance Science in Eighteenth-Century America* (New York, 1976), 71; and Richard Weisman, *Witchcraft, Magic, and Religion in 17th-Century Massachusetts* (Amherst, Mass., 1984), 96–97.

5. Paul Bayer and Stephen Nissenbaum, *Salem Witchcraft Papers: Verbatim Transcripts*, 3 vols. (New York, 1977), 3:755 (hereafter *SWP*).

6. All references to Tituba's testimony in this article are taken from the transcripts reprinted in *SWP* (see note 5), 2:361–62, 745–57. The dearth of Indian women's voices in the written records makes her confession a unique document. On the difficulties of extracting evidence about American Indian women from literary sources see Clara Sue Kidwell, "Indian Women as Cultural Mediators," *Ethnohistory* 39 (1992): 97–107.

7. On the association of Indians and devil worship see Alden T. Vaughan, "Early English Paradigms for New World Natives," *Proceedings of the American Antiquarian Society* 102 (1992): 35–40; Alfred A. Cave, "Indian Shamans and English Witches in Seventeenth-Century New England,"

Essex Institute Historical Collections 128 (1992): 242–49; William Kellaway, *The New England Company, 1649–1776: Missionary Society to the Indians* (London, 1961), 82–83; William S. Simmons, "Cultural Bias in the New England Puritan Perception of Indians," *William and Mary Quarterly*, 3rd ser., 38 (1981): 56–64; Slotkin, *Regeneration through Violence* (see note 1), 128–45, 199; and Charles W. Upham, *Salem Witchcraft*, 2 vols. (1867; rpt. Boston, 1971), 1:8.

8. Chadwick Hansen, "The Metamorphosis of Tituba, or Why American Intellectuals Can't Tell an Indian Witch from a Negro," *New England Quarterly* 47 (1974): 3–12.
9. Ibid., 6–11. On the other hand, the most recent fictional work on Tituba attempts to rescue the Tituba-as-African theme and use her as a metaphor for twentieth-century African-American women. See Maryse Condé, *I, Tituba, Black Witch of Salem*, trans. Richard Philcox (Charlottesville, Va., 1992). The African motif is also the foundation of Peter Hoffer's highly dramatized narration of the Salem happenings, *Devil's Disciples: Makers of the Salem Witchcraft Trials* (Baltimore, Md., 1996), esp. 1–16, 205–10. Hoffer bases his argument solely on the similarity of the first syllable of Tituba's name to a single Yoruba word, but he cannot explain why, if she were an African, she is so consistently identified as an Indian in the seventeenth-century records.
10. George Lincoln Burr, ed., *Narratives of the Witchcraft Cases, 1648–1706* (New York, 1914), 162, 413; Robert Calef, *More Wonders of the Invisible World* (1700; rpt. Boston, 1828), 238–39.
11. Lorenzo Johnston Greene, *Negro in Colonial New England* (New York, 1968), 198.
12. *SWP* (see note 5), 1:113, 179; Calef, *More Wonders* (see note 10), 93; Upham, *Salem Witchcraft* (see note 7), 2:136, 215. See also William D. Piersen, *Black Yankees: The Development of an Afro-American Subculture in Eighteenth-Century New England* (Amherst, Mass., 1988), 70–71.
13. Larry D. Gragg, "The Barbados Connection: John Parris and the Early New England Trade with the West Indies," *New England Historical and Genealogical Register* 140 (1986): 103–11; Barbados Archives, Wills and Testaments, RB6/14, 453–55. See also G. Andrews Moriarty, "Genealogical Notes on the Rev. Samuel Parris of Salem Village," *Essex Institute Historical Collections* 49 (1913): 354–55. For commentary on Tituba and John's married status see John Hale, "A Modest Inquiry into

the Nature of Witchcraft" (1702), in Burr, *Narratives of the Witchcraft Cases* (see note 10), 413; Calef, *More Wonders* (see note 10), 238; and Upham, *Salem Witchcraft* (see note 7). 2:2.

14. Elaine G. Breslaw, "Prices — His Deposition: Kidnapping Amerindians in Guyana, 1674;" *Journal of the Barbados Museum and Historical Society* 39 (1991): 47–51. On slave-catching ventures in South America see Neil L. Whitehead, *Lords of the Tiger Spirit: A History of the Caribs in Colonial Venezuela and Guyana* (Providence, R.I., 1988), 180–86. On the Arawak Indians of South America see W. Edwards and K. Gibson, "An Ethnohistory of Amerindians in Guyana; *Ethnohistory* 26 (1979): 161–75; William Henry Brett, *Indian Tribes of Guiana: Their Condition and Habits* (London, 1868); "A Description of Guyana," in *Colonising Expeditions to the West Indies and Guiana, 1623–1667*, ed. Vincent Harlow (London, 1925), 132–48; Fred Olson, *On the Trail of the Arawaks* (Norman, Okla., 1974); James Rodway, *Guiana: British, Dutch, and French* (London, 1912); and Irving Rouse, "The Arawak," in *Handbook of South American Indians*, ed. Julian H. Steward, 7 vols. (New York, 1963), 4:507–46.

15. Barbados Archives, Recopied Deeds, RB3/10, 451. See also Elaine G. Breslaw, "The Salem Witch from Barbados: In Search of Tituba's Roots;" *Essex Institute Historical Collections* 128 (1992): 217–38. A similar name, Tutúba, appears among the eighteenth-century maroons (runaway African slaves) of Guiana, who absorbed local Indians during the formative years of their society. See Richard Price, *First-Time: The Historical Vision of an Afro-American People* (Baltimore, Md., 1983), 9, 144–45, 162. Price argues that Tutúba's descendants attempted to clarify their ancestor's racial origins by claiming that she was not "red" (light-skinned) but "absolutely black," implying that the name had strictly African and not Indian roots. Despite the explicitly African ending *uba*, Tituba and Tutúba may both be traceable to an Arawak clan, the Tetebetanas, in the Orinoco-Amacura River valleys in the seventeenth century. See Everard F. im Thurn, *Among the Indians of Guiana* (London, 1883), 183. Such names, with their combined American Indian, African, and Spanish roots, reflect the multicultural influences in the circum-Caribbean area. For additional information regarding Tituba's South American name origins see Elaine G. Breslaw, *Tituba, Reluctant Witch of Salem: Devilish Indians and Puritan Fantasies* (New York, 1996), 12–14.

16. On Caribbean Creole culture see Joseph J. Williams, *Voodoos and Obeahs: Phases of West India Witchcraft* (New York, 1932); Eugene D. Genovese, *Roll, Jordan, Roll: The World the Slaves Made* (New York, 1974), 209–10; Roger Bastide, *African Civilisation in the New World*, trans. Peter Green (New York, 1971); Lawrence W. Levine, *Black Culture and Black Consciousness: Afro-American Folk Thought from Slavery to Freedom* (New York, 1977); Sidney W. Minz and Richard Price, "An Anthropological Approach to the Afro-American Past: A Caribbean Perspective" (Philadelphia, 1976), 18–21; Margaret E. Crahan and Franklin W. Knight, eds., *Africa and the Caribbean: The Legacies of a Link* (Baltimore, Md., 1979), 8–9; and Edward Brathwaite, *The Development of Creole Society in Jamaica, 1770–1820* (Oxford, 1971). On Barbados in particular see Jerome Handler and Frederick W. Lange, *Plantation Slavery in Barbados: An Archeological and Historical Investigation* (Cambridge, Mass., 1978), 33; P. F. Campbell, *The Church in Barbados in the Seventeenth Century* (St. Michael, Barbados, 1982), 82–83; and Neville Connell, trans., "Father Labat's Visit to Barbados in 1700," *Journal of the Barbados Museum and Historical Society* 24 (1957): 168.
17. A. Gunkel and J. Handler, "A Swiss Medical Doctor's Description of Barbados in 1661: The Account of Felix Christian Sporri," *Journal of the Barbados Museum and Historical Society* 33 (1966): 7.
18. Walduck, a military officer stationed in Barbados, noted that both American Indians and Africans used image magic with such materials as clay, wax, and dust fashioned into a form, which they then stuck with a variety of objects to cause pain. See "T. Walduck's Letters from Barbados, 1710," *Journal of the Barbados Museum and Historical Society* 15 (1948): 148–49. Jerome S. Handler identifies several types of obeah practitioners in Barbados, from approved healers and diviners to the most antisocial sorcerers, in "Slave Medicine and Obeah in Barbados" (paper presented at Hamilton College, Clinton, N.Y., October 1992), 11–16.
19. Bastille, *African Civilisation* (see note 16), 30. See also Genovese, *Roll, Jordan, Roll* (see note 16), 181; Harry Hoetink, "The Cultural Links," in Crahan and Knight, *Africa and the Caribbean* (see note 16), 28; and Levine, *Black Culture* (see note 16), 60.
20. Jerome S. Handler, "Amerindian Slave Population of Barbados in the Seventeenth and Early Eighteenth Centuries," *Caribbean Studies* 8 (1969):

47-51; Handler "Slave Medicine" (see note 18), 5. See also Breslaw, *Tituba, Reluctant Witch* (see note 15), 45–51.
21. The most important source on Arawak belief systems is the nineteenth-century text of im Thurn, *Among the Indians* (see note 15), 328–34, 41–70. See also Raphael Karsten, *The Civilization of the South American Indians, with Special References to Magic and Religion* (1926; rpt. London, 1968); Andrew Landers, "American Indian or West Indian: The Case of the Coastal Amerindians of Guyana," *Caribbean Studies* 16 (1976): 121–22; and Lewis Spence, "Brazil: The Arawaks," in *Encyclopedia of Religion and Ethics*, ed. James Hastings (New York, 1926), 2:85.
22. "Walduck's Letters" (see note 18), 148–49.
23. Calef, *More Wonders* (see note 10), 224; Deodat Lawson, "A Brief and True Narrative of Witchcraft at Salem Village" (1692), in Burr, *Narratives of the Witchcraft Cases* (see note 10), 163.
24. Samuel Parris, "Records of Salem Village Church, March 17, 1692," in *Salem Village Witchcraft: A Documentary Record of Local Conflict in Colonial New England*, ed. Paul Boyer and Stephen Nissenbaum (Belmont, Calif., 1972), 278. See also Calef, *More Wonders* (see note 10), 225; and Upham, *Salem Witchcraft* (see note 7), 1:405.
25. The practice of sympathetic magic postulated a connection between all parts of the physical world. Thomas, *Religion and the Decline of Magic* (see note 1), 437–38, describes a belief in the cosmos as "an organic unity in which every part bore a sympathetic relationship to the rest," and thus the nail parings or urine continued to be connected to the person. Therefore manipulating one substance would affect the other. See also Bastide, *African Civilisation* (see note 16), 103; Williams, *Voodoos and Obeahs* (see note 16), 163–64; im Thurn, *Among the Indians* (see note 15), 349; Robert Galbreath, "Explaining Modern Occultism," in Kerr and Crow, *Occult in America* (see note 4), 16; and Alvin O. Thompson, *Colonialism and Underdevelopment in Guyana, 1580–1803* (Bridgetown, Barbados, 1987), 12.
26. Karsten, *Civilization of the South American Indians* (see note 21), 190, 202, describes several procedures similar to the preparation of the witchcake. See also Walter E. Roth, *An Inquiry into the Animism and Folk-Lore of the Guiana Indians* (Washington, D.C., 1915), 356.
27. Simmons, "Cultural Bias" (see note 7), 64–68; Kenses, "Some Unexplored Relationships" (see note 1), 86–91.

28. Quoted in Godbeer, *Devil's Dominion* (see note 1), 192.
29. Slotkin, *Regeneration through Violence* (see note 1), 124–29. See also Cotton Mather, "Brand Plucked from the Burning" (1693), in Burr, *Narratives of the Witchcraft Cases*, 255–87.
30. *SWP* (see note 5), 2: 768–69.
31. There is little evidence of John's complicity in earlier occult practices, but his role at Salem is different from Tituba's and requires a separate analysis.
32. That Tituba was a practitioner of the occult in some form has been assumed by many historians, starting with Upham, *Salem Witchcraft* (see note 7), 2:3. See, for example, Leventhal, *In the Shadow* (see note 4), 68–69; James Duncan Phillips, *Salem in the Seventeenth Century* (Boston, 1933), 292; Piersen, *Black Yankees* (see note 11), 81; and especially Marion Starkey, *Devil in Massachusetts* (New York, 1949), 34–36
33. *SWP* (see note 5), 2:587; see Parris, "Records of Salem Village Church" (see note 24), 178–79.
34. *SWP* (see note 5), 2:612, 3:708, 756.
35. See especially the testimonies against Bridget Bishop, Mary Bradbury, Sarah Good, and Ann Pudeator in *SWP* (see note 5), 1:92–94, 124–25; 2:368–69, 375.
36. Hale, "Modest Inquiry" (see note 13), 414. Compare, for instance, the four accusers during the examination of Tituba on 1 March and the larger number of "afflicted" complaining about Martha Corey on 19 March; the latter group included the Ann Putnams (mother and daughter), Mrs. Pope, Goodwives Bibber and Goodall, Mary Walcott, and the original three girls. *SWP* (see note 5), 1:247; Lawson, "Brief and True Narrative" (see note 23), 143–46; *SWP* (see note 5), 3:745, 756.
37. *SWP* (see note 5), 1:260; 3:603–4.
38. Hale, "Modest Inquiry" (see note 13), 414.
39. Parris, "Records of Salem Village Church" (see note 24), 278.
40. We have only Calef's word that the beating took place (*More Wonders* [see note 10], 225), but there is no doubt that Tituba was pressured to give evidence. Hale confirms that she was questioned before the warrant was issued and before she was brought before the magistrates ("Modest Inquiry" [see note 13], 414). The use of violence against accused witches was not unusual in 1692. The successful use of force against Tituba probably encouraged the later tortures. For a discussion of the use of

torture and psychological pressure in 1692, see Godbeer, *Devil's Dominion* (see note 1), 206-11.
41. *SWP* (see note 5), 3:749, 752; Hale, "Modest Inquiry" (see note 13), 413-16.
42. Im Thurn, *Among the Indians* (see note 15), 328-34. See also Landers, "American Indian" (see note 21), 121-31; Peter Rivière, "Factions and Exclusions in Two South American Village Systems," in *Witchcraft Confessions and Accusations*, ed. Mary Douglas (London, 1970), 245-56; and Thompson, *Colonialism and Underdevelopment* (see note 25), 12.
43. See especially Lawson, "Brief and True Narrative" (see note 23), 156, 159-61; and Calef, *More Wonders* (see note 10), 246, 254, 284.
44. On the differences between popular and elite beliefs regarding the occult see Godbeer, *Devil's Dominion* (see note 1), 35-46; George L. Kittredge, *Witchcraft in Old and New England* (1929; rpt. New York, 1956), 7-22; and Joseph Klaits, *Servants of Satan: The Age of the Witch Hunts* (Bloomington, Ind., 1985), 173.
45. Handler and Lange, *Plantation Slavery* (see note 16), 213. See also Orlando Patterson, *The Sociology of Slavery: An Analysis of the Origins, Development, and Structure of Negro Slave Society in Jamaica* (London, 1967), 183; and John Mbiti, *African Religions and Philosophy* (New York, 1969), 158-61.
46. According to Edward Phillip's 1671 lexicography, witchcraft was "a certain evill art, whereby with the assistance of the Devil, or evill Spirits, some Wonders may be wrought which exceed the common Apprehension of Men." Quoted in Samuel Drake, *Witchcraft Delusion in New England*, 3 vols. (Roxbury, Mass., 1866), 1:xi. On the history of this notion see Norman Cohn, *Europe's Inner Demons: An Enquiry Inspired by the Great Witch Hunt* (New York, 1975), 225-57; Klaits, *Servants of Satan* (see note 44), 22-47; Brian I. Levack, *The Witchhunt in Early Modern Europe*, 2nd ed. (New York, 1995), 29-44; and Thomas, *Religion and the Decline of Magic* (see note 1), 253-79.
47. Godbeer, *Devil's Dominion* (see note 1), esp. 162-74.
48. Geoffrey Parrinder, *Witchcraft: European and African* (London, 1963), 128.
49. Leventhal, *In the Shadow* (see note 4), 122; Hansen, *Witchcraft at Salem* (see note 3), 37; Godbeer, *Devil's Dominion* (see note 1), 18; Thomas, *Religion and the Decline of Magic* (see note 1), 255.

50. On the South American Indian concept of evil see Marc Simmons, *Witchcraft in the Southwest: Spanish and Indian Supernaturalism on the Rio Grande* (Flagstaff, Ariz., 1974), 14; William Curtis Farabee, *The Central Caribs* (Philadelphia, 1924), 75; and Åke Hultkrantz, *The Religions of the American Indians*, trans. Monica Setterwall (Berkeley, Calif., 1979), 32–33.
51. See especially im Thurn, *Among the Indians* (see note 15), 328–34; Landers, "American Indian" (see note 21), 121–22; and Lawrence E. Sullivan, *Icanchu's Drum: An Orientation to Meaning in South American Religions* (New York, 1988), 445–47.
52. Lawson, "Brief and True Narrative" (see note 23), 160–61; *SWP* (see note 5), 1:164, 2:659.
53. *SWP* (see note 5), 2:680.
54. Ibid., 1:239.
55. Ibid., 1:151.
56. Ibid., 1:313–15.
57. John Putnam Demos, *Entertaining Satan: Witchcraft and the Culture of Early New England* (New York, 1982), 60.
58. Ibid., 62.
59. Of the 22 men accused before 1692, 10 were suspect by association with an accused woman; the major exceptions were John Godfrey of Andover and Henry Wakely of Wethersfield, Connecticut. In 1692 some of the men, such as John Proctor and Philip English, were accused before the women in their families, and others particularly Nehemiah Abbott, George Burroughs, John Willard, John Alden, Nicholas Flood, and Job Tookey, had no association with the women suspected of witchcraft. There is no detailed analysis of the backgrounds of all the men accused at the time. Information on many of them is available in Karlsen, *Devil in the Shape* (see note 2); and Boyer and Nissenbaum, *Salem Possessed* (see note 1).
60. Karlsen, *Devil in the Shape* (see note 2), 50.
61. *SWP* (see note 5), 2:429.
62. Karlsen sees the attacks on elite women as part of a trend to discredit women who inherited property or were successful in business (*Devil in the Shape*, see note 2, 116). Tituba's evidence gave impetus to this class bias. Her words rang true to people already primed to see diabolical action in the growing number of such women in the community.

63. Parrinder, *Witchcraft: European and African* (see note 48), 128–40; Simmons, *Witchcraft in the Southwest* (see note 50), 55–59, 88.
64. Examples are reported by James Axtell, *The European and the Indian: Essays in the Ethnohistory of Colonial North America* (New York, 1981), 73; Parrinder, *Witchcraft: European and African* (see note 48), 38–39, 128–40; Williams, *Voodoos and Obeahs* (see note 16), 129; Notestein, *History of Witchcraft* (see note 1), 237; Lamer, *Enemies of God* (see note 2), 10; and Cohn, *Europe's Inner Demons* (see note 46), 206–23.
65. SWP (see note 5), 3:751.
66. On the Arawak interpretation of dreams see im Thurn, *Among the Indians* (see note 15), 329, 343–49, 358–59; and Sullivan, *Icanchu's Drum* (see note 51), 241–43.
67. SWP (see note 5), 3:750.
68. Ibid., 2:423. Ann Foster later confirmed Abigail Hobbs' story (ibid., 2:343). See also Boyer and Nissenbaum, *Salem Village Witchcraft* (see note 24), 99, 103–5; SWP (see note 5), 1:164, 172, 409–11.
69. Breslaw, *Tituba, Reluctant Witch* (see note 15), 144.
70. SWP (see note 5), 3:752.
71. Landers, "American Indian" (see note 21), 131; Williams, *Voodoos and Obeahs* (see note 16), 130.
72. Patterson, *Sociology of Slavery* (see note 45), 200.
73. The reinterpretation and incorporation of alien traits also occurred among the Spaniards and Indians in Central America, as described by Julian Pitt-Rivers, "Spiritual Power in Central America," in Douglas, *Witchcraft Confessions* (see note 42), 197–99; and Simmons, *Witchcraft in the Southwest* (see note 50), 39–54. For similar transference between Algonquin Indians and the French in Canada see Richard White, *The Middle Ground: Indians, Empires, and Republics in the Great Lakes Region, 1650–1815* (New York, 1991), 50–93.
74. The blood practices were noted among maroon societies in Guiana in the eighteenth century and may well have been found earlier in Barbados. See Richard Price, *Maroon Societies: Rebel Slave Communities in the Americas* (Baltimore, Md., 1979), 301–2. On the American Indian use of red paint and its origin in blood rituals see Roth, *Inquiry into the Animism* (see note 26), 290; and Karsten, *Civilization of the South American Indians* (see note 21), 4, 40–42.
75. SWP (see note 5), 3:752.

76. Im Thurn, *Among the Indians* (see note 15), 119, 183; Roth, *Inquiry into the Animism* (see note 26), 274–75.
77. Weisman, *Witchcraft, Magic, and Religion* (see note 4), 63–64. Carlo Ginzburg, in *Night Battles: Witchcraft and Agrarian Cults in the Sixteenth and Seventeenth Centuries*, trans. John Tedeschi and Anne Tedeschi (1966; rpt. Baltimore, Md., 1983), 17-21, finds that trancelike behavior did continue in the folk traditions of Italy as late as the sixteenth century.
78. On the role of the trance in African religions see Parrinder, *Witchcraft: European and African* (see note 48), 128–30; and Bastide, *African Civilisation* (see note 16), 120–22. On the Indians see im Thurn, *Among the Indians* (see note 15), 343–49, 358–59; and Hultkrantz, *Religions of the American Indians* (see note 50), 87–90.
79. Cotton Mather, "Memorable Provinces Relating to Witchcraft and Possessions" (1689), in Burr, *Narratives of the Witchcraft Cases* (see note 19), 115.
80. On Indian diplomacy and strategies for survival see Axtell, *The European and the Indian* (see note 64), 79; Elise M. Brenner, "To Pray or to Be Prey: That Is the Question: Strategies for Cultural Autonomy of Massachusetts Praying Town Indians, *Ethnohistory* 27 (1980): 135–52; Gerald Sider, "When Parrots Learn to Talk and Why They Can't: Domination, Deception, and Self-Deception in Indian-White Relations," *Comparative Studies in Society and History* 29 (1987): 3–23; and Simmons, "Cultural Bias" (see note 7), 71. On the Puritan attitude toward lies see Hansen, *Witchcraft at Salem* (see note 3), chap. 6 ("A Country Full of Lies"); Demos, *Entertaining Satan* (see note 57), 77–79; and Karlsen, *Devil in the Shape* (see note 2), 147.
81. Pitt-Rivers, "Spiritual Power" (see note 73), 198.
82. Norman Cohn, "Myths of Satan and His Human Servants," in Douglas, *Witch-craft Confessions* (see note 42), 11. On the growth of these legends see especially Cohn, *Europe's Inner Demons* (see note 46), 225–57; and Klaits, *Servants of Satan* (see note 44), 173. See also Richard P. Gildrie, "Salem Witchcraft Trials as a Crisis of Popular Imagination," *Essex Institute Historical Collections* 128 (1992): 284.
83. The report of these events is in Lawson, "Brief and True Narrative" (see note 23), 160–61.
84. On the similarities between Congregational practice and these supposed satanic rites see Richard Godbeer, "Chaste and Unchaste Covenants:

Witchcraft and Sex in Early Modern Culture," in *Wonders of the Invisible World, 1600–1900*, ed. Peter Benes (Boston, 1995), 62–69.

85. Cotton Mather, "Wonders of the Invisible World" (1693), in Burr, *Narratives of the Witchcraft Cases* (see note 10), 246. See also Chever, "Prosecution of Philip English" (see note 3), 73–78.

86. Tituba was held in the Boston jail until April 1693, was never tried for any crime, and finally, when Parris refused to take her back into his household, was sold for the cost of her imprisonment to an as-yet-unidentified person. Her subsequent fate is unknown. See Calef, *More Wonders* (see note 10), 343.

Chapter Eight
New England's Well-Ordered Society

Carol Karlsen

The women of early New England were used to an active religious role. As Puritans, many of the first settlers had been schooled since childhood in opposition to established authority. During the years of religious ferment that preceded Puritan political victories in England, ministers may have expressed misgivings about openly encouraging women to disobey Anglican rule. But after the Puritans came to power in England, the implications of women's training in issues of religious doctrine became clear. And in New England, Puritan rule obtained from the very first.

Even before Anne Hutchinson challenged the Puritan authorities in the mid-1630s were signs of an ensuing battle between women and their religious and secular leaders. Like their male companions, most of the first female settlers had risked the dangerous ocean voyage to New England specifically to participate in setting up God's kingdom. They shared no single vision of what that kingdom would be like, but they were not easily deterred. Anne Hutchinson's excommunication and banishment sent a clear and emphatic message to her female followers and to other religiously aggressive women who might, like Hutchinson, assert their own spiritual authority.

The message was not immediately heeded by women in Boston or in other communities. Mary Dyer, Jane Hawkins, and at least four other women were prosecuted for religious defiance in Boston in the wake of Hutchinson's expulsion: Judith Smith in 1638, for "obstinate persisting" in "sundry Errors"; Katherine Finch that same year, for "speaking against the magistrates, against the Churches, and against the Elders"; Widow Hammond in 1639 for saying "that Mrs. Hutchinson neyther deserved the Censure which was putt upon her in the Church, nor in the Common Weale"; and Sarah Keayne in 1646, for "irregular prophesying in mixed assemblies."[1]

New Haven experienced a similar pattern of female recalcitrance in the mid-1640s. Anne Eaton, wife of the governor of the colony, was excommunicated in 1644 for "her disavowal of infant baptism" and for other offences that mounted after she refused to admit her error. Two years later, Lucy Brewster was accused of "sympathizing with Eaton and of saying [the minister John] Davenport made her 'sermon sick.'" During the same court, a Mrs. Moore and her daughter, Mrs. Leach, were prosecuted for their outspoken denigration of ministerial authority.[2]

In Salem, the authorities found female dissent an even greater problem. At least seven women were called before church or court officials for disorderly religious behavior in the late 1630s and the 1640s. Several men committed religious crimes in Salem during these years, but in all but one of their cases the charges were minor ("fowling" on the Sabbath, for example).[3] The religious crimes of the women, on the other hand, were interpreted as heresy. Elinor Truslar, who was said to have "question[ed] the government ever since she came," was accused of declaring that the town's minister and its principal magistrate were unfaithful to the church and that the minister "taught the people lies." Mary Oliver, who simply insisted on her right "as a Christian" to church membership, was eventually charged with "disturbing the peace of the church," reproaching the elders and the magistrates, and propounding dangerous opinions.[4] To John Winthrop, Oliver was "far before Mrs. Hutchinson ... for ability of speech, and appearance of zeal and devotion" and therefore was "the fitter instrument to have done hurt, but that she was poor and had little acquaintance."[5]

A few dissenting women recanted their positions and were simply admonished or fined. But most persisted in their "errors" until excommunicated, officially banished, or driven from the colony. According to their opponents they bore their punishments with what Winthrop described as a "masculine spirit."[6] This display of female obstinacy was part of an energetic debate that covered a whole range of women's religious behavior: whether a woman could prophesy; whether she could publicly relate the religious experience marking her acceptance of grace (which was necessary, some argued, if church members were to judge her fitness for membership); whether she should be considered an individual, as opposed to a wife, with regard to church membership or dismissal; whether St. Paul's injunction that women be silent in the churches extended to propounding questions to the minister after the sermon, voting in church meetings, or participating in decisions about membership in the church; and even whether the sound of women's voices in the singing of psalms would offend God's ear.[7]

This debate — like women's religious activism itself — grew as much out of the diverse experiences of settlement as it did out of the contradictions in Puritan doctrine. In early New England, the minister and the laity had considerable power to decide the practices of their own churches.[8] Some congregations emphasized the view that women enjoyed spiritual equality with men. In those churches women could prophesy, or relate their conversion experiences as men did, publicly to the whole congregation rather than privately to their husbands or their ministers. Although we do not know how most churches arranged their gender relations, in the wake of the Antinomian controversy liberal readings of Puritan doctrine regarding women were increasingly frowned upon by the established clergy.

The debate over women's position within the church, then, was occasioned both by the latitude earlier afforded women in some congregations and by women's own vocal assertions of spiritual equality. This debate may have been stimulated also by the growing visibility of women as church members: despite the disproportionate numbers of men in the larger population, in the 1640s women already composed majorities of the elect in some congregations, and by the 1650s in most.

By the late 1640s, however, the outcome of the conflict over women's spiritual status was foreshadowed by the abrupt decline in Puritan women's opposition to their male leaders, and by the growing numbers of women who were called to account for their behavior in both the church and the commonwealth. As the historian Mary Maples Dunn has noted, not only were women disciplined within the church "in numbers out of proportion to their share of congregational populations," but "their offenses were increasingly connected with social behavior, not with heresy."[9] Much of this aberrant social behavior was sexual.

During the early years of settlement, Puritans in Massachusetts Bay were also uncertain about how to translate their sexual beliefs into public policy. As early as 1631, Massachusetts passed its first adultery law, stating "that if any man shall have carnall copulation with another mans wife, they both shal be punished by death."[10] The act was originally provoked by John Dawe's adultery with an unnamed Indian woman. The magistrates decided not to hang either of the offending parties, possibly because the woman involved was not the wife of a colonist or perhaps, as later cases would suggest, because Puritan magistrates were reluctant to administer in full measure the punishment that legally fit the crime. In this case, they simply ordered Dawe "severely whipped for intiseing an Indian woman to lye with him." No charges were filed against the woman.[11]

In the ensuing several years the Massachusetts magistrates attempted to articulate more precisely the forms and degree of punishment appropriate to the different varieties of sexual offenses. In 1632, they ordered that Robert Huitt and Mary Ridge be "whipt for committing fornication togeather."[12] Here the Court of Assistants set out what was to become a common punishment for sexual misdemeanors among the unmarried, or among married men and single women. In 1635 the authorities turned their attention to the problem of fornication between persons who later married. They fined two men, Edward Gyles and John Galley, for "knoweing" their wives "carnally before marriage," but they did not punish either of the two wives.[13] In 1638, they ordered John Hathaway, Robert Allen, and Margaret Seale whipped and banished for adultery but simultaneously confirmed their 1631 law stipulating that the punishment for adultery was death.[14]

In at least three of these cases, the magistrates did not hold the woman responsible for her sexual misbehavior. This was not unusual. In Massachusetts in the 1630s and early 1640s, many more men than women were prosecuted for sexual offenses. Although a few of these cases involved forced sexual acts, legal actions against men predominated largely because the most common sexual offense was premarital intercourse resulting in pregnancy and the courts did not prosecute the woman involved if she subsequently married the father of the child. Between 1630 and 1639, seventeen men were charged with fornication-related crimes in Massachusetts' two highest courts, while only two women were so charged.[15]

Even considering the inconsistencies in Puritan sexual beliefs, this differential treatment of men and women is surprising. We might expect the courts either to hold men and women equally responsible for their sexual behavior or, considering the place of Eve in the Puritan worldview, to place the greater blame on women. Perhaps the legal response spoke to the scarcity of women during these years and the magistrates' desire to ensure the colony's survival. By marrying and legitimizing the children of their illicit unions, women who committed the sin of fornication may have sufficiently redeemed themselves in the eyes of the authorities. In any event, the courts' leniency with women was short-lived.

For the period 1640–44, 18 men and 10 women were charged with fornication-related offenses in the two highest Massachusetts courts.[16] The ratio of male to female offenders had changed since the 1630s from roughly 4:1 to just less than 2:1. After 1644 the higher courts no longer handled any but the most serious sexual crimes, but in Essex County, Massachusetts, the direction of the change was even more evident. Between 1636 and 1650, the Essex courts adjudicated 56 sexual offense cases: 30 of the offenders (54%) were women. The tendency to hold women more responsible than men for violations of sexual norms, which would become more obvious over the rest of the century, dates from the 1640s.[17]

The increased proportion of women among those charged with sexual offenses in Essex County arose in part from the magistrates' new willingness, first evidenced in Essex in 1643, to hold women equally responsible with men for incontinence before marriage. But the courts also displayed a growing reluctance to prosecute men for some sexual crimes and a growing inclination, present even during the early years, to conceive of certain crimes in images of female sexuality. In a 1650 letter to Connecticut governor John Winthrop, Jr., minister Roger Williams condemned adultery as "that filthy devill of whorish practices."[18] Williams' words suggest that the idea that women led men to sexual sin was too deeply embedded to be eradicated easily by the Puritans' more enlightened ideas about women. Yet there was no theologically consistent way to punish only women for men's and women's assertion of sexual independence. The resolution to this problem, like the resolution to the problem of women's religious and economic independence, was never openly acknowledged, but a resolution was found.

Witchcraft accusations, trials, and executions began in earnest in New England in 1647. The accused were from the start primarily women who had violated gender norms — norms that had not always been clearly articulated or agreed upon during the early years of settlement but which by the mid-1640s were being enforced. Most of the accused were women who had no brothers or sons, women who either had inherited or were likely to inherit property. Many of these same women had committed or were thought to have committed fornication, infanticide, or other sexual or sexually related offenses. A few others were women who stubbornly maintained their own versions of religious truth. Except for this last group, witches were not normally accused by the religious or secular authorities but by their own neighbors. This suggests that by the mid-1640s, signs of female independence had also become objectionable to the larger community. [...]

[...] By treating female dissent as evidence of witchcraft as well as heresy, the authorities may have effectively silenced Puritan women's opposition. Indeed, by 1660 the debate over women's participation in the church had all but ended — and women had lost many of the gains of the early years.[19] After 1660 Puritan ministers increasingly found reasons to celebrate rather than vilify their most active female congregants, but women's religious activity had taken on a decidedly submissive character. Women continued to join the church in proportionately larger numbers than men for the rest of the century, but if the ministers can be believed, female congregants now listened more than they spoke — and when they spoke, it was not in church.[20]

Ironically, the clergy's success in bringing women to God may have fostered witchcraft accusations in other areas. The growing visibility of women in the church did not go unnoticed: by 1692, with no more than a quarter of his congregation male, even Cotton Mather was forced to speculate that women might be more religious than men.[21] As women's religious commitment became more obvious over the second half of the seventeenth century, the contradictions in Puritan beliefs about women intensified, encouraging those who lived with those contradictions to associate some women with the evil of Satan. The new religious submission of women might have quieted fears about certain kinds of female independence but aroused fears about other kinds.

If religious tensions became submerged in other issues, the tensions evident in the first outburst of witchcraft accusations continued to grow. Fornication and adultery aroused greater and greater concern in New England as the century wore on. [...]

[...] After 1680, except for the poor, Essex County men were only infrequently whipped or fined for fornication with women they did not subsequently marry, or for what we would call adultery with a single woman. Adultery with a married woman continued to bring harsh penalties, except in some cases where the woman's husband was without influence. Women, however, continued to be held responsible for both the illicit sexual act and its consequences. Women were liable for the child's care and sometimes for his or her maintenance — in some cases even when the child was put out to service. Beyond that, women were still whipped or sometimes fined for fornication and were punished more often and more severely — by public humiliation as well as beatings — for adultery of any kind.[22] By the late seventeenth century, the stigma of having an illegitimate child and the difficulty of caring for and maintaining that child were, along with the fines and public degradations, the principal deterrents to sexual misbehavior: all were burdens borne primarily if not exclusively by women.[23]

The combination of economic concerns and the increasing incidence of illegitimacy go a long way toward explaining New England's double standard of sexual accountability — and its witchcraft accusations and trials. As the seventeenth century wore on, more and more men were refusing to marry the mothers of their children. Illegitimate children and their mothers were becoming a greater financial burden not only to the community but also to these women's parents and siblings.[24] [...]

[...] The problem of "overcrowding" in settled New England communities was not only demographic. It was economic as well, and this dimension also affected the lives of second and third generation women. It seems a paradox to find constricting local conditions in a region that in comparison to England offered apparently boundless economic opportunity.[25]

Nevertheless this process was real, and it influenced inheritance patterns, mobility, and the polarization of rich and poor, especially in seaport and river towns.

Salem was one of these seaport communities. The areas surrounding Salem had been settled early, and most of the lands within its borders had been taken by the first generation of settlers. Beginning in the 1650s there were continual boundary disputes between Salem's residents and those of surrounding towns. Most second and third generation Salem children lived as adults on subdivided lands or moved on. Those sons and daughters who continued to farm within Salem found themselves less well-off than their parents, if not poor in absolute terms. The resulting tensions were heightened by the concentration of land ownership in the hands of a relative few and by the spread of commercial farming for local and foreign markets. Trade networks expanded so rapidly that by 1650 Salem was already a thriving mercantile center. Distinctions had always existed between the prosperous and the not-so-prosperous, but they became even more visible as the seventeenth century progressed, particularly as merchants became the most economically and politically powerful group in the community.[26]

Springfield, Massachusetts, experienced extensive commercial development and economic inequality even earlier. From its founding in 1636 as a Connecticut River fur-trading post, Springfield was oriented toward an international as well as a New England market. A single family, the Pynchons, dominated the direction of the economy from the beginning and controlled most of its resources. For other townspeople, most of whom depended on the Pynchons' good will for their livelihoods, access to these resources came hard. Even after the town shifted its economic base from furs to agricultural products in the 1650s and 1660s, land ownership continued to be restricted and individual holdings remained small. Few families could prosper easily, let alone provide all their sons with land, even in their wills. Parents and children who remained in Springfield faced the ongoing frustration of their economic goals.[27]

Land problems also afflicted towns without a mercantile orientation. Andover, for instance, was one of those farming communities in which a high birth rate combined with low child and adult mortality rates to constrict the process of land transmission. Though most second and third generation Andover sons were settled on lands by the late seventeenth century, they commonly had to wait for many years to gain ownership of their inheritance, because their fathers were unwilling to relinquish full control. Even in Andover's unusually healthy economic environment, fathers had to maintain their continuing prosperity and economic independence at the expense of their sons. In a society in which land ownership determined men's political and economic status, most Andover men could not secure autonomy until long after they had come of age, many of them until their fathers' deaths.[28]

We know little about the impact of these material conditions on women or on the relations between men and women. In Salem, however, the probate records disclose that some men responded to the plight of second and third generation sons by adjusting the portions of their estates that went to their wives and daughters.[29]

These Salem records show that at least until 1681, magistrates disposed of intestate property much as they had done during the early years of settlement. They upheld the widow's right to dower, usually leaving her about one-third of the estate for her use during her life. They divided the rest of the estate among the children. The eldest son received a double share, the daughters and younger sons equal shares. When there were no sons, daughters inherited equally. The exceptions were almost always in cases where the estate was quite small and the children young. In these cases the widow was likely to be awarded most if not all of the estate to help her raise the children.[30] Early in the century, we find several intestate records of widows' estates, since women were still inheriting property in significant numbers. After 1670, so few women were in that position that only one intestate record shows the disposition of a woman's property.

Wills written in Salem followed fairly closely the principle of leaving the eldest son a double portion of the estate, but there were many exceptions. These wills deviated in other ways too from the intestate cases. Before 1650, there were too few inheritance cases involving families with both sons and daughters surviving to warrant any conclusions, but after that time the records show that most fathers were not conforming to the intestate pattern of allotting equal shares of estates to daughters and younger sons (see table 8.1). Although it is conceivable that these fathers gave their daughters part of their portions earlier as dowries while withholding their sons' full shares, this does not seem to have been the

Table 8.1
Relative Inheritances of Daughters and Younger Sons as Revealed in Wills, Salem, Massachusetts, 1651–1700

Period	Number of Cases	Dispositions in Favor of Younger Sons	Equal Dispositions among Younger Sons and Daughters
1651–1660	9	6 (67%)	3 (33%)
1661–1670	9	7 (78%)	2 (22%)
1671–1680	21	19 (91%)	2 (9%)
1681–1690 *	11	10 (90%)	1 (9%)
1691–1700 *	10	9 (90%)	1 (10%)

* incomplete data

case; even when a man's children were still quite young at the time he wrote his will, the pattern held. The pattern also became more obvious over the course of the century. Whereas 25–33% of the fathers who left wills in Salem in the 1650s and 1660s treated their younger sons and their daughters equally, only about 10% did so in the last three decades of the century.[31] If fathers in Salem and other settled communities were responding to the difficulty of settling their sons on land in this manner, their actions may account for the increasing numbers of spinsters, even in towns such as Andover or Hingham where the sex ratios were still favorable to men. In Hingham, for instance, rather than marry downward economically men tended to marry women from other towns.[32]

The treatment of wives in wills also changed in Salem during the seventeenth century. Though half of the men who wrote wills prior to 1650 left their widows ownership of property rather than merely its use, less than one-third of them did so after mid-century (see table 8.2). This suggests that the earlier deviation from the pattern of dower established in intestate law and practice was only a temporary expedient to deal with the special conditions of those years. As men lived longer and more of their sons survived to inherit, fewer men were inclined to leave their widows economically independent. The number of women leaving wills also decreased — from 35% of the total in the years prior to 1650 to 8% in the 1690s — indicating the gradual decline of a group of women who inherited property despite the presence of sons (see table 8.3).

Table 8.2
Patterns of Widow Inheritance, Salem, Massachusetts, 1638–1700

Period	Number of Cases	Ownership of Property	Property Use Only
1638–1650	10	5 (50%)	5 (50%)
1651–1660	13	4 (31%)	9 (69%)
1661–1670	16	5 (31%)	11 (69%)
1671–1680	26	8 (31%)	18 (69%)
1681–1690*	19	4 (21%)	15 (79%)
1691–1700*	24	6 (25%)	18 (75%)

* Incomplete data

Table 8.3
Wills and Intestate Cases by Sex of Estate Holder, Salem, Massachusetts, 1638–1700

Period	Number of Cases	Female	Male
1638–1650	17	6 (35%)	11 (65%)
1651–1660	32	6 (19%)	26 (81%)
1661–1670	53	7 (13%)	46 (87%)
1671–1680	80	6 (7.5%)	74 (92.5%)
1681–1690*	20	2 (10%)	18 (90%)
1691–1700*	24	2 (8%)	22 (92%)

* Incomplete data

The declining frequency with which men left women property of their own coincided with other important changes in Salem's inheritance practices. As we have seen, most men left their widows the use of one-third of their real property. Sometimes a man stipulated that his widow was to have more than one-third, but only rarely less. But whereas women's dower rights were interpreted in intestate cases as the use of this property for life, as often as not Salem men limited its use to their wives' widowhood. As a result, many widows who remarried did not bring their dower right to the new marriage. Instead, their "thirds" were immediately passed on to their husbands' heirs. This practice eliminated any economic advantage widows may have had over single women as potential marriage partners.

In making decisions that would benefit their children at their wives' expense, men were not necessarily acting out of callous disregard for their wives. As Salem widows faced an increasingly narrow access to estates, elaborately worded protection clauses appeared in Salem men's wills. Virtually absent prior to 1650, and only occasionally present during the 1650s, by the 1660s and 1670s these clauses had become an established pattern. They spelled out in painstaking detail the exact rights of the widow in what had become her son's house — from the rooms she could use to the number of cords of wood she could burn to the amount of space she could cultivate in the garden plot, even to her right of access to the house. While these clauses expressed men's genuine concern for their widows' well-being, they also reveal men's fears that their sons would not provide even the most fundamental necessities for their aging mothers and stepmothers. [...]

[...] If men found it hard to acknowledge, let alone express, their resentment against other men, they encountered less difficulty in expressing their resentment against women. Even mothers were vulnerable. By the early eighteenth century, ministers found scorn and neglect of mothers so common that they felt compelled to denounce what Increase Mather described as adult children's tendency to "despise an Aged Mother" and what Cotton Mather called the "Barbarity of Ingratitude."[33] By that time the economic plight of widows was so extreme that ministers wrote as if widowhood were synonymous with poverty. The clergy said little about why so many women had to be entirely supported by their offspring, but they were appalled that so many adult children did not willingly provide for their mothers and implied that some actually wished their mothers dead.[34]

The roots of sons' resentment are clear. No matter what decisions father and mothers made about their own or their sons' economic futures, simply by living long lives mothers, like fathers, threatened their sons' economic interests. Whether a woman remained a widow or remarried, whether she held on to her means of support or relinquished them, she competed with her sons for precious resources.

The Puritan emphasis on the respect due both mother and father may have strengthened the bonds of affection, preventing most seventeenth-century sons from expressing hostility toward their mothers. But this may have made the frustrations of sons even more explosive, especially since they knew that their mothers' predicament was inescapable. Fathers who maintained full control over their property until their deaths, or who provided well for their widows and daughters, would have heightened the animosity of their sons — not only toward themselves but toward the women who continued to stand in the way of inheritances long denied.

These resentments came out, but they were not directed at the men who were their principal sources. Rather they were expressed as witchcraft accusations, primarily aimed at older women, who like accusers' own mothers vied with men for land and other scarce material resources. Whether as actual of potential inheritors of property, as healers or tavern-keepers or merchants, most accused witches were women who symbolized the obstacles to property and prosperity. This was as apparent in Springfield at mid-century as it was in Salem and Andover near the century's close. My research does not support the idea (as Boyer and Nissenbaum's argument about Salem suggests) that these women were beneficiaries of the new economic order. Some witches clearly were, but most were not. And in a more fundamental way, all witches stood symbolically opposed to — and were therefore subversive of — that order, in that they did not accept their assigned place within it.[35]

Puritan belief made it easy to hold women responsible for the failures of the emerging economic system. Discontent, anger, envy, malice, and pride were understandable responses to the stresses of social and economic change. Yet the clergy's repeated descriptions of these responses as sins against the hierarchical order of Creation, and their association of women with these sins and with the devil, encouraged the conviction among men that if anyone were to blame for their troubles it was the daughters of Eve.

Sexual tensions also fostered witchcraft accusations, and these too were endemic to the social arrangements of colonial New England. In allowing for their own sexual freedom, men had to live with the fear, and the reality, of women's interference with the orderly transfer of property from father to son. In requiring women's sexual and economic dependence, they were compelled to support women in that dependence. In claiming for themselves the privilege of deciding how property would be transmitted, they had to live with other men's decisions about who would inherit and when. It was a formula that invited the devil.

We already know the stories of many of the women who were New England's witches — women like Katherine Harrison and Ann Hibbens, who maintained their economic independence until the end, and women like Rachel Clinton and Sarah Good, who were forced into dependency. Only rarely, though, do we have enough information on the relationships of individual women with their neighbors to see the day-to-day dynamics that generated the fear that these women were practicing witchcraft. For the most part the connections between New England's social structure and its witchcraft beliefs emerge only when we look generally at land scarcity, sexual and economic tension, and demographic change. Yet elusive as they were, we can catch glimpses of these connections, even in the history of one of New England's most unlikely witches.

Early in 1675, Edmund Faulkner settled his eldest son, twenty-four-year-old Francis Faulkner, on land he had purchased from the town of Andover several years before.[36] Later that year, Francis took advantage of the opportunity his father provided and married Abigail Dane, the daughter of Andover's minister, the Reverend Francis Dane. A year and a half after that, Edmund Faulkner deeded his son roughly half of his own accumulated estate, thereby making him one of the youngest landowners in town.

In both his decisions, the elder Faulkner stood out as an exception among his peers. Most Andover men could not easily afford to purchase land for their sons, and they gave up control of their estates only with their own deaths. Most of Francis' contemporaries would wait until their late twenties or their thirties to marry, and usually much longer for economic independence. Francis' good fortune came at the expense of his brother and sisters. His brother was not able to marry until he was twenty-eight, and his portion was small. His sisters' portions may have been smaller still: when Edmund Faulkner wrote his will in 1684, he bequeathed his daughters very little of his £388 estate. To one of his sons-in-law he left a pillow, "being willing," he said, "would my Estate have reach it, to have manifested my love towards him in a larger manner."[37]

Abigail Faulkner's story, like that of most witches, comes to us largely from the records of her witchcraft trial.[38] At first glance, her personal history would never lead us to suspect her for one of Satan's allies. Her age is unknown, but she probably married young, and she was still bearing children when she was accused. Between her marriage and her imprisonment seventeen years later, she had given birth to two sons (both of whom were still alive in 1692) and four daughters (one of whom had died), and she was pregnant at the time of her incarceration. She also had brothers, and by all accounts the Dane and Faulkner families were unusual in both their prosperity and social status. No sexual misconduct or other witchlike behavior is discernible in her past — at least not before 1687. The same cannot be said for several of Abigail's female relatives. Her sister, widow Elizabeth Johnson, had many years before been prosecuted for fornication. Her sister-in-law, Deliverance Dane, was still married but had no surviving sons. Her stepmother, Hannah Dane, exerted almost full control of a £587 estate left to her by her first husband.[39]

In 1687, Abigail herself began to resemble a witch. In that year, her father-in-law died and her husband came into the rest of his sizeable inheritance. More significantly, her husband became too ill to manage his own affairs. The exact nature of his illness is unclear, but he suffered from convulsions, and his memory and understanding were impaired. He was unable to do anything for himself. With no adult sons to assume responsibility, Abigail took charge of the family estate.

We can only speculate about the response of the men of Abigail's generation, most of whom were still waiting for the kind of privilege her husband had been accorded, when that privilege devolved to a woman. In 1692, in the midst of the Salem outbreak, Abigail Faulkner was "cried down" as a witch. Accused with her were two of her daughters, her sister, her sister-in-law, and two nieces and a nephew. Apparently even her father was suspected, though he was never formally accused.[40]

The origin of the complaint against her is obscure, but it was evidently filed by one of several neighbors, all of whom had children who testified that she afflicted them. Abigail initially denied any witchcraft, but later she acknowledged that the devil might have taken advantage of the malice in her heart. She owned that "she was angry at what folk said" when one of her nieces was accused and at their laughter when they suggested that her sister would be next. She also admitted that in her anger she "did look with an evil eye on the afflicted persons and did consent that they should be afflicted, becaus they were the caus of bringing her kindred out."[41] To her judges, this may have been evidence enough, for they convicted her and sentenced her to die. Her pregnancy, however, delayed her execution — and ultimately saved her life.

In 1703, a decade after the end of the Salem outbreak, Abigail Faulkner submitted a petition to the Massachusetts magistrates that captures the full force of witchcraft beliefs in seventeenth-century New England and their relentless, awesome presence in women's lives. It was not the first petition Abigail and her family had filed since she was released from prison in 1693, but the others were concerned with the effect of her conviction on the Faulkner estate. This one spoke more plaintively of its effect on her state of mind. In it, she asked the court for an official purging of the record and the full vindication of her name. "I am yet suffred to live," she said,

> but this only as a Malefactor, Convict[ed] upon record of the most heinous Crimes that mankind Can be supposed to be guilty of, which besides its utter Ruining and Defacing my Reputation, will Certainly Expose my selfe to Iminent Danger by New accusations, which will thereby be the more redily believed, [and] will Remaine as a perpetuall brand of Infamy upon my family ... [42]

Abigail could not know, of course, what only time would reveal: that the witchcraft prosecutions were at last over, that the accusations were virtually over, and that the image of woman-as-evil was even then passing into its more purely secular form, to be played out in the class and racial dynamics of a modern industrial economy.

BRANDS PLUCKED OUT OF THE BURNING

[...] The power struggle enacted through possession had another dimension. The possessed and their ministers were engaged in a fierce negotiation, initiated by the possessed, about the legitimacy of female discontent, resentment, and anger. It was a legitimacy the clergy never conceded. If the clergy had God on their side, the possessed had a formidable ally in the devil. If the outcome of the ensuing battle was preordained in Puritan New England, the possessed did not lose it without a sustained struggle.

We can see this dimension best in Elizabeth Knapp's relationship with Samuel Willard. When not possessed, Knapp was in every way respectful of the man who was both her minister and master. When the demons were in her, however, she expressed an intense hostility toward him. She railed at him and called him a liar. She castigated her father and others for listening to him. She challenged his authority in the community and his power over her. Among those she wanted to kill were Willard and his children.

Willard's account reveals the sources of this deep, painful ambivalence. Elizabeth Knapp was a young woman who had accepted the Puritan explanation for her troubles, who deeply appreciated Willard's concern for her plight and his dedication to freeing her from the demons that held her in their power. But she had cause to resent him. He was a young, well-off, Harvard-educated minister whose life was full of promise; she was a young woman with little schooling and little prospect of anything but service to others, whether as a servant, daughter, or wife. He spent most of his time reading, writing, and traveling; she had never been taught to write, seldom left Groton, and spent her time sweeping his house, caring for his children, carrying in his wood, keeping his fires burning — all so he could continue his work in peace and comfort.[43]

These were the surface resentments, and Knapp found ways to talk about these openly, even as she agreed that they were signs of her deplorable sinfulness. But the intensity of her fits and the violence of her response to Willard spoke of a deeper resentment that was so fundamentally a part of her being that she could not acknowledge it, even to herself. Only when taken over by the Prince of Evil could she express the full force of her feelings — her *desire for* the independence and power embodied in the symbol of the witch and her rage at the man who taught that independence and power were the ultimate female evils. When possessed, she could assert the witch within, she could rebel against the many restrictions placed upon her, she could dismiss the kind man in the black robe who himself symbolized her longed-for independence and power and tell him what a rogue she thought he was. For the moment, she could be as powerful as he.

Other possessed females indicated a similar ambivalence toward their ministers and their faith and struggled as vigorously to assert what their culture deemed unacceptable in women. When not possessed, they too treated their ministers with the respect due God's representatives. But when possessed, they stopped their ears when their ministers preached or mocked them in their pulpits. They were blinded when the Puritan Bible was placed in front of them or deafened when people prayed for their souls. Martha Godwin had no trouble reading Catholic or Quaker books, Cotton Mather explained, or books that argued that witches did not exist. But she could not get near the Bible, books that argued for the existence of witches, or Puritan catechisms for children without falling into what he described as "hideous Convulsions."[44] Ministers were not surprised that witches and demons would afflict the possessed in these ways — after all, they were trying to draw these young women away from their faith — but they were taken aback, they said, because the possessed were for the most part pious and godly young women who up until the time of their possessions were model young Christians. As astonishing to ministers was how often the possessed lashed out at them in their fits, and how articulate these diatribes were. They described the possessed as more intelligent than they had previously thought, more knowledgeable about religion, and exceptionally witty in attacking it.[45] With the restraints temporarily broken, the possessed were, like Elizabeth Knapp, barely recognizable to their ministers — and impossible to control.

We must remember, however, that the possessed did not deliberately confront, let alone substantially alter, the cultural values or hierarchical relations of their society. To the contrary, possession was acceptable, if not actively encouraged, because it ultimately affirmed existing gender and class arrangements, specifically the subordinate position of the possessed and, finally all women.[46] If during their possessions these women obliquely challenged Puritan beliefs and social arrangements, it was only their residual support of religious and social norms that was finally allowed recognition. Indeed, during their brief respite from powerlessness, the possessed continued to blame both themselves and other (older, seemingly more independent and powerful) women for their condition. In their fits, most of their anger was directed inward, on themselves, and, more overtly, outward on women their culture designated as their arch-enemies. While their accusations of "unlikely" witches helped to bring witchcraft prosecutions to an end and contributed to the dramatic alteration of witchcraft beliefs, colonial society did not change in fundamental ways. New ways would be found in the eighteenth century to keep most women in their place.

One remaining dimension of possession is revealed by removing it from the context of colonial New England. Taking away the language of witches and the devil, we are still left with the convulsions, the trances, the inability to talk, the paralyzed limbs, and the several other physical manifestations of possession. We can attribute them simply to the possessed's fear of witches, both within and without, but these physical responses might have existed even New Englanders and their ancestors had never created witches. They have manifested themselves in women in most cultures of the world, many of which employed no concept of witchcraft.

Anthropologists have begun to decipher the mysterious physical behaviors of possession. They suggest that the possessed disengage themselves from "the socially constructed world of everyday life" and enter a state in which what is deemed socially dangerous within their psyche is allowed freer reign. Here their discontent, anger, resentment, and other unacceptable feelings can be expressed without the usual reprisals. From this perspective, possession appears to be a special, altered state of consciousness which some women enter as an involuntary reaction to profound emotional conflict. This conflict emerges from the need simultaneously to embrace social norms and to rebel against them — to live out more autonomous, self-directed lives. With no legitimate way to express this conflict directly, the unbearable psychic tensions are expressed physically — through women's bodies.[47]

The New England possessed were frequently unable to speak: their tongues curled upward toward the roofs of their mouths or curled downward and outward to extraordinary lengths; their throats were constricted or swelled to many times their normal sizes; their words would not come, however hard they tried to speak, and their breath simply would not catch. They strove to communicate through these many physical disabilities what they so much wanted but so much feared to say: that their situations enraged them. Their fits expressed that rage, but not in a way that brought to the surface of normal consciousness the enormous psychic pain that they were experiencing. Their "socially constructed selves" had not been — and could not be — totally obliterated.

The same kind of symbolic expression is apparent in the other physical manifestations of possession. Their hearing impaired, or lost in a trance, the possessed simply could not hear the accustomed call to duty. Their arms, legs, or hands paralyzed, they simply could not do the spinning, sweeping, hauling, and serving customarily required of them. When pinched, bitten, beaten by forces others could not see or touch, they expressed both their sense of victimization and their own desire to attack the sometimes barely visible and equally untouchable sources of their frustrations. In their complaints of being starved, and in their inability to eat for days on end, they spoke to the depths of their emotional hunger and deprivation, perhaps as well to the denial of their sexual appetites. Both the emotional and the sexual seem to be represented in their overpowering convulsions, the symbolic release of their many pent-up tensions.

This physical response to their plight would have been most common in women raised in particularly religious households. They were the ones who were most pressured to internalize their society's values, who most frequently heard their parents and ministers warning them of the dangers of rebelling against God's laws. And they had the most to lose by overt rebellion. If these women allowed their conflicts to surface in any other manner, they risked not only society's vengeance but also the loss of approval and love of the people closest to them — most particularly their own fathers or the godly men whom many of the possessed identified as fathers.[48] Elizabeth Knapp was probably not alone in her fear that her extraordinary anger would alienate the man who seemed both to care the most and to insist most strongly on her self-renunciation.

Witchcraft possession in early New England, then, was an interpretation placed upon on a physical and emotional response to a set of social conditions that had no intrinsic relationship to witches or the devil. These conditions were in some respect specific to Puritan New England, but they are also evident in other societies. Like women in other times and places, the New England possessed were rebelling against pressures to internalize stifling gender and class hierarchies.[49] Puritans understood that reaction as "witchcraft possession" or "diabolical possession"; other historical and contemporary cultures call it "spirit possession." In modern Western cultures, it is called "hysteria" or some other form of individual psychopathology. The specific label, however, only tells us how certain cultures resist the knowledge of female dissatisfaction and anger with their condition.

Like women in other societies, the New England possessed were able, through this culturally sanctioned physical and emotional response, to affect some of these hierarchical arrangements, if only temporarily. They were also able to focus the community's concern on their difficulties. For once, they were the main actors in the social drama. And the more attention they received, the more they dramatized their socially, generated anguish and their internally generated desire to rebel. As the community looked on, their bodies expressed what they otherwise could not: that the enormous pressures put upon them to accept a religiously based, male-centered social order was more than they could bear. To accept the community truth was to deny the self. To assert the self was to suffer the response of a threatened community. Given this choice, they chose a world of their own.

This world, though, offered no real escape. Their religious beliefs led the possessed finally to confirm the only reality their culture allowed, the reality articulated by their ministers and affirmed by most men and women in their communities. There were only two kinds of women: godly women and witches. If witches symbolized female resistance to this dualism, so too did the possessed. But the possessed also represented female capitulation.

Epilogue

[...] Images of Eve gradually disappeared from ministerial sermons and women were increasingly portrayed as passive, dependent, chaste, powerless, and content.[50] Secular literature written for the middle and upper classes in both England and New England told women that it was their nature to be passionless, signaling what one historian had called "a pivotal point in the transformation from external to internal controls of sexual behavior."[51] Simultaneously, the witch figure herself took on a less intimidating shape in the minds of the larger population. Ideologically, both the virtuous woman and the witch had been desexed and domesticated.

The old fear of female sexual power had not disappeared. Indeed, the increasing emphasis on women's lack of sexual power was simply a new way of diminishing it, part of a larger eighteenth-century reconstruction of womanhood.[52] The celebration of the Puritan helpmeet of the seventeenth century had not, as the witchcraft trials attest, converted women to submission. The elaboration of a more diffident, self-sacrificing, innately spiritual but more secularly based female ideal would have greater success.

By the early nineteenth century, the new formulation of womanhood was fully developed, and it expressed the fears and goals of the emerging industrial society. The ideology of domesticity proclaimed that "woman" embodied a moral purity that distinguished her from man and that required women to spread their moral influence as the "mothers of civilization."[53] Created to serve the needs of the new middle class, this ideology gained widespread acceptance in part because it explicitly asserted that all women shared the same nature, but it implicitly excluded from "womanhood" those who could not or would not aspire to the ideal. Woman-as-evil had gradually taken on not a single but a dual shape — one formed by race, the other by class. By the nineteenth century, black women and poor white women were viewed as embodying many of the characteristics of the witch: they were increasingly portrayed as seductive, sexually uncontrolled, and threatening to the social and moral order.[54] To be a "woman" was to eschew the powers once identified with the witch and to use one's newly celebrated "influence" in defense of domesticity. Acceptance of the ideology's explicit and implicit truths assured white women of the middle and upper classes that the evil was not in them.

Notes

1. Lyle Koehler, "The Case of the American Jezebels: Anne Hutchinson and Female Agitation during the Years of Antinomian Turmoil, 1636–1640," *William and Mary Quarterly*, 3rd ser., 31 (January 1974): 69–70.
2. Mary Maples Dunn, "Saints and Sisters: Congregational and Quaker Women in the Early Colonial Period," *American Quarterly* 30 (winter 1978): 587; Isabel Calder, *The New Haven Colony* (New Haven, 1934), 93–94.
3. Richard Gildrie, *Salem, Massachusetts, 1626–1683: A Covenant Community* (Charlottesville, Va., 1975), 78. On male heretics in other early New England communities, see David S. Lovejoy, *Religious Enthusiasm in the New World: Heresy to Revolution* (Cambridge, Mass., 1985); Philip F. Gura, *A Glimpse of Sion's Glory: Puritan Radicalism in New England, 1620–1660* (Middletown, Conn., 1984).
4. These Salem cases are discussed in Gildrie, *Salem, Massachusetts* (see note 3), 78–83: Koehler, "American Jezebels," 70; John Winthrop, *Winthrop's Journal: "History of New England," 1630–1649*, 2 vols., ed. James Kendall Hosmer (New York, 1908), 1:281–82 (hereafter cited as Winthrop, *Journal*). On Mary Oliver, see also *Records and Files of the Quarterly Courts of Essex County, Massachusetts*, 9 vols. (Salem, 1912–75) 1:8, 12, 34, 99, 138, 152, 154, 160, 173, 180, 182–83, 185–86 (hereafter cited as *Essex Court Records*); *Records of the Court of Assistants of the Colony of Massachusetts Bay, 1630–1692*, ed. John Noble and John F. Cronin (Boston, 1901–28), 2:80 (hereafter cited as *Mass. Assistants Records*); *Records of the Governor and Company of the Massachusetts Bay in New England*, 6 vols., ed. Nathaniel B. Shurtleff (Boston, 1853–54), 1:247, 2:258, 283, 3:140 (hereafter cited as *Mass. Records*).
5. Winthrop, *Journal* (see note 4) 1:281–82.
6. Ibid., 282.
7. Many of the issues in this debate are discussed in Dunn, "Saints and Sisters" (see note 2) 588–90.
8. See Gerald F. Moran, "'Sisters' in Christ: Women and the Church in Seventeenth-Century New England," in *Women in American Religion*, ed. Janet Wilson James (Philadelphia, 1980), 53–4.

9. Dunn, "Saints and Sisters" (see note 2) 589–90.
10. *Mass. Records* (see note 4) 1:92.
11. Ibid., 91.
12. *Mass. Assistants Records* (see note 4) 2:30.
13. Ibid., 60.
14. *Mass. Records* (see note 4) 1:225.
15. See Koehler, "American Jezebels" (see note 1), 71 n.
16. Ibid.
17. These figures are compiled from *Essex Court Records* (see note 4), 1. It is often impossible to distinguish cases of male sexual coercion from cases involving mutually consenting parties (see, for instance, the prosecution of Auld [old?] Churchman in 1643 "for having the wife of Hugh Burt locked with him alone in his house," ibid. 1:56); therefore, these figures include all recorded sexual offenses, and they necessarily understate the degree to which a sexual double standard was developing in Essex County.
18. Cited in William K. Holdsworth, "Adultery or Witchcraft? A New Note on an Old Case in Connecticut," *New England Quarterly* 48 (September 1975): 400.
19. Dunn, "Saints and Sisters" (see note 2), 589–90.
20. For a discussion of the post-1660 ministerial literature on women, see Laurel Thatcher Ulrich, "Vertuous Women Found: New England Ministerial Literature, 1668–1735," in *A Heritage of Her Own*, ed. Nancy F. Cott and Elizabeth Pleck (New York, 1979), 58–80. Although we have little information on the actual gender arrangements within individual congregations after 1660, women still participated actively in at least some church controversies. See, for instance, Paul Boyer and Stephen Nissenbaum, *Salem Possessed: The Social Origins of Witchcraft* (Cambridge, Mass., 1974), 60–81.
21. Cotton Mather, *Ornaments for the Daughters of Zion. Or the Character and Happiness of a Vertuous Woman* ... (Cambridge, Mass., 1692), 44–45. On the increase in female church membership after 1660, see Moran, "'Sisters' in Christ" (see note 8), 47–65; Dunn, "Saints and Sisters" (see note 2) 590–95; Edmund S. Morgan, "New England Puritanism: Another Approach," *William and Mary Quarterly*, 3rd ser., 18 (April 1961): 236–42.
22. By 1699, clauses enjoining single men to marry the mothers of their illegitimate children had disappeared from the Massachusetts legal records,

as had those clauses calling for disenfranchisement of men convicted of fornication. At the same time, the magistrates had set limits on the fines and whippings allowed as punishments for these men, deleted requirements that they assist in the "bring[ing] up" of the children, and clarified that mothers were to assist them with the financial burdens of raising the children. See John D. Cushing, comp., *The Laws and Liberties of Massachusetts, 1641–1691: A Facsimile Edition*, 3 vols. (Wilmington, Del., 1976), 1:205 and John D. Cushing, *Massachusetts Province Laws, 1692–1699* (Wilmington, De., 1978), 29–30, for the subtle and not-so-subtle changes in the bastardy law between 1668 and 1699.

23. On the continuation of this process in New Haven Colony in the 18th century, see Cornelia Hughes Dayton, "Women Before the Bar: Gender, Law, and Society in Connecticut, 1710–1790" (Ph.D. diss., Princeton University, 1986), 89–186. For the colonies as a whole, see David Flaherty, "Law and the Enforcement of Morals in Early America," *Perspectives in American History* 5 (1971), esp. 213–17, 225–49; Robert V. Wells, "Illegitimacy and Bridal Pregnancy in Colonial America," in *Bastardy and Its Comparative History*, ed. Peter Laslett, Karla Oosterveen, and Richard M. Smith (London, 1980), esp. 355–61.

24. In New Haven County, at least, women and their parents shouldered most of this burden by the early 18th century. See Dayton, "Women Before the Bar" (see note 23), 178–79. I suspect this was the case earlier, and in other parts of New England as well.

25. See Kenneth A. Lockridge, "Land, Population and the Evolution of New England Society, 1630–1790," *Past and Present* 39 (April 1968): 62–80. Lockridge discusses this process in the 18th century, when it had its worst effects, but its characteristic social tensions were already present in some communities in the seventeenth century.

26. This description is drawn from Boyer and Nissenbaum, *Salem Possessed* (see note 20), esp. 44, 86–91; Gildrie, *Salem, Massachusetts* (see note 3), esp. 105–8, 116–22; Donald Warner Koch, "Income Distribution and Political Structure in Seventeenth-Century Salem, Massachusetts," *Essex Institute Historical Collections* 105 (1969): 50–71; William I. Davisson, "Essex County Wealth Trends: Wealth and Economic Growth in 17th Century Massachusetts," *Essex Institute Historical Collections* 103 (1967): 291–342.

27. This discussion of Springfield is based on Stephen Innes, *Labor in a New Land: Economy and Society in Seventeenth-Century Springfield* (Princeton, N.J., 1983), esp. chaps. 1–5.
28. See Philip Greven, *Four Generations: Population, Land, and Family in Colonial Andover, Massachusetts* (Ithaca, N.Y., 1970), chaps. 1–6,
29. The following analysis of Salem's inheritance patterns is based primarily on the published Salem probate records, collected in Essex County Probates (Registry of Probates, Essex County Courthouse, Salem, Mass.), doc. 6001, 1–3. These include 99 wills and 83 intestate records. I have also used 20 wills from the period 1682 to 1689, most of them published in *Essex Court Records* (see note 4), 8–9, and 24 manuscript wills for the years 1691–1700. These latter documents are found in the Registry of Probate, Essex County Courthouse, Salem, Mass.
30. Children whose fathers died young and whose mothers did not remarry were, with their mothers, among the poorest members of the community.
31. Interestingly, while adhering fairly closely to the principle of a double share for the eldest son, women who left wills rarely discriminated between daughters and younger sons. Their estates, however, were few and usually quite small; hence the impact of their actions was more psychological than material.
32. Daniel Scott Smith, "Population, Family, and Society in Hingham, Massachusetts, 1635–1800" (Ph.D. diss., University of California, 1973), 121–23. Smith also notes that in Hingham the "relative wealth of the father of the wife" was "an excellent predictor of the direction of intergenerational mobility."
33. Increase Mather, *Two Discourses, Shewing ... II, The Dignity and Duty of Aged Servants of the Lord* (Boston, 1716), 100–101; Cotton Mather, *Maternal Consolations, An Essay on the Consolations of God ... on the Death of Mrs. Maria Mother ...* (Boston, 1714), 9. This paragraph is based on Jeanne Boydston, "Aged Handmaidens of the Lord: Views of Widowhood in Boston, 1679–1728" (seminar paper, Yale University, 1978). Especially useful are her comparisons of the clergy's treatment, in their writings, of old men and old women, passim.
34. See, for example, Thomas Foxcroft, *The Character of Anna, the Prophetess ... In a Sermon Preached after the Funeral of ... Dame Bridget Usher ... Being a Widow of Great Age* (Boston, 1723), 36–37, 56. On the economic realities of widowhood for women at this time,

see Alexander Keyssar, "Widowhood in Early Eighteenth-Century Massachusetts: A Problem in the History of the Family," *Perspectives in American History* 8 (1974): 83–119.
35. This interpretation owes a great deal to Edmund Morgan's insights into the way in which economic and political discontent among elites and among different classes of white men in late seventeenth-century Virginia was vented in racial hatred during Bacon's Rebellion. See *American Slavery, American Freedom* (New York, 1975), esp. chaps. 11–13. Bernard Bailyn's "Politics and Social Structure in Virginia," in *Seventeenth-Century America: Essays in Colonial History*, ed. James Morton Smith (Chapel Hill, 1959), 90–115, was also helpful in my thinking on this issue.
36. The following discussion of Francis Faulkner is drawn primarily from Philip Greven, "Family Structure in Seventeenth-Century Andover, Massachusetts," in *The American Family in Social-Historical Perspective*, 2nd ed., ed. Michael Gordon (New York, 1978), esp. 32; *Four Generations* (see note 28), esp. 95–97.
37. Essex County Probates (see note 29), doc. 9305.
38. See Paul Boyer and Stephen Nissenbaum, *The Salem Witchcraft Papers: Verbatim Transcripts of the Legal Documents of the Salem Witchcraft Outbreak of 1692*, 3 vols. (New York, 1977), 1:327–34; 3:966–68, 970, 972–73, 991–92, 1010–19, 1034–37 (hereafter cited as *Witchcraft Papers*). Unless otherwise noted, the following discussion of Abigail Faulkner is drawn from these documents.
39. See *Essex Court Records* (see note 4) 3:5; *Vital Records of Andover, Massachusetts, to the End of the Year 1849*, 2 vols. (Topsfield, Mass., 1912), 1:117–19; James Savage, *A Genealogical Dictionary of the First Settlers of New England* (Boston, 1860), 1:2, 2, 5–6, 148, 557; Essex County Probates (see note 29), doc. 43.
40. *Witchcraft Papers* (see note 37), 1:267, 2:335–37, 499–505; Sarah Loring Bailey, *Historical Sketches of Andover, Massachusetts* (Boston, Mass., 1880), 199.
41. *Witchcraft Papers* (see note 37), 1:328.
42. *Witchcraft Papers* (see note 37), 3:967–68.
43. Samuel Willard, "A Brief Account of a Strange and Unusual Providence of God Befallen to Elizabeth Knapp of Groton," in *Remarkable Providence, 1600–1760*, ed. John Demos (New York, 1972), passim.

44. See esp. Cotton Mather, "Memorable Providences, Relating to Witchcrafts and Possessions," in *Narratives of the Witchcraft Cases, 1648–1706*, ed. Charles Lincoln Burr (New York, 1914), 112–14, 119–21 (hereafter cited as C. Mather, "Memorable Providences").

45. Ibid., 119–20; Cotton Mather, "A Brand Plucked Out of the Burning," in Burr, *Narratives* (see note 44), 267–72; Deodat Lawson, "A Brief and True Narrative of Some Remarkable Passages Relating to Sundry Persons Afflicted by Witchcraft, at Salem Village," in Burr, *Narratives* (see note 44), 154.

46. My understanding of the way possession reinforced New England's social structure is deeply indebted to discussions of status reversal rituals in Victor Turner, *The Ritual Process: Structure and Anti-Structure* (Ithaca, N.Y., 1967), chap. 5, and Natalie Zemon Davis, "Women on Top," in *Society and Culture in Early Modern France*, (Stanford, 1975), 124–51.

47. Vincent Crapanzano and Vivian Garrison, *Case Studies in Spirit Possession* (New York, 1977), 120; I. M. Lewis, *Ecstatic Religion: An Anthropological Study of Spirit Possession and Shamanism* (Middlesex, England, 1971), esp. 100–26; Erika Bourguignon, "Culture and the Varieties of Consciousness," Addison-Wesley Module in Anthropology, 3–6, 13–18. The quotation is from Crapanzano and Garrison, *Case Studies in Spirit Possession*, 9. My thinking on these issues has also been greatly influenced by Carroll Smith-Rosenberg, "The Hysterical Woman: Sex Roles and Role Conflict in Nineteenth-Century America," *Social Research* 39 (winter 1972), 652–79; Marc H. Hollander, "Conversion Hysteria: A Post-Freudian Reinterpretation of Nineteenth-Century Psychosocial Data," *Archives of General Psychiatry* 26 (April 1972), 311–14.

48. See, for instance, Cotton Mather, "Another Brand Pluckt Out of the Burning, or, More Wonders of the Invisible World" in Burr, *Narratives* (see note 44), 316–17.

49. See Bourguignon, "Culture and the Varieties of Consciousness" (see note 47), 11–13, for a discussion of the relationship between possession and hierarchical social structures. Possessed individuals in other cultures tend to be either women, or men who share with women inferior, marginal, or ambiguous social positions in their societies. See Lewis, *Ecstatic Religion* (see note 47), 100–7; Crapanzano and Garrison, *Case Studies in Spirit Possession* (see note 47), xi–xii.

50. Lonna M. Malmsheimer, "Daughters of Zion: New England Roots of American Feminism," *The New England Quarterly* 50 (September 1977): 497–504.
51. Laurel Thatcher Ulrich, *Good Wives: Image and Reality in the Lives of Women in Northern New England, 1650–1750* (New York, 1982), 103–5; Nancy F. Cott, "Passionlessness: An Interpretation of Victorian Sexual Ideology, 1790–1850," in *A Heritage of Her Own*, ed. Nancy F. Cott and Elizabeth H. Pleck (New York, 1979), 162–181. See also John Putnam Demos, *Entertaining Satan: Witchcraft and the Culture of Early New England* (New York, 1982), 389–92.
52. This analysis owes much to Ulrich's discussion of the role of the witch figure in Samuel Richardson's *Pamela*, the English novel which achieved considerable popularity in the colonies in the mid-eighteenth century. See *Good Wives* (note 51), 104–5.
53. See Nancy F. Cott, *Bonds of Womanhood: "Woman's Sphere" in New England, 1780–1835* (New Haven, 1977), for a thorough discussion of the tenets of domesticity.
54. *Black Women in White America: A Documentary History*, ed. Gerda Lerner (New York, 1973), 149–215; Deborah Gray White, *Ar'n't I a Woman?: Female Slaves in the Plantation South* (New York, 1985), 27–61; Charles E. Rosenberg, "Sexuality, Class and Role in 19th-Century America," *American Quarterly* 25 (May 1973), 131–58; Kathy Peiss, *Cheap Amusements: Working Women and Leisure in Turn-of-the-Century New York* (Philadelphia, 1986). In the South, black women had taken on the image of evil as early as the beginning of the eighteenth century. See Winthrop Jordon, "Fruits of Passion: The Dynamics of Interracial Sex," in *Our American Sisters*, ed. Jean E. Friedman and William G. Shade, 3d ed. (Lexington, Mass., 1982), 154–69.

Chapter Nine
The Six Nations Indians in the Revolutionary War

Barbara Garymont

In 1863, when the United States was undergoing its most trying period in history, President Abraham Lincoln memorialized the achievement of a previous generation that in 1776 had "brought forth on this continent a new nation, conceived in liberty, and dedicated to the proposition that all men are created equal." And in dedicating the battlefield at Gettysburg, Lincoln reminded his hearers: "Now we are engaged in a great civil war testing whether that nation or any nation so conceived and so dedicated can long endure." Two hundred years after the revolution we are now engaged in a reassessment of our history; from the vantage point of two centuries' distance, we can deal more objectively with aspects of the revolutionary war that our ancestors overlooked in their fervent patriotism glorifying the victorious achievements of white participants in that war.

Historians in recent years have given far more attention to the role of black Americans and Indian Americans in the revolution. We know now, as Indians have always known, that Indians fought, bled, and died to make the white man free. We know also that other Indians fought, suffered, and eventually lost their homes and their lands as loyal allies of King George III. And, we know that, tragically, Indian nations were frequently divided among themselves during that war — brother against brother.

Indians were then "engaged in a great civil war" that had powerful repercussions in their society, testing whether their nations could long endure. Worthy of particular consideration is the role of the Six Nations, or Iroquois Confederacy, in the conflict.

The American Revolution sundered the British Empire; it also sundered the Six Nations Confederacy. At the same time that it brought forth "a new birth of freedom" for the people of the thirteen colonies, it led eventually to the decline of freedom for the Iroquois people. For these reasons, the American Revolution is one of the most profound events in both American and Iroquois history.

Why did the Iroquois become involved in the war? A careful examination of the documentary sources indicates that most of them actually wanted to remain neutral. In fact, the Americans had concluded a neutrality treaty with the Six Nations in 1775. Furthermore, General George Washington was not eager to have Indians in the war on the side of the Americans because the expense of maintaining an Indian department would be enormous, and both supplies and money were scarce. The British were more eager for Indian support in the early stages of the war and they placed much pressure on the Indians of Canada to declare themselves for the British and to provide warriors to repulse the American invasion of Canada.[1] By and large, however, the British could not nudge most of the Six Nations Indians into the hostility in the early stages of the war. Some few among them, though, took sides immediately. Mary Brant, Mohawk widow of Sir William Johnson, was active as a conveyor of intelligence to the British. She also sheltered and fed British Loyalists.[2] Her younger brother, Joseph Brant, did his utmost to persuade the Six Nations to break their treaty of neutrality with the Americans. Various Oneidas also carried intelligence to Americans during the early stages of the conflict. In the end, it was a combination of several factors which determined Indian allegiances in the revolution. These included long-standing connections and friendships of the various Iroquois nations with their white neighbours, religious preferences of the Indians and influence of missionaries, military needs of the British and of the Americans, and the availability of trade goods and other services from whites.

The strong Iroquois warrior tradition also played a significant part in drawing respective nations into the war. Being a warrior was a large part of being a man in Iroquois society. Hunting, fishing, waging war, diplomacy, and oratory were prized male virtues. Iroquois warriors actually had been involved in all intercolonial wars between the English and French fought on the American continent. Once before the Iroquois Confederacy had been partially split when, in the French and Indian War, some Senecas supported the French and the Mohawks supported the British.

Their success on the warpath had made the Iroquois fearsome to white and Indian alike, and it established their confederacy as a power to be reckoned with. But constant warfare had also reduced drastically their numbers. The Mohawks, who had been most active for the British in wars against the French, suffered a population decline as a result of continuing casualties among their warriors. The Senecas, however, seemed to have gained population as a result of warfare, for their losses were replenished by large-scale adoption of neighbouring tribes whom they had defeated.

Although individual Iroquois were fighting in Canada for the British or actively spying for one side or another, the actual break in their neutrality did not come until 1777 with Burgoyne's invasion of New York. A number of Oneida and Tuscarora warriors, under the leadership of the Caughnawaga, Louis Atayataghronghta, offered their services to the Americans and assisted General Horatio Gates at the Battle of Saratoga.[3] In the western part of the confederacy, Colonel John Butler, with the assistance of a number of militant Indian leaders, persuaded the Iroquois, particularly the Senecas and Cayugas, to break their treaty of neutrality with the Americans. He accomplished this feat by means of persuasive oratory, the display of an old covenant belt linking the Iroquois and British in an alliance of perpetual friendship, and a large bribe of rum and trade goods.[4] This successful manipulation of the Iroquois netted the British a large number of Indian allies for St. Leger's campaign against Fort Stanwix and for the Battle of Oriskany. The presence of Oneida warriors on the side of Americans at Oriskany assured a continuing enmity throughout the war between pro-American and pro-British factions among the Iroquois.

Confederacies are structurally the weakest form of government. A large measure of autonomy is retained locally and the central government frequently has difficulty enforcing its authority. In the Iroquois Confederacy, decisions affecting the entire organization had to be unanimous. When unanimity broke down, the confederate form of government broke down and the league separated into its various national, and even village, components. For instance, Big Tree, a Seneca chief, supposedly maintained a friendly neutrality towards the Americans, even though other Seneca villages ultimately enlisted in the British cause. The invading army of Generals Sullivan and Clinton, however, evidently did not put much stock in Big Tree's alleged neutrality, for the American soldiers destroyed his village, along with the others, in 1779. Also, early in the war, the Onondagas had split into pro-American, pro-British, and neutral factions. The Van Schaick expedition of 1779 destroyed the neutral Onondaga village and thus thrust all Onondagas into the British column.

Oneidas and Tuscaroras favoured the Americans largely because of the availability of American trade goods and the long-standing influence of their missionary, Samuel Kirkland; and of James Dean, who had been raised among the Oneidas and spoke their language perfectly. Both men were American patriots. Support for the Oneida mission had come also from the New England churches and the missionary society at Boston. The Oneidas and Tuscaroras throughout most of the war maintained a loyal support for those who had shown them this friendship. A serious break in their loyalty did not come until 1780.

Mohawks were influenced not only by the Brants and Guy Johnson and Sir John Johnson, successors to Sir William Johnson, but also by the Loyalist Anglican missionary John Stuart. These personal and family ties and religious preference were decisive in drawing their allegiance to the British government. Even so, a handful of Mohawks at Fort Hunter refused to follow their pro-British brethren to Canada but instead remained behind in a friendly neutrality to the Americans.

Families also were divided at times. An Oneida named Hanyost Thaosagwat received a lieutenant's commission in the Continental army and accompanied the Sullivan-Clinton expedition as one of several Indian guides and scouts. He was captured in Seneca territory by Indian allies of the British, along with Lieutenant Thomas Boyd's advance scouting party. His brother, enlisted with the British, confronted and upbraided him for making war against the Six Nations, telling him he deserved death but that, as a brother, he could not perform the deed. The Seneca Little Beard thereupon dispatched Lieutenant Thaosagwat. The Americans subsequently found his body hacked to pieces and gave him and his luckless companions a burial with full military honours.[5]

As allies, the Iroquois were of inestimable value to both the Americans and the British. General Horatio Gates praised his 150 Oneida, Tuscarora, and Caughnawaga warriors at the Battle of Saratoga. He reported after the battle: "The Six Nations Indians having taken up the hatchet in our favour has been of great service and I hope the Enemy will not be able to retreat from them." A New Yorker who knew many of these Indians and who fought beside them at that battle said that they were all "brave men and fought Like Bull dogs" until Burgoyne surrendered.[6] In 1780, sixty Oneida warriors, under the command of Colonel Louis Atayataghronghta, joined Colonel Marinus Willett and the militia in pursuit of the invading force of Major John Ross, Captain Walter Butler, and their Indian allies; it was an Indian who subsequently shot and killed Butler. Willett considered Indians to be "the best cavalry for the wilderness."[7]

About five hundred Indians served with St. Leger in his 1777 campaign against Fort Stanwix. According to the adopted Mohawk, John Norton, "there was not provided a sufficient Quantity of Arms for these Warriors, so that nearly one half of them fought with no other arms than a Short Spear or Tomohawk." When word came of the advance of General Herkimer with eight to nine hundred Tryon County militia to relieve Fort Stanwix, four hundred Indians, John Butler and twenty Rangers, and John Johnson and fifty Royal Yorkers detached themselves to ambush the Americans. The force was about half the size of the American militia contingent. Because of the shortage of firearms, the Indians would have to fight the Americans in close combat. During the engagement, the vastly outnumbered Indians and Tories inflicted a devastating slaughter upon the Americans and thwarted their plan to relieve the fort. John Norton, evidently repeating what he had heard from his friend Joseph Brant or one of the other participants, said "that in the commencement, the Warriors of the Five Nations immediately advancing in the front, were much annoyed by the Loyalists in the rear keeping up an inconsiderate Fire, — which they were mixed in combat with the Enemy, did equal injury to both: A celebrated War Chief of the Ondowaga [Seneca], (of the Ottigaumi race,) appeared to have fallen by their Fire — as he was found after the Battle shot through the Back, with his face towards the Enemy."[8]

In all seasons of the year, pro-British Iroquois warriors continued to carry on a deadly guerrilla warfare against American frontier settlements and American forces in New York, Pennsylvania, Virginia, and Ohio. Their effectiveness can be gauged from a report by Governor George Clinton to Congress concerning New York's tribulations since the beginning of the war. Speaking of the year 1778, he said: "In the course of the Campaign the native Barbarians conflagrated the antient and valuable Settlements of Burnetsfield, German Flatts, and German Town, and reduced a People who had lived in Comfort and Ease, in a Country on which nature had bestowed inexhaustible Fertility, to Indigence and Want. This Disaster was followed by the entire Destruction of Kobell's Kill, the thriving district of Cherry Valley, Anderson's Town and Wagoners Town, and reduced almost the whole of Tryon County on the South Side of the Mohawk to the Settlements on the Banks of that River."[9]

The year 1779 saw some respite because of the invasion of Indian country by the Continental army, but the Indians still managed to destroy settlements in Ulster and Orange Counties and areas "Westward and Northward of Albany." In 1780, the year after the Sullivan-Clinton expedition that was supposed to have smashed the power of the confederacy, the Indians again devastated much of Tryon County. The districts of Caughnawaga and Canajoharie in Tryon County were destroyed in that year, as was the settlement of Schoharie. The enemy then, continued Clinton's report, "moved to the Mohawk River and laid waste many valuable Habitations on its Banks, and penetrating to Stone Arabia destroyed great Part of that antient Settlement, and would have completed the entire Destruction of Tryon country, had not the Militia and Oneida Indians overtaken and obliged them to retire with precipitation."[10] In summarizing the situation in the year 1781, when he was writing his report, Clinton concluded: "We are now ... deprived of a great Portion of our most valuable and well inhabited Territory, numbers of our Citizens have been barbarously butchered by ruthless Hand of the Savages, many are carried away into Captivity, vast numbers entirely ruined, and these with their Families become a heavy Burthen to the distressed Remainder ... Without help from other states, we shall soon approach the Verge of Ruin."[11]

The war was often brutal on both sides. Indians fought total war and the British were frequently embarrassed by their attacks on women and children. But Indians always complained that Indian captives in American hands could expect no quarter and the Onondaga women captured on the Van Schaick expedition were shamefully treated. White captives, on the other hand, if they could stand the ordeal of the march back to Indian territory, generally were treated humanely, although torture and burning of captives occasionally did happen right after a battle. Forcing captives to run the gauntlet in Indian villages was common also. Although the British had tried to impress upon the Indians that this war was different and that the king's rebellious subjects were not to be adopted but turned in to British authorities for imprisonment, Indians occasionally disobeyed this injunction and adopted white captives. Those fortunate enough to be adopted had a far more pleasant life in the Indian villages than in British prison camps.

As previously mentioned, the Oneidas and Tuscaroras, with few exceptions, remained for several years staunch allies of the Americans. On 13 September 1779, after the American army's devastation of Iroquoia, General Frederick Haldimand wrote to Lord George Germain expressing fears that their Indian allies in the Ohio region — but not the Iroquois — were being disaffected by the rebels: "It is not so with the Six Nations, the Oneidas & a great part of the Tuscaroras excepted, who from the beginning have strongly espousd the Interest of the Rebels, their attachment is as affixed as ever, but the regular advances made by the Rebels into their country in force, & the impossibility of their resisting them unassisted has alarmed their fears, but not shaken their fidelity."[12]

The situation with the Oneidas and Tuscaroras would soon change.

Early in 1780 General Philip Schuyler sent a delegation of two leading men from the Oneidas and two from the Fort Hunter Mohawks to Niagara to persuade the Six Nations in the British cause to make peace with the Americans. The delegates were treated with contempt by the Indians and thrown into prison by the British, where eventually one of them died.

Evidently there was a certain amount of factionalism at Old Oneida, a village several miles distant from the main Oneida settlement of Kanowalohale, for some of the Loyalist Indians had been receiving messages of friendship from some of these Oneidas, promising to join the British. Accordingly, on 24 June 1780, a party under David the Mohawk and John McDonell of the Rangers reached Old Oneida and held council with the chiefs in an attempt to persuade them "to come off and join the rest of the six nations." Instead of the acquiescence expected, the Oneidas expressed resentment at the treatment their chiefs had received at Niagara and asked for their release. The next day, however, the visitors had better luck. Spruce Carrier of the Senecas came in with his party of warriors and held another council with the Oneidas. McDonell reported the favourable outcome to Colonel Mason Bolton at Fort Niagara: "whether the Spruce-Carrier's arguments were more forcible, or that they had deliberated on what had been told them the day before, I cannot pretend to say — They have, however, unanimously agreed to come off. They beg of me to inform you, that they are very sorry for their past Behaviour; but that they will, for the future, behave like dutiful Children — They request that their Chiefs may be allowed to return, as they have vary large families, and no men in them to take care of them, the instant they arrive the Whole of them are to be set off."

Eleven warriors of Old Oneida departed immediately to serve with the British. But the chiefs held captive at Fort Niagara were never released to return home. The three of them who survived were forced instead to join Indian war parties going against the Oneidas and the American settlements.[13]

On 2 July 1780, 294 men, women, and children who had formerly been pro-American joined the pro-British Iroquois who were living in the vicinity of Fort Niagara. This total included 123 Onondagas from Onondaga, sixty-one Onondagas from the mixed Onondaga-Tuscarora settlement of Ganaghsaraga, seventy-eight Tuscarora from the same village, and thirty-two Oneidas from Kanowalohale. Eighty-eight of this group were men, most of whom presumably were capable of bearing arms. On 11 July 1780, a war party of 314 left Niagara under the command of Joseph Brant. In this party were 59 of the formerly pro-American Iroquois who had just come over to the British side.[14]

Except for the Onondagas, who had recently had their villages destroyed by the Americans, the motives of the other Iroquois in joining the British are more difficult to discover. The break may have been a result of sympathy aroused for the neutralist Onondagas who had their village destroyed and the subsequent American treatment of the Onondaga women. It may also have been a result of some long-standing or recent factionalism within the villages coupled with British offers of supplies and protection, which the Americans obviously could not provide.

Brant's main objective on the July 1780 campaign was the destruction of the Oneida and Tuscarora villages, which he and his party accomplished towards the end of the month. About one hundred more Oneidas were persuaded to desert to the British, but 406 Oneidas, Tuscaroras, and Caughnawagas chose continued loyalty to the Americans and fled to the American settlements for protection.

We have said much of Iroquois warriors. It would not be just to neglect the role of Iroquois women in the war. The Oneida Good Peter aptly described the high esteem in which women were held in Iroquois society when he said: "Our Ancestors considered it a great Transgression to reject the Council of their Women, particularly the female Governesses. Our Ancestors considered them Mistresses of the Soil. Our Ancestors said who brings us forth, who cultivate our Lands, who kindles our Fires and boil our Pots, but the Women ... they are the Life of the Nation."[15]

The warrior Silver Heels, in presenting a wampum belt on behalf of the women to Major DePeyster at Detroit during the course of the American Revolution, succinctly summarized the part of the women in the war effort. "This Belt," he said, "is in behalf of the Women who are the Support of us Warriors as they mend their Shoes, plant Corn and without their assistance we would not continue the War."[16]

Women could block the decision of a party to depart on the warpath by refusing to perform these functions. It was therefore entirely necessary for the women to agree to and co-operate in a decision for war. Mary Jemison, the adopted white captive of the Seneca and a resident of Little Beard's village on the Genesee River, has recounted her experience in helping both white and Indian warriors: "During the revolution, my house was the home of Col's Butler and Brandt, whenever they chanced to come into our neighborhood as they passed to and from Fort Niagara, which was the seat of their military operations. Many and many a night I have pounded samp for them from sun-set till sun-rise, and furnished them with necessary provision and clean clothing for their journey."[17]

In the matrilineal Iroquois society, it was the elder of the mothers who became the female governesses to whom Good Peter referred. These women were empowered to choose the sachems, or peace chiefs, for their respective clans. It was the clan mother also who could dehorn, or remove from office, a sachem who misbehaved. The women could not only veto a declaration of war, but also free or adopt captives and give their advice on matters of diplomacy. Thus Iroquois women in their own society enjoyed more power and higher status than did white women of the day in their society.

The Iroquois woman who performed the most outstanding service and who wielded the greatest influence during the war was Mary Brant, a

Mohawk who was head of a society of Six Nations matrons. This society, and Mary Brant as its head, had much influence with the warriors.[18]

Although she and Sir William Johnson were undoubtedly married according to Indian rites, Johnson never recognized the legality of the marriage, referring to her in his will as his "housekeeper" and to his children by her as his natural children. There was, however, no doubt of their affection for each other and of his high regard for her and his children by her, for whom he provided handsomely in his will. Mary Brant was always highly respected by all who knew her, both before and after Sir William's death.

Mary Brant obviously had dual loyalties — to her people and to her husband's king. Although she came from a prominent Mohawk family, she doubly enhanced her status by the connection with such a powerful British official as Sir William. Both as his widow and as a capable leader in her own right, she enjoyed much prestige in the Six Nations. She did not use this power in an opportunistic way. Her support of the British cause was sincere, for she put her life in jeopardy and lost her home, her lands, and her possessions as a result of her decision.

After the battles of Fort Stanwix and Oriskany, when the Iroquois began counting the cost of their service to the British and began wondering aloud if peace would not be the better policy, Mary Brant held them steady to the king's service. She publicly rebuked the noted Seneca war chief Sayenqueraghta in council for wavering in his loyalty to the king and Sir William, and gave an impassioned oration that carried the day. That a woman spoke in council at all was remarkable; usually a warrior was appointed spokesman for the women. But Mary Brant was no ordinary woman, either in status or in ability. Throughout the war, she continued to use her influence to steady the warriors, encourage them after setbacks, and bolster their morale and strengthen their loyalty to the king's interest, which she felt to be the Indians' best interest.[19]

Even an elder white woman who had the respect of the Indians could upon occasion take the initiative in matters of diplomacy. Such an incident happened at Cayuga after the campaign of 1777. General Philip Schuyler had sent a wampum belt westward to the tribes telling of the American victory at Saratoga. A Tory woman named Sarah Magines,[20] widow of Tedy Magines, had fled to St. Leger's lines and, after the battle, was settled by the British among the Cayugas where, because of her loyalty and her knowledge of the Indian language, she was expected to render what service she could in keeping the Indians firmly attached to the British. When Schuyler's belt bearing the news of the American victory reached Cayuga, Mrs. Magines, availing herself of the prerogative of an Iroquois clan mother, seized the belt and cancelled it and had the Indians send on a message more favourable to the British cause.

Upon occasion, Iroquois women accompanied their men on their campaigns, and even, when necessity demanded, fought beside them. There were some women with the pro-British Indians at Fort Stanwix in 1777, and undoubtedly their tasks were to perform the usual camp chores. The Cherry Valley campaign of 1778 entailed a particularly arduous march in inclement weather; we know that there were women along on that fatiguing journey. Cherry Valley was a sorry affair, which shocked and embarrassed the British greatly, for their Indian allies — except for those under Captain Joseph Brant, who acted humanely — did not confine their attacks to men in arms but spread through the settlement, massacring helpless settlers indiscriminately, making no distinction between Loyalist friends and Whig foes. In the memoirs of Governor Blacksnake, the Seneca chief, there is an interesting but all too brief mention of the Indian women, who, he wrote, had armed themselves with tomahawks for protection and waited in the rear lines until it was safe for them to loot the settlement.[21]

During the battle of Oriskany, approximately sixty Oneida warriors fought on the side of the Americans. In the course of the conflict, the Oneida commander, Thawengarakwen (Honyery Doxtater), was wounded in the right wrist. His wife, who had accompanied the army, came to his rescue, loading his gun for him, and also using her own gun against the enemy, fighting as bravely as any warrior in this furious engagement.[22]

Thus the Iroquois women also shared with their men the rigours, the dangers, and the horrors of war.

Finally, we should not let ourselves be led astray by the contemporary British and American description of Indians as savages. The word *savage* actually did not have all of the unfavourable connotations in the seventeenth and eighteenth centuries that it does today. It meant a person who lived in the woods, or who lived in a state of nature. But by the middle of the eighteenth century there was very little difference between the material way of life of the Indians and the white frontier families. Sometimes the homes and farms of the Indians were even superior to those of the whites.

A tremendous amount of important ethnological information on Iroquois material culture can be gained from the diaries kept by soldiers on the Sullivan-Clinton expedition and from the very accurate sketch maps made by army surveyors.[23]

Traditional Indian bark houses were still in use, but there were also, throughout Iroquoia, many log houses and even some built of hewn planks. The various house styles indicated a gradual adoption of the building techniques of whites, whenever these suited Indian preferences.[24] The soldiers also remarked favourably upon the very fine and extensive fields of corn, beans, squash, pumpkins, melons, cucumbers, potatoes, and other vegetables that they found everywhere surrounding the Indian villages.[25] At a number of places they also discovered apple and peach orchards, some of them quite old, indicating a long-standing Iroquois development of fruit culture.[26] There is abundant evidence also that the Iroquois were raising not only horses, but cattle and pigs. At least in one village, a large amount of hay had been cut and stacked, indicating adoption of European methods of feeding cattle.[27]

Colonel Peter Gansevoort was ordered by Sullivan to destroy the Mohawk village of Fort Hunter, despite the fact that the few remaining families were friendly to the Americans. Gansevoort arrested the remaining Mohawks but refrained from destruction of the settlement because the whites who had lost their homes wished to move in. In reporting on his actions, Gansevoort noted that the Mohawk village "is in the Heart of our Settlements, and abounding with every Necessary so that it is remarked that the Indians live much better than most of the Mohawk River farmers their Houses very well furnished with all necessary Household utensils, great plenty of Grain, several Horses, cows and waggons."[28]

It was this way of life that was entirely destroyed during the war. With the coming of peace, the Iroquois painstakingly tried to recapture and rebuild what they had once known. They succeeded only partially, for peace brought also land speculators and white settlers in droves, gobbling up Iroquoia by the millions of acres. The white man's gain was, inevitably, the Indian's loss.

NOTES

1. "Journal of Treaties at German Flats and Albany, 15 August–September, 1775," *MS* 13431, New York State Library; Edmund B. O'Callaghan, ed., *Documents Relative to the Colonial History of the State of New York* (Albany: Weed, Parsons & Co, 1857), 7: 605–31; John C. Fitzpatrick, ed., *The Writings of George Washington from the Original Manuscript Sources, 1745–1799* (Washington: U.S. Government Printing Office), 4: 280; Memorial of Guy Johnson to Lord's Commissioners of His Majesty's Treasury, 28 March 1776, no. 147, British Headquarters Papers, New York Public Library (NYPL); Claim of Guy Johnson, American Loyalists, 44: 58–59, NYPL; Claim of Daniel Claus, American Loyalists, 3:4–9, 43:397–38.
2. Claim of Mary Brant's Children, American Loyalists, 44:118, NYPL.
3. Draper MSS 11U264, State Historical Society of Wisconsin (SHSW).
4. Ibid., 4F190, 16F121–34, 4S17–23.
5. James E. Seaver, *Narrative of the Life of Mrs. Mary Jemison* (New York: Corinth Books, 1961), 79–81; "Journal of Lieut. Erkuries Beatty," in Frederick Cook, ed., *Journals of the Military Expedition of Major General John Sullivan against the Six Nations* (Auburn, N.Y.: Knapp, Pack and Thomson, 1887), 32.
6. Draper MSS IIU264, SHSW (see note 3); Gates to Hancock, Oct. 12, 1777, Emmet, no. 4347, NYPL.
7. William M. Willett, *A Narrative of the Military Actions of Colonel Marinus Willett, Taken Chiefly from His Own Manuscript* (New York: G. & C. Carvill, 1831), 85–7; Jeptha R. Simms, *History of Schoharie County and the Border Wars of New York* (Albany: Munsell & Tanner, 1845), 479; Jeptha R. Simms, *The Frontiersmen of New York* (Albany: Geo. C. Riggs, 1882, 1883), 2:259.
8. Carl F. Klinck and James J. Talman, eds., *The Journal of Major Norton 1816* (Toronto: Champlain Society, 1970), 272–3.
9. George Clinton to President of Congress, 5 February 1781, Papers of the Continental Congress (microfilm Columbia University), item 67, 346.
10. Ibid., 347, 349–50.
11. Ibid., 351.
12. Haldimand to Germain, 13 September 1779, Haldimand Transcripts, B 54, 144, National Archives of Canada (NA).

13. McDonell to Bolton, 1 July 1780, B 100, 418–19, NA; Draper MSS 11U204–9, 237–44, SHSW (see note 3).
14. Return of Indians, 2 July 1780, B 100, 422, NA; Return of a Party of Indians who are gone to War, under the command of Capt. Joseph Brant, 11 July 1780, B 100, 438.
15. Franklin B. Hough, *Proceedings of the Commissioners of Indian Affairs Appointed by Law for the Extinguishment of Indian Titles in the State of New York* (Albany: Munsell, 1861), 279–80.
16. Council at Detroit, 1 May 1782, Indian Records, RG 10, series 2, vol. 12, 103, NA.
17. Seaver, *Mary Jemison* (see note 5), 77.
18. Claus Papers, 6 September 1779, vol. 25, 119, NA; Haldimand to Germain, 13 September 1779, B 54, 155–6, NA (see note 12).
19. Claus to Haldimand, 30 August 1779, Claus Papers, vol. 2, 131–3, NA; Anecdotes of Brant, ibid., 51.
20. Her name is variously spelled. In 1760, when she bound herself out to Harme Gansevoort in Albany, she signed her name "Sarah Magines." In the American Loyalist Transcripts it is "McGinn." Daniel Claus spelled it "McGinnis" and "Maginnes." Harme Gansevoort, Letters and Documents, vol. 1, 17 November 1760, Gansevoort-Lansing Collection, NYPL; Claus to Haldimand, 30 September 1779, B 114, 76–7, NA.
21. Blacksnake Conversations, Draper MSS 4S28–31, SWSH (see note 3).
21. Draper MSS 11U196–7, 200, 215–17, SHSW (see note 3).
23. Cook, ed., *Journals*. Some of these maps have been published as endpapers in ibid. Others are in the Erskine-Dewitt Collection, New York Historical Society.
24. John W. Jordan, "Adam Hubley, Jr., Lt. Colo. Commandant 11th Penna. Regt., His Journal, Commencing at Wyoming, July 30th, 1779," *Pennsylvania Magazine of History and Biography* 33 (1909): 298–99.
25. The observation is made in numerous journals in Cook, ed., *Journals* (see note 5).
26. "Journal of Major James Norris," ibid., 233–4; Jordan, ed., "Adam Hubley," 294–7 (see note 24).
27. "Journal of Sgt. Moses Fellows," in Cook, ed., *Journals* (see note 5), 90; "Journal of Major James Norris," ibid., 234.
28. Gansevoort to Sullivan, 8 October 1779, Gansevoort Military Papers, vol. 5, NYPL.

Chapter Ten
Political Dialogue and the Spring of Abigail's Discontent

Elaine Forman Crane

One of the ironies of American history is that the Revolutionary movement produced no female Revolutionaries ready to initiate a public dialogue about male tyranny. English women had already associated their cause with civil unrest more than a century earlier, and French women would demand liberté and égalité for themselves a dozen years in the future, but American women of the 1770s resisted discussing openly the parallels between British oppression and male domination. Notwithstanding their inhibitions, however, American women were acutely aware of the inequities imposed by one sex upon the other, and literate women steeped in popular literature and the classics surely realized that the implications of Revolutionary rhetoric were as applicable to men and women as they were to Great Britain and her colonies.

Abigail Adams made that association. Yet, even though she recognized the correlation between contemporary politics and gender, her willingness to engage in theoretical debate was tempered by the radical nature of the subject and the boundaries of permissible female behavior. John Adams, no less than Abigail, had internalized the codes governing female conduct, making outright advocacy of women's rights all but impossible — unless Abigail was willing to alienate John or humiliate herself. Abigail compromised by negotiating with John privately, but, when John responded to her opening salvo with a patronizing retort, Abigail retreated into a literary playground replete with hidden meanings, text out of context, and allusions to the more progressive writers of her time. As a rereading of the three letters discussed below reveals, Abigail expropriated republican ideology and gave it a gendered twist that was both subtle and nuanced. She connected political philosophy to women's rights, but she did so deviously — and in the grand tradition of eighteenth-century European literature.

That she was able to do so with such competence resulted from the intellectual sponsorship of her father, husband, and other assorted kin. The Reverend William Smith was a permissive parent with an extensive library, a combination that allowed his daughter Abigail to cut her wisdom teeth on William Shakespeare, Joseph Addison, John Dryden, Alexander Pope, and John Milton. Her cousin Isaac, five years Abigail's junior, also shared books and ideas with her as he prepared for Harvard. Richard Cranch, suitor and then husband of Abigail's sister Mary, obliged his prospective sister-in-law by tutoring her in French and challenging her mind with the fine points of English literature. In 1764, when she was twenty, Abigail married the up-and-coming lawyer John Adams, a man nine years her senior. She married into his library as well. Thus, by the time Abigail Smith Adams entered her thirties, her intellectual social climbing had placed her in the company of Homer, John Harrington, and George Savile, marquis of Halifax. Plato, John Trenchard and Thomas Gordon, Plutarch, Joseph Priestley, Polybius, the 3rd earl of Shaftesbury, John Shebbeare, Robert Molesworth, Jean-Jacques Rousseau [...]

At least part of Abigail's outlook on women must have been distilled from what she had read over time. Issues of *The Spectator* in her father's library contained articles debating women's status in eighteenth-century England. Her long-standing familiarity with that journal allowed her to quote from it on occasion. The ten-volume edition of Montaigne's essays in John's collection surely included his critique of people who applauded male scholarship and disparaged female learning. A long passage from Montaigne appears in Abigail Adams' letter to Royall Tyler in the summer of 1784. A perusal of John Shebbeare's Letters in the Adams library would have revealed his low regard for female educational standards in England compared to those enjoyed by French women. The impression made by Shebbeare's work is indicated in Abigail's comment to John, "I have entertained a superiour opinion of the accomplishments of the French Ladies, ever since I read the Letters of Dr Sherbeer." Madame de Sévigné's letters to her daughter on the freedom of widowhood, the gendering of politics, and a well-balanced female educational curriculum were also on the shelves at home — all eight volumes. Even John seems to have read them.[1]

Furthermore, Adams' unslaked thirst for learning might have made her conscious of the overwhelmingly male authorship of her reading material and reinforced the idea that publications by women were rarely circulated, much less advanced. Female authors with male sponsors were most likely to achieve recognition — even acclaim — if they embraced political or historical subjects with which a reading public could identify. The Englishwoman Catharine Sawbridge Macaulay was such an author, and both Adamses claimed unbounded admiration for her.[2]

John and Abigail Adams were also admirers of Mercy Otis Warren, whose education had been fostered by her brother, James Otis. Mercy Warren solicited and received John's support for her dramatic works, thereby achieving recognition from a man positioned to satisfy her ambitions as a political writer. Indeed, she was the first American woman to publish political works in her own name. Mercy Warren wrote about women only indirectly in the 1770s. She accepted the *status quo* for women and men, even as she herself challenged prevailing attitudes about female aptitude. Her pre-Revolutionary writing includes few female characters, although she subsequently recognized their importance to the war effort. In theory, Warren linked republicanism to domestic virtue; in fact, she saw women as the victims of war.[3] She, like many other spokespeople on both sides of the Atlantic, advocated greater educational opportunities for women, but Warren never called for an expansion of women's political or legal rights. Nor did any other American woman in the prewar years.[4]

English women, on the other hand, were heirs to a reform tradition that erupted from time to time and of which Abigail Adams could hardly have been totally unaware. It is impossible to say whether Adams ever read Mary Astell, whose turn-of-the-century protofeminism stirred such great controversy, and it is doubtful that she came into contact with "Sophia" or the petition about "The Hardships of the English Laws in Relation to Wives" in the mid-eighteenth century.[5] What is not doubtful is that Abigail Adams was familiar with the grievances and arguments articulated by these English critics who spoke openly of male tyranny and female slavery.

Beyond her own reading, it is difficult to know how Abigail Adams became tainted with such radicalism. Early British women's rights advocates were relegated to the background by the generation of British women writers known as the Bluestockings, a group that was most prolific in the period 1756–1776, when Adams was voraciously devouring literature of all kinds.[6] This circle of writers (which included Elizabeth Carter, Elizabeth Montagu, and Catherine Talbot) published poetry and translations of classical authors but did not advance egalitarian ideas about women, at least not for publication. In private correspondence, they discussed women's issues raised by *The Spectator, Tattler,* and *Gentleman's Magazine* and ruminated about male tyranny or marriage as imprisonment, but Abigail Adams would not have been privy to such letters. Nor does it appear that letters containing similar sentiments circulated among colonial women to the extent that they did in England.[7]

At midcentury, two American women, Esther Edwards Burr and Sarah Prince, exchanged letters in the form of journals, and Burr even referred to a group of Boston women as "the Sisterhood," but their common experiences were rooted in religion rather than rights. Yet their correspondence reveals that both women were conscious of their female identity and the inescapable demands imposed upon them because of it. And, although Burr and Prince were reluctant to protest prevailing attitudes toward women in a public forum, their frustrations occasionally surfaced through irony and satire in their private letters. They never called for the social changes that would have improved their status, but they surely would have welcomed such innovations.[8]

American women wrote poetry and essays as well as letters, and some even circulated their manuscripts, but a salon culture only slowly took hold on this side of the Atlantic. Evidence of an exchange of manuscripts in the pre-Revolutionary period seems concentrated in the Philadelphia region among Quakers, an unsurprising pattern given the prominent role of women in Quaker tradition. At the same time, the extent to which manuscripts passed from family to friends to associates is unclear, and allusions to women's rights in such writing appears to have been rather limited.[9]

A powerful exception to these general observations (and in the context of Quaker tradition) is a poem by Susanna Wright entitled "To Eliza Norris — at Fairhill," which excoriates marital hierarchy and male domination.[10] In her poem, probably written sometime prior to 1773, Wright explicitly rejects the institution of marriage on the grounds that it is inequitable and hostile to the interests of women. Conversely, by advocating and applauding female celibacy she appears to be resigned to the idea that marriage could not be purged of hierarchy. In short, Wright urged resistance to the *status quo* by repudiating marriage altogether — but she did not call for institutional reform. Wright's position is strikingly different from Abigail Adams' stance, which was predicated on legal change. Moreover, because Wright's poem circulated among Quakers, it was not likely to have raised eyebrows since more conservative writers also warned against relinquishing "the ease and independence of a single life to become the slaves of a fool or a tyrant's caprice."[11] Wright's more egalitarian audience, therefore, would not have seen such ideas as particularly radical. Adams, however, was contesting the basic assumptions of her husband's world when she challenged common-law rules governing married women. [...]

[...] Although American women advocated educational advancement for themselves in the years preceding the Revolution, no one called for an expansion of political or legal rights. American women lacked both the proliferation of journals and the group consciousness that encouraged English debate about women's rights. These disadvantages make Abigail's subsequent excursion into political feminism (albeit disguised and expressed privately) all the more notable.[12] Her pronouncements on tyranny, her recognition of marital oppression, her theoretical and creative merger of the political and domestic, and her attempt (however tentative) to initiate change tempt one to argue that she looks backward to Mary Astell and forward to Mary Wollstonecraft in the context of a radical Anglo-American tradition. Even her husband concluded as much: she was, he charged in 1794, a "Disciple of Wolstoncraft."[13]

Most historians are ambivalent about Adams' literary sorties, however and are unwilling to take her at her word. She was either "half joking" or her language revealed a "polite, if somewhat lighthearted request for limits of the power of husbands." She was coaxing John "playfully but frankly, to accept her ideas." At best, her biographers say "she was not entirely serious"; at worst, they insist she has been miscast as a radical feminist. Endorsing this position, still another historian adds that there was little reason to expect Adams to have propounded feminist principles.[14] True enough.

At the same time (and perhaps somewhat paradoxically), a few historians concede that Abigail expressed, in Edith Gelles' words, "unusual gender awareness for her time." Rosemary Keller and Alfred F. Young agree that she was both unique and innovative in her approach to women's issues, and Phyllis Lee Levin credits Abigail with more serious intentions than other historians are willing to allow. Lynne Withey recognizes the way in which Adams "linked the cause of women to the cause of the Revolution" but stops short of pursuing this line of thought in her biography. Mary Beth Norton also gives Adams' protest serious consideration, even in the absence of a sustained discussion about Adams' intentions and methods. Adams "chose to make a significant observation about women's inferior status by putting a standard argument to new use."[15]

Yet, if at least a few historians acknowledge that Abigail might have been the first American advocate of women's rights, they and others refuse to accept her pleas for constitutional protection of women or legal protection of wives from common-law abuses as part of a feminist canon. Although admitting that Adams was urging a separate legal existence for married women, Charles W. Akers argues simultaneously (and inconsistently) that such a demand was neither "a declaration of the principle of sexual equality" or "a revolution in the roles of men and women."[16] Yet it is difficult to understand how a quest for legal and constitutional protection where none existed, or a call for a separate legal existence for married women where none was contemplated, could be anything less than egalitarian and revolutionary in 1776. If Abigail Adams was an eighteenth-century woman incapable of challenging contemporary *social* codes, she was still an avant-garde thinker who resisted a *political status quo* where the rights of one sex were dependent on the subjugation of the other. In that limited sense she was a feminist.

"Remember the Ladies," wrote Abigail. Remember the ladies. Thus begins the most familiar of Abigail Adams' words and the most oft-quoted entreaty of any eighteenth-century American woman. She penned this earnest enjoinder to her husband on the last day of March 1776, just as spring approached a chastened, yet optimistic Boston.[17] John Adams was in Philadelphia at that time, engaged in a series of intellectual wrestling matches with those who did not see what he saw and who seesawed between reconciliation and secession.

Abigail Adams was as concerned as John about the escalating crisis with Great Britain, and she acted as his eyes and ears in Boston while the town underwent one upheaval after another. Yet, on this particular March day, after discharging her duties as local commentator and reminding John of her desire for Independence, she seized the opportunity to expound on what must have been long-percolating ideas about power and authority. This would not be the first time that Abigail Adams revealed her republican tendencies, however. A decade earlier, she had expressed negative views about the motivating force of self-interest, and by 1775 her words demonstrated just how deeply antiauthoritarian roots had taken hold. "I am more and more convinced that Man is a dangerous creature, and that power whether vested in many or a few is ever grasping, and like the grave cries give, give."[18] It remained only for Abigail to apply abstract republican principles to her concrete female world.

In her letter to John of 31 March 1776, Abigail began her assault with what she considered to be an unassailable premise: common law favored "Husbands" by giving them "unlimited power." Yet her next sentence suggests that it was not just married men who took advantage of unchecked sovereign authority. "Remember," she urged for the second time, "all Men would be tyrants if they could." As a result, the legal code, originally generated by those Abigail disdainfully labeled "your ancestors," exacerbated a latent, even inherent, male propensity to tyrannize others — in this case, women. Yet, although Abigail Adams was writing in the context of a heated debate on empire and tyranny, there was a subtle difference between her gendered assessment of the relationship between law and tyranny and the evolving political discourse couched in the same language. Abigail was arguing that the male-constructed body of law relating to women was intrinsically tyrannical, whereas standard Revolutionary rhetoric held that British oppression sprang from a deliberate and calculated *departure* from a just and enlightened legal/constitutional framework.

Such ideas weighed heavily on Adams' mind because she had already given serious consideration to the legal structure that would materialize once separation from England was assured. "What Code of Laws will be established[?]" she asked John as early as November 1775. And as a political strategist who knew that liberty and power were always poised for conflict, she posed other questions: "How shall we be governd so as to retain our Liberties?" "Who shall frame these Laws?" And, finally, Abigail ruminated, "When I consider ... the prejudices of people in favour of Ancient customs and Regulations, I feel anxious for the fate of our Monarchy or Democracy or what ever is to take place."[19] Thus, the allusion to a "new Code of Laws" in her letter of 31 March 1776 — a code that would supplant the one imposed by their ancestors — was entirely consistent with Abigail's previously expressed ideas.

This time, however, Abigail Adams' pronouncements on tyranny were a way of leading up to related and pressing concerns about women. Could (or would) male legislators devote the "care" and "attention" necessary to rectify the inequities of the past? History and experience offered reason for doubt on this point, permitting Adams to invoke a standard natural rights argument: women would not be "bound" by laws made without their "voice, or Representation." American men had already made this case in the context of parliamentary representation, and Abigail's startling assertion simply extended the logical implications of the same theory. It is a leap, of course, to maintain that Adams was demanding female suffrage, since she threatened "to foment a Rebelion" with a nonexistent band of rebels. Nevertheless, it is puzzling how she would have resolved the hypothetical question of female representation without giving at least some propertied women the right to vote. Furthermore, one is left to wonder whether Abigail Adams' reference to a "Rebelion" was an innocent slip of the quill or a calculated literary wink at a word that was identified with *unjustified* resistance to male authority.

The idea of women's voting must have been intoxicating, even if Adams did not pursue it. Enfranchisement of women would soon become more than theoretical in New Jersey, where vigilant women would seize upon a loophole in the state constitution of 1776 and actually exercise the right to vote in local elections for the next two decades. The sources do not reveal how or when Abigail Adams became aware of the privilege temporarily extended to some New Jersey women, but her reaction to that excursion in political participation was unequivocal. In 1797, as the experiment neared its end, Adams admitted to her sister, Mary Cranch, that, had the Massachusetts Constitution "been equally liberal," she "certainly" would have added her name to the list of voters.[20] In the meantime, it must have been particularly galling for Adams to know that her husband had drafted the Massachusetts Constitution of 1780 that specifically disenfranchised women. In fairness to John, that provision appears to have reflected prevailing sentiment and had not been challenged in the abortive Constitution of 1778. More to the point, however, the Convention emended two exclusionary sections of Adams' 1780 draft by converting his overly restrictive "man" to "subject." This might have been a minor detail, but it was one that commanded the Convention's attention.[21]

As bona fide eighteenth-century Whigs who were well attuned to opposition oratory, both Abigail and John Adams were, no doubt, comfortable with a range of self-evident propositions. Thus, Abigail could advance the next point in her letter of 31 March 1776, without fear of contradiction by insisting, "That your Sex are Naturally Tyrannical is a Truth so thoroughly established as to admit of no dispute." Nevertheless, continued Abigail, not all men took advantage of the "unlimited power" granted to them by law or the tendency bestowed by nature to oppress women. Perhaps as a concession to her relationship with John, perhaps stimulated by eighteenth-century sentimental rhetoric, perhaps as a nod to rational theory, Abigail modified her previous stand: "But such of you as wish to be happy willingly give up the harsh title of Master for the more tender and endearing one of Friend."

Abigail Adams' analysis of the potential despotism of family government rested on two assumptions. First, that men instinctively drifted toward tyranny and, second, that, although existing legal codes were inherently unfavorable to women, reframed laws would act as a buffer between "tyrannical" men and subordinate women. The latter construction paralleled John's insistence that, although uncurbed selfish passions always prevailed over social passions, governmental rule was capable of restraining excessive power. It was also an argument openly propounded by the most assertive eighteenth-century English advocates of women's rights.[22]

Yet, if Abigail truly believed that men who sought happiness would willingly forgo the role of master, she was actually conceding the ability of men to change for the better. In short, she recognized a self-imposed malleability that John would have surely denied. And if, on this point,

"Cato" had convinced John Adams that "almost every tyrant grows worse and worse," Abigail's alternative assessment rejects the idea of irrevocable depravity.[23] In this instance, she may have been persuaded by a writer she professed to admire, James Fordyce, who argued that men had the ability "to choose" happiness by cultivating female good will.[24] Nevertheless, despite the possibility of an affectionate marriage, Abigail was not quite willing to leave such matters to male whims, and, in the last paragraph of her 31 March 1776, letter, she returned to her insistence on the necessity of legal safeguards to restrain male passion — a notion John could hardly refute. [...]

[...] Whatever the ratio of satire to seriousness in Abigail Adams' letter that day, John's response two weeks later suggests his unwillingness to consider his wife's petition with anything but humor. He "cannot but laugh," he tells her, admitting at the same time that "we [delegates? husbands? men?] know better than to repeal our Masculine systems." John acknowledges male power but dismisses Abigail's objections by insisting that in reality men are "subjects" who "have only the Name of Masters."[25]

John might have shrugged off Abigail's appeal, but he did so knowing that eventually her arguments would have to be addressed. And, although he refused to engage in a serious dialogue with her on 14 April, six weeks later he responded to James Sullivan's "Investigation" of representative government with a strong statement that clarified his position on female political participation.[26] Sullivan had not broached this proposition in his own analysis, but John's heated reply to a question that had not been raised hints that his wife had been more than a little successful in her role as gadfly. It was almost as if Adams was responding to her through his letter to Sullivan.

John approached the issue by probing the basis of representation. "Whence arises the Right of the Men to govern Women, without their Consent?" What might have been a dilemma for someone seeking consistency in his Lockean interpretation was easily put to rest by John Adams. He resolved the problem by comparing all women to propertyless men whose lack of worldliness rendered them politically incompetent and whose dependence precluded "a Will of their own." That the husband of Abigail Adams could have reached a conclusion at odds with his own experience says much about the blind spots of republican thinking. And, even if his point of reference was *economic* dependence, his statement merely confirmed (albeit unwittingly) the oppressive effects of these very man-made laws against which his wife protested. Convinced of the propriety of his position and oblivious to the potential for rebuttal, Adams rendered a final judgment: because civil society would not be served by the inclusion of such persons in the political process, he could not advise "any alteration in the Laws, at present, respecting the Qualifications of Voters." Such a move would not only stimulate "Controversy and Altercation," but there would be "no End of it." Young and propertyless men would be among the new claimants. "Women will demand a Vote." This result was "dangerous" because such an electorate would "destroy all Distinctions, and prostrate all Ranks, to one common Levell." Thus, despite the witticisms with which John responded to Abigail's overture, he did, in fact, have serious misgivings about extending the political base to women.[27] It was far easier to explain all this to James Sullivan than to his wife.

It took from two to three weeks for letters to travel between Philadelphia and Braintree, so Abigail could have been in possession of John's reply of 14 April only a short time when she complained to her friend Mercy Otis Warren on 27 April that her husband's rejoinder to her "List of Female Grievances" had been very "sausy" — a word that John and Abigail used from time to time to describe spirited (and sometimes unwelcome) behavior.[28] The tone of Abigail's letter to Warren suggests that she was wounded by her husband's cavalier attitude — as if he betrayed her expectations of a more positive reaction to her political foray. But why she should think he would be sympathetic is a mystery. Abigail Adams had not written a stirring patriotic treatise with which her husband could identify; she had advanced ideas that shook his comfortably patriarchal world. She had strayed from those topics that were acceptable to this particular husband/wife, male/female dialogue.

Given the blossoming friendship between Abigail Adams and Mercy Otis Warren, that Abigail shared her ideas with Mercy only after receiving John's rebuff is also curious.[29] The sequence (as well as the recipients) of the letters hint that Abigail was unconnected to any female network where ideas — such as those propounded in her 31 March letter — could be circulated. If such a network even existed in the Boston area at this time, it has not been uncovered, and it is plausible that Abigail turned to John first not only because he was in a position to effect change but because she had few other sounding boards for such advanced ideas.

When the frustrated Abigail Adams confided in Mercy Otis Warren at the end of April, she recounted the contents of her 31 March letter to John in some detail, possibly in the hope of enlisting her friend's support. She reached out to Warren, knowing of John's esteem for Mercy's intellect, adding, "I think I will get you to join me in a petition to Congress" in favor of more equitable laws for women. Abigail's light tone might have belied the seriousness of her message. Petitions had long been the means by which American women sought redress in civil actions and English women in search of rights attempted to achieve their goals. Thus, if Abigail had been able to elicit Warren's support, her stature would have lent weight to the cause. As it was, Abigail said, she herself had "help'd the Sex abundantly" — which meant, of course, exactly the opposite. No response from Warren survives, and it is unlikely one ever existed. Had she expressed support for Abigail's aims knowing that John disapproved, Mercy might have jeopardized her own relationship with John. John Adams supported Mercy Otis Warren's public writing in 1776 because it was solidly mainstream and non-threatening. If Mercy had advocated women's rights, no doubt John would have reacted just as negatively as he did to his wife's private missive. Why take the chance? The irony, of course, is that Mercy's brother, James Otis, was among the first Revolutionaries to suggest that female suffrage was integral to the formation of a legitimate compact.[30] [...]

[...] Abigail's affection for John notwithstanding, there is no reason to believe that she was merely bantering with her husband on 31 March 1776, particularly if she had either memorized the lines about marital happiness or had copied them from a source familiar to her. After receiving John's playful response on or about 27 April, she did not write to him again until 7 May because, she admitted, "I have not felt in a humour to entertain you." "If I had taken up my pen perhaps some unbecomeing invective might have fallen from it." But what would have precipitated such invective? Emotions stimulated by the preceding paragraph in the same letter where she unwillingly acquiesces in the "painfull Seperation" from her husband? The succeeding paragraph where she describes Boston's precarious situation? Or was it, perhaps, further on where she finally refers to John's response to her letter of 31 March and charges him with inconsistencies in his political philosophy? "I can not say that I think you very generous to the Ladies, for whilst you are proclaiming peace and good will to Men, Emancipating all Nations, you insist upon retaining an absolute power over Wives."[31]

Abigail Adams' petulant response suggests that such issues were of great concern to her. But why? Her own husband was far from tyrannical, and the "absolute power" with which he was invested touched her only lightly. Yet, as an observant woman, Adams could not help but notice the local conditions that placed other women in disadvantageous — even precarious — situations. Boston's sex ratio was extremely low, its female poverty rate excessively high. Widowhood always hovered in the background, waiting to impoverish middle-class women who had lost their means of support.[32] As a result, much of the male power against which Abigail Adams railed was economic in nature: control of marital assets, control of independent income, control of wages. Abigail might have circumvented the worst aspects of a patriarchal legal code in John's absence, but the inability to obtain credit or enter a valid contract or demand legal recourse in a court of law jeopardized the well-being of female friends, neighbors, and family. Not that Abigail Adams sought the same independent status enjoyed by men. Indeed, in any redistribution of power, she appears quite willing to renounce an equal share as long as men took it upon themselves to abdicate their "absolute power over Wives." Unfortunately, John Adams' resistance to change confirmed that renunciation of male power in any brave new American world was wishful thinking. [...]

NOTES

The author wishes to thank Pauline Maier, Mary Beth Norton, and Sheila Skemp for their insightful reading and suggestions for refining the argument. She is grateful as well to Karen Kupperman and the members of the Columbia University Seminar in Early American History, who also proposed points for revision.

1. Abigail Adams to John Adams, June 30, [1778], to John Thaxter, Apr. 29, July 1, 1783, to Royall Tyler, July 10, 1784, and introduction, in *Adams Family Correspondence*, 6 vols. ed. L.H. Butterfield et al.,

(Cambridge, Mass., 1963–1993), 1:xxxii, 3:52, 5:191, 148, 391; Edith B. Gelles, *Portia: The World of Abigail Adams* (Bloomington, Ind., 1992), 27; Sylvia H. Myers, *The Bluestocking Circle: Women, Friendship, and the Life of the Mind in Eighteenth-Century England* (Oxford, 1990), 123, 183; John Shebbeare, *Letters on the English Nation*, 2 vols. (London, 1755), 1:168, 223, 2:171, 193–94. The copy of de Sévigné's letters to her daughter in John Adams' collection was in French (Marie de Rabutin-Chantal, marquise de Sévigné, *Recueil des lettres de Madame le Marquise de Sévigné, à Madame la Comtesse de Grignan, sa fille* [Paris, 1775]).

2. See Abigail Adams to Catharine Sawbridge Macaulay, [1774], in *Adams Family Correspondence*, ed. Butterfield et al., (see note 1), 1:xiii, 177–79.

3. Jeffrey H. Richards, *Mercy Otis Warren* (New York, 1995), 3, 5; Rosemarie Zagarri, *A Woman's Dilemma: Mercy Otis Warren and the American Revolution* (Wheeling, Ill., 1995), xvi, 75–76, 92; Nina Baym, "Mercy Otis Warren's Gendered Melodrama of Revolution," *South Atlantic Quarterly* 90 (1991), 536, 539.

4. Even during and following the Revolution, the first tentative voices in favor of women's rights called for improved education, rather than for political or legal changes. Although Judith Sargent Murray's proposals in the 1780s were progressive for their time and place, they were not radical compared to what earlier English feminists had urged.

5. Mary Astell, *The First English Feminist: Reflections upon Marriage and Other Writings*, ed. Bridget Hill (New York, 1986). Excerpts from "Sophia's" writings (1739–1740) may be found in Moira Ferguson, ed., *First Feminists: British Women Writers, 1578–1799* (Bloomington, Ind., 1985), 266–83; "The Hardship of the English Laws in Relation to Wives," in *Women in the Eighteenth Century: Constructions of Feminists*, ed. Vivian Jones, (London, 1990), 217–25.

6. Myers, *The Bluestocking Circle* (see note 1), 122, 123, 125, 188–89.

7. Historians have not discovered a running commentary about the confining nature of marriage in letters written by American women until after the Revolution. See Cathy N. Davidson, *Revolution and the Word: The Rise of the Novel in America* (New York, 1986), 119.

8. Carol F. Karlsen and Laurie Crumpacker, eds., *The Journal of Esther Edwards Burr 1754–1757* (New Haven, Conn., 1984), vii, 20, 34, 35, 38, 39.

9. Catherine La Courreye Blecki and Karin A. Wulf, eds., *Milcah Martha Moore's Book: Commonplace Book from Revolutionary America* (University Park, Pa., 1997), 24, 27, 60.
10. For a perceptive analysis of this poem, see Karin A. Wulf, "'My Dear Liberty': Quaker Spinsterhood and Female Autonomy in Eighteenth-Century Pennsylvania," in *Women and Freedom in Early America*, ed. Larry I. Eldridge, (New York, 1997), 87–98.
11. John Gregory, *A Father's Legacy to His Daughters* (1765; reprint, London, 1784), 110.
12. The word "feminism" was not in use in Adams' time. Today there are many different feminists and feminisms and thus several alternative and overlapping definitions of the words. I am applying "feminism" broadly to include any theory that advocates egalitarian rights for women. Such rights may be social, economic, legal, educational, or political — or any combination thereof.
13. John Adams to Abigail Adams, Jan. 22, 1794, in *Letters of John Adams, Addressed to His Wife*, 2 vols., ed. Charles Francis Adams, (Boston, 1841), 2:139.
14. Alfred F. Young, ed., *Beyond the American Revolution: Explorations in the History American Radicalism* (DeKalb, Ill., 1993), 13; Joan Hoff, *Law, Gender, and Injustice: A Legal History of U.S. Women* (New York, 1991), 60, 78; Linda Grant DePauw, "The American Revolution and the Rights of Women: The Feminist Theory of Abigail Adams," in *The Legacy of the American Revolution*, ed. Larry R. Gerlach, (Logan, Utah, 1978), 203; Rosemary Keller, *Patriotism and the Female Sex: Abigail Adams and the American Revolution* (Brooklyn, N.Y., 1994), 97; Gelles, *Portia* (see note 1), 1.
15. Gelles, *Portia* (see note 1), 48; Keller, *Patriotism and the Female Sex* (see note 14), 90; Young, *Beyond the America Revolution* (see note 14), 324; Phyllis Lee Levin, *Abigail Adams: A Biography* (New York, 1987), 81–82; Lynne Withey, *Dearest Friend: A Life of Abigail Adams* (New York, 1981), 81; Mary Beth Norton, *Liberty's Daughters: The Revolutionary Experience of American Women, 1750–1800* (Boston, 1980), 226–27.
16. Keller, *Patriotism and the Female Sex* (see note 14), 90; Young, *Beyond the American Revolution* (see note 14), 324; Hoff, *Law, Gender, and Injustice* (see note 14), 78; Charles W. Akers, *Abigail Adams: An American Woman* (Boston, 1980), 43.

17. Abigail Adams to John Adams, Mar. 31, 1776, in Butterfield et al., eds., *Adams Family Correspondence* (see note 1), 1:369–71. See also Abigail Adams to Mercy Otis Warren, Apr. 27, 1776, ibid., 1:396–98.
18. Abigail Adams to Mary Smith Cranch, Oct. 6, 1766, to John Adams, Nov. 27, 1775, ibid., 1:55–56, 329.
19. Abigail Adams to John Adams, Nov. 27, 1775, ibid., 1:329–30.
20. Abigail Adams to [Mary Cranch, Nov. 15, 1797, in Stewart Mitchill, ed., *New Letters of Abigail Adams, 1788–1801* (Boston, 1947), 112. According to Richard Henry Lee, widowed women with property were not barred from voting in Virginia either. Responding to a complaint from his sister, Hannah Lee Corbin, Lee argued that nothing "forbid widows having property from voting notwithstanding it has never been the practice either here or in England." Concerning voting rights for propertied widows and "never married women who have lands in their own right," Lee declared he "would at any time" give his consent "to establish their right of voting." Richard Henry Lee to Hannah Lee Corbin, Mar. 17, 1778, in James Curtis Ballagh, ed., *The Letters of Richard Henry Lee*, 2 vols. (New York, 1970), 1:392. For a brief synopsis of the events in New Jersey, see Norton, *Liberty's Daughters* (see note 15), 191–93.
21. Adams' draft proposal included the stipulation that "every man has a right to be secure from all unreasonable searches and seizures." Further on in the document, he wrote that "no man ought ... to be declared guilty of treason or felony by any act of the legislature." In both cases, the Convention substituted the word "subject" for "man." See Charles Francis Adams, ed., *The Works of John Adams, Second President of the United States*, 9 vols. (1850–1856; reprint, Freeport, N.Y., 1969), 4:217, 226, 229.
22. John Adams, "An Essay on Man's Lust for Power ...," in *Papers of John Adams*, 10 vols., ed. Robert J. Taylor et al., (Cambridge, Mass., 1977–1996), 1:82; "Hardship of the English Laws," 217–18.
23. [John Trenchard and Thomas Gordon], *Cato's Letters; or, Essays on Liberty, Civil and Religious, and Other Important Subjects*, 4 vols., 3rd ed. (New York, 1969), 3:48–49. This edition is reproduced from a set in the collection of the New York Public Library. I would like to thank Steven Spishak, graduate student in history, Fordham University, for his insights on this point as well as for the amount of research time he spent on this project.

24. See James Fordyce, *Sermans to Young Women*, 2 vols. (London, 1766), 1:208.
25. John Adams to Abigail Adams, Apr. 14, 1776, in Butterfield et al., eds., *Adams Family Correspondence* (see note 1), 1:381–83.
26. John Adams to James Sullivan, May 26, 1776, in Taylor et al., eds., *Papers of John Adams* (see note 22), 4:208–13.
27. Adams would continue to have such reservations. A little more than a decade later, he still found it acceptable to leave "women and children out of the question" when considering the source and nature of political authority. See John Adams, "Defence of the Constitutions" (1787–1788), in Adams, *Works*, ed. Adams (see note 21), 4:301.
28. Abigail Adams to Mercy Otis Warren, Apr. 27, 1776, in Butterfield et al., eds., *Adams Family Correspondence* (see note 1), 1:396–98. Although John, in his use of the word "saucy," might have meant that Abigail was merely impertinent (in a good-humored way), Abigail herself might have been angry enough to have used the word in another sense: rude, insolent, presumptuous — or even scornful. See "saucy" in the *Oxford English Dictionary*.
29. See Edith B. Gelles, *First Thoughts: Life and Letters of Abigail Adams* (New York, 1998), chap. 3, for a discussion of the correspondence between Abigail Adams and Mercy Otis Warren.
30. James Otis, "The Rights of the British Colonies Asserted and Proved" (1764), in *Pamphlets of the American Revolution, 1750–1776*, vol. 1, 1750–1765, ed. Bernard Bailyn and Jane N. Garrett, (Cambridge, Mass., 1965), 420.
31. Abigail Adams to John Adams, May 7, 1776, in Butterfield et al., eds., *Adams Family Correspondence* (see note 1), 1:402.
32. For an extended discussion of these issues, see Elaine Forman Crane, *Ebb Tide in New England: Women, Seaports, and Social Change, 1630–1800* (Boston, 1998).

Chapter Eleven
The Black Population of Canada West on the Eve of the American Civil War: A Reassessment Based on the Manuscript Census of 1861

Michael Wayne

There is a tour you can take through southwestern Ontario that stops at a number of historical sites associated with runaway slaves, including the home of Josiah Henson, once thought to be the model for Harriet Beecher Stowe's Uncle Tom. This tour, known as "The Road to Freedom," provides a good illustration of the extent to which fugitive slaves dominate popular perceptions of the history of blacks in nineteenth-century Ontario. So do the books that schoolchildren read about the exploits of the men and women of the Underground Railroad. So too do the stories that appear in newspapers each year during Black History Month recounting the trials and triumphs of slaves who made their way to Canada.

Scholars have raised doubts about the more extravagant claims made for the Underground Railroad and have brought an appropriately critical eye to the reminiscences of individual runaways.[1] Otherwise, however, they have presented a picture of the past that is largely in accord with the popular view. Indeed, it is the interpretation historians have offered of the demography of the period that provides the principal justification for placing the fugitive slave at the centre of nineteenth-century black history. That interpretation is built on four separate but related arguments: there were approximately 40,000 blacks in Canada West in 1860; an overwhelming majority of these 40,000 were runaway slaves and their children; the black population concentrated itself narrowly in a small number of communities along the western edge of Lake Ontario and in southwestern Ontario; and the great majority of blacks returned to the United States after the Civil War.[2]

It comes as a surprise, then, to discover that this interpretation is apparently wrong in all its particulars. The enumerators' schedules from the 1861 census for Canada West, hardly flawless but substantially more reliable than any other available source, suggest that historians have exaggerated the size of the black population in general, significantly overstated the proportion of that population who were fugitives from slavery, underestimated the degree to which blacks were dispersed throughout the province, and misrepresented the extent of return migration.

We can begin with the question of the number of blacks in the province before the war. The opinion of commentators varied at the time, with estimates ranging between 15,000 and 75,000. The historian who has done the most thorough survey of contemporary views, Robin Winks, argues that the most frequently quoted figure, 40,000, is probably reasonably accurate. As Winks acknowledges, however, it is difficult to know how seriously to take the impressionistic evidence. Most commentators had little upon which to base their estimates beyond personal observation, hearsay, and infrequent reports about blacks in local newspapers.[3] Furthermore, abolitionists, because they were determined to bring the horrors of slavery to the forefront of public consciousness, had reason to exaggerate the number of fugitives; so did the many white Canadians who were opposed to black immigration.

Because the census of 1861 provided for the collection of data on colour, in theory at least historians have always had the means to go beyond the speculation of contemporaries.[4] Until now, however, it has been assumed that the enumeration was so flawed as to make the data collected worthless.[5] The final report published by the Census Department indicated that there were only 11,223 blacks in Canada West.[6] Since that figure was almost 4,000 below even the lowest estimates made at the time, it seemed evident to historians that enumerators had neglected to record a significant proportion of the black population.

Examination of the original manuscript schedules, however, suggests that it was the clerks who transcribed the data who were at fault, not the enumerators. The census rolls include entries on 17,053 blacks, not the 11,000 quoted in the published report. The former figure falls within the low range of estimates made at the time. For example, Samuel Gridley Howe of the American Freedman's Inquiry Commission, described by Winks as "on the whole a careful man," claimed in 1863 that there were 15,000 to 20,000 blacks in the province.[7] There are also other more convincing reasons for accepting the results of the manuscript census. Instructions to enumerators regarding column 13 of the schedules, in which information on colour was to be recorded, stated: "In this column mark a figure (1) after every *Colored* person's name, i.e. Negro or Negress. This was much neglected last Census and the number of colored persons was not ascertained."[8] In other words, enumerators were under express orders to secure an accurate count of blacks. Not that we should assume that they were invariably diligent in carrying out all their assigned duties. The Prescott County representative wrote his superiors asking how much information on blacks they wanted him to gather: "It would be difficult in most cases to ascertain their Names Religion birth Place ages or any thing else ... "[9] Negligence in recording data on religion, age, or even names is not the same as leaving individuals off the rolls entirely, however, and there is little evidence to suggest that enumerators failed to take seriously their responsibility to provide Bureau officials with an accurate count.

The most compelling corroborating evidence is based on statistics. In 1854 the abolitionist Benjamin Drew came to Canada West to interview fugitive slaves. He accepted uncritically the claim by the Anti-Slavery Society that there were almost 30,000 blacks in Canada in 1852.[10] At the same time, in each community he visited he was able to ascertain through conversation with residents what was presumably a reasonably accurate figure on the size of the local black population. The figures he recorded for individual communities can be compared with the figures derived from the 1861 manuscript schedules. As Table 11.1 clearly indicates, the numbers that Drew reported — they total more than 1,000 fewer individuals than enumerators recorded seven years later — are far too low to support the estimate made by the Anti-Slavery Society. On the contrary, taking into account population growth over the last half of the decade through natural increase and especially immigration, they lend substantial support to the argument that the enumeration of 1861 should be regarded as reliable.

Table 11.1
The Black Population of Designated Communities in Canada West as Recorded by Benjamin Drew in 1854 and in the Manuscript Census Schedules of 1861

	Drew	Census
St. Catharines	800	609
Toronto	1,000	987
Hamilton	274	476
Galt	40	31
London	350	370
Chatham	800	1,252
Windsor	250	533
Sandwich	100	95
Amherstburg	400–500	373
Colchester	450	937
Gosfield	78	101
Total	4,642	5,764

Sources: Canada West Manuscript Census Schedules, 1861, for Essex County, Kent County, Lincoln County, Waterloo County, City of Hamilton, City of London, City of Toronto (see note 6); Drew, *A North-Side View of Slavery* (see note 10), 17–18, 94, 118, 136, 147, 234, 321, 341, 348, 367, 378.

Further support comes from statistics collected by Samuel Gridley Howe during his investigation of the black population in 1863. As already indicated, Howe concluded that no more than 15,000 to 20,000 blacks were living in the province at that time, although he was aware that most contemporaries thought the true figure was much higher. In his report he cited presumably reliable estimates for the number of blacks in St. Catharines, Hamilton, Chatham, Toronto (provided by George Barber, Secretary of the Board of School Trustees), and Windsor (provided by Reverend A. R. Green, a black minister from the community). As Table 11.2 demonstrates, his estimates correspond closely to the figures based on the 1861 manuscript census.

> **Table 11.2**
> **The Black Population of Designated Communities in Canada West as Recorded by Samuel Gridley Howe in 1863 and in the Manuscript Census Schedules of 1861**
>
> | | Howe | Census |
> |---------------|-------|--------|
> | St. Catharines | 700 | 609 |
> | Hamilton | 500+ | 476 |
> | Chatham | 1,300 | 1,252 |
> | Toronto | 934 | 987 |
> | Windsor | 500 | 533 |
> | Total | 3,934 | 3,857 |
>
> Sources: Canada West Manuscript Census Schedules, 1861, for Essex County, Kent County, Lincoln County, City of Hamilton, City of Toronto (see note 6); Howe, "The Self-Freedmen of Canada West" (see note 7), 25, 101, 125.

All this does not mean that the number 17,053 should be taken as definitive. Numerous studies have indicated that there were substantial undercounts in the nineteenth-century American censuses — as much as 20 per cent in certain communities.[11] Canadian schedules are unlikely to be more reliable in this regard. Even if we assume that enumerators did miss fully one-fifth of the black population in Canada West, however, that would still leave a total of only about 20,500. Add another 2,000 or so for individuals passing as white — a phenomenon apparently fairly common in Toronto, although less so elsewhere — and we end up with a figure of maybe 22,500 or 23,000.[12] The conclusion seems inescapable: historians have significantly overestimated the black population of Canada West in 1860, probably by 75% or more.

Once the figure for the black population is corrected downward, a second part of the standard interpretation has to be discarded: there was no mass migration of blacks back to the United States at the end of the Civil War. The claim that such a migration took place has always been based less on testimony by contemporaries than on statistical inference. The published census of 1871, considered a far more reliable source than the report produced a decade earlier, indicated that there were approximately 13,500 blacks in Canada West at that time.[13] If the correct figure for 1861 was 40,000, then fully two-thirds of the black population had left the province by the end of the decade, presumably emigrating, or returning, to the United States. Since in reality enumerators found about 17,000 blacks in 1861, it follows that only a minority left Canada West in the aftermath of the Civil War. If we assume that the 1871 census was no more or less likely to suffer from an undercount than the census a decade earlier, and if we conclude that the proportion of individuals passing as white remained roughly constant, then the black population of Canada West decreased by about 20% during the period of 1861 to 1871. While this represents a substantial decline, it hardly amounts to an exodus. Apparently an overwhelming majority of blacks chose to remain in the province after the Civil War.

Although contemporaries differed widely over the size of the black population, there was unanimous agreement on another point: the great majority of blacks were fugitive slaves. The *First Report of the Anti-Slavery Society of Canada* noted in 1852 that "nearly all the adults and many of the children have been fugitive slaves from the United States."[14] In his autobiography, published in 1854, the fugitive Samuel Ringgold Ward observed, "I do not believe that with the exception of the children born in Canada, there are 3,000 free-born coloured persons in the whole colony."[15] When he travelled through Canada West seven years later the American abolitionist William Wells Brown was struck by the size of the fugitive population at each locality he visited. Of St. Catharines, he noted: "Out of the eight hundred in St. Catharines, about seven hundred of them are fugitive slaves." Of Chatham: "The population here is made up entirely from the Slave States, with but a few exceptions." Of Buxton: "There are now nearly 600 persons in this settlement ... Most of these people were slaves in the South." Of Windsor: "a place of 2,500 inhabitants, 600 of whom are colored, and most of the latter class are fugitives from slavery."[16]

Historians have always recognized that such estimates cannot be taken at face value. As already noted, it was in the interests of abolitionists to exaggerate the number of fugitives. As well, the prejudices of the times led most white Canadians to assume that any black person they encountered was a runaway slave.[17] But the main objection to contemporary estimates is simply that they are inconsistent with what we know about the incidence of successful flight by American blacks from slavery. No more than 1,000 or so slaves escaped during any given year, and of these the vast majority settled in the free states.[18] It is no doubt true that, following the passage of the restrictive Fugitive Slave Act of 1850, when life became much less secure for runaways in the North, the numbers continuing to Canada increased,[19] but it is unreasonable to assume that more than a small fraction took up residence outside the United States. Still, well aware of the problems with contemporary estimates, historians have without exception embraced the view that a significant majority of the blacks in Canada West before the Civil War were fugitive slaves and their children. Winks, for example, puts the figure at approximately 75%.[20]

The manuscript census tells a different story. By 1861, of the total enumerated black population of over 17,000, approximately 9,800, or only about 57%, were originally from the United States. Over 6,900, more than 40%, were native-born Canadians (see Table 11.3). While most American blacks listed their birthplace in the schedules as "United States," a sizable number, 744, indicated the particular state in which they had been born. As Table 11.4 shows, the results confirm the popular impression that the great majority of blacks who came from the United States were natives of the slave states — over 70%, in fact. Not all blacks from the South were fugitive slaves, however. Most had been born in either Maryland, Virginia, or Kentucky.[21] Over 150,000 free blacks lived in these three states in 1860. Free blacks represented 49.5% of the black population in Maryland, 10.6% in Virginia, and 4.5% in Kentucky.[22] It was obviously far easier for a free person to get to Canada than it was for a slave, and conditions for free blacks were deteriorating rapidly in the 1850s. By the eve of the Civil War nearly every Southern state was considering legislation to relegate some or all of its free black population to slavery.[23] Even without any other evidence, it would be reasonable to assume that a significant proportion of the Southern blacks who came to Canada were free immigrants, not fugitive slaves.

As it happens, however, additional evidence is available. We can use the data on sex in the census schedules to make credible inferences about the percentage of the black population from the slave states that was free. As the statistics on blacks born in the Northern states make clear, it can be assumed that free men and women were more or less equally likely to relocate to Canada.[24] Historians agree that males made up a

Table 11.3
Distribution of the Black Population of Canada West by Birthplace and Age, 1861

	Age Unknown	Under 20	20 & over	Total	%
Africa	1	1	18	20	0.1
West Indies	-	1	43	44	0.3
British Isles	-	15	50	65	0.4
Maritime Provinces	-	2	8	10	0.0
Canada East	-	30	48	78	0.5
Canada West	21	5,765	1,120	6,906	40.5
United States	28	2,739	7,039	9,806	57.5
Other	-	0	7	7	0.0
Unknown	-	69	48	117	0.7
Total	50	8,622	8,381	17,053	100.0

Source: Canada West Manuscript Census Schedules, 1861 (see note 6).

disproportionate number of the fugitives from slavery.[25] Men were more likely than women to have opportunities to travel beyond the plantation and to learn to read and write. Furthermore, women were less likely to be sold away from their children and as a result arguably had stronger emotional ties to family. The best estimates suggest that somewhere around 75–80% of runaways were men. As Table 11.5 indicates, out of a total of 521 blacks in Canada West who indicated in the census schedules that they had been born in the slave states, 197 (or 38%) were women and 324 (or 62%) were men. If we assume that males would have made up 75% of the fugitives from slavery, then simple algebra establishes that only 49% of blacks from the Southern states were runaway slaves while 51% were free.[26] This means that out of the total of approximately 9,800 blacks born in the United States, only 34% were fugitives. Since American-born blacks represented only 57.5% of all blacks in Canada West, slightly under 20% of all the blacks in the province were fugitives.[27]

Of course, children made up a large proportion of the black population. As Table 3 indicates, a little over half the individuals recorded in the census were under twenty years of age. More to the point, at the time of the enumeration a substantial number of Canadian-born blacks,

Table 11.4
Distribution of the Black Population of American Origin by State of Birth, 1861

Slave states	No.	Free states[a]	No.
D.C.	20	Massachusetts	4
Delaware	17	Vermont	8
Maryland	162	Connecticut	6
Virginia	169	"New England"	1
Kentucky	101	New York	75
Missouri	6	New Jersey	11
North Carolina	8	Pennsylvania	53
Tennessee	4	Ohio	28
South Carolina	7	Michigan	27
Georgia	7	Indiana	1
Alabama	2	Illinois	5
Louisiana	4	Kansas	1
"South States"	14	New Mexico	2
		Wisconsin	1
Total	521	Total	223
Proportion	70.0%	Proportion	30.0%

a) Kansas and New Mexico were territories, not states, at the time of the Canadian census. Under the terms of the doctrine of popular sovereignty applied to Kansas by the Kansas-Nebraska Act of 1854 and to New Mexico by the Compromise of 1850, it was up to the residents of the individual territories to decide for themselves whether they wanted to allow slavery. The issue was still unresolved in both jurisdictions at the outbreak of the Civil War. I have arbitrarily grouped both territories with the free states. The two individuals born in New Mexico and the one in Kansas were children of a tailor named George Washington and his wife, Frances, both of whom listed their birthplace as "United States." The family almost certainly was free.

Source: Canada West Manuscript Census Schedules, 1861 (see note 6).

more than 4,500, were living with at least one parent who had either fled or migrated to the province from the United States.[28] How many of these American parents of Canadian-born children had escaped from slavery is impossible to say, but there can be little reason to accept Robin Winks's claim that fugitives and their sons and daughters represented 75% of the black population. Somewhere between 30 and 40% would seem to be a much more reasonable estimate.

Table 11.5
Distribution of the American-Born Black Population by Sex, According to State of Birth, 1861

	Male	Female	Total
Slave states			
D.C.	9	11	20
Delaware	6	11	17
Maryland	98	64	162
Virginia	116	53	169
Kentucky	61	40	101
Missouri	4	2	6
North Carolina	5	3	8
Tennessee	3	1	4
South Carolina	4	3	7
Georgia	5	2	7
Alabama	1	1	2
Louisiana	3	1	4
"South States"	9	5	14
Total	324	197	521
Percentage	62.2%	37.8%	100.0%
Free states			
Massachusetts	1	3	4
Vermont	5	3	8
Connecticut	2	4	6
"New England"	1	0	1
New York	36	39	75
New Jersey	4	7	11
Pennsylvania	24	29	53
Ohio	16	12	28
Michigan	13	14	27
Indiana	1	0	1
Illinois	5	0	5
Kansas	0	1	1
New Mexico	2	0	2
Wisconsin	1	0	1
Total	111	112	223
Percentage	49.8%	50.2%	100.0%

Source: Canada West Manuscript Census Schedules, 1861 (see note 6).

In the fall of 1861 William Wells Brown came to Canada West to promote the cause of Haitian emigration among blacks. He began his journey in Toronto, stopped for a time at Hamilton and St. Catharines, turned west to London, and finally made his way to Chatham, Dresden, Windsor, Amherstburg, Colchester, and the all-black Elgin settlement at Buxton. His itinerary was much like the one the abolitionist Benjamin Drew had followed in 1854 when he came to the province to interview fugitive slaves. Two years after Brown, Samuel Gridley Howe took a similar route when he travelled through the province gathering information for the Freedmen's Inquiry Commission.[29]

Brown, Drew, and Howe thought that they could take the measure of the black population by going to a limited number of centres where blacks had located in large numbers. Historians have, if anything, carried this reasoning even further by focusing on the handful of all-black communities that were established in the province. Winks reserves almost an entire chapter of his authoritative *The Blacks in Canada* for discussion of such communities. The Elgin settlement alone has been the subject of a book, several articles, and at least one doctoral dissertation.[30] Under the circumstances, it is scarcely surprising that many people appear to be under the impression that the great majority of blacks lived in separate enclaves in and around the Chatham area.

As the 1861 manuscript census reveals, however, the black population of Canada West was much more widely dispersed than anyone has ever imagined. Blacks appear in a total of 312 townships and city wards in the schedules, representing every county and city of the province and the Algoma district (see Appendix C). Of course, they were much more heavily concentrated in some localities than others. By 1861 there were over 1,250 blacks in Chatham and over 1,300 in Raleigh township, where Elgin was located. Many whites in such communities claimed that they were being inundated by fugitive slaves, but it is important to go beyond the perspective of Canadian whites. Imagine, for instance, how things must have looked to an immigrant from Virginia. In his or her native state, 57% of all blacks lived in counties in which blacks were in the majority. By contrast, the heaviest concentration of blacks in Canada West was in Raleigh township, where they represented only about one-third of the total population. In Virginia less than 1% of all blacks lived in counties in which they constituted under 3% of the population. In Canada almost 30% of blacks lived in townships or city wards in which this was the case; over 12% lived in communities where blacks were less than 1% of the population.[31] As well, the concentration of blacks was substantially greater in Deep South states than it was in Virginia. To a fugitive slave who had escaped from Georgia or a free black who had emigrated from South Carolina, the contrast between his or her present and former surroundings must have been all that much more striking.

There are serious objections to treating the all-black settlements as windows into the black experience as a whole. Their fraction of the total black population was never significant. Furthermore, with the exception of Elgin, they were notoriously unsuccessful. No more than 150 to 200 individuals ever resided at Oro on Lake Simcoe or Wilberforce, the two earliest settlements, or at the Refugee Home Society, established in the 1850s outside Windsor. The population of Dawn near Dresden rose as high as 500 for a brief time in the early 1850s, but was never stable.[32] As for Elgin, William Wells Brown found about 600 people there in 1861.[33] That represented less than 3% of the total black population of the province on the eve of the Civil War.

In sum, it appears that historians have overstated the importance of the all-black settlements and given far too little attention to the apparent willingness of blacks to settle in communities where they were outnumbered, often vastly so. A comparison is suggestive. The only immigrant group in the middle of the nineteenth century that was roughly comparable in size to the black population was the Germans.[34] About 35% of German settlers took up residence in a single county, Waterloo. Under 28% of all blacks lived in Kent, the county of heaviest black concentration.[35]

The pattern of settlement and the free origins of the majority of American immigrants suggest new directions for historical research into the black experience in Canada West. Before looking at what those directions may be, however, it would be useful to spend a moment considering some sources of bias in the existing impressionistic evidence. The issue of slavery dominated public debate in the United States during the 1850s, dividing the nation. There was no accompanying difference of opinion over race, however. With few exceptions whites from both sections subscribed to what George Fredrickson has called "*herrenvolk* egalitarianism": a belief that black subservience was a precondition for white equality.[36] Almost all Northern states imposed substantial legal disabilities on blacks, which is why in the famous Dred Scott case Chief Justice Roger Taney felt justified in arguing that blacks had always been treated as if "they had no rights which the white man was bound to respect," and why several thousand blacks from the free states decided to emigrate.[37] This state of affairs — conflict over slavery but consensus over race — clearly influenced what was written at the time about blacks in Canada. There was great interest in runaway slaves — in the conditions they faced under slavery, the means by which they escaped, their adjustment to life in a free land.[38] By contrast, there was comparatively little attention paid to the background or experiences of free blacks. Indeed, as mentioned earlier, many whites seem to have assumed that any black they encountered was a runaway slave. Under the circumstances, it is scarcely surprising that fugitive slaves have come to play a disproportionately large role in both scholarly and popular histories of the period.

A second source of bias is directly related to the pattern of settlement. Where blacks concentrated in large numbers — and especially in areas where racial tensions were high — separate institutions emerged. The records of institutions can be a rich resource for historians. They are much more likely than the private papers of ordinary families to end up in archives and libraries, they frequently are clearly written and organized, and more often than not they contain a wealth of valuable information. There is a danger, however, that a scholar who relies heavily on such records may be inclined to exaggerate the extent to which members of a given institution are representative of other individuals of the same race, class, sex, or ethnicity. Historians of Ontario, like historians of the Northern states, have drawn extensively on documents from black churches, schools, and charitable organizations, along with surviving issues of black newspapers, to gain insight into nineteenth-century black life. Similarly, they have produced interpretations of the black experience that devote considerable attention to the development of separate institutions and take as their central theme the formation of a black "community."[39] But as the historical record makes quite clear, even in localities where blacks were heavily concentrated, many people decided against attending separate churches, objected in principle to separate schools, and chose not to subscribe to black newspapers (as the editors frequently complained). Those men and women who did make the decision to settle in towns such as Bowmanville or Sidney, where the number of black families was small, could hardly have done so in the expectation that they would be part of a separate black community or that their children and grandchildren — or they themselves, if they were single — would find black marriage partners. It is noteworthy that 385 black men listed in the census had white wives, mainly immigrant women from Europe or the British Isles. This represented approximately 1 out of every 7 black married men, or almost 1 in 5 if we exclude those individuals from the United States who we can infer from the census were already married when they arrived in Canada.[40]

It is time, then, that historians gave serious attention to the men and women who chose to settle in localities where the black population was too small to sustain separate institutions or a separate culture. Obviously the lives of such people would have differed dramatically from the lives of blacks in, say, Chatham or St. Catharines. Perhaps so, too, did their assumptions about the meaning and significance of race. In addition, we need to know more about the free blacks who came to Canada West and about the blacks who were born in the province. The literature is not silent on these individuals, but at the moment we only have a slight understanding of how their experiences compared and contrasted to those of runaway slaves. Finally and most importantly, we need to know much more about how the different elements of the black population related to each other. A traveller passing through the townships or city wards where blacks resided in 1861 was liable to come across field hands escaped from cotton or tobacco plantations, artisans and clergymen from the Northern states, native-born farmers, labourers, and professionals, perhaps even one or two free blacks from the South who had themselves owned slaves.[41] At this point we really know very little about how men and women of such divergent backgrounds and, perhaps, material interests viewed each other. The truth is, we cannot even say with certainty that most blacks shared the assumption of both nineteenth-century whites and present-day historians that race mattered more than class, gender, religious affiliation, or nationality in defining who they were or in determining their place in Canadian society.

Whatever the direction of future research, it must take as its starting point an accurate picture of the demography of the period. Perhaps the most unfortunate consequence of the prevailing view is that it tends to perpetuate the nineteenth-century perception of blacks as outsiders. If most blacks were fugitives, if they lived by themselves in a limited number of communities near the border, and if the overwhelming majority returned to the United States after the Civil War, then clearly they were not truly part of the Canadian immigrant experience. Certainly one can find instances of American blacks who held what might be described as an "exile mentality."[42] They spoke with passion of their love for the United States and their dreams of returning home once the blight of slavery had been eliminated. More compelling, however, is the testimony of the many individuals, both slave and free, who saw Canada as a land of new possibilities. Listen to Alexander Hemsley, for example. Born a slave in Maryland, he escaped to Canada when he was in his thirties. After spending a short time in Toronto he moved to the St. Catharines area where, with another man, he acquired five acres of cleared land and started farming:

> We were then making both ends meet. I then made up my mind that salt and potatoes in Canada were better than pound-cake and chickens in a state of suspense and anxiety in the United States. Now I am a regular Britisher. My American blood has been scourged out of me ... [43]

Finally, there is the testimony of the census itself. By 1861 blacks had made their way to all corners of Canada West and had become an integral part of the provincial economy. A great many — more than half — were from the United States. Contrary to popular opinion, however, they were mainly free blacks, not runaway slaves — immigrants not fugitives. In many respects Canada was unkind to both groups of Americans. Although entitled to equality before the law, they experienced persistent discrimination. Whites called them "nigger" to their faces, and worse. Still, when the Civil War ended most chose to remain. Canada was not all they had hoped for, perhaps, but, despite what their white neighbours may have believed, it had become home. For the 40% of the black population who had been born in the province, it had never been anything else.

Notes

The author is indebted to Marnee Gamble, Shannon Lee, and Ken McLeod for assistance in compiling data from the manuscript census; to Harpreet Dhariwal and Yodit Seifu for computer programming; and to Ian Radforth, Franca Iacovetta, Arthur Silver, Allan Greer, Larry Powell, Richard Reid, Kris Inwood, Nancy Anderson, Joey Slinger, and Sandra Tychsen for their helpful comments.

1. See, for example, Larry Gara, *The Liberty Line: The Legend of the Underground Railroad* (Lexington, Ky.: D.C. Heath, 1967); Robin Winks, *The Blacks in Canada: A History* (New Haven: Yale University Press, 1971), 180–195, 240–244.
2. The most influential study is Winks, *The Blacks in Canada* (see note 1) (see especially pp. 233–240, Appendix). Other important works include C. Peter Ripley et al., eds., *The Black Abolitionist Papers: Volume II, Canada 1830–1865* (Chapel Hill: University of North Carolina Press, 1986); William H. Pease and Jane H. Pease, *Black Utopia: Negro Communal Experiments in America* (Madison, Wis.: State Historical Society, 1963); Jason Silverman, *Unwelcome Guests: American Fugitive Slaves in Canada, 1830–60* (Millwood, N.Y.: 1985). Two useful dissertations are Donald George Simpson, "Negroes in Ontario from Early Times to 1870" (Ph.D. dissertation, University of Western Ontario, 1971); and Jonathan William Walton, "Blacks in Buxton and Chatham, Ontario, 1830–1890: Did the 49th Parallel Make a Difference?" (Ph.D. diss., Princeton University, 1979).
3. Winks, *The Blacks in Canada* (see note 1), 233–240.
4. The instructions directed enumerators to "mark a figure (1) after every Colored person's name, i.e. Negro or Negress ... If Mulatto, marked [sic] M after his or her name — thus, (1) M; and if Indian, mark 'Ind.'" For the purposes of this article I have treated both "Negroes" and "Mulattoes" as part of the black population since that is how they were viewed at the time. National Archives of Canada (hereafter NAC), RG31, "Instructions to Enumerators," Census Returns, Algoma District, 1861. For discussion of the problems involved in retrieving data on blacks from the census and in assessing the distinction drawn by enumerators between "Negroes" and "Mulattoes," see Michael Wayne, "Blacks in the Canada West Census of 1861," paper delivered at the Conference on the Use of Census Manuscripts for Historical Research, Guelph, Ontario, 5 March 1993.

5. Winks, *The Blacks in Canada* (see note 1), 492. Even contemporaries raised doubts about the enumeration. See, for example, John Langton, "The Census of 1861," *Transactions of the Literary and Historical Society of Quebec,* New Series, Part 2 (1864), 105–124. Langton suggested that in certain instances the "figures were cooked." His investigation was confined to Lower Canada, however. Recently Bruce Curtis has demonstrated that the enumeration was carried out in a most careless and haphazard manner. Bruce Curtis, "The Local Construction of Statistical Knowledge, or Mistaking the 1861 Census," paper delivered at the Conference on the Use of Census Manuscripts for Historical Research, Guelph, Ontario, 4 March 1993.
6. *Census of the Canadas. 1860–1861. Personal Census. Vol. I* (Québec, 1863), 78–79. Curiously, the census of 1871, which included a recapitulation of previous census findings, reported the number of blacks in 1861 as 13,566. *Censuses of Canada. 1665 to 1871. Statistics of Canada. Vol. IV* (Ottawa, 1876), 266.
7. National Archives (United States), RG94, Letters Received by the Adjutant General's Office, 1861–70, microcopy 619, roll 199, "The Self-Freedmen of Canada West. Supplemental Report (A) of the American Freedmen's Inquiry Commission," 26–27; Winks, *The Blacks in Canada* (see note 1), 489. The Commission was set up by Abraham Lincoln to help him formulate a set of policies for dealing with the emancipated slaves.
8. NAC (see note 4), RG31, "Instructions to Enumerators."
9. NAC (see note 4), RG17, vol. 2419, Charles Waters, Prescott County, 2 February 1861. I am indebted to Bruce Curtis for this reference.
10. Everyone recognized that the vast majority of these 30,000 lived in Canada West. Benjamin Drew, *A North-Side View of Slavery. The Refugee: Or the Narrative of Fugitive Slaves in Canada. Related by Themselves, With an Account of the History and Condition of the Colored Population of Upper Canada* (1856; New York: 1968), p. v. On the anti-slavery movement in Canada West, see Allen P. Stouffer, *The Light of Nature and the Law of God: Antislavery in Ontario 1833–1877* (Montreal and Kingston: McGill-Queen's University Press, 1992).
11. This problem is discussed in Richard Reid, "A Preliminary Report on Black Underenumeration and the 1870 Census," paper delivered at the Conference on the Use of Census Manuscripts for Historical Research, Guelph, Ontario 5 March 1993. See also Richard H. Steckel, "The

Quality of Census Data for Historical Inquiry: A Research Agenda" *Social Science History* 15 (1991): 579–599; John B. Sharples and Ray M. Shortridge, "Biased Underenumeration in Census Manuscripts: Methodological Implications," *Journal of Urban History* 1 (1975): 409–439; Peter R. Knights, "Potholes in the Road of Improvement? Estimating Underenumeration by Longitudinal Tracing: U.S. Censuses, 1850–1880," *Social Science History* 15 (1991): 517–526; Peter R. Knights, *Yankee Destinies: The Lives of Ordinary Bostonians* (Chapel Hill: University of North Carolina Press, 1991), 176–178. On the political implications of the enumeration of slaves and free blacks in the United States, see Margo J. Anderson, *The American Census: A Social History* (New Haven: Yale University Press, 1988), 58–82.

12. William Wells Brown may have come up with the most accurate assessment. He wrote in the fall of 1861: "The colored population of the Canadas have been largely over-rated. There are probably not more than 25,000 in both Provinces, and by far the greater number of these are in Canada West ... " Ripley et al., eds., *Black Abolitionist Papers: Volume II* (see note 2), 461, 463, 466.
13. Winks, *The Blacks in Canada* (see note 1), 233–234; *Censuses of Canada. 1608 to 1876. Statistics of Canada. Vol. V* (Ottawa, 1878), 20.
14. Quoted in Howe, "The Self-Freedmen of Canada West" (see note 7), 26–27.
15. Samuel Ringgold Ward, *Autobiography of a Fugitive Negro: His Anti-Slavery Labours in the United States, Canada, and England* (London, 1855), 154.
16. Ripley et al., eds., *Black Abolitionist Papers: Volume II* (see note 2), 465, 470, 475, 477.
17. Winks, *The Blacks in Canada* (see note 1), 234.
18. Eugene Genovese, *Roll, Jordan, Roll: The World the Slaves Made* (New York: Pantheon Books, 1974), 648; Winks, *The Blacks in Canada* (see note 1), 235.
19. Fred Landon, "The Negro Migration to Canada After the Passing of the Fugitive Slave Act," *Journal of Negro History* 5 (1920): 22–36. On the origins and consequences of the law itself, see Stanley W. Campbell, *The Slave Catchers: Enforcement of the Fugitive Slave Law, 1850–1860* (Chapel Hill: University of North Carolina Press, 1968). Under the act life became much less secure for free blacks as well.
20. Winks, *The Blacks in Canada* (see note 1), 240.

21. This reflects in part the fact that it was easier for slaves in border states to escape than it was for slaves living in more distant regions. Early in the century the centre of the slave population lay much farther north and east than it did at the time of the Civil War, however. An undetermined proportion of the fugitive slaves who made their way to Canada West had been born in Maryland and Virginia but would have been taken or sold to the Deep South and presumably escaped from there. Kenneth Stamp, *The Peculiar Institution: Slavery in the Ante-Bellum South* (New York: Vintage Books, 1956), 118; Genovese, *Roll, Jordan, Roll* (see note 18), 648.
22. Jos. C. G. Kennedy, *Preliminary Report on the Eighth Census. 1860* (Washington, D.C., 1862), 261, 263, 286–289. For insight into the unique situation in Maryland, where slaves and free blacks were about equal in number, see Barbara Jeanne Fields, *Slavery and Freedom on the Middle Ground: Maryland During the Nineteenth Century* (New Haven: Yale University Press, 1985).
23. Ira Berlin, *Slaves Without Masters: The Free Negro in the Antebellum South* (New York: Oxford University Press, 1974), 343–380; Michael Johnson and James Roark, *Black Masters: A Free Family of Color in the Old South* (New York: Norton, 1984), 153–287.
24. The fact that roughly equal numbers of men and women reported being born in the free states suggests that virtually no fugitive slaves saw an advantage in claiming birth in the North. On the life of blacks in the free states before the Civil War, see James Oliver Horton, *Free People of Color: Inside the African American Community* (Washington, D.C.: Smithsonian Institution Press, 1993); Leonard P. Curry, *The Free Black in Urban America, 1800–1850: The Shadow of the Dream* (Chicago: University of Chicago Press, 1981); Leon Litwack, *North of Slavery: The Negro in the Free States, 1790–1860* (Chicago: University of Chicago Press, 1961); Gary B. Nash, *Forging Freedom: The Formation of Philadelphia's Black Community, 1720–1840* (Cambridge, Mass.: Harvard University Press, 1988).
25. Deborah Gray White, *Ar'n't I a Woman? Female Slaves in the Plantation South* (New York: Norton, 1985), 70–74; Genovese, *Roll, Jordan, Roll* (see note 18), 648; Gerald W. Mullin, *Flight and Rebellion: Slave Resistance in Eighteenth-Century Virginia* (New York: Oxford University Press, 1972), 40.

26. Let x equal the number of females from the South who were fugitive slaves and y the number of females who were free. Then $x + y = 197$ (the total number of women indicating they had been born in the slave states). Similarly, $3x + y = 324$ (the total number of males born in the slave states), since it is assumed that males represented three out of every four runaways and that free men and women came to Canada West in more or less equal numbers. Solving for x and y allows us to determine the percentage of all blacks from the slave states who were fugitives.

27. If 80% of the fugitives were men, this figure drops to around 16%. The objection might be raised that perhaps the 744 who indicated their state of birth were not representative. But men made up a slightly lower proportion of those who registered "United States" as their birthplace than of those who indicated a specific state (56% as compared to 58%), suggesting that the estimate of 20% fugitives is, if anything, marginally too high. It is worth noting that likely a small number of elderly blacks from the North had fled to Canada as slaves before emancipation was carried out in their individual states, and no doubt at least a few of the blacks from the West Indies were also fugitives.

28. In fact, the census does not specify family relationships. However, they can be inferred with what appears to be a reasonable degree of accuracy from the data recorded on individuals and households. For a discussion of the methodology involved, see Wayne, "Blacks in the Canada West Census of 1861," The schedules allow us to identify 2,851 children born in Canada living with both mother and father who were American and another 1,652 living with one parent from the United States. However, the need to use the person listed first in each household as the reference point for determining family relationships precludes the possibility of easily identifying sons and daughters of any individual who was not the household head — for example, a widow from Maryland who had moved with her children into the home of a married brother or sister.

29. Ripley et al., eds., *Black Abolitionist Papers: Volume II* (see note 2), 461–498; Drew, *A North-Side View of Slavery* (see note 10); Howe, "The Self-Freedmen of Canada West" (see note 7).

30. Winks, *The Blacks in Canada* (see note 1), 156–162, 178–218; Pease and Pease, *Black Utopia* (see note 2); Victor Ullman, *Look to the North Star: A Life of William King* (Boston: Beacon Press, 1969); Walton,

"Blacks in Buxton and Chatham" (see note 2); Howard Law, "'Self-Reliance is the True Road to Independence': Ideology and the Ex-Slaves in Buxton and Chatham," *Ontario History* 77 (1985): 107–121.

31. A county in Virginia was on average somewhat larger than a township, but considerably smaller than a county, in Canada West.
32. Winks, *The Blacks in Canada* (see note 1), 147, 156, 180, 205.
33. Ripley et al., eds., *Black Abolitionist Papers: Volume II* (see note 2), 475.
34. Keep in mind, though, that approximately 40% of all blacks were native-born.
35. The census reported a total of 22,906 individuals born in "Prussia, German States, and Holland." *Census of the Canadas. 1860–1861. Personal Census. Vol. I,* 78–79. This assumes that the data on birthplace in the published report are more reliable than the data on colour. Such an assumption is not necessarily invalid. Entries on colour were made in a separate column of the schedules with some but not all enumerators including totals at the bottom of the page. It seems that likely one of the reasons clerks understated the number of blacks in particular communities is that they made their tabulations on the basis of the listed totals. Where no total was listed, the clerk may have assumed no blacks had been found. The entries on birthplace, often varying from household to household and sometimes from person to person, allowed for no totals at the bottom of the page, and presumably clerks had no choice but to check individual entries in compiling the data.
36. George M. Fredrickson, *The Black Image in the White Mind: The Debate on Afro-American Character and Destiny, 1817–1914* (New York: Harper Torchbooks, 1971), 58–96. David Roediger has recently made a compelling case for use of the term "*herrenvolk* republicanism" to describe the political ideology of American working men. See David R. Roediger, *The Wages of Whiteness: Race and the Making of the American Working Class* (London: Verso, 1991), 59–60.
37. Quoted in James M. McPherson, *Ordeal by Fire: The Civil War and Reconstruction* (New York: Alfred A. Knopf, 1982), 100.
38. Needless to say, we know next to nothing about the relatively small number of blacks who came from outside North America.
39. James Oliver Horton writes in reference to the United States: "Today almost all scholars accept the historical existence of a highly structured

and dynamic community among antebellum free African Americans." Horton, however, shares a mistaken impression with other scholars that, by the second quarter of the nineteenth century, blacks "clustered in small urban communities in sizable cities." Horton, *Free People of Color* (see note 24), 13, 2. As Kenneth Kusmer has observed, "It is seldom realized that throughout most of the nineteenth century most blacks — like most whites — lived in rural areas or small towns." Kenneth L. Kusmer, *A Ghetto Takes Shape: Black Cleveland, 1870–1930* (Urbana: University of Illinois Press, 1976), 24fn. The same was true of Canadian blacks. For a recent example of a Canadian study that makes community formation central to its analysis, see Patricia J. Yee, "Gender Ideology and Black Women as Community-Builders in Ontario, 1850–70," *Canadian Historical Review* 75 (March 1994), 53–73.

40. I have assumed that a husband and wife were married prior to their arrival in Canada if they were both recorded in the census as having American birthplaces and if their oldest child was also born in the United States. Of course, some of the married couples who came to Canada from the United States did not have children until after they settled in the province — some did not have children at all — while others had American-born children who were not living with them at the time of the enumeration. Hence, the figure "almost 1 in 5" is clearly understated, probably substantially so.

41. Charles J. Johnson, who settled in Toronto, was the son of a prominent free black tailor from Charleston who had owned six slaves. South Carolina's free black elite is discussed in Johnson and Roark, *Black Masters* (see note 23). Correspondence involving the Johnson family can be found in Michael P. Johnson and James L. Roark, eds., *No Chariot Let Down: Charleston's Free People of Color on the Eve of the Civil War* (Chapel Hill: University of North Carolina Press, 1984). Patricia J. Yee has recently drawn attention to distinctions between the experiences of black men and women in "Gender Ideology and Black Women" (see note 39).

42. Ripley et al., eds., *Black Abolitionist Papers: Volume II* (see note 2), 39.

43. Drew, *A North-Side View of Slavery* (see note 10), 39.

Chapter Twelve
Queen's Bush

Benjamin Drew, ed.

This name was originally given to a large, unsurveyed tract of land, now comprising the townships of Peel and Wellesley, and the country extending thence to Lake Huron. While it was yet a wilderness, it was settled mainly by colored people, about the year 1846. The following, communicated by a resident of Galt, gives the main features of the settlement of the Queen's Bush. The testimonials following Jackson's, are from that part of the scarcely reclaimed wilderness now known as the township of Peel.

WILLIAM JACKSON

My father and myself went to the Queen's Bush in 1846. We went four and a half miles beyond the other farms, to Canestogo, where he cleared up and had a farm; for years scarcely any white people came in, but fugitive slaves came in, in great numbers, and cleared the land. Before it was surveyed, there were as many as fifty families. It was surveyed about two years after we went there. The colored people might have held their lands still, but they were afraid they would not be able to pay when pay-day came. Under these circumstances, many of them sold out cheap.

They now consider that they were overreached — for many who bought out the colored people have not yet paid for the land, and some of the first settlers yet remain, who have not yet been required to pay all up.

Some colored people have come in from the free States, on account of the fugitive slave bill, and bought land. The farms are usually from fifty to one hundred acres. The timber is hard wood. The soil is productive, and it is a good wheat country.

A great many who sold out went to Mr. King's settlement, and to Owen Sound. The health of the colored people was very good — there was hardly any sickness at all: indeed, the climate of Canada agrees with them as well as with the white people. It is healthy for all.

I have heard white people who lived at Queen's Bush say, that they never lived amongst a set of people that they had rather live with as to their habits of industry and general good conduct. I never knew of but one to be taken before a court, for any thing but debt, and I lived there seven years.

In regard to riding in coaches or cars, I never had any trouble in Canada. I have heard of some who have suffered from prejudice, but I never did. The amount of prejudice is small here, and what there is grows out of slavery: for some, when they first come, feel so free, that they go beyond good limits, and have not courtesy enough. But I find that they get over this after a while.

Thomas L. Wood Knox

I was born free in the eastern part of Pennsylvania, but removed to Pittsburg. I should not have left the States only that I was not treated with respect. I would go to market with provisions off a farm I rented in New Brighton. When I got into Pittsburg, other farmers would drive in with their teams into the tavern yard, and get their breakfasts and go and sell out, before I could get any thing to eat: so that by the time I would get to market, the best of it would be over. The same thing would run through all the conduct of the whites. In the place where I went, they were opposed to my coming, — but after four years they were grieved to have me come away. But I could not stand it, and left for Canada. I have been in Canada eleven years — eight in the Queen's Bush. When I came here it was a complete wilderness: I took hold and cleared a farm. I would rather have remained in my native country, among my friends, could I have had such treatment as I felt that I deserved. But that was not to be, and I came into the wilderness.

Most of the colored people living here are doing as well, if not better, than one could reasonably expect. Most of the grown people among them are fugitive slaves. I know of but one, free-born, from Pennsylvania, and that is myself. The number here I cannot speak of with any certainty. Many have removed to Owen's Sound and other places: there may be now five hundred persons. All are equal here: I have been about here a great deal, but have seen no prejudice at all.

Sophia Pooley

I was born in Fishkill, New York State, twelve miles from North River. My father's name was Oliver Bur then, my mother's Dinah. I am now more than ninety years old. I was stolen from my parents when I was seven years old, and brought to Canada; that was long before the American Revolution. There were hardly any white people in Canada then — nothing here but Indians and wild beasts. Many a deer I have helped catch on the lakes in a canoe: one year we took ninety. I was a woman grown when the first governor of Canada came from England: that was Gov. Simcoe.

My parents were slaves in New York State. My master's sons-in-law, Daniel Outwaters and Simon Knox, came into the garden where my sister and I were playing among the currant bushes, tied their handkerchiefs over our mouths, carried us to a vessel, put us in the hold, and sailed up the river. I know not how far nor how long — it was dark there all the time. Then we came by land. I remember when we came to Genesee, — there were Indian settlements there, — Onondagas, Senecas, and Oneidas. I guess I was the first colored girl brought into Canada. The white men sold us at Niagara to old Indian Brant, the king. I lived with old Brant about twelve or thirteen years as nigh as I can tell. Brant lived part of the time at Mohawk, part at Ancaster, part at Preston, then called Lower Block: the Upper Block was at Snyder's Mills. While I lived with old Brant we caught the deer. It was at Dundas at the outlet. We would let the hounds loose, and when we heard them bark we would run for the canoe

— Peggy, and Mary, and Katy, Brant's daughters and I. Brant's sons, Joseph and Jacob, would wait on the shore to kill the deer when we fetched him in. I had a tomahawk, and would hit the deer on the head — then the squaws would take it by the horns and paddle ashore. The boys would bleed and skin the deer and take the meat to the house. Sometimes white people in the neighborhood, John Chisholm and Bill Chisholm, would come and say 'twas their hounds, and they must have the meat. But we would not give it up.

Canada was then filling up with white people. And after Brant went to England, and kissed the queen's hand, he was made a colonel. Then there began to be laws in Canada. Brant was only half Indian: his mother was a squaw — I saw her when I came to this country. She was an old body; her hair was quite white. Brant was a good looking man — quite portly. He was as big as Jim Douglass who lived here in the bush, and weighed two hundred pounds. He lived in an Indian village — white men came among them and they intermarried. They had an English schoolmaster, an English preacher, and an English blacksmith. When Brant went among the English, he wore the English dress — when he was among the Indians, he wore the Indian dress, — broadcloth leggings, blanket, moccasins, fur cap. He had his ears slit with a long loop at the edge, and in these he hung long silver ornaments. He wore a silver half-moon on his breast with the king's name on it, and broad silver bracelets on his arms. He never would paint, but his people painted a great deal. Brant was always for making peace among his people; that was the reason of his going about so much. I used to talk Indian better than I could English. I have forgotten some of it — there are none to talk it with now.

Brant's third wife, my mistress, was a barbarous creature. She could talk English, but she would not. She would tell me in Indian to do things, and then hit me with any thing that came to hand, because I did not understand her. I have a scar on my head from a wound she gave me with a hatchet; and this long scar over my eye, is where she cut me with a knife. The skin dropped over my eye; a white woman bound it up. [The scars spoken of were quite perceptible, but the writer saw many worse looking cicatrices of wounds not inflicted by *Indian* savages, but by civilized (?) men.] Brant was very angry, when he came home, at what she had done, and punished her as if she had been a child. Said he, "you know I adopted her as one of the family, and now you are trying to put all the work on her."

I liked the Indians pretty well in their place; some of them were very savage, — some friendly. I have seen them have the war-dance — in a ring with only a cloth about them, and painted up. They did not look ridiculous — they looked savage, — enough to frighten anybody. One would take a bowl and rub the edge with a knotted stick: then they would raise their tomahawks and whoop. Brant had two colored men for slaves: one of them was the father of John Patten, who lives over yonder, the other called himself Simon Ganseville. There was but one other Indian that I knew, who owned a slave. I had no care to get my freedom.

At twelve years old, I was sold by Brant to an Englishman in Ancaster, for one hundred dollars, — his name was Samuel Hatt, and I lived with him seven years: then the white people said I was free, and put me up to running away. He did not stop me — he said he could not take the law into his own hands. Then I lived in what is now Waterloo. I married Robert Pooley, a black man. He ran away with a white woman: he is dead.

Brant died two years before the second war with the United States. His wife survived him until the year the stars fell. She was a pretty squaw: her father was an English colonel. She hid a crock of gold before she died, and I never heard of its being found. Brant was a freemason.

I was seven miles from Stoney Creek at the time of the battle — the cannonade made every thing shake well.

I am now unable to work, and am entirely dependent on others for subsistence: but I find plenty of people in the bush to help me a good deal.

JOHN FRANCIS

I was twenty-eight years old when I came into the Queen's Bush from Virginia. My usage down South was hard. I was sold three times: first, for debt; then I was traded off: the third time I sold myself to myself.

I came in ten years ago. Then there were few families. More kept coming, — colored people, — there were not many white. The land was not surveyed. We settled down where we saw fit. We knew nothing about price nor terms. After considerable many settlers had come in, we called a meeting, and sent a man to get a grant of the land if he could; or, if not that, to find the terms. The answer was, that we were on clergy reserves, and they could give no grant. Still we kept at work, clearing and planting. The land came into market about seven years ago, being surveyed and a price set on it.

Then came a land agent, to sell and take payments. He put up public notices, that the settlers who had made improvements were to come and pay the first instalment, or the land would be sold from under them. The payment was to be in ten annual instalments of 15s. 6d. currency, 5s. to the dollar. It was then hard times in Canada, and many could not meet the payment. The agent, as we now know, transcended his powers, for some people, white and colored, still hold their lands, not having made payments. The agent had a percentage for collecting. His course in driving people for money, ruined a great many poor people here in the bush. Fearing that the land would be sold, and they get nothing for their betterments, they sold out for very little and removed to other parts. The agent himself told me he would sell my land unless the instalment was paid. I sacrificed my two cows and a steer, to make the payment that I might hold the land. Others did not do that and yet hold. One man, fearing to lose all he had done, sold out for ten dollars, having cleared eight or ten acres — that property is now estimated at $15,000. Some borrowed money on mortgages, and some paid a heavy per cent. for money to meet that instalment: which was very hard on the poor settlers who had their hands full in trying to live, and clearing land so that they could live. But it was done: and it has kept many back by trying to meet that borrowed money, and others by their moving where they would have to begin again: that is what has scattered the colored people away from here. There are now about three hundred, — there were three times as many. Some went where they got grants of fifty acres for settling.

The young men growing up here have not so much knowledge as desirable, as there were no schools here when they were growing up. Now it is different, and many send their children. The teachers generally have not the feelings in regard to slavery that we have. It would be well to have the young taught, that they should improve themselves as a means of elevating their race. When my children get old enough to read, I intend to instruct them about slavery, and get books to show them what we have been through, and fit them for a good example.

My mother was sold away from me, when I was about eleven years old. In escaping, I sailed over two hundred miles on the sea in an open boat with my father, a day without eating, and ten days without drinking. One night we were near being lost in a storm. We put in to get water and were taken: but we made out to clear ourselves.

The colored people in the Queen's Bush, are doing pretty well — they have many drawbacks: as they can keep no books nor accounts, they are liable to be overreached — and are overreached sometimes.

JOHN LITTLE

[The hero of the following narrative is much respected, wherever he is known — in Canada West. And in that country of good farms, Mr. Little's is one of the best, and among the best managed.]

I have been bought and sold by several masters. I was born in N. C., Hertford Co., nigh Murfreesboro': I lived there more than twenty years. My first master, was just a reasonable man for a slaveholder. As slaveholders go, he used his people very well. He had but seven, — my mother and her six children; of the children, I was the oldest. I was never sent to school a day in my life, and never knew a letter until quite late in life. I was not allowed to go to meeting. My business on Sundays was looking after the mules and hogs, and amusing myself with running hares and fishing.

My master broke down, and I was taken by the sheriff, and sold at public auction in Murfreesboro'. I felt miserably bad to be separated from my mother and brothers and sisters. They too felt miserably about it, especially my poor old mother, who ran all about among the neighbors trying to persuade one and another to buy me; which none of them would promise to do, expecting the traders to give more. This she did on Sundays: week-days, she had to work on the farm.

Finally I was sold to a man in the same county, about ten miles from the first place. He abused me like a dog — worse than a dog, — not because I did any thing wrong, but because I was a "nigger." My blood boils to think about him, let me be where I will. It do n't seem to me that even upon the Lord's day, and now I know that there is a hereafter, it would be a sin before God to shoot him, if he were here, he was so bad:

he so abused me, — he, a wise man, — abused me because I was a fool, — not naturally, but made so by him and others under the slave laws. That is God's truth, that I was inhumanly abused.

At the time of this sale I was about twenty-three, but being a slave, I did not know my age; I did not know any thing. He came and said to me, "Well, boy, do you know who's bought you?" I answered, "I do not, sir." "Well," he said, "I've bought you: do you know me ?" I told him "I did." "I have bought you, and I'll give you a pass (for there a colored man cannot go without a pass even from an auction,) to go to my farm; go down there, to the overseer, and he'll tell you what to do." I went on Sunday morning, the day after the sale, and delivered myself up. Said he, "Go down there to the quarters, with the rest of the *niggers,* and to-morrow I'll tell you what to do. When I got down there I found about seventy men, women, and children. They told me Mr. E—— was a hard man, and what I had better do to avoid the lash. They do that among themselves any time. It was in the winter time, and when the horn sounded for us to rise, we were allowed fifteen minutes to get to the overseer's house about a quarter of a mile off. I wish he were here now to hear me tell it, to see whether it's the truth, — I could look right in his face the whole time. Breakfast was not even talked about. We were dismissed from work at different hours, but never till after dark. Then we would go to our cabins, and get up our little fires, and cook, or half cook, our victuals. What we did not eat that night, we put into little old baskets that we made ourselves, and put it handy, so that when the horn sounded, we could take it and clear to the overseer's. This provision served us all the next day. We usually ate it at the time the horses ate. We were not allowed to eat during work, under penalty of fifty lashes. That was the law laid down by the master to the overseer. We had to plan and lay schemes of our own to get a bite. "A nigger could always find time to eat and smoke and shuffle about, and so he wouldn't allow it to us. He would n't have his work hindered by eating." I do n't put the blame of cruelty on the overseer: I put it on the master who could prohibit it, if he would. No man ought to take the place of overseer, — I blame the scoundrel who takes the office; but if he does take it, he must obey orders.

After being there three weeks, I wanted to go back to see my mother who was broken-hearted at the loss of her children. It seemed as if the evil one had fixed it so, — for then two daughters were taken and carried off to Georgia. She had been sold before for the fellow's debts, — sold close by at private sale. I asked leave of my master Saturday night. I went to him, pulled off my hat, and asked him, if he would please give me a pass to go and see my mother, and I would come back Sunday evening. "No! I do n't allow my niggers to run about Sundays, gawking about; I want you to-morrow to look after the mules and the horses along with the rest of the niggers." He was the greatest gentleman in that neighborhood. The white men all looked up to him. He was what is called a "nigger-breaker." If any one had a stubborn slave, that they could n't bend just as they wanted to, they would hire him to S—— E—— for a year. I have known them to be sent from as much as fifty miles, to be broke, because he had so much cruelty: he was a hard-hearted, overbearing scoundrel: the cries and groans of a suffering person, even if ready to die, no more affected him, than they would one of my oxen in the field yonder. This I have seen and known, and partly endured in my own person.

His refusing the pass, naturally made me a little stubborn: I was a man as well as himself. I started and went without the pass, and returned on Sunday evening, after dark. Nothing was said until Monday morning, — then we went to the overseer, and were all told to go to the gin-house. As soon as I got there, the overseer and two colored men laid right hold of me, and tied me fast to an apple-tree with some of the baling-rope, and then sent for the master. He came, — "Well, Sir, I suppose you think you are a great gentleman." I thought, as they had me tied, I would try to beg off as well as I could, knowing that sauciness would not make it any better for me. "I suppose," he went on, "you think you can come and go whenever you please." I told him "No: I wanted to see my mother very bad, and so I ran over there and came back as I told you." Said he, "I am your master, and you shall obey me, let my orders be what they may." I knew that as well as he, but I knew that it was devilishness, that he would n't give me a pass. He bade the overseer hit me five hundred lashes, — *five hundred lashes* he bade the overseer hit me! Men have received them down south, this morning since the sun rose. The overseer ordered two slaves to undress me, which they did: they turned my shirt over my head which blindfolded me. I could not see who put on the blows, but I knew. It was not the master, — he was too much of a gentleman: but he had a plenty of dogs to set on. What I tell you now, I would tell at the judgment, if I were required. 'T is n't he who has stood and looked on, that can tell you what slavery is, — 't is he who has endured. I was a slave long enough, and have tasted it all. I was black, but I had the feelings of a man as well as any man.

The master then marked on me with his cane where the overseer was to begin, and said, "Whip him from there down." Then the overseer went at it, the master counting aloud. He struck me a hundred lashes right off before he stopped. It hurt me horribly, but after the first hundred, sensation seemed to be beaten out of my flesh. After the first hundred, the master said, "Now, you cursed, infernal son of a b——, your running about will spoil all the rest of my niggers: I do n't want them to be running about, and you shan't be running about." I answered, "Master, I did n't mean any harm; I wanted to go and see my mother, and to get a shirt I left over there." He then struck me over my head twice with his cane, and told me to "hold my jaw." I said no more; but he told the overseer, "put it on to him again like the very devil." I felt worse on account of the blows with the cane than for the overseer's whipping: that's what makes me feel so towards him now. It poisons my mind to think about him. I do n't want to think about him. I was as much a man as my master. The overseer then went on with the bull whip. How many they put on, I do n't know, but I know that from the small of my back to the calves of my legs, they took the skin clear off, as you would skin beef. That's what they gave me that day — the next day, I had to have some more. One of the slaves then washed me with salt and water to take out the soreness. This almost put me into a fit. It brought the pain all back — the abominable scoundrel knew it would. Then I was taken up to the blacksmith's shop to be fettered: that was the way S—— E—— broke "niggers." His name sounded around there as if he had been Satan himself: the colored people were as afraid of him as they would be of a lion out in these bushes.

Iron rings were put about my ankles, and a short chain to the rings. I was given in charge to two slaves. Some may deny that the slaveholders are so bad, but I know it's true, and God knows it's true. A stranger may go there, and they are not such fools as to put such punishment on a man before him. If he is going to do that, he will send him over the fields out of the way, and while they are enjoying themselves in the house, the slave is suffering under the whip. A regular slaveholder has got no conscience. A slaveholder knows the difference between a northerner and a southerner. If a man came from any other part, he never saw me in irons. G——

L—— might have seen me, or L—— K——, or any other slaveholder might come and see it, and hold a council over it, and blackguard me for it: "Boy, what have you got that on you for? That shows a d—d bad nigger: if you war n't a bad nigger you would n't have them on."

The two slaves took me in charge, with orders to kill me if I tried to escape. At night, my feet were made fast in the stocks, without removing the irons. The stocks were of wood with grooves for the ancles, over which laid an iron bar. I could lie on my back, but could not turn. The next morning, I was taken to the gin-house to receive fifty blows with the bucking-paddle. This was my master's order. I received three blows, and then fainted. When I came to, only one slave was with me, who took me to the field to work, — but I was in so bad state that I could not work that day, nor much for a week. After doing a hard day's work in the fetters which had now worn to the bone, for they would get wet with dew in the morning, and then sand would work in, I was placed in the stocks — my ankles sore, bleeding, and corrupted. I wished I could die, but could not.

At the end of three months, he found I was too stubborn for *him* to subdue. He took off the fetters from my ankles, put me in handcuffs, and sent me to Norfolk jail, to be shipped for New Orleans. But when I arrived, the time that niggers were allowed to be shipped to New Orleans was out, and the last boat for that spring had sailed. After two weeks, I had the measles. My master was written to, but neither came nor sent any answer. As the traders were coming there with slaves, the turnkey put me into the kitchen to avoid contagion. I soon got better, — the turnkey said, "You are well now, and must be lonesome, — I'll put you in with the rest in a day or two." I determined to escape if I could.

At night I took a shelf down and put it against the inclosure of the yard, and climbed to the top, which was armed with sharp spikes, fourteen inches long, and, risking my life, I got over the spikes. Just as I had done this, the nine o'clock bell rung the signal for the patrols. I fell on the outside and made for the river, where I found a skiff loaded with wood. I threw over half a cord in a hurry, and pushed off for the opposite shore, to go back into the neighborhood of my old place, hoping, by dodging in the bush, to tire out my master's patience, and induce him to sell me running. I knew nothing about the North then — I did not know but the northerners were as bad as the southerners. I supposed a white man would be my enemy, let me see him where I would. Some of the neighbors there would have bought me, but he refused to sell me in the neighborhood, being ashamed to sell there a slave whom he could not break. He gave up first, but I was the worse beaten. I was as big-hearted as he was: he did not like to give up, and I would not give in — I made up my mind that if he would find whips, I would find back.

Having lightened the skiff, I paddled across, and went back to North Carolina to my mother's door. I ran about there in the bush, and was dodging here and there in the woods two years. I ate their pigs and chickens — I did not spare them. I knew how to dress them, and did not suffer for want of food. This would not have taken place had my master complied with my reasonable request for a pass, after I had done my work well, without any fault being found with it. But when I found out that, and by his cruel punishment, that he was a devil, I did not care what I did do. I meant he should kill me or sell me.

My master did not advertise me when he got the news of my escape, saying it was their loss, as I was placed in their charge. He sued, but was beaten. After this he advertised for me, offering fifty dollars for my capture, dead or alive. A free-born colored man, whom I had known, betrayed me. Some poor white fellows offered him *ten dollars* if he would find out where I was. He put them on my track. At ten one morning, they found me lying down asleep. I partially aroused, and heard one say, "Do n't shoot: it may be somebody else lying down drunk." I arose with my face towards them: there were six young white men armed with guns. I wheeled, and ran; they cried out, "Stop, or I'll shoot you." One of them, a real youngster, hit me, firing first. [...]

[Much later ...] I went back to the house in the village — at the door I saw a person with our things. They gave them to me, and bade me Godspeed, and that, if ever I was taken, not to betray them. I then put forth, and, with my wife, reached Canada. God save the Queen!

From Jackson to the Ohio River was called one hundred and forty miles, — crossed the river to Cairo; then we footed through Illinois to Chicago; all the way we lay by days, and travelled nights. I forgot the name of that city, and wandered out of the way, and got to a river. It was the Mississippi, but I did not know it. We crossed into Black Hawk territory. There I was so lost and bewildered, that I had at last to go up to a house to inquire the way. I found there a man with true abolition principles, who told us the route. He said a man and his wife had been carried back to slavery from that neighborhood. He did not take us across the river, but we found a way over. Then we walked on, — my wife was completely worn out: it was three months from the time we left home before we slept in a house. We were in the woods, ignorant of the roads, and losing our way. At one time we came to a guideboard, which said "5 miles to Parks's Landing." I had learned to spell out print a little. This was Sunday night. I took the direction I wanted to travel as near as I could, and we went on. On Wednesday afternoon we came back to the same guide-board — "5 miles to Parks's Landing." Many such roundabout cruises we made, wearing ourselves out without advancing: this was what kept us so long in the wilderness and in suffering. I had suffered so much from white men, that I had no confidence in them, and determined to push myself through without their help. Yet I had to ask at last, and met with a friend instead of an enemy. At Chicago money was made up to help me on, and I took passage for Detroit, and then crossed to Windsor, in Canada. That was the first time I set my foot on free soil.

Work was dull among the French at Windsor. We stayed there about six months. We heard of the Queen's Bush, where any people might go and settle, colored or poor, and might have a reasonable chance to pay for the land. We set out to find the Queen's Bush — went to Buffalo — thence to Black Rock — thence to St. Catharines, and there I got straight instructions. We had not a second suit of clothes apiece; we had one bedquilt and one blanket, and eighteen dollars in money. I bought two axes in Hamilton, one for myself, and one for my wife; half a dozen plates, knives and forks, an iron pot, and a Dutch oven: that's all for tools and furniture. For provisions I bought fifty weight of flour, and twenty pounds of pork. Then we marched right into the wilderness, where there were thousands of acres of woods which the chain had never run round since Adam. At night we made a fire, and cut down a tree, and put up some slats like a wigwam. This was in February, when the snow was two feet deep. It was about fourteen years ago. We made our bed of cedar boughs from a swamp. Thus we travelled three or four days, seeing plenty of deer: wolves, as plenty as sheep are now, were howling about us, and bears were numerous.

At last I came to a place where I judged, from the timber, the land was good — and so it proved. My nearest neighbor was two miles off. I felt thankful that I had got into a place where I could not see the face of a white man. For something like five or six years, I felt suspicious when I saw a white man, thinking he was prying round to take some advantage. This was because I had been so bedevilled and harassed by them. At length that feeling wore off through kindness that I received from some here, and from abolitionists, who came over from the States to instruct us, and I felt that it was not the white man I should dislike, but the mean spirit which is in some men, whether white or black. I am sensible of that now.

The settlers were to take as much land as they pleased, when it should be surveyed, at various prices, according to quality. Mine was the highest price, as I had taken of the best land. It was three dollars seventy cents an acre. I took a hundred acres at first, and then bought in fifty.

Myself and wife built us here a little log hut amid the snow. We made it ourselves, shouldering the logs to bring up to the place. We went to the cedar swamp, and split out boards for the roof. We had plenty of firewood, which served instead of blankets. Wolves, any quantity, were howling about us constantly, night and day — big, savage wolves, which alarmed the people. Some men carrying meat, were chased by them. Isaac Johnson was obliged to take up a tree. We got used to them on our way here, and did not fear them at all. In the spring, plenty of bears came about us after sheep and hogs. One day my wife and I were walking out, and we saw four bears in the cherry-trees eating the fruit. My wife went for my gun, called some neighbors, and we killed all four. Now the wolves are all gone, and the deer and the bears are scarce. There are idle men enough about here, colored and white, to drive them away, when they had better be chopping and clearing land.

We went to chopping, day and night; there was no delay; we logged the trunks with our own hands, without cattle, or horses, or help, — all with our own hands, and burned them. I raised that year one hundred and ten bushels of spring wheat, and three hundred bushels of potatoes on land which we had cleared ourselves, and cultivated without plough or drag. All was done with the hoe and hand-rake. This I can prove by my nearest neighbors. I got the seed on credit of some Dutchmen in the towns, by promising to work for them in harvest. They put their own price on the seed, and on my labor.

In the next winter we went to clearing again. My wife worked right along with me: I did not realize it then, for we were raised slaves, the women accustomed to work, and undoubtedly the same spirit comes with us here: I did not realize it then; but now I see that she was a brave woman. I thank God that freedom has never overweighted us: some it has, but I have worked to support it, and not to discourage it. I thought I ought to take hold and work and go ahead, to show to others that there is a chance for the colored man in Canada; to show the spirit of a man, and a desire to improve his condition. As it is so often said by slaveholders, that if the "niggers" were free, and put in a place where they would be together they would starve to death, I wanted to show to the contrary. I have one hundred and fifty acres of land: one hundred and ten of it cleared, and under good cultivation: two span of horses, a yoke of oxen, ten milch cows and young cattle, twenty head of hogs, forty head of sheep; I have two wagons, two ploughs, and two drags. I would like to show this to that everlasting scoundrel, E——, my former master, and tell him, "All this I would have done for you cheerfully, and thought myself at home, and felt happy in doing it, if you would have let me: but I am glad that you scarred and abused me, as it has given to myself and my family the fruits of my own labor." I would like to show it to those stout, able men, who, while they might be independent here, remain in the towns as waiters, blacking boots, cleaning houses, and driving coaches for men, who scarcely allow them enough for a living. To them I say, go into the backwoods of Queen Victoria's dominions, and you can secure an independent support. I am the man who has proved it; never man came into an unsettled country with lesser means to begin with. Some say, you cannot live in the woods without a year's provisions, — but this is not so: I have come here and proved to the contrary. I have hired myself out two days to get things to work on at home one. If there is a man in the free States who says the colored people cannot take care of themselves, I want him to come here and see John Little. There is no white blood in me; not a drop. My mother's father was imported from Africa, and both my grandparents on the father's side were also imported. I can prove to him that every thing which was due on the land is paid; that I raised seven hundred bushels of wheat last year, two hundred bushels of potatoes, one hundred bushels of peas, two hundred and fifty bushels of oats, ten tons of hay; fattened fifteen hundred weight of pork, one ox, besides other produce of less consequence. I have now growing fifty acres of wheat, eighteen acres of oats, ten of peas, one acre of potatoes, and twenty acres of meadow grass: I have horses, oxen, cows, hogs, sheep, and poultry in abundance. The man who was "a bad nigger" in the South, is here a respected, independent farmer. I thank God that I am respected in this neighborhood by the best men the country can afford — can lend or borrow two thousand dollars any time I am asked, or choose to ask for it. I do n't say this for the sake of boasting — I say it to show that colored men can take care of themselves, — and to answer any who deny that Canada is a good country.

The "*nigger*" who was so "BAD" among Southerners, as to be scarred with whips, put in the stocks, chained at his work, with ankles sore from the irons, months together, legally shot and maimed for life by a boy who was too young to be trusted with a gun, sold into Tennessee, his character "*bad,*" sent after him to debase him there, put in jail after jail, hunted by hounds — stands up here at the North, a man respectable and respected. I don't ask any one to take my word for it, merely. Ask the people of Peel, Wellesley, Woolwich, and Waterloo — those are the places where I am known, and where they can get acquainted with my character; and I am willing it should be compared with that of any slaveholder whatever.

The abuse a man receives at the South is enough to drive every thing good from the mind. I sometimes felt such a spirit of vengeance, that I seriously meditated setting the house on fire at night, and killing all as they came out. I overcame the evil, and never got at it — but a little more punishment would have done it. I had been so bruised and wounded and beset, that I was out of patience. I had been separated from all my relatives, from every friend I had in the world, whipped and ironed till I was tired of it. On that night when I was threatened with the paddle again, I was fully determined to kill, even if I were to be hanged and, if it pleased God, sent to hell: I could bear no more. If any man thinks slavery a proper thing, let him go and be abused as I was for years in North Carolina, much of the time in agony from irons and whips and paddles — then let him be sold off a thousand miles into Tennessee, and begin to live it over again, and I think he would be tired of it too.

I want every man that has the heart of a man, to put down upon slavery with all his heart and soul, — because it is a curse — because it makes the feeling of dislike to color, leading the white to abuse a "nigger" because he is a "nigger," and the black to hate the white because he abuses him.

In making my escape, my main difficulty was in crossing the Ohio Bottoms, before reaching the river. The water was black and deep. I bound our packages on my wife's back, placed her on a log as a man rides on horseback, and I swam, pushing the log, holding it steady, to keep her up. Had the log turned right or left, she would have slipped off, and the packs would have sunk her. It would have been death, sure — but worse than death was behind us, and to avoid that we risked our lives. When we had crossed one, we would presently come on another, and had to go through the same again. By and by, I would think, this must be the last, — but when we had crossed this, and gone over some little island, there would be another. Oh dear! it seems as if I could see it now, — I almost repented I had started, but on I went. There was another and another — good swimming creeks: but when I had crossed the last one, my spirits rose again — my heart cheered up, and I thought I could go through all.

After we had got to a place where we intended to pass the night, I would leave my wife, and go and look all around, to see if there was any white man. I was like an old hunting dog, who, when he has treed a coon, will not believe his eyes, but goes scenting about to see if the track has left the tree: if not, he will come back, look at the coon, bark, and then scent again.

I was hunted like a wolf in the mountain, all the way to Canada. In three months I had to go to many places to steal our food. I would have asked for it, but if I did, it was, "Where is your pass?" To avoid this meanness, and the risk of capture, I was obliged to look out for myself, and I made good use of my time. One night, on entering a dairy near a farm-house, the door creaked, and an old man called out, "Sa-a-l!" But I took some cakes, and Sal made no answer.

When I was travelling in the North, I found that men worked days, and slept nights without fear, because they were honest. At the South they do not have this comfort. The overseer watches through the day, and the master is on the look-out in the night. I know this, for many times, after my hard day's work, being but half fed, I went out to steal a chicken, or a goose, or a pig, as all slaves have to do, — at night, if the dog barked sharp, I would see master at the window with a gun. Sometimes the window would fly up — "who's that?" — then the man must give an account of himself. They are doing wrong in robbing the slaves, and so they are uneasy nights. When I first got into the North, and heard a dog at night, I would dodge away from the house, expecting to see the man of the house start out with a musket, as I had down south: but I was much astonished to find that they let a dog's bark go for what it was worth. I saw then the difference between free labor and slave labor: the northern man labors in the day, and sleeps soundly all night. He does not spend his day in laying deep schemes to whip a "nigger's" back, and then start up at night, in unexpected places, like a ghost.

One night, in Tennessee, my master heard a dog bark; he started up and ran out in his shirt, like a madman, to the quarters. When he got there, he called to us by name, saying some one had gone up to the house to see his girls — two slave girls he kept at the house. Every man was in his own cabin, but one old man of sixty, who was out getting a little wood. He accused him of going up to the great house to trouble his people: the old man begged off, and finally was excused.

How can men, who know they are abusing others all the day, lie down and sleep quietly at night, with big barns of corn, and gin-houses full of cotton, when they know that men feel revengeful, and might burn their property, or even kill them? Even now the thought of my cruel abuses begins sometimes to creep up and kindle my feelings, until I feel unhappy in my own house, and it seems as if the devil was getting the better of me; I feel, then, that I could destroy that tyrant, who, knowing that I was a man, cut me with a whip in a manner worse than I will name. Then I think, "What is the use? here I am, a free man in Canada, and out of his power." Yet I feel the stirrings of revenge. I know that thousands at the South feel the same, for we have counselled upon it; the slaveholders know this — how will they sleep nights? The slaveholder is afraid of his slaves: it cannot be otherwise. Some have been round the borders of slavery, and seen a little of the edges of it, and they think they know a great deal about it, but they are mistaken. I have been in slavery, and know its worst is hid from them. They have all the laws and customs of the country in their favor, and yet they find something to grumble about: how then can they expect the slaves, whose feelings are wretched, even when they are best used, can be happy and contented? They say the slaves are happy, because they laugh, and are merry. I myself, and three or four others, have received two hundred lashes in the day, and had our feet in fetters: yet, at night, we would sing and dance, and make others laugh at the rattling of our chains. Happy men we must have been! We did it to keep down trouble, and to keep our hearts from being completely broken: that is as true as gospel! Just look at it, — consider upon it, — must not we have been very happy? Yet I have done it myself — I have cut capers in chains!

Mrs. John Little

I was born in Petersburg, Va. When very young, I was taken to Montgomery county. My old master died there, and I remember that all the people were sold. My father and mother were sold together about one mile from me. After a year, they were sold a great distance, and I saw them no more. My mother came to me before she went away, and said, "Good by, be a good girl; I never expect to see you any more."

Then I belonged to Mr. T—— N——, the son of my old master. He was pretty good, but his wife, my mistress, beat me like sixty. Here are three scars on my right hand and arm, and one on my forehead, all from wounds inflicted with a broken china plate. My cousin, a man, broke the plate in two pieces, and she said, "Let me see that plate." I handed up the pieces to her, and she threw them down on me: they cut four gashes, and I bled like a butcher. One piece cut into the sinew of the thumb, and made a great knot permanently. The wound had to be sewed up. This long scar over my right eye, was from a blow with a stick of wood. One day she knocked me lifeless with a pair of tongs, — when I came to, she was holding me up, through fright. Some of the neighbors said to her, "Why do n't you learn Eliza to sew?" She answered, "I only want to learn her to do my housework, that's all." I can tell figures when I see them, but cannot read or write.

I belonged to them until I got married at the age of sixteen, to Mr. John Little, of Jackson. My master sold me for debt, — he was a man that would drink, and he had to sell me. I was sold to F—— T——, a planter and slave-trader, who soon after, at my persuasion, bought Mr. Little.

I was employed in hoeing cotton, a new employment: my hands were badly blistered. "Oh, you must be a great lady," said the overseer, "can't handle the hoe without blistering your hand!" I told him I could not help it. My hands got hard, but I could not stand the sun. The hot sun made me so sick I could not work, and, John says if I had not come away, they would surely have sold me again. There was one weakly woman named Susan, who could not stand the work, and she was sold to Mississippi, away from her husband and son. That's one way of taking care of the sick and weak. That's the way the planters do with a weakly, sickly "nigger," — they say "he's a dead expense to 'em," and put him off as soon as they can. After Susan was carried off, her husband went to see her: when he came back he received two hundred blows with the paddle.

I staid with T—— more than a year. A little before I came away, I heard that master was going to give my husband three hundred blows with the paddle. He came home one night with an axe on his shoulder, tired with chopping timber. I had his clothes all packed up, for I knew he would have to go. He came hungry, calculating on his supper, — I told him what was going. I never heard him curse before — he cursed then. Said he, "If any man, white or black, lays his hand on me to-night, I'll put this axe clear through him — clear through him:" and he would have done it, and I would not have tried to hinder him. But there was a visitor at the house, and no one came: he ran away. Next morning, the overseer came for him. The master asked where he was; I could have told him, but would not. My husband came back no more.

When we had made arrangements for leaving, a slave told of us. Not long after, master called to me, "Come here, my girl, come here." I went to him: he tied me by the wrist with a rope. He said, "Oh, my girl, I do n't blame you, — you are young, and do n't know; it's that d—d infernal son of a ——; if I had him here, I'd blow a ball through him this minute." But he was deceived about it: I had put John up to hurrying off.

Then master stood at the great house door, at a loss what to do. There he had Willis, who was to have run away with us, and the man who betrayed us. At last he took us all off about half a mile to a swamp, where old A—— need not hear us as he was going to meeting, it being Sunday. He whipped Willis to make him tell where we were going. Willis said, "Ohio State." "What do you want to be free for? G— d— you, what do you know about freedom? Who was going with you?" "Only Jack." "G— d— Jack to h—, and you too." While they were whipping Willis, he said, "Oh, master, I'll never run away." "I did n't ask you about that, you d—d son of a ——, you." Then they tried to make him tell about a slave girl who had put her child aside: but he knew nothing about that. As soon as they had done whipping him, they put a plough clavis about his ankle to which they attached a chain which was secured about his neck with a horse-lock.

Then they took a rheumatic boy, who had stopped with us, whom I had charged not to tell. They whipped him with the paddle, but he said he was ignorant of it: he bore the whipping, and never betrayed us. Then they questioned him about the girl and the child, as if that boy could know any thing about it! Then came my turn; they whipped me in the same way they did the men. Oh, those slaveholders are a brutish set of people, — the master made a remark to the overseer about my shape. Before striking me, master questioned me about the girl. I denied all knowledge of the affair. I only knew that she had been with child, and that now she was not, but I did not tell them even that. I was ashamed of my situation, they remarking upon me. I had been brought up in the house, and was not used to such coarseness. Then he (master) asked, "Where is Jack?" "I don't know." Said he, "Give her h——, R——," That was his common word. Then they struck me several blows with the paddle. I kept on telling them it was of no use to whip me, as I knew nothing to tell them. No irons were ready for me, and I was put under a guard, — but I was too cunning for him, and joined my husband.

My shoes gave out before many days, — then I wore my husband's old shoes till they were used up. Then we came on barefooted all the way to Chicago. My feet were blistered and sore and my ankles swollen; but I had to keep on. There was something behind me driving me on. At the first water we came to I was frightened, as I was not used to the water. It was a swift but shallow stream: my husband crossed over, and I was obliged to follow. At the Ohio Bottoms was a great difficulty, — the water was in some places very deep, — it was black, dirty water. I was scared all but to death: but I had become somewhat used to hardship. If I had seen a white face, I would have run into the river.

By and by, we succeeded in crossing the last one. Then we struck a light at a shingle-getter's shanty, made a fire with the clapboards and dried ourselves. We were merry over our success in getting so far along, and had a good laugh as we burned the boards and part of the shanty itself. I felt afraid at getting into a boat to cross the Ohio River: I had never been in any boat whatever. Now to get on this in the night, frightened me. "John," said I, "don't you think we'll drown?" "I don't care if we do," said he. We reached Cairo well enough.

We never slept at the same time; while one slept, the other kept watch, day or night. Both of us never slept at one time, — if we had, we would not have reached Canada. One morning, as I was watching by a fire we had made, John sleeping, I saw a dog, and told John. Said he, "'t is some old white man hunting a hog, — however, we had better go from this fire." We went down into a valley and there remained. In the afternoon, an hour before sunset, a white man came suddenly upon us, while we were getting ready for a night's march. I started to run: John stood. The man said, "Stop, there!" But I kept on; his face was so white, that I wanted nothing to do with him. John said, "What did you say?" " Stop, there." John said, "I'll do no such thing." Then hard language passed between them. The man said, "I'll have a pack of hounds after you before night." John answered him with an oath to frighten him, "You had better do it, and be off yourself, or I'll blow a ball through you." The man never had heard a negro swear at him before. They are generally so cowed down, that John's swearing at him, alarmed him more than a bullet from a white man. It showed that he was desperate, — and that was the only reason why he used such language. The man struck spurs to his horse, and went off in a hurry. We followed him, as he went the same way we were going, and kept as close to him as we could: for, if the man got hounds he would start them at the place where he had seen us; and coming back over the same route with hounds, horses, and men, would kill our track, and they could not take us. But we saw no more of the man.

Soon after dark, we came to a lake. We found an old white man there in a shanty, who was caring for a slave that had been shot by his master a few days before. We went in and saw him, — he was an old, gray-headed man. His master had threatened him with a flogging, and he took to the river: just as he reached the water, his master shot him behind. But he got across. He was wounded, and without hat or shoes. In this place we were informed about our route. It was in Kentucky.

While we were stopping at the shanty, a day or two, John went out one evening with the old man, to hunt for provisions. I went to bed. By and by the dogs barked; the door opened, and by the fire I saw five white men. One said, "Who you got here ?" "Only, my own family." I was afraid, and crept out slyly on my hands and knees, and hid behind an ash-barrel until they were gone.

In a few days we crossed the ferry. Then we went on, and were without provisions, except some corn, which we parched. We met here a runaway slave, who knew the route of the country above us. He was returning to his master, where he had a wife and children.

At Cairo, the gallinippers were so bad, we made a smoke to keep them off. Soon after I heard a bell ring. Said I, "John, somebody's dead." It was a steamboat bell tolling. Presently there she was, a great boat full of white men. We were right on the river's bank, and our fire sent the smoke straight up into the calm. We lay flat on the ground. John read the name — Maria. No one noticed us: after the boat was gone, we had a hearty laugh at our good luck. Thinking there was no more trouble, we did not put out our fire. Presently came a yawl boat: they saw our fire, and hailed, "Boat ashore! boat ashore! runaway niggers! runaway niggers!" We lay close, and the boat kept on. We put out our fire, and went further back from the river, but the mosquitoes were so bad, we made another fire. But a man with a gun then came along, looking up into the trees. I scattered the fire to put it out, but it smoked so much the worse. We at last hid in a thicket of briers, where we were almost devoured by mosquitoes, for want of a little smoke.

Next day I lay down to sleep, while John kept watch. When I awoke, I told him I had dreamed about a white cow, which still seemed a white woman, and that I feared we would be caught. We were in the woods, in a low, damp place, where there was no bit of a road, and we knew not where the road was. We started to find a road, and then met with a white woman. I reminded John of my dream. "Good evening, good evening," said she. My husband asked if she would sell him some bread: this was to make conversation, so he could inquire the road. "Oh yes, just come to my house, I'll give you some bread." We went to the house, and presently her husband came in. He asked, "Have you got, free papers?" John answered, "No." "Where are you travelling to?" "To the upper lakes." "We are not allowed to let a colored man go through here without free papers: if we do, we are liable to a fine of forty dollars." He allowed us to remain all night, — but in the morning we were to go before a squire at Dorrety, and, if we were free, we would go on. This was the woman's arrangement: the man did not seem inclined to stop us. She said, "If we stop you, we shall get fifty dollars apiece for you: that's a — good — deal — of — money, — you know." The man asked John if he had a pistol. John produced one. The man said 't was no harm, he would take care of it for him, — and locked it up. They lived in a little, dirty log hut: they took the bed off the bedstead, and lay down on it close to the door, so that it could not be opened without disturbing him. The man took a nice silver-mounted pistol from a cupboard, loaded it, and placed it where he could reach it in the night. We lay on the bedstead — they on the floor. She was the evil one: she had made the plans. Their name was Smith.

At about three o'clock in the morning, husband aroused me, — "I'm going away from here; I do n't value them, now other folks are asleep." We both got up. John spoke roughly, "Mr. Smith! Mr. Smith!" He aroused: "we are unwell, and must pass out, — we'll be back very soon." Mr. Smith got up very readily, and pulled the bed away a little, so we could slip out. As John passed by the pistol, he put his hand on it, and took it in exchange for his old one. It is a beautiful rifle pistol, percussion lock, — John has been offered fifteen dollars for it. If the man will come here with John's old flint lock, my husband will exchange back, and give him *boot*. I am very sorry for my friend, Mrs. Smith, that she did not get the hundred dollars to go a shopping with in Dorrety — am much obliged to her for our night's lodging. We went across a small stream, and waited for daylight. Then we went on to Dorrety, and passed through the edge of it, without calling on the squire, as we had not time.

One Sunday morning, being on a prairie where we could see no house — about fifty miles west of Springfield — we ventured to travel by day. We encountered an animal, which we at first supposed to be a dog; but when he came near, we concluded it to be a wolf. He yelped something like a dog: he did not attack us. We went on and crossed a stream, and then we saw three large wood-wolves, sneaking around as if waiting for darkness. As we kept on, the three wolves kept in sight, now on one hand, and now on the other. I felt afraid, expecting they would attack us: but they left us. Afterward we made a fire with elder-stalks, and I undertook to make some corn bread. I got it mixed, and put it on the fire, — when I saw a party of men and boys on horseback, apparently approaching us. I put out the fire; they turned a little away, and did not appear to perceive us: I rekindled the fire, and baked our bread. John managed to keep us well supplied with pies and bread. We used to laugh to think how people would puzzle over who drank the milk and left the pitchers, and who hooked the dough.

I got to be quite hardy — quite used to water and bush-whacking; so that by the time I got to Canada, I could handle an axe, or hoe, or any thing. I felt proud to be able to do it — to help get cleared up, so that we could have a home, and plenty to live on. I now enjoy my life very well — I have nothing to complain of. We have horses and a pleasure-wagon, and I can ride out when and where I please, without a pass. The best of the merchants and clerks pay me as much attention as though I were a white woman: I am as politely accosted as any woman would wish to be.

I have lost two children by death; one little girl is all that is spared to me. She is but four years old. I intend to have her well educated, if the Lord lets us. […]

Chapter Thirteen
Black Parents Speak: Education in Mid-Nineteenth-Century Canada West

Claudette Knight

During the mid-nineteenth century, many black residents of Canada West were ardent advocates of public education for their children. Government policy officially supported black access to public education, although local white prejudice often limited its scope. Some black children attended common schools regularly, but others were denied public education or were forced to enroll in separate schools. Despite the increasing regulation and centralization of education during this period, local white opposition to integrated schooling ultimately shaped the policy that governed black students and, in some circumstances, was ultimately more powerful than the law.

Black parents seeking education opportunities amid anti-integrationist white communities resorted to a variety of strategies to combat local prejudice. Appeals to local officials, letters of protest to government education officers, and civil suits were initiated by black parents committed to educating their children. These initiatives not only document the history of black access to education in mid-nineteenth-century Canada West, but also serve as an important social barometer.

> I'm on my way to Canada
> That cold and distant land

> The dire effects of slavery
> I can no longer stand —
> Farewell, old master,
> Don't come after me.
> I'm on my way to Canada
> Where coloured men are free.[1]

This excerpt from George Clark's song, "The Free Slave," depicts Canada as a desirable refuge from the indignities and injustice suffered by American blacks under slavery. During the mid-nineteenth century, especially between 1850 and 1860, Canada West received a substantial influx of American blacks. The enslaved and the free sought to enjoy the freedom, equality, and justice that they were denied in the United States. According to Robin Winks, blacks migrating from the United States prior to the 1830s were generally well received in Canada West. During this period the number of blacks in Canada West was relatively small, and cheap labour was needed in many frontier communities to fell trees, lay roads, cut ties, and introduce tobacco farming.

After 1840 several significant changes altered these conditions. First, during the 1840s blacks faced increased competition from Irish immigrants, who were equally willing to embrace physically demanding, low-wage work, and whose skin colour was less likely to create social opposition. Secondly, as the availability of cheap land declined, blacks tended to drift towards towns where racial and real or imagined social differences would be more easily observed. Finally, and perhaps most significantly, the number of black fugitives fleeing to Canada West increased substantially after the passage of the Fugitive Slave Act in 1850. This act required all Americans to assist in the recapture and return of fugitive slaves, regardless of whether these blacks had obtained freedom in the northern states. Prior to September 1850, ten thousand blacks lived in Canada West; ten years later, this figure had increased to between thirty and thirty-five thousand.[2]

Initially, black fugitives tended to settle near the border in order to farm in regions most geographically familiar. Lack of funds and easy return access to the United States also determined that small groups settled in Welland, St. Catharines, Colchester, Windsor, Amherstburg,

London, Chatham, and Dresden. Settlement occurred more slowly in Toronto, Oro, and the Queen's Bush. It is not surprising that later arrivals tended to settle in these regions where the small, established black communities could provide assistance to incoming fugitives.

Employment opportunities for the fugitives varied in Canada West, but most were farmers. Nevertheless, during the 1830s and 1840s many waiters in hotels near Niagara Falls were black, while others were employed on road construction or hired themselves out as field hands in Oro, and a small number operated their own small businesses in various towns. Some worked as brakemen on the Great Western Railway, made rope, were fishermen, or laboured in brickyards and slaughterhouses. Black women worked on farms and as servants. Despite the opportunities and prosperity enjoyed by some of these fugitives, the majority struggled financially, were often poorly prepared for the winter months, and many suffered from consumption.[3]

Proscriptions placed on black education in both northern and southern states meant that most black fugitives were illiterate. Blacks residing in the free states were often barred from public schools or forced to attend separate schools. Educating blacks was illegal in all slave states except Kentucky. A Virginia state representative summarized southern white sentiment: "We have as far as possible closed every avenue by which light may enter their minds ... if we could extinguish the capacity to see the light our work would be completed."[4]

Despite their restricted access to education in the United States, once in Canada West black fugitives eagerly sought access to public schools. Many believed that the popular myth of black inferiority would be quickly destroyed when blacks gained educational opportunities. Educated blacks would undermine racist ideology, obtain superior employment, and gain voting privileges. On 22 October 1851, three black abolitionists (Henry Bibb, John Fisher, and James Tinsely) summarized the importance of education in their *Address to the Coloured Inhabitants of North America*:

> As we value education as being one of the most important items connected with our destiny, and it is more dreaded by the slaveholders than bowie-knives or pistols, we therefore

recommend that there should be no time or opportunity lost in educating people of colour. Let there be put into the hands of the refugee as soon as he crosses Mason's and Dixon's Line, the Spelling Book. Teach him to read and write intelligibly, and the slaveholder won't have him on the plantation among his slaves. It is emphatically the most effectual protection to personal or political liberty with which the human family can be armed.[5]

Recognizing the value of education, blacks sought to enroll their children in Canada West's common schools. Susan Houston and Alison Prentice state that black children, like their white peers, attended schools "when and where they could."[6] Local prejudice of varying intensity resulted in the segregation of black youth. The exclusion of many black children from public schools was not inconsistent with the aims of the elites who promoted centralized education in Canada West. Furthermore, the success of white opposition to integrated schooling reflected the inability of government officials to wholly usurp educational authority from local communities.

The School Act of 1816 provided for the establishment of schools by property owners. These local citizens were permitted to construct a school, hire a teacher, and select trustees; during this period the schools provided basic literacy for their communities. The nature of public education in Canada West was altered throughout the latter half of the nineteenth century by elite Upper Canadians who sought to wrest educational authority from local communities. These elites were not concerned with economic or social mobility for the lower classes; instead, they sought to inculcate the attitudes and values that would respect their power and authority to rule. Bruce Curtis contends that these elite school promoters "consistently stressed both the necessity and beauty of class differences and of the social subordination of women."[7] It is not unreasonable to suggest that education reformers seeking to maintain class divisions in the white community would also have preferred Canada West's black community to maintain its inferior status.

The creation of the office of the superintendent of schools, legislated in the School Act of 1841, launched the beginning of centralized education in Canada West. School acts introduced between 1843 and 1871 resulted in a significant increase in the number of public schools and a serious erosion of local control over schooling. The educational bureaucracy expanded its power through increased regulation and the appointment of regional and central education officials. Whereas the pace of bureaucracy was rapid in Canada West, the actual authority of education officials to implement school policy emerged more slowly. For example, the School Act of 1841 provided for the superintendent of education to inspect common schools, manage the provincial school funds and distribute funds to district councils, and create and publicize plans to improve the education system. It did not, however, legislate power to enforce new school policies. Furthermore, the superintendent of education technically had no power to resolve local educational disputes.

In 1844 Egerton Ryerson, a well-known Methodist minister and former principal of Victoria College, accepted the position of superintendent of education of common schools in Canada West. To support policy development and funding responsibilities, this office expanded to include collecting educational data, resolving educational disputes, and discouraging "inappropriate behaviour." Despite the wide range of administrative responsibilities, the superintendent's power to enforce school policy was limited to withholding school funds from uncooperative communities. Egerton Ryerson was passionately committed to the development and expansion of schooling in Canada West. He sought the successful training of youth whose Christian values and developed mind and body would ensure political and moral order. It is likely that Ryerson's commitment to the expansion of Canada West's education system created a reluctance to withhold funding from disobedient school districts; his vision of a vast and regulated school system was dependent on the increase, not decline, of functioning public schools.

Before 1850, whites often used "creative" strategies to deny blacks their legal right to attend common schools; for example, they would gerrymander school districts or declare that local common schools were private. As a last resort, white parents would simply remove their children from the common school, which invariably closed due to the reduction in attendance. In a response to the exclusion of black youth from common schools, several black women established separate schools. In 1851 Mary Bibb opened a school for black children in her home, eventually expanding to a larger building. Similarly, in 1856 Amelia Freeman operated a grammar school for Chatham blacks. Between 1851 and 1853 Mary Ann Shadd, partially under the auspices of the American Missionary Association, operated a school in Windsor and eventually joined Amelia Freeman in the teaching and management of the Chatham Separate School. By providing independent education for black children, these black teachers made a valuable contribution to their communities, but their schools were plagued by financial difficulties. Since black communities were often small and relatively poor, funding was meagre. Enrolments varied and school grants, which were based on attendance, suffered as a result.[8]

Although much of black education in Canada West took place in separate schools, integrated schooling was accepted in some regions. In the late 1830s white children attended the renowned "black" school in Brantford. Similarly, the excellent reputation of the Buxton school, in the black settlement of Kent County, as well as the Church of England's Mission School, founded in London in 1854, attracted both black and white students. Even though the residents in larger, more socially heterogeneous communities such as Toronto and Hamilton were not wholly committed to racial integration, these urban centres did have some integrated schools. Prentice and Houston suggest that the central administration of these commons schools, combined with teachers, trustees, and politicians who were committed to racial integration, were important components that permitted and supported integrated schooling.[9]

The voices of individuals who did not gain access to public schools are difficult for the historian to detect. Fortunately, letters written to education officials between 1840 and 1860 provide some indication of the history of black access to education. These letters articulate parents' tenacity and commitment to public education and illuminate the opposition mounted by their prejudiced white neighbours. Despite laws that granted equal citizenship, racism was a component that circumscribed black life in Canada West.

One of the earliest available records of the black struggle for access to education was a petition to Governor General Charles Metcalfe from Hamilton's community. In a letter dated 15 October 1843, these parents protested that although they paid taxes, their children were denied access to local common schools. They had emigrated to Canada to escape racism in the United States believing that "there was not a man to be known by his colour under the British flag." Yet they encountered verbal and physical abuse from their white neighbours. The local police board, whose members were also the public school trustees, refused to protect their access to education. The letter concludes apologetically: "[We are] sorry to annoy you by allowing this thing, but we are grieved much, we are imposed on much, and if it please your excellency to attend to this grievance."[10]

Charles Metcalfe's office responded immediately to this petition. On 19 October 1843, it sought additional information from George Tiffany, president of the Hamilton Board of Police, about the number of black children in Hamilton, the attitudes of whites toward blacks attending the public schools, and requested a summary of police action concerning black education. Tiffany's response confirmed that racism was prevalent in the Hamilton community. He concluded that the Board of Trustees should not yield to prejudice, but "should enforce the law without distinction of colour ... a firm stand will eventually destroy prejudice."[11] It appears that these board officials chose to ignore the plight of their black neighbours until queries from Metcalfe's office prompted them to reverse their discriminatory enrolment practices. As a result of their parents' petition, black children gained access to Hamilton's common schools.

Similar circumstances existed in Amherstburg in 1846, but the outcome here was not so favourable. The Reverend Isaac Rice, a white Presbyterian missionary, wrote a letter on behalf of the black citizens of Amherstburg on 23 January 1846. Addressed to the Reverend Alexander McNab, the former acting superintendent of education, the letter complained that black children were barred from the common school by prejudiced whites. These white residents stated that, rather than send their children "to school with niggers, they will cut their children's heads off and throw them in the road side ditch." The letter asserted that Amherstburg's black students, children of tax-paying parents, deserved access to the public school. Nonetheless, the school trustees and white residents falsely claimed that the school was private and barred black students. The white teacher's response to black children was to "turn them out doors."[12]

Egerton Ryerson responded promptly to the concerns of the Amherstburg residents. Before replying, he sought additional information from Robert Peden, Amherstburg's former education superintendent. In a letter of 23 February 1846 Robert Peden concurred with the black residents' assessment of their exclusion from educational opportunities. Peden had attempted unsuccessfully to assuage these black parents by creating a separate school, but they had adamantly rejected segregated education.[13]

Ryerson's response to Amherstburg's black community was sympathetic: "the exclusion of your children from the school was at variance with the letter and spirit of the law, and the ground of exclusion is at variance with the principles and spirit of British institutions, which deprive no human beings of any benefit which they can confer on account of the colour of their skin." Unfortunately the affirmation of black citizens' rights as British citizens was the extent of Ryerson's assistance. He acknowledged the recent election of Amherstburg school trustees and concluded that he "trusts that a sufficient remedy will be provided against the recurrence of the inquiries [sic] of which you complain."[14]

Although Egerton Ryerson's written response to the residents of Hamilton and Amherstburg was of little tangible use, he was not wholly insincere in the sympathy that he expressed. Ryerson was committed to educational opportunities for all children, but he was unwilling to jeopardize his burgeoning universal common school program by directly confronting racist opponents to integrated schooling. Instead he opted for an indirect resolution. Recognizing the possible destabilizing effects of attempting to compel local whites to accept integrated schooling, Egerton Ryerson chose to push for legislation aimed at ensuring that all black children had educational opportunities. The School Act of 1850 included a provision for the creation of separate schools for blacks which would permit any group of five black families to ask local trustees to establish a school for their children. Theoretically, this legislation was to provide an option for black parents seeking education for their children, and it was in fact used by some black communities. But racist whites also used to establish separate schools for blacks who did not want segregated education. In the 1859 School Act, Egerton Ryerson encouraged more active separation by legislating that any "12 or more heads of families, Protestant or Negro, could open their own institutions and receive apportionments from the common school fund."[15] Again, this provision was problematic because white school supporters interpreted it as a legitimate way of barring black youth from local common schools and forcing them to establish their own schools. As a result, many black children were excluded from local common schools, and those who did not have access to separate schools received no education at all.

The School Act of 1850 received mixed reviews from Canada West's black residents. Despite the misuse of the separate school provision by some white school supporters, this legislation was welcomed in several black communities. Separate schools were established in Amherstburg, Chatham, Colchester, and Windsor and these parents embraced the opportunity for their children to learn on their own terms protected from prejudice.[16] Other blacks were passionately opposed to this legislation because it often prevented access to a superior common school, and they believed that such segregation encouraged racism. In the March 1857 edition of the *Provincial Freeman*, black editor H. F. Douglas condemned religious and educational segregation: "Separate schools and churches are nuisances that should be abated as soon as possible, they are dark and hateful relics of Yankee Negrophobia." It is difficult for the historian to determine whether the overall effect of the 1850 School Act was favourable or detrimental to black children. Clearly, the existence of separate schooling remained a contentious issue in Canada West's black community. Nonetheless, it is probable that black advocates, on both sides of the debate, were governed by a belief in the value of education and a commitment to uplifting the black race.

On 12 December 1851, black residents of Simcoe questioned the intent of the 1850 School Act. The community petitioned Egerton Ryerson because their children were denied access to the local common schools. Their letter stated that school trustees and teachers excluded black students even though their parents paid municipal taxes. These parents had "no desire for separate schools" and requested Ryerson's assistance since they had attempted by "every possible means" to gain access to the public schools. They were particularly distressed because their poverty eliminated the prospect of private tutoring: "We are poor and can't provide education for our kids." Aware of the provision for separate schools, the Simcoe residents requested a specific interpretation of the law: did they have the right to attend the public schools with their white neighbours?[17]

Again, Ryerson's response expressed his dismay and sympathy for the Simcoe residents: "I deeply grieve the painful circumstances which you state." He cited the 1850 act to prove that black children enjoyed the same rights and privileges as their white peers unless their parents chose separate schooling. If black parents did not establish separate schools they "have the same right of access for their children as the parent of any other children residing in the section." He advised the Simcoe parents to pursue legal action. He suggested they should sue the school trustees for denying their children the right to education. Egerton Ryerson's final remarks compassionately reaffirmed Simcoe blacks' rights and privileges as British citizens, declaring that it was a "deplorable calamity to be denied access to education ... more especially for those who are seeking it ... who have been greatly wronged and oppressed in a neighbouring country and who are assured of all the rights and privileges of British subjects in this country, which ought not be infected with the spirit any more than it is cursed with the curse of slavery."[18]

The battle to gain access to public schools in Canada West continued in Camden Township, Kent County. In November 1852 Dennis Hill, a black resident, wrote to Ryerson asking: "Is it presumptuous to expect my eleven year old be educated with whites?" White residents had denied Hill's son access to the public school for "no crime other than skin a few shades darker." Hill sought Ryerson's advice because he "refused to allow his children to grow up in ignorance." He was particularly angry because he had significant landholdings and paid more taxes than most of his white neighbours. Hill was further incensed by white school trustees who barred local black children yet invited white students from other districts to attend the Camden Common School.

Ryerson's response was again supportive in emphasizing his disgust at yet another case of injustice. "It is mean beyond expression as well as unjust for the Trustees and other supporters of the school to levy and receive taxes from you," he wrote, "for the education of their children and then refuse admission to yours." He again cited the 1850 School Act, highlighting black students' fundamental right to public education unless a separate school had been established for their benefit. Ryerson advised Hill to prosecute for damages.[19]

Letters concerning black access to education were not exclusively written by black parents. The provincial education office received several letters from white school supporters who were frustrated by their black neighbours' determined efforts to gain access to Canada West's common schools. In 1856 James Douglas, the school superintendent of West Flamborough, Wentworth County, sought Ryerson's advice on segregated schooling. In his letter he outlined the ongoing racial conflict that threatened the survival of the local common school. West Flamborough school trustees demanded that their public school teacher physically separate black and white students in the classroom. This action provoked the wrath of a black parent who disrupted classroom proceedings in his attempt to eliminate this segregation. Superintendent Douglas summarized the anti-black sentiment that dominated his township: "old Canadian families are unwilling to allow their children to sit promiscuously with Negroes and Mulattos."[20] James Douglas feared that his school would soon close because white parents would withdraw their children unless black students were relegated to a separate area of the classroom.

Discrimination against black students was also the topic of Samuel Atkinson's letter of 29 December 1856 to Ryerson. This school trustee from Malden, Essex County, explained that a separate school established for black students had fallen into disuse, and black parents were seeking admission to the local common school. Atkinson was firmly opposed to integrated schooling. He stated that "a mixed school with them [blacks] at present cannot be had!" Again, school closure would result if black parents persisted in their efforts to gain access to the public school because white parents would refuse to send their children to the school. Certain that the black residents would continue to "push themselves on us," Atkinson advocated the legitimacy of rejecting blacks from public schools. Ryerson responded immediately and succinctly. "The Trustees," he wrote, "are not required by law to admit into the public school the children of persons, whether Roman Catholic or coloured people for whom a separate school has been established. Should the persons for whom a Separate School has been established not keep open the Separate School they do not thereby acquire a right to send their children to the public school."[21] It is probable that Malden's black children received no education following Ryerson's decision that supported their exclusion from the local common school.

The persistence of black citizens in seeking public education was also a source of aggravation for white residents of the township of Harwich, Kent County. In March 1862, Duncan Campbell, a white school trustee, wrote to Ryerson asserting that blacks did not request separate schools because they rarely possessed the funds to maintain these institutions. As a result of the attendance of eight black students in the local common school, fifty white children had been withdrawn because "the white people are determined that they shall not send their children to any school while the coloured people have the privilege of sending their children." Anger at his inability to relegate blacks to a separate school had led him to resign as a school trustee, a position that he had held for ten years. Harwich school trustees corroborated his testimony, stating that their black neighbours had "never contributed to the support of our school as there is not one of them who owns a single foot of land." Legally unable to exclude blacks from the classroom, the Harwich trustees proposed to the construction of a connecting classroom in order to segregate black and white students.[22]

The struggle to gain access to common schools was also seen in Dresden, Kent County. In January 1852 William Newman informed Ryerson, on the behalf of his black neighbours, that he needed clarification of the 1850 Common Schools Act. These black citizens frankly inquired if "the spirit of the law was to aid Blacks or the prejudice against colour?"[23] As Dresden's black children were denied access to the common school, they were forced to attend a separate school seven miles away. Exasperated by the inequity of contributing taxes towards the Dresden Common School, these citizens asked whether "the law was intended to give blacks the same rights as whites?"

An incident in Windsor showed that although Egerton Ryerson was committed to the education of black children, he was resigned to the racism that relegated blacks to separate schools. In February 1859, Clayborn Harris wrote to a barrister, William Horton, on behalf of the blacks in Windsor who sought legal assistance to enable their children to attend the local common school. Confident in their rights and privileges as British subjects, their letter asked: "Shall the Trustees use government money to support a prejudice of one class of Her Majesty's subjects against another?"[24]

All levels of Windsor's educational hierarchy had united to exclude black students from the public school. The local school administration refused to teach or admit these students. The regional superintendent of education stated that he was subordinate to the trustees and "consequently he, too, must reject Black students." These white officials provided blacks with a separate school, described as a "16 by 24 feet coop," in order to satisfy their black neighbours' desire for education. Windsor blacks were adamantly opposed to separate education. They believed that segregated schooling provided inferior education and thus defied British principles of equity and justice. The "idea of us asking for a separate school when it will debar us from all the higher branches of literature," Clayborn Harris wrote, "would be like cutting off our noses to spite our faces ... We as a people feel to love British Law and will ever defend it, but we shall equally stand up for all the rights that the law provides for us, otherwise we would be unworthy of the rights that we are guaranteed." Harris concluded his letter to Horton by suggesting that Superintendent Ryerson might provide some valuable assistance. The postscript remarked that black residents of Sandwich encountered similar injustices. Their children were barred from the local common school and forced to attend a separate school four miles from their homes.

In addition to retaining William Horton, the black residents of Windsor wrote to Egerton Ryerson themselves. These parents were willing to abide by the laws of their new homeland, but were angered by the "use of the general Government as a means of fostering for a moment that hydra-headed monster [prejudice] at the cost of any class either on account of complexion or religion." Their letter addressed the fundamental legislative obstacle encountered by blacks pursuing public education after 1850: "Have they [school trustees] power to decide without our request according to Section 19 that the coloured children shall go in a separate school?" William Horton also wrote to Ryerson on behalf of his clients. He stated that he had advised Windsor's black parents to seek separate education, but that they were either unwilling or unable to accept his suggestion. Unable to advance an alternative, Horton requested Ryerson's advice.[25]

Ryerson came to the point quickly in replying that if no separate school had been established, black children had the right to attend the local common school. It seems that an increased awareness of the strength of local racism led Ryerson to qualify his view: "If however public feeling is very strongly expressed against such a course it may be expedient with the consent of the parties concerned to establish a Separate School under the section quoted by you [section 19], but it is very undesirable that such a prejudice be sustained."[26] In 1862 a separate schoolhouse was constructed for Windsor's black community. Defeated in their attempt to gain access to the local common school, these black parents probably resigned themselves to segregated education.

Petitioning Superintendent Ryerson was clearly not an effective strategy for black parents seeking integrated education. Although Ryerson supported principles of equity and justice for blacks, he reluctantly concluded that "the prejudice and feelings of people are stronger than the law."[27] Perhaps it was the recognition of the education system's inability to overcome white racism that prompted several black parents to pursue legal action. Between 1855 and 1864 four cases concerning black access to public education were resolved in Canada West's civil courts. The justices presiding over these legal disputes acknowledged the prejudice that restricted black children's education. Nonetheless, they were firmly committed to the education of black youth, either through integrated or segregated schooling.

The first case occurred in 1855 when a black man named Washington prosecuted the school trustees of Charlotteville. The plaintiff's son, Solomon Washington, was barred from the local common school, yet there was no separate school in the district. Previously, this child had attended the common school and his father had been assessed and billed for school tax. Mr. Washington continued to pay school taxes despite his son's exclusion from the school. The Charlotteville school trustees defended their actions by stating that Solomon Washington had exhibited poor behaviour when he attended the school. In 1850 two of the school trustees had altered the boundaries of the school district so as to exclude Washington's fifty acres of land, and had instructed the local school teacher to bar Solomon Washington because his attendance promoted conflict and the potential dissolution of the school. These trustees used the new school boundaries to legitimize their expulsion of the black student from the school.

John Beverley Robinson, the chief justice of Upper Canada from 1830 to 1862, presided over this case. Robinson's ruling favoured Washington. He declared the case to be a clear example of gerrymandering. He was particularly concerned that, due to the lack of a local separate school, Solomon Washington had been denied access to public education. Robinson's concluding comments acknowledged that the formation of the School Act of 1850 was predicated on an acceptance of racism, but he believed that prejudice should not wholly deny black children their right to education. "The legislation," he found, "does seem to have meant, though reluctantly, to give way so far to any prejudice that may exist in the minds of white inhabitants as to allow the establishment of separate schools for the coloured people, if thought expedient, but not to shut them out from the only public schools that do exist, by leaving it discretionary in the school trustees to deny them arbitrarily, when they have no other school to go to."[28]

Washington's legal triumph over the Charlotteville school trustees was financially debilitating. The defendants possessed no property that could be sold and Washington was forced to sell his farm to pay for legal expenses. *Washington v. Trustees of Charlotteville* established a precedent rendering gerrymandering of school districts illegal and unacceptable, especially if there was no proximate separate school.[29] The issue of segregated education surfaced again in *Dennis Hill v. The School Trustees of Camden and Zone*. Failing in his attempt to elicit a solution from Ryerson in 1852, Dennis Hill resorted to legal action in 1855. On several occasions he had requested permission to send his two sons to the local common school. The school trustees, both individually and collectively, had refused to admit Hill's sons because they were black. Dennis Hill was particularly distressed because there was no proximate separate school and his children received no public education.

Contrary to Dennis Hill's testimony, the school trustees of Camden alleged that a separate school, located at the British American Institute, had been established for the exclusive benefit of black residents under a bylaw passed in 1850. One of the defendants explicitly stated that the establishment of the separate school was a direct response to the prejudice displayed by white residents.

Chief Justice Robinson's decision favoured the Camden school trustees. He concluded that the "legislature did not intend at that time that separate schools should be resorted to or not according to the choice of the persons in whose behalf they have been established, by which I understand not only applicants of the school, but those individuals belonging to the class of persons in whose behalf they have been established." In addition to ruling that black children must attend separate schools in their district, Robinson identified the prejudice that supported segregated schooling:

> We are of the opinion that separate schools for coloured people were authorized, as the defendants have suggested, out of deference to the prejudice of the white population,

prejudices which the Legislature evidently, from the language they used, disapproved of and regretted and which arise, perhaps not so much from the mere difference of colour, as from the apprehension that the coloured people, many of whom have lately escaped from a state of slavery, may be, in respect to morals and habits, unfortunately worse trained that the white children in general, and that their children might suffer from the effect of the example.[30]

Robinson's ruling suggests that white racism fuelled the legislation for separate schools. His theory that white prejudice arises not from race but from substandard morals and behaviour exhibited by blacks may have some validity. Certainly, life in Canada West must have been considerably different from slavery in the American South. Many of the blacks in Canada West, however, had not recently escaped plantation slavery. Several writers, including Mary Ann Shadd, Benjamin Drew, Henry Bibb, and Samuel Gridley Howe, stressed the high moral standards and temperance exhibited by blacks. It is most likely that white prejudice stemmed from a variety of sources, including "mere difference of colour."

In 1861 gerrymandering was again at issue in the case of Simmons and the Corporation of the Township of Chatham. Simmons, a black parent, prosecuted the local school trustees who had established a school section according to the presence of black inhabitants. Chatham's School District No. 1 was vaguely defined and fluctuating because it included "every lot or parcel of land occupied, or which shall be occupied by any coloured person in front of the said township." By establishing a separate school in this manner, Chatham school trustees compelled all black residents to attend this school regardless of their proximity to the school. Their exclusionary objectives were addressed in Chief Justice Robinson's ruling. Identifying the trustees' attempt to deny all blacks access to local common schools, Robinson quashed the bylaw responsible for School District No. 1. He concluded that Chatham's school districts were "not intelligibly confined, ... uncertain in nature and do not give the school section any limits that can be said to [be] ascertained or known at any point in time."[31]

In 1864, George Stewart, of Sandwich, Essex County, successfully prosecuted local school trustees for refusing to admit his daughter Lively to the local common school. This black parent requested permission to send his child to the common school on several occasions, but his requests were rejected by school trustees because "he and his daughter were coloured people." Despite Lively's exclusion from the school, George Stewart regularly paid school taxes. The Sandwich East school trustees attempted to justify Lively Stewart's exclusion from school by stating that a separate school had been established at the request of local blacks. The trustees also alleged that George Stewart had not been taxed to support the common school. Although a separate school had been established by the Refugee Home Society, financial difficulties had forced its closure in 1861.

Chief Justice William Draper's ruling favouring Stewart was predicated on his belief in the immutability of black children's right to receive public education. He concluded that "coloured people are not to be excluded from the ordinary common schools if there be no separate school established and in operation for their use. The creation of a separate school suspends but does not annul those privileges [conferred by the common school act], and when the separate school ceases to exist the rights revive." Draper awarded Lively Stewart the right to attend the Sandwich East common school, but his judgment recognized the prejudice that motivated the school trustees. "We do not question the sincerity of those who state their apprehension of the consequences of allowing coloured children to enter the common schools," his judgment read, "but this is an argument against the law itself, if it can have any weight. The law does give such a right, subject to certain defined exceptions. The existence of these exceptions is not proved in this case."[32]

Canada West's black community continued to seek access to public schools until the outbreak of the American Civil War. The war launched a massive exodus of blacks back to their homeland. By 1865 approximately three quarters of Canada West's black community had returned to the United States.[33] A desire to renew family ties and friendships, as well as to participate in the civil war and reconstruction, are plausible explanations for their departure. However, white racism in Canada was also a catalyst as William Henry Bradley, a black Dresden resident, accurately and succinctly summarized:

> There is a great deal of prejudice here. Statements have been made that coloured people wished for separate schools;

some did ask for them and they have been established, although many coloured people have prayed against them as an infringement of their rights. Still we have more freedom here than in the United States, as far as the government guarantees ... There are many respectable coloured people moving in, but I have not much hope of a better state of things. Public sentiment will move a mountain of laws.[34]

The history of black education in mid-nineteenth-century Canada West establishes the presence of racism in the formation of Ontario's public education system. Although unpalatable to modern sensibilities, the introduction of segregated education in Canada West seems to have been a reasonable response to blacks who sought educational opportunities for their children and racist whites who opposed integrated schooling. Separate schools gradually fell into disuse during the 1890s, but the 1859 Separate School Act remained until 1964. Nonetheless, even today black parents struggle against the more subtle racism in academic curricula and the assessment of student ability. It is likely that the tradition of active concern for educational rights, initiated by black parents in the mid-nineteenth century and currently exhibited by blacks, will continue to influence the development of Ontario's education system.

NOTES

I am indebted to Professor Ian Radforth and *Ontario History* for their faith and invaluable criticism. Many thanks to Guy and my family for providing constructive criticism and encouragement throughout the evolution of this manuscript.

1. Quoted in Daniel Hill, *The Freedom Seekers: Blacks in Early Canada* (Agincourt: The Book Society of Canada Limited, 1981), 25.
2. Robin Winks, *The Blacks in Canada* (Montreal: McGill-Queen's University Press, 1980), 142–44. James Walker, *The History of Blacks in Canada* (Quebec: Government Publications, 1980), 55. Alison Prentice and Susan Houston, *Schooling and Scholars in Nineteenth-Century Ontario* (Toronto: University of Toronto Press, 1988), 298.
3. Winks, *Blacks in Canada* (see note 2), 144, 246.

4. Jason Silverman and Donna Gillie, "Pursuit of Knowledge under Difficulties: Education and the Fugitive Slave in Canada," *Ontario History* 74 (1982), 95. See also Donald G. Simpson, "Negroes in Ontario from Early Times to 1870" (Ph.D. diss., University of Western Ontario, 1971), 26–29.
5. "Address to the Coloured Inhabitants of North America," in *The Black Abolitionist Papers*, Volume II, *1830–1865*, ed. Peter C. Ripley, (Chapel Hill and London: The University of North Carolina Press, 1986), 173.
6. Prentice and Houston, *Schooling and Scholars* (see note 2), 299.
7. Bruce Curtis, *Building the Educational State: Canada West, 1836–1871* (London: The Falmer Press, 1988), 13–15. See also 54–56, 102, 115.
8. Prentice and Houston, *Schooling and Scholars* (see note 2), 299. See Afua Cooper, "Black Women and Work in Nineteenth Century Canada West: Black Woman Teacher Mary Bibb," in *We're Rooted Here and They Can't Pull Us Up*, ed. Peggy Bristow, (Toronto: University of Toronto Press, 1994), 144, 155, and Walker, *Blacks in Canada* (see note 2), 65.
9. Prentice and Houston, *Schooling and Scholars* (see note 2), 301.
10. Public Archives of Ontario, Incoming General Correspondence 1842–1871 [hereafter RG2 C6C], petition, People of Hamilton to Charles Metcalf, 15 October 1843.
11. Public Archives of Ontario, Outgoing General Correspondence 1842–1860 [hereafter RG2 C1], Robert Murray to George Tiffany, 19 October 1843. RG2 C6C, George Tiffany to Robert Murray, 9 November 1843. Silverman and Gillie, "Pursuit of Knowledge," 99.
12. RG2 C6C (see note 10), Isaac Rice to Reverend Alexander McNab, 23 January 1846.
13. RG2 C6C (see note 10), Robert Peden to Egerton Ryerson, 23 February 1846.
14. RG2 C1 (see note 11), Egerton Ryerson to Isaac Rice, 5 March 1846.
15. Winks, *Blacks in Canada* (see note 2), 368, 370. Simpson, "Negroes in Ontario" (see note 4), 498–500. Cooper, "Black Woman Teacher" (see note 8), 148.
16. Walker, *Blacks in Canada* (see note 2), 61.
17. RG2 C6C (see note 10), Coloured Inhabitants of Simcoe County to Egerton Ryerson, 12 December 1851.
18. RG2 C1 (see note 11), Egerton Ryerson to R. Henderson, 17 December 1851.

19. RG2 C6C (see note 10), Dennis Hill to Egerton Ryerson, 22 November 1852. RG2 C1 (see note 11), Egerton Ryerson to Dennis Hill, 30 November 1852.
20. RG2 C6C (see note 10), James Douglas to Egerton Ryerson, 3 February 1856.
21. Ibid. (see note 10), Samuel Atkinson to Egerton Ryerson, 29 December 1856. RG2 C1 (see note 11), Egerton Ryerson to Samuel Atkinson, 29 January 1857.
22. RG2 C6C (see note 10), Duncan Campbell to Egerton Ryerson, 14 March 1862; Harwich School Trustees to Egerton Ryerson, 17 March 1862.
23. Ibid. (see note 10), William Newman to Egerton Ryerson, 13 January 1852.
24. Ibid. (see note 10), Clayborn Harris to William Horton, 15 February 1859.
25. Ibid. (see note 10), Committee for the Coloured People of Windsor to Egerton Ryerson, 2 March 1859; William Horton to Egerton Ryerson, 16 February 1859.
26. RG2 C1 (see note 11), Egerton Ryerson to William Horton, 21 February 1859. Silverman and Gillie, "Pursuit of Knowledge" (see note 4) 103.
27. Quoted in Winks, *Blacks in Canada* (see note 2), 112.
28. Report of the Cases Decided in the Court of Queen's Bench, Vol. 11 (Toronto: Harry Rowswell, 1854), *Washington v. Charlotteville*, 569–70.
29. Robin Winks, "Negro Education in Ontario and Nova Scotia," *Canadian Historical Review* 50, 175.
30. Court of Queen's Bench, Vol. 11 (see note 28), *Dennis Hill v. The School Trustees of Camden and Zone*, 574, 575–78.
31. Ibid. (see note 28), Vol. 21, *In The Matter of Simmons v. The Corporation of the Township of Chatham*, 75–79.
32. Ibid. (see note 28), Vol. 22, *Re Stewart v. Sandwich East School Trustees*, 636–38.
33. Winks, *Blacks in Canada* (see note 2), 61.
34. William Henry Bradley, in *A North-Side View of Slavery*, ed., Benjamin Drew (New York: John P. Jeweth, 1856), 312.

Chapter Fourteen
American Mariners and the Rites of Manhood, 1830–1870

Margaret S. Creighton

In 1862, the *Golden Cross,* a merchant vessel employed in the bird dung trade to Peru, shipped a female steward. The ship's logbook suggests that this was not a successful placement. On 24 June, the steward addressed the shipmaster in "verry improper" language. When she was sent to her cabin as punishment she threatened the captain with a "mark" that he would "carry to his grave." Furthermore, she said she would "be prepared for him the next time." She was true to her word and in an altercation with the ship's officers on 5 October, she "hove a jug" at the captain's temple (lacerating it) and then left without liberty.[1]

The steward of the *Golden Cross* was that rare employee in American merchant and whaling vessels in the nineteenth century: a woman. A survey of crew lists, ship logs, sailors' diaries, and secondary literature indicates that the female deepwater sailor was nearly a contradiction in terms.[2] This is not to say, however, that women were not present on extended voyages. Not only did some traders and whalers carry passengers, but some sea captains sailed with their spouses. Captains' wives, in fact, went to sea in increasing numbers in the nineteenth century. By one contemporary estimate (1853) nearly twenty per cent of whaling masters carried their wives. Overcoming the reluctance of whaling agents, who sometimes worried that a married couple might interfere with the business objectives of a voyage, these daring women moved themselves, their household furnishings, and sometimes their children into ships' aftercabins.[3]

These women were not welcomed with universal enthusiasm by their shipmates. An examination of seafaring diaries produced by nearly two hundred white American sailors at all levels of the ship's hierarchy suggests that while the shipmaster himself may have enjoyed close (very close) companionship, working seamen frequently regarded the presence of "bluewater" wives with distinct antipathy. "Capt. woman sick and I wished she would dye," complained whaleman Edward Kirwin in 1871. "A disgusting woman," remarked sailor Robert Weir, of a shipmaster's spouse. Marshall Keith echoed these sentiments. "I think you wished me very ill when you told me you were glad that the Capt. was going to carry his wife," he commented, "for she is a source of trouble."[4]

Two other sailors vented their contempt for masters' wives with remarkable specificity, focusing their indignation on the women's noses. A Mrs. Brown of the *Northern Light* was, according to seaman Lewis Williams, blessed with a striking facial protuberance: "My descriptive powers fail me here and I will say it was a Nose but what a Nose. I shall not proceed any farther with my description for that Nose looms up before me in such magnificent proportions I can see nothing else." Edward Mitchell was not quite so dumbstruck when it came to describing the nose of Elizabeth Harriman, his shipmaster's wife. He even put his contempt into verse: "She walks the deck with majestic grace. With her cherry picker nose all over her face."[5]

Eric Sager recently asked whether or not seafaring was, among other things, an escape from the company of women and from shore-based domestic responsibilities.[6] Certainly this sailor invective suggests some, if not a lot of ambivalence about the presence of women on nineteenth-century deepwater vessels. Examination of other sailor opinions and beliefs, as well as shipboard ritual and behaviours, indicates, however, that the matter is a complicated one. Seafaring diaries tell us that deepwater voyaging was and was not an escape. They indicate that sailors may have fled certain women, but at the same time they moved closer to others. They tell us, in general, as a number of historians of gender have recently argued, that in this period of massive social and economic renegotiation, when gender spaces were increasingly distinct, that male and female cultures intersected and overlapped, and that relationships between women and men were fraught with ambivalence.[7]

Sex-segregation may be one of the most striking aspects of American deepwater sail in the nineteenth century, but it is one of the least examined. Neither historians working from the "top down," who have focused on the experiences and concerns of shipowners or masters, nor historians of the "bottom up," who have centered their attention on the common seaman, have adopted a gender analysis. Social and labour historians, who must be credited with moving maritime studies light-years over the past decade, have considered fraternity at sea, but largely in terms of class relations.[8] It is time, certainly, to approach the maleness of the sailing ship in the same way that we have treated such circumstances as ship autocracy — that is, not as a given or a timeless happenstance, but as a variable social construction. It is time we took a look at the various ways that the sailing voyage made men, and how men *as men* shaped the sailing voyage.[9]

Any examination of the way that gender ideology or behaviour influenced or reflected seafaring will inevitably have to disentangle or at least acknowledge how gender is linked to age, race and class. The hostility that sailors directed at women aboard ship, for instance, was clearly not informed by gender antagonism alone, but was complicated by sailors' resentment of the privilege, power, and wealth of the aftercabin. Shipmaster's wives flaunted their elevated station, sailors claimed, when they ate the ships' provisions, and when they demanded extra work of seamen. Some seafaring women seem to have sought to soften the hardships of shipboard hierarchy by disapproving of their husband's use of punitive violence, but, more often than not in the cases examined here, they underscored their own power and that of their spouse. At the same time they often helped to fragment the solidarity of the forecastle. By selecting favourites among the men before the mast, and by rewarding these "upstanding" sailors with special favours and foods, they challenged forecastle unanimity.[10]

But if captains' wives elicited negative responses from mariners because they seemed to exacerbate class divisions within the sailing ship, they also drew criticism because they challenged, both spatially and socially, notions of women's "proper" place. The sailing spouse, having chosen to abandon her land-based home and her functions within it, seemed to exert an unnatural power at sea. Mariners saw her as the dominant party in the marital relationship, and, by extension, a pretender to the throne of shipboard power. Mrs. Elizabeth Harriman, the woman who allegedly walked the deck "with her cherry picker nose all over her face" was the "Captain of the ship Ivanhoe," a ship that had a "double skipper." Mrs. Hamblin, wife of the master of the *Eliza Adams,* who stayed in bed late, kept officers waiting for their breakfasts, and was prone to childbearing, was also seen as a co-captain. Abram Briggs, the fourth mate who sailed with this woman, asserted that when he sailed with another woman "it will [not] be one that wears the breeches ... God preserve me from that."[11]

There are a number of reasons why sailors might have been particularly sensitive to women who appeared to exert an unseemly degree of control in the aftercabin, but many of them centre around the fact that allegedly powerful women were impediments to men who sought, throughout a voyage, to establish their own power and independence. Most of the foremast hands studied here were, like many deepwater sailors of the period, in their late teens and early twenties,[12] and they looked to the sailing voyage as a means to enhance a mature masculinity. Not only did they speak frequently of aspects of the voyage as a "test" that they might fail or survive, but as a mechanism for pushing them forward in the progress of life. That the King Neptune Ceremony was the centrepiece of ritual activities on deepwater ships points clearly to seafaring as a vehicle for male adulthood. This Equator-crossing ritual, which usually featured a paternal figure who evaluated young boys, counselled them, and then shaved and baptized them, demonstrates the importance of sailing in masculine maturation.[13]

Not surprisingly, the indoctrination of neophyte seamen into adult manhood was a complicated business. As one whaleman remarked, mariners were a "hetregenious mass of incongruity"[14] and they espoused many ideals of masculinity. Many of the diarists surveyed, for instance, looked forward to what the voyage promised them in terms of providership. They hoped for earnings that would help them buy a farm or start a small business on shore, and a number voiced the hope that their wages (or, in the case of whaling, their share of the take) would enable them to attract a wife.

Seafaring not only potentially offered these men the means to an independent and hence "manly" life, it also provided a setting in which men could, with little interruption, practise distinctive social behaviours. Greenhands (first-time sailors) became, under the tutelage of experienced shipmates, adept at smoking, swearing, gambling, and, in sailortown, drinking and having sex with strange women. While such traditionally masculine attributes may not have made these men more appealing to prospective spouses on the home front, they probably made these men more acceptable to members of the same sex. (Men, of course, had to satisfy the gender ideals of both sexes, and in a period when these ideals were sometimes sharply variant, this was no easy task.)[15]

But other sailors had different gender ambitions. Men who described themselves as individuals of "talent and information" (i.e., wealth) hoped to use the voyage to adopt that *sine qua non* of the new business culture: self-discipline. These men, who comprised only about one-fifth of this sample, revelled in the idea that shipboard life involved an ascetic routine, which did not tempt them with opportunities for heterosexual dalliance, intemperance, or gustatory sprees. Anxious to cultivate habits of self-restraint, they found the ship offered them ample opportunities to do so. Indeed, Sylvester Graham, that antebellum guru of abstinence, might well have turned to the American sailing ship as an alternative to his boarding houses. Other reformers recognized as much, for some middle-class social agencies viewed sailing ships as alternatives to reformatories.[16]

To outline two "modes" of masculinity within this mariner population is not to suggest, of course, that these were the only or even the dominant expressions of gender. Research on sailors of different ethnic and national backgrounds, of different races, of different ages and sexual orientations will add necessary complexity to our understanding of the diverse ambitions and aspirations of seamen. Even within this seemingly homogeneous group of white middle-class mariners (the minority described above), for instance, there were several who espoused a Christian manhood, and who viewed seafaring, particularly its dangers, not as means of elevating themselves, but as evidence of God's omnipotence. Other men spoke not only of female attachments but of male romantic friendships, and expressed vehement ardour for their shipmates who, while of widely different social backgrounds, appealed to them as "nature's noblemen."[17]

Seafaring spoke to men of various interests and masculine inclinations, then, and their differing ambitions sometimes clashed. Within the forecastle, for instance, veteran seamen sought to enforce a behavioural consensus. Drawing on the power of social ridicule, old salts (rarely older than twenty-five years of age) tried to shape neophyte seamen into tough-minded men who could sever sentimental attachments to women at home, particularly family members — sisters, mothers, and grandmothers. Acceptance in the forecastle was contingent upon this shift of allegiance from home to ship, and upon the adoption of a veneer of steely fortitude. It was not always an easy transition for greenhands to make. A New Hampshire boy named Orson Shattuck, for example, found himself in serious trouble when he became watery-eyed over the thought of home and his sisters. He got a grip on himself, though. "I must stop this," he insisted, "for I can hardly hide the tears from the rough men around me." A sailor named Smith aboard the *Sunbeam* in 1868 was less stoic, and he suffered for it. "His love for his Grandmother is very strong," explained a shipmate, " ... a few days since he was discovered sitting upon his chest bathed in tears, weeping excessively over a bed quilt which he informed his shipmates was the gift of his Grandmother, who was upwards of 90 years of age and in all probability he would never see again. A strong proof of filial affection, a commodity not very troublesome to sailors as a general thing." For this emotional display, Smith was subject to his shipmates' jeers, and was labelled the "ship's fool."[18]

The old salts who called on new sailors to suppress tears also encouraged them to distance themselves from their main sources of empathetic concern — their mothers. Writer-sailor Charles Nordhoff described greenhands as men who "cut loose from [their] mammy's apron strings." Seaman George Blanchard echoed those sentiments. As his ship struggled with a fierce gale in the South Atlantic, he congratulated himself on his ability to brave the world on his own. "The poor devils on shore," he remarked, "who cannot muster courage enough to leave their Mammas for a week have all my pity."[19]

These sailors were not the only men in the mid-nineteenth century, of course, who worked to sever maternal attachments. Even though many "poor devils" on shore did not go to sea, this does not necessarily mean that they did not struggle with filial affection. Anthony Rotundo, in a recent study of nineteenth-century middle-class "boy culture," claims that one of the salient features of this youthful culture was the ridicule that was directed at young men who appeared to be attached to their mothers. "The worst fate a youngster could suffer at the hands of his peers," he notes, "was to be labeled a 'Mama's boy.'" At the same time, boys taught youngsters "to control their inner world of emotions," and boys fearful of being taunted as crybabies learned to "overcome pain, fear, and the need for emotional comfort."[20]

Sailing ships might be seen as floating extensions of boy culture, with some differences. There is little evidence in these diaries to suggest that the veteran seamen who initiated neophyte sailors into a tear-less, mother-less world were trying to prepare these men for the rigors of commercial rivalries (as Rotundo suggests is the ultimate goal of the middle-class, land-based experience). If anything, mariners emphasized fraternity and co-operation over competition, and in day-to-day shipboard prank-playing, they underscored the dangers of self aggrandizing or individualistic behaviour.[21]

Sailors' emphasis on emotional restraint, then, was not meant to encourage social isolation. In further contrast to the "mainland" boys who, according to Rotundo, learned to negotiate between the demands of two different worlds — a female one of co-operation and nurture and a male one of competition and conflict — sailors were called on to forfeit the female world of nurture for the *male* world of interdependence. Significantly, King Neptune, the veteran mariner (and foremast hand) who initiated new sailors into a deepwater brotherhood, was also known as Father Neptune. In the ritual process, he gave birth to his sons, he baptized them, and he made sailors promise that they would take care of each other at sea and on shore.[22]

Sailors before the mast who put mutualism into practice would find it eminently useful. All seamen, and Marcus Rediker has made this abundantly clear for the eighteenth-century case, were fully dependent on each other in order to sail a ship safely through a volatile environment. Foremast hands, in particular, found solidarity helpful in challenging shipboard authoritarianism and comforting when those challenges were less than successful.[23]

The emphasis on communalism in the forecastle was not only relevant to demands on men at sea, of course. We know too little about where mariners came from and where they went (most of these native-born sailors did not plan to become permanent sailors), but certainly some entered male occupations or trades where an ethos of community prevailed. Even if they went headlong into the marketplace, it is quite possible that they sought and found a place outside of work for social brotherhood. The proliferation of fraternal organizations at this time —

especially those which secretly espoused nuturance — suggests the degree to which men valued group culture.[24]

The emphasis at sea — particularly in the forecastle — on the all-male family (complete with "procreative" potential) suggests ways that we might consider some of the relationships between women and mariners. Many middle-class women on shore found seafaring troubling in the 1830s and 1840s, and joined social agencies in droves to "assist" and reform sailors. One of the reasons that they did so could be that mariners not only threatened middle-class programs with their flagrantly oppositional behaviours (intemperance, sexual licence, gambling, etc.) but that they also threatened women's benevolence by virtue of *similar* intentions. Women in the anti-Masonic movement at this time, Mary Ann Clawson tells us, were concerned that Masons' claims to moral autonomy through brotherhood co-opted or competed with women's (newly acquired) moral authority through the family. Seaman's reformers did not have to worry about sailors claiming to be custodians of virtue, certainly, but they may well have been disturbed by men who, to some extent, took over "family" caretaking.[25] The confrontation between the sexes that we saw expressed in sailors' gestures of hostility towards shipmasters' wives may have centred around this sort of conflict. Sea captain's wives not only sought to bring class-based programs to the forecastle, but sometimes maternal compassion as well. Sailors who spent a good deal of energy in learning how to take care of themselves may have deemed their ministrations unnecessary.

Deepwater sailing ships, as exclusive domains of working men and as institutions of masculine indoctrination, presented their participants with a peculiar challenge. They were self-contained worlds in which, seemingly, the sexual division of labour was an impossibility. Men who, on the one hand, were called on to divorce themselves from female behaviours, were, on the other, asked to perform those tasks — cleaning, cooking, washing, sewing — that were almost invariably assigned to women on shore.[26] As a first mate named Isaac Baker put the matter: at sea there were no "mosquitoes to molest us, no flies to annoy us, and *no women to wash our dirty clothes.*"[27] A necessary evil, according to Baker, was sadly missing at sea. But how did men protect the sanctity of their masculine mission and at the same time accomplish women's tasks? Men aboard these ships could avoid the taint of women's work if they had the correct credentials — if they were, in other words, white native-born Americans with some spending money.

On the vessels examined here, the job of the captain's housekeeper (the steward) and the work of the ship's cook were often conducted by black men. These were men who had limited access to conventional masculine roles on shore, and who, partly as a consequence, were viewed as marginally masculine by many antebellum whites.[28] Deepwater industries had, in the early national period, offered black men possibilities for regular employment as sailors before the mast, but by the 1850s blacks more commonly served as shipboard "servants." The forecastle, in the words of Jeffrey Bolster, "increasingly became the province of white men." The racial division of labour was an outgrowth, according to Bolster, of rising class stratification at mid-century and accompanying racial discrimination.[29] It also reflected, no doubt, the intensifying prescriptions for a gender division of labour with rigid work roles for women and for men. At sea, the white power structure could "protect" white male sailors from the taint of women's work by assigning service roles to racial minorities who already seemed to violate gender role norms.

Men who were exclusively assigned to housekeeping or homemaking work on shipboard were often distinctive by virtue of their race. Not surprisingly, these men were sometimes delegated separate living space at sea, and were assigned quarters in the ship's steerage, located amidships. Their job mobility within the ship was impressively non-existent. They were not regularly trained in sail handling, boat pulling, or helmsmanship. On some occasions they were required to assist in an all-hands call, but they were not part of watch duty and they slept through the night. Left out of the power politics that ran from the afterdeck to the forecastle, they were, like the women whose work they performed, excluded from the dynamics of government. As steward Charles Benson remarked succinctly in 1862, "I have little to do with a sailor."[31]

While cooks and stewards could not easily move into positions as skilled seamen, or into officers' roles, there were some compensations to these jobs. As several historians have recently pointed out, a galley worker or steward frequently earned higher wages than seamen.[32] Thus, even though a man might perform women's work under sail, he might as a consequence be better equipped to act as a "manly" provider.

Higher wages were not enough compensation to make service work widely attractive, however. Shipmasters who were left with vacant galley jobs on the ships reviewed here did not find many willing applicants, especially among foremast hands. Seaman William Townsend, called in to handle the galley aboard the merchant ship *Imaum*, insisted that it was a "berth which I will throw off as soon as possible." Likewise Henry Davis, after a stint as cook in 1862, laughed bitterly at the idea of repeating the experience: "He [the captain] wants me to go Cook as if I was going Cook again now."[33]

Not only were the men who performed kitchen and housekeeping work physically and professionally ostracized within the ship, they were regularly reminded of their social inferiority through teasing and abuse from the ship's officers. The sources examined here are replete with accounts of particularly harsh disciplinary actions against cooks and stewards. Ships' officers meted out severe physical punishments to cooks for such "crimes" as wasting food, burning meals, and cooking and serving rotten or spoiled food. On one occasion a cook was force-fed a pudding he had prepared for the entire crew because he had scorched it. And in another incident a captain attacked a drunken steward with a hammer and an ax until he was seriously "mutilated."[34]

The aftercabin, of course, did not have a monopoly on antagonism towards stewards and cooks. White forecastle sailors could and frequently did vent hostility on the cook (they had few dealings with the steward). Sailors on the *Lucy Ann* put gunpowder in the cook's stove in 1842, and, claimed journal-keeper John Martin, "play all sorts of tricks on the old cook ..." When that man left the ship, the crew accosted his successor, and according to Martin, the "crew runs all sorts of rigs upon him." On the morning of 7 July 1843, for instance, the cook was told that one of the "coloured men" was having a fit in the forecastle. When he went to see him, "the scuttle was closed & the deck lights were covered over which made it so dark that he could see no one. They that were below commenced whetting their knives & swearing all sorts of oaths that they had him safe & were going to make sea pie of him, the poor Doc was terribly frightened & begged they would not hurt him as he came down with no evil intention." The forecastle lynching squad eventually let him out, but not until he was "covered from head to foot with flour & chalk."[35]

Categorization of the conflicts between cooks and sailors is difficult. To what extent did galley workers take abuse from sailors that was really directed at shipmasters and owners, and emerged from the hardships and sufferings associated with inadequate fare and provisions? To what extent is racial antagonism separable from tensions evolving out of rigid gender role definitions? The line that separated gender from race and class prejudice in these instances was very indistinct, but it does seem that men could be doubly or triply damned. Larkin Turner, a shipmaster's son, was able to accommodate a number of antipathies in this assessment of the steward aboard the brig *Palestine* in 1832: "You must know we here, in our house, have a kitchen girl — Oh! but this said personage is a black man! No matter he answers our purpose ... a red shirted, raged pantalooned, holed-stocking-heeled, laughing shoed, be dirted, black faced rascal ..."[36]

Cooks and stewards were delegated much of the "women's" work that was generated by a ship's company. There remained a number of tasks, though, that were not handled by these men alone. Sailors before the mast did their own sewing and washing, for instance, and they performed housekeeping jobs like washing decks, scrubbing fittings, and sweeping. As we shall see next, mariners approached this female work variously. Some mariners saw it as a kind of amusing curiosity. Other men recast it into men's work, and a large number of sailors "sent it out" to hired servants.

The experience of washing or sewing was enough of a novelty that it offset some of the prejudices against the practice. Francis Moreland aboard the *Sooloo* in 1861 had a "grand wash" with his shipmates. James Haviland, like other sailors, saved his washing until he could stand it no longer, but claimed that he could "do it as quick and as well as any washwoman." Robert Weir was pleased to be able to make himself a patchwork cap, and thought of those at home who were more familiar with such work: "How often do I think of my dear sisters while engaged upon all this kind of work wouldn't they laugh and criticize — but they may yet find out I am not so poor a Knight of the Needle after all."[37]

Sailors who performed domestic work might avoid its female taint, as did Robert Weir, by translating it into bona fide male work. Needlework could, by a stretch of the imagination, be recast into tailoring. (And sailmakers sewed, too, after all). But most seamen were not willing to make this cognitive adjustment and washing in particular did not translate well into a male job. The best solution for the men who could afford to do so, it seems, was to send the work out to be done. Robert Weir hired "Manuel" to wash his clothing. Lewis Williams paid "Antone" a pair of pants to wash his clothes, and Elias Trotter made a bargain with "Valentine Millet (a Colored man) that He should do my washing, mending, & shaving during the whole voyage for 17 dollars."[38]

As these excerpts indicate, racial and ethnic minorities were, again, the most likely men to take on women's traditional work. The gender division of labour was a luxury not all men could afford, and, as on land, it served as a mark of social distinction.[39] The shipmaster, as befitted his elevated station, had his own women or "wife" in the way of the private steward, the cook, and the cabin boy. The crew could only hope that in the future they, too, would have enough money to distance themselves from stigmatized tasks.

Deepwater sailors, in distancing themselves from female relatives and women's work, sought to protect and enhance distinct masculine identities. At the same time, though, many of these men sought to demonstrate convincingly their heterosexual prowess and power, and to this end they needed female partners.[40] Ashore in foreign ports, of course, these men displayed such a potent virility that shock waves went reeling back to the shores of Victorian America. But on shipboard, sailors needed to be more creative in expressing their ability to attract, command, and, to some extent, dismiss the opposite sex. What they did was to bring women as symbol and image into seafaring life and shipboard ritual. Mariners did not diminish their seafaring fraternity or threaten the gender division of labour in doing so, and at the same time they were able to control the appearance of women and manage their own response to social relations between the sexes.

Many of the young men aboard these whaling and merchant ships had left American shores at the height of their courting years, and they entertained thoughts of specific sweethearts whenever they wished. They did not allow sweet and erotic memories to impinge on shipboard commitments, however. Letter-writing was restricted to the dogwatch (off-duty hours) or to Sundays, and a ritual that honoured loved ones at home was similarly timed so that it did not seriously affect the work routine. On Saturday nights, particularly in the aftercabin, mariners set aside time (and alcohol on non-temperance ships) for a toast to "sweethearts and wives."

"Saturday night!" exulted Isaac Baker, "'Wives and Sweethearts!' Well here's to the little ones at home. 'And the big ones too.' 'Aye, and the big ones too.'" John Alden, a passenger aboard the *Albatross* in 1847, enjoyed a whisky punch in toasting the health of sweethearts and wives and asserted that he believed it "is an old established custom to devote Saturday evening to this cause, and although it may in some instances be needful to remind one of his duties to those he left behind him — such is not the case with me."[41]

Alden's remarks point to the tension that existed between a sailor's attachment to his ship and his mates and his commitment to home, and it is echoed in a "Saturday Night" sea song that a sailor recorded in 1843:

> A sailor loves a gallant ship
> And messmates bold and free
> And even welcomes with delight
> Saturday night at sea
>
> One hour each week we'll snatch from care
> As through the world we roam
> And think of dear ones far away
> And all the joys from home.[42]

Men might take the idea of restricting homeward thoughts to one or two hours out of three hundred quite literally. Captain Albert Goodwin, for instance, allowed (forced?) himself once a week to get out daguerreotypes of his wife and family. For a short period of time he paraded them before him and he kissed each one. Then he retired them for the next six days.[43]

Sailors honoured hometown women, then, but they celebrated these individuals in carefully circumscribed ways. They welcomed the generic sort much more readily at sea. As Caroline Moseley has pointed out, sailors' forecastle songs and shanties championed two well-known female types: the easily available [if not costly] sexual partner and the dutiful and constant wife or sweetheart.[44]

Sailors' glorification of loyal women found expression not only in song but in artwork. Scrimshaw was an especially effective medium for the aspirations and anxieties of whalemen, and enterprising sailors made gifts for mothers and sisters, and rewards, no doubt, for special friends who had played their prescribed roles with solitary patience. Seamen were prolific manufacturers of yarn-winders, pie crimpers, hair pins, and workboxes. On these items, and on the ubiquitous sperm whale's tooth, sailors carved scenes that underscored their most fervent prayers: scenes of tearful partings and joyful reunions. At the same time, of course, they celebrated their sexual interests. They carved toothpicks, whistles, and pipe-tampers in the shape of a female leg. They etched and sketched figures of women half clothed.[45]

Sea songs and scrimshaw allowed sailors to indulge their double fantasies of females, and the ship itself, in a peculiar way, was also a medium for sailors' social aspirations. Many vessels in the nineteenth century had female figureheads. On the one hand this wooden statue on the prow of the ship could be a reminder of wife, home, and family. According to folklorist Margaret Baker, captains "hated losing a figurehead through storm or accident," and one master reportedly refused to replace his lost figurehead because of its association with domesticity. 'Do I seem,' exclaimed the offended master,' [like someone] one who would pick up another's cast off figurehead? I'd sooner think of taking up with a new wife!'" Baker also claims that a figurehead on the *Alice Knowles,* which sported "high button boots and country day dress, sturdy, domestic, redolent of apple pie and warm kitchens," was for her crew a "better reminder of home than a portrait." And on the *Princess,* reports Baker, a lovesick crew repeatedly crept forward after dark "to pour their troubles into sympathetic wooden ears."[46]

Captains' and owners' daughters might serve as models for figureheads, and thus sent symbols of domestic middle-class purity to sea. But, as Margaret Baker points out, the wooden figures were often bare-breasted. "It is an ancient nautical belief," she claims, "that a storm will quieten if a woman exposes herself to it *nuda corpore.*"[47] Thus, sailors who consulted the figurehead under the cover of darkness may have visited a sister or a sexually pure sweetheart. Others might have projected onto this inanimate being their fondest wish for a sexual object.

Sailors' double fantasies of women extended onto the ship itself. While no more than a third of the vessels described here carried female names, all of the vessels were firmly feminine in gender. And the feminization and anthropomorphizing of the ship carried well beyond the simple assignation of the pronoun "she." Ships were lively animate things, and caused no little emotion on the part of sailors. John Crimblish was one such affected mariner. The bark *Palestine,* claimed Crimblish, "rides [the waves] with such ease and alacrity as to make me in raptures with her she seems to hold the billows in contempt and mounts them 'like a thing of life.'" Isaac Baker compared his merchant vessel under full sail to a "beautiful belle of a ball room." Even in the absence of wind, he insisted, when her sails were listlessly flapping against the ship's mast "still she resembles woman, lovely woman languishing under the effects of ennui and of course 'en dishabille.'" Baker carried the analogy even further. When the wind blew a gale and the ship "buffets the waves in triumph and scatters the spray around vehemently without respect to persons, still she is a true emblem of the fair sex when hurrying through the labours of a washing day!"[48]

Not surprisingly, sailors tended to see in their vessels the woman they could "own" as property and the woman they could command sexually. The ship, as Isaac Baker pointed out, could be a woman enticingly undressed. Sailors could "ride" her and "witness the motions ... as she plunges and rears her proud head to the sea." They could discuss her "bottom" which might be "so full of barnacles that it takes nearly a gale o' wind to set her going" or which might simply be plump: "The Taskar is the thing to roll/ O ee roll & go/Her bottom's round as any bowl!/ O ho roll & go!"[49]

At the same time the ship could be a sailor's treasured possession. He drew a competitive pride in her "good looks" if she had them, and in her sailing abilities. Augustus Hamblet made explicit what other mariners expressed more tacitly: " ... next to his girl," explained the merchant seaman, "a sailor loves his ship and takes an honest pride in seeing her look neat and trim and never will let any other vessel go ahead of him if he can help it and if they do it puts them (generally) in about as good humour as making a breakfast of vinegar would. But if he beats and goes ahead he is as happy a clam at high tide."[50] In translating the ship into a girl and the barren ocean into a social street, sailors could parade their women past each other, puff themselves up with masculine pride, and compare notes.

Sailors brought generic or objectified women into shipboard culture, I think, for several reasons. By dismissing attachments to particular women ashore (or by formally relegating them to the margins of ship society), they reinforced the fraternity that was necessary for the work of the ship as a whole and, within the forecastle, for political solidarity and power. The process of objectification, though, was relevant not only to these men as sailors, but to them as men who struggled to maintain control over sexual and social partners. Woman in generic form, as the subject of song or art, or as the ship itself, could be molded into whatever the mariner wished. The sexy and available woman could validate his virility and express his freedom from social ties at home. "The sailor is true to his Sal or his Sue," went a capstan shanty, "as long as he's able to keep them in view."[51] And when the Sal or Sue was accessible and attractive, all the more comforting.

The dutiful, faithful woman demonstrated a mariner's attractiveness, too, of course, but more than that she underscored his ability to keep her in tow. Or rather she represented his wish to keep her in tow. In their diaries, sailors speak privately of deep anxieties and doubts about female loyalty. The sailing voyage, they say, could be seriously disempowering. Not only did odious "landsmen" court women away from them while they were away, but women themselves, wives included, were actively unfaithful. Victorian purity was a dim hope for sailors who felt sure that women at home were not only capable of expressing sexuality but switching partners to satisfy their needs. Captain Samuel Braley likened women at home to the roving sailor. "How many poor Sailors," he remarked, "have ... had unfaithfull wives and they none the wiser for their slips, but it is only tit for tat." A mate named Marshall Keith heard the same thing. "I have been listening," noted Keith, "to ... the captain tell how untrue women were to their husbands while they were away. I have come to the Conclusion that there is not one likely woman in Provincetown and he trys to make me think that they Are so in all other places, but he can talk, it will be some time before he makes me believe that my wife Is not true to me."[52]

Most of these seamen were not as confident as Keith, particularly when it came to the loyalty of sweethearts, not wives. A scarcity of letters or a scrap of hometown gossip that made its way round the world to them undermined hopes of constancy. Some unhappy sailors sought to remedy their misery by purchasing commitment. Walter Brooks of the *Gladiator* hoped to "buy" a letter from his shipmates. Ezra Goodnough found a shipmate willing to pay a heavy price for one of his hometown letters: "I sold a letter that I received from a young lady of Salem ... for two heads of tobacco, it being a very scarce article."[53]

Ashore in foreign ports, sailors attempted to rectify the problem of constancy by purchasing loyalty with sex. At least a dozen mariners in this sample mention marrying prostitutes temporarily. They called them their "wives" and they asked for monogamous commitment. Whaleman Ezra Goodnough, who cruised on the Indian Ocean in 1847, explained both the necessity and difficulty of establishing shore commitments. If his vessel did not see whales, he would not have enough money to get his girl in Mahe a new dress. And if he did not get her a new dress, "she will forget me." "You see," he explained, "we can hire the girls in Mahe to remember us, that is more than the girls at home will do."[54]

The cases of sailors who "married" prostitutes necessitates a re-evaluation of a familiar sailor's ditty, offered in this case by first mate Isaac Baker:

> How happy is a sailor's life
> From coast to coast to roam
> In every port to find a wife
> In every land a home.[55]

In addition to regarding this poem as a jab at married sailors who were adulterous or even polygamous, we can also see it as a description of men, most of whom were unattached, who attempted to formalize what could have been a casual relationship. When we ask, then, why these sailors might have objectified women, one of the answers is that they wanted to hold on to them better. Justin Martin, a veteran of both merchant sail and whaling, put the matter succinctly in a letter to his brother. "Find a good woman," he urged, and "cage her up."[56]

Caging women up meant keeping them, of course, but it also meant restraining them. Women were an ascending power in the nineteenth century, not only in the home, but through church and social organizations, in the world at large.[57] Sailors were all too well aware of the fact that some mothers and wives, while they might be prohibited or discouraged from sailing, did not wait passively at the dock or, hanky in hand, pace a widow's walk. Shipmasters' wives, as we know well by now, occasionally chose to go to sea with their husbands, and many of them made concerted efforts to reshape the social behaviour of sailors to their liking.[58] Some mariner mothers persistently followed their sons to the far corners of the world with their letters and anxiously sought to exert a distant maternal influence over their moral and physical well-being. The mother of Willie Reed, a young merchant seaman from Boston, pursued her son by mail at every port of call in 1862. Did he, she wondered, remember to wear his wool socks? Had he placed flannels next to his bowels to prevent diarrhea? Had he spilled his writing ink? Had it stained his clothing? Mostly, though, she "trembled" at the influences around him. She cautioned him against drinking, chewing tobacco, and using "words you may have cause to be sorry for." And as for sailortown, she pleaded with him not to go to a "house — or place of amusement." She asked him to bear in mind one question as he encountered new and strange opportunities: "Would Mother be willing?"[59]

Through ritual, too, wives and sweethearts challenged sailors to acknowledge them and their concerns. Even though their presence at sea was circumscribed by such carefully timed events as the "Saturday Night" toast, they inserted themselves into their men's consciousness with their own celebration: the ritual of the Home Cake.

Home Cakes were tasty concoctions that women at home sent aboard ship upon departure. They were well preserved with alcohol — so much so, in fact, that to open one could be a dangerous enterprise. Marshall Keith's Home Cake, made by Sarah Pope, his betrothed, was so explosive by the time he opened it five months after sailing that he "nocked [it] higher than a kite." It was "in good order," though, and he relished it.[60]

Marshall Keith's cake had been made specifically for him to honour his financée's birthday. Thus this woman was able to carry herself along with Keith and to direct his thoughts homeward. George Bowman, a married second mate on the *Albion,* was also reminded of his woman at home because she had sent with him a box of cake for their anniversary. "It caused," said Bowman, "my mind to wander back to her." Captain Edmund Jenings opened a Home Cake on Thanksgiving day, and the process, plus the comparison of his present circumstances with the imagined happiness of the domestic holiday, sent him into a fit of despondency: "This is your thanksgiving Day with you how different it is with us a gale of wind, Our Bark tossed about. I cut Aunt Dyers Cake, and gave it to the Steward and then went into my room and had a good crying spell. I wondered if they missed my place at the Table. Or if [they] thought of me. I suppose Some thinks of me on all such occasions. May God bless and keep you all."[61]

Women at home made their presence felt beyond gustatory nostalgia, of course. Middle-class women, even when they could not go to sea themselves, worked energetically to reform the sailing ship by domesticating it. As enthusiastic participants in sailor reform societies, they made tireless efforts to improve the physical conditions of seafaring life and to "uplift" seamen morally. By means of shipowners and shipmasters sympathetic to their causes, they sent oceanward social programs which discouraged swearing, gambling, dancing, and sabbath-breaking at sea. Seaman's reform agencies also sought to establish "Homes" in port and encouraged sailors to take cover in them from the hustlers of sailortown. The American Seaman's Friend Society, the largest of these organizations, made repeated claims in the 1840s that their agency was slowly succeeding in "civilizing" American sailing ships and they had brought about "marvellous" changes among mariners.[62]

The American Seaman's Friend Society was overly optimistic, for, ultimately, it never attracted the numbers of sailors it sought, and other organizations faced similar problems.[63] Seamen may not have taken kindly to the attempted reform of the sailing ship for reasons having to do with class interests, of course, (Judith Fingard went into that subject some time ago),[64] but also because, as we have seen, the feminization of sail threatened the gender objectives of seamen. Some ships' officers and other "older" veterans may also have been hostile to the attempted domestication of the ship because (and here we come full circle to Eric Sager's question about "escape") they may have been reluctant to forfeit a place of masculine refuge. Seafaring represented, for many men, the means of owning a home with a wife and children, but it also represented a way to avoid living there.

Consider the case of a sea captain named Stetson, for instance. According to a foremast hand in 1844, Stetson was worth $100,000 "in cold cash," (implying, in other words, that Stetson had no economic reason to be at sea). When this shipmaster first got home from a voyage, he "always made up his mind not to go to sea anymore" and he "would take his seat in the chimney corner and smoke his pipe." After a while, though, "his return got to be an old story in the house," and "the women began to shove him from one corner to another and he could not stand it, so he was obliged to come away."[65]

First Mate Ambrose Bates found himself in similar difficulties. While not as explicit as Stetson about power struggles between the sexes, he was not able to adjust himself to living with his wife in his "happy home." Although he yearned for the comforts of the domestic circle, at the same time he felt he could not relinquish the satisfactions of seafaring. He translated his double-edged dilemma into verse:

> It was morning and I longed for evening
> It was evening and I longed for home
> I was at home and I longed for the sea
> Now whire shall I fly to amuse myself
> But alas [I] know of no place excepting
> I could combind Land and sea together.[66]

Ambrose Bates, who solved his conundrum in part by finding himself a "home on the rolling deep" was deeply troubled by his persistent sailing. "In vain I have sought a place upon the globe that I might settle down in quiet contentment," he wrote. "Although I have been blessed with all the heart could ask still as it seems almost against my will I find myself volunteerly flying from all I love on earth."[67] Bates saw himself as singularly divided. but he was certainly not alone. Historians date the origins of companionate marriage at a later period, and suggest that in the mid-1800s men and women, even after marriage, played minor roles in each others' physical and emotional lives. They cite examples of men who joined fraternal orders in droves, who met together by the hundreds of thousands on the battlefields in Mexico and the American South, and who went together to California and to the mining country of the West.[68] Men who would never know the rigors of deepwater life took the same tack Ambrose Bates had. On dry land, they, too, found ships and fellow sailors, and tests of physical courage, and like him, they carried on the joint task of loving women but living in worlds without them.

NOTES

1. Diary of first mate, *Golden Cross*, 24 June 1862; 5 October 1862, Shipping Logbook #1862G2, Manuscript Collections, Essex Institute, Salem, Massachusetts, hereafter cited as EI.
2. This survey includes the examination of over 3,200 crew lists from New London, Connecticut, Salem, Massachusetts, and New York City from 1818–1878, as well as close study of over 200 ship logs and diaries produced on deepwater vessels from the northeastern United States. Women disguised as men, of course, would have been overlooked in this assessment.
3. The numerical estimate of sailing spouses appears in the "Whalemen's Shipping List and Merchants' Transcript," 1 February 1853. On the matter of whaling wives and agents' objections see Lisa Norling, "Contrary Dependencies: Whaling Agents and Whalemen's Families 1830–1870," *The Log of Mystic Seaport* 42 (spring 1990): 10. The subject is also discussed more generally in Joan Druett, "More Decency and Order: Women and Whalemen in the Pacific," *The Log of Mystic Seaport* 39 (summer 1987): 67.
4. Diary of Edward Kirwin, *William Gifford,* 16 November 1871, The Kendall Whaling Museum, Sharon, Massachusetts, U.S.A. (hereafter cited as KWM); Diary of Robert Weir, *Clara Bell,* 26 January 1856, Manuscript Collection of the G.W. Blunt White Library at Mystic Seaport Museum, Mystic, Connecticut, hereafter cited as MSM; Diary of Marshall Keith, *Brewster,* n.d. (1864?), KWM.
5. Diary of Lewis Williams, *Gratitude,* 13 January 1860, Peabody Museum of Salem, Salem, Massachusetts, hereafter cited as PMS; Diary of Edward Mitchell, *Ivanhoe*, 16 April 1867, International Marine Archives in the Whaling Museum Library of the Old Dartmouth Historical Society, New Bedford, Massachusetts (Original at the Penobscot Marine Museum, Searsport, Maine).
6. Eric Sager, *Seafaring Labour: The Merchant Marine of Atlantic Canada 1820–1914* (Montréal, 1989), 237.
7. See Nancy F. Cott, "On Men's History and Women's History," in *Meanings for Manhood: Constructions of Masculinity in Victorian America*, ed. Mark C. Carnes and Clyde Griffen, (Chicago: The University of Chicago Press, 1989), 205-11.

8. See Marcus Rediker, *Between the Devil and the Deep Blue Sea: Merchant Seamen, Pirates, and the Anglo-American Maritime World, 1700–1750* (Cambridge, 1987); and Sager, *Seafaring Labour* (see note 6). Jesse Lemisch's "Jack Tar in the Streets: Merchant Seamen in the Politics of Revolutionary America," *William and Mary Quarterly* 25 (July 1968): 371–407 is recognized as the pioneering essay of the "new" maritime history.

9. On the still-limited literature on the construction of masculinity see Carnes and Griffen, *Meanings for Manhood* (see note 7), 1–7.

10. Margaret S. Creighton, "Fraternity in the American Forecastle, 1830–1870," *New England Quarterly* (December 1990): 531–57.

11. Mitchell diary (see note 5), 16 April 1867; Diary of Abram Briggs, *Eliza Adams*, 12 July, 27 July 1874; 4 February 1873; 29 November 1872; 12 November 1873; 23 May 1875, Whaling Museum Library of the Old Dartmouth Historical Society, hereafter cited as OD.

12. On the ages of merchant seamen in the early national period see Ira Dye, "Early American Merchant Seafarers," *Proceedings of the American Philosophical Society* 120 (October 1976): 331–69; On the ages of antebellum seamen see W. Jeffrey Bolster, "'To Feel Like a Man': Black Seamen in the Northern States, 1800–1860," *Journal of American History* 76 (March 1990): 1190, and Margaret S. Creighton, "The Private Life of Jack Tar" (Ph.D. diss., Boston University, 1985), appendix.

13. Margaret S. Creighton, "Fraternity" (see note 10), 534–39.

14. Diary of Richard Boyenton, *Bengal*, 30 May 1834, Shipping Logbook #1832B, Manuscript Collections, EI (see note 1).

15. On the relationships between masculine and feminine ideals in the mid-nineteenth century among the middle classes see Mark C. Carnes, *Secret Ritual and Manhood in Victorian America* (New Haven, 1989): 107–27; E. Anthony Rotundo, "Body and Soul: Changing Ideals of American Middle-Class Manhood, 1770–1929," *Journal of Social History* 16 (summer 1983): 23–38.

16. Stephen Nissenbaum, *Sex, Diet, and Debility in Jacksonian America* (Westport, Conn., 1980); David Rothman, *The Discovery of the Asylum: Social Order and Disorder in the New Republic* (Boston, 1971): 263; Judith Fingard, *Jack in Port: Sailortowns of Eastern Canada* (Toronto, 1982): 19.

17. Weir diary (see note 4), 18 August 1855–4 May 1858; Diary of Elias Trotter, *Illinois*, 1 July 1845–23 July 1847, OD (see note 11); Diary of

William Abbe, *Atkins Adams*, 10 October 1858–September 1859, OD; Diary of Orson Shattuck, *Frances*, 1 September 1850–18 October 1852, OD.

18. Shattuck diary (see note 17), 19 October 1850; Diary of Silliman Ives, *Sunbeam*, 10 July 1868, OD (see note 11).

19. Charles Nordhoff, *Whaling and Fishing* (New York, 1895), 28; Diary of George Blanchard, *Solomon Saltus*, 18 November 1845, OD (see note 11).

20. E. Anthony Rotundo, "Boy Culture: Middle-Class Boyhood in Nineteenth-Century America," in *Meanings for Manhood*, ed. Carnes and Griffen (see note 7). John Faragher, in his study of gender roles among Overland Trail participants, also emphasized the stigmatization of male tears. In Faragher's words, "The male horror of tears was well founded, for cultural consensus about masculine strength and feminine weakness meant that a public display of sentiment might mark a man indelibly." See John Mack Faragher, *Women and Men on the Overland Trail* (New Haven, 1979), 92.

21. Creighton, "Fraternity" (see note 10), 539–40.

22. *Ibid.*

23. Rediker, *Between the Devil* (see note 8), 77–115; 205–53.

24. Nancy Cott, citing recent labour histories by David Montgomery, Ava Baron, and Steven Hahn, has suggested that there seem to be more "group" values to be found in nineteenth-century male workplaces and within male culture than many historians have previously acknowledged. See "On Men's History and Women's History" (see note 7), 210. On the rise of fraternal groups see Carnes, *Secret Ritual* (see note 15).

25. Judith Fingard, "Masters and Friends, Crimps and Abstainers: Agents of Control in 19th Century Sailortown," *Acadiensis* 8 (autumn 1978): 38; *Fourth Annual Report of the American Seaman's Friend Society* (New York, 1832), 21–22; Hugh Davis, "The American Seaman's Friend Society and the American Sailor, 1828–1838," *American Neptune* 34 (January 1979): 45–57; Mary Ann Clawson, *Constructing Brotherhood: Class, Gender, and Fraternalism* (Princeton, 1989), 185–86.

26. On the sexual division of labour in nineteenth-century America see Julie A. Matthaei, *An Economic History of Women in America: Women's Work, the Sexual Division of Labor, and the Development of Capitalism* (New York, 1982), 74–114.

27. Diary of Isaac Baker, *John Caskie*, 20 August 1855, PMS (see note 5).
28. Leon Litwack, *North of Slavery* (Chicago, 1961), 174; James Oliver Horton, "Freedom's Yoke: Gender Conventions among Antebellum Free Blacks," *Feminist Studies* 12 (Spring 1986): 51–76. Other discussions of black manhood and African-American gender roles in the antebellum period are to be found in the literature on free and enslaved black women. See, for example, Christie Farnham, "Sapphire? The Issue of Dominance in the Slave Family, 1830–1865," in *'To Toil the Livelong Day': America's Women at Work, 1780–1980*, ed. Carol Groneman and Mary Beth Norton (Ithaca, 1987), 68–83.
29. Bolster, "To Feel Like a Man" (see note 12): 1194–6.
30. Ruth H. Bloch, "Untangling the Roots of Modern Sex Roles: A Survey of Four Centuries of Change," *Signs* 4 (winter 1978): 237–52.
31. Diary of Charles Benson, *Glide*, 14 May 1862, Charles Benson Papers, Manuscript Collections, EI (see note 1).
32. Bolster, "To Feel Like a Man" (see note 12), 1183; Lance E. Davis, Robert E. Gallman, Teresa D. Hutchins, "Risk Sharing, Crew Quality, Labor Shares and Wages in the Nineteenth-Century American Whaling Industry," *NBER Working Paper Series* 13 (May 1990): 62.
33. Diary of William Townsend, *Imaum*, 1 May 1858, MSM (see note 4); Diary of Henry Davis, anonymous merchant vessel, 15 September 1862, MSM.
34. Diary of Edwin Pulver, *Columbus*, 7 January 1852; 23 November 1852, The Nicholson Whaling Collection, Providence Public Library, Providence, Rhode Island, hereafter cited as PPL.
35. Diary of John Martin, *Lucy Ann*, 3 July 1842; 7 July 1843, KWM (see note 4).
36. Diary of Larkin Turner, *Palestine*, 16 February 1832, MSM (see note 4).
37. Diary of Francis Moreland, *Sooloo*, 12 October 1861, PMS (see note 5); Diary of James Haviland, *Baltic*, 26 January 1857, PPL (see note 34); Weir diary (see note 4), 16 April 1856.
38. Weir diary (see note 4), 18 April 1858; Williams diary (see note 5), 29 March 1859; Trotter diary (see note 17), 22 August 1845.
39. Stephanie Coontz, *The Social Origins of Private Life: A History of American Families 1600–1900* (London and New York, 1988), 193.
40. The paucity of records on sexual relations between men at sea among the sources reviewed here cautions us against speculation on that

important subject. Suffice it to say that there were many reasons why such attachments might have been considered normative at sea, such as the need to accommodate sexual drives and the emotional bonding that invariably took place between seamen, but also many reasons why such behaviour might have been discouraged or outlawed, such as prevailing shore-based injunctions against sodomitic acts, and, within the forecastle, an ethos of mutuality that discouraged exclusive pairing of any sort. On the last point see Creighton, "Fraternity in the American Forecastle" (see note 10).

41. Baker diary, *John Caskie* (see note 27), 8 September 1855; Diary of John D. Alden, *Albatross*, 5 June 1847, PMS (see note 5).
42. Gale Huntington, *Songs the Whalemen Sang* (Barre, Mass, 1964), 65.
43. Diary of Albert Goodwin, *Tuscaloosa*, 28 December 1845, PMS (see note 5).
44. Caroline Mosely, "Images of Young Women in Nineteenth Century Songs of the Sea," *Log of Mystic Seaport* 35 (1984), 132–39 discusses the representation of women in sailors' songs.
45. E. Norman Flayderman, *Scrimshaw and Scrimshanders/Whales and Whalemen* (New Milford, Conn., 1972), 26–6l.
46. Margaret Baker, *Folklore of the Sea* (North Pomfret, Vt., 1979), 19–20.
47. *Ibid*.
48. Diary of John Crimblish, *Palestine*, 31 August 1839, Shipping Logbook #1839P, Manuscript Collections, EI (see note 1); Diary of Isaac Baker, *Taskar*, 29 May 1842, PMS (see note 5).
49. Alden diary (see note 41), 8 June l847; Baker diary, *Taskar* (see note 48), 11 September 1842; 15 October 1841.
50. Diary of Augustus Hamblet, *St. Paul*, 29 June 1839, PMS (see note 5).
51. Frederick Pease Harlow, *Chanteying Aboard American Ships* (Barre, Ma., 1962), 43.
52. Diary of Samuel Braley, *Arab,* date in question (1852?), KWM (see note 4); Diary of Marshall Keith, *Edith May*, 4 April 1868, OD (see note 11).
53. Walter Brooks to his mother, 26 February 1854, MSM (see note 4); Diary of Ezra Goodnough, *Ann Perry*, 23 March 1847, PMS (see note 5).
54. Goodnough diary (see note 53), 8 July 1847, PMS (see note 5).
55. Diary of Isaac Baker, *Warsaw*, 6 April 1841, PMS (see note 5).
56. Justin Martin to Charles H. Martin, 29 November 1844, MSM (see note 4).

57. Bloch, "Untangling the Roots of Modern Sex Roles" (see note 30), 248–50; Mary Ryan, "The Power of Women's Networks: A Case Study of Female Moral Reform in Antebellum America," *Feminist Studies* 5 (1979): 66–85; Ann Douglas, *The Feminization of American Culture* (New York, 1977).
58. Lisa Norling, "Contrary Dependencies" (see note 3), 10.
59. Eliza Howard Reed to William B. Reed, 8 December 1862; 2 June 1863; 3 February 1863, Cheever and Howard Family Papers, Manuscript Collections, EI (see note 1).
60. Diary of Marshal Keith, *Brewster,* 9 February 1864, PPL (see note 34).
61. Diary of George Bowman, *Albion,* 21 June 1869; 28 February 1868, PPL (see note 34); Diary of Edmund E. Jennings, *Mary and Susan,* 29 November 1877, PPL.
62. See, for example, *The Fifteenth Annual Report of the American Seaman's Friend Society* (New York, 1843); *The Sixteenth Annual Report of the American Seaman's Friend Society* (New York, 1844).
63. Davis, "American Seamen's Friend Society" (see note 25).
64. Judith Fingard, *Jack in Port: Sailortowns of Eastern Canada* (see note 16), 194–241.
65. Diary of William Allen, *Samuel Robertson,* 9 October 1844, OD (see note 11).
66. Diary of Ambrose Bates, *Millwood,* June 1867; August 1867, KWM (see note 4).
67. *Ibid.*
68. Carroll Smith-Rosenberg, "The Female World of Love and Ritual," *Signs* 1 (1975): 1–29; Margaret Marsh, "Suburban Men and Masculine Domesticity, 1870–1915," *American Quarterly* 40 (June 1988), 165–86; Mark C. Carnes, *Secret Ritual* (see note 15).

Chapter Fifteen
The Sentimentalization of American Seafaring: The Case of the New England Whalefishery, 1790–1870

Lisa Norling

A poem was printed in an evangelical publication, *The Sailor's Magazine and Naval Journal*, in 1861. Titled "The Sailor's Wife," it went like this:

THE SAILOR'S WIFE
Thou o'er the world, and I at home
But one may linger, the other may roam,
Yet our hearts will flee o'er the bounding sea
Mine to thy bosom, and thine to me.

Thy lot is the toll of a roving life,
Chances and changes, sorrow and strife
Yet is mine more drear to linger here
In a ceaseless, changeless war with tear.

I watch the sky by the stars' pale light,
Till the day — dawn breaketh on gloomy night,
And the wind's low tone hath a dreary moan
That comes to my heart as I weep alone.

> With the morning light. Oh! would I could see,
> Thy white sail far on the breaking sea,
> And welcome thee home o'er the wild wave's foam
> And bid thee no more from my side to roam.[1]

What we have here (aside from a rather corny poem) is the rendering into maritime terms of the ideology of separate gendered spheres, that conceptual construct by which Victorian Americans organized their sex/gender system. Here is the manly sailor, whose occupation takes him roaming over the world, in an active life full of chances and strife. In explicit contrast is the setting and role of his wife: she is at home, alone, passively waiting, watching and weeping. Her main activity (in addition to the constant weeping) is to welcome the sailor home *and* urge him to stay there, which is implicitly a futile gesture since his "lot" is that of a "roving life." The set of oppositions is mitigated only by the brief and ineffectual mention of the tie that binds them together — their hearts, fleeing over the bounding sea — in other words, an exclusive romantic relationship that exists without reference to social or economic context, a relationship that somehow survives prolonged and repeated separations.

This translation into maritime terms of the idea of two opposing spheres, male and female, linked exclusively through emotional bonds, is symbolic of what I call the "sentimentalization of seafaring." By this I mean a reconceptualization of seafaring that shifted attention away from the sea to the land, from maritime work to maritime home. One of the many sometimes competing interpretations of seafaring current in the nineteenth century, "sentimentalization" affected the ways in which land, society, and seamen interacted on a number of levels. For maritime women, sentimentalization represented an ideal that played down female agency and women's substantive contributions to the seafaring enterprise, emphasizing instead women's emotional role and (as the poem suggests) their experience of deprivation and loss.

My focus here is on a particular group of maritime women, those associated with a specific occupational group within the New England whalefishery: the pool of local, native-born, white men, primarily of yeoman and artisanal background, from which the whaling masters and mates were drawn. This group formed a stable segment within the industry's labor force on which, I believe, the shipowners and whaling agents depended entirely to counteract the anarchic tendencies of the fishery itself.[2] As the owners and agents depended on the group of local men to sustain the industry in distant seas, so did the industry at large depend on the mariners' female connections — their mothers, daughters, and especially their wives — to sustain family and community ashore.[3] Whaling was certainly distinctive among the deep-sea industries, with its own peculiar demands, work rhythms and relationships. Yet, I think, the process of sentimentalization occurred in the whaling communities not differently but rather in particularly exaggerated form: mariners' wives, more than the men themselves, were the most influenced by the sentimentalized interpretation of seafaring that emerged in the mid-nineteenth century.

In the earlier years of the industry, women's relationship to it and their role within the whaling community had been understood quite differently. Particularly on Nantucket, the centre of the colonial fishery, the ways in which women's activities on shore made possible the men's endeavors at sea were both acknowledged and applauded. J. Hector St. John Crevecoeur, who visited Nantucket in the 1760s, praised the women's material contributions: "as the sea excursions are often very long," he wrote, "[the whalers'] wives are necessarily obliged to transact business, to settle accounts, and, in short, to rule and provide for their families .... This employment," he remarked, "ripens their judgment, and justly entitles them to a rank superior to that of other wives .... The men, at their return, weary with the fatigues of the sea ... cheerfully give their consent to every transaction that has happened during their absence, and all is joy and peace."[4] Indeed, Crevecoeur wondered, "what would the men do without the agency of [their] faithful mates?" The young age at which Nantucket men married suggests not only that they could afford to do so on their whaling profits but also that Nantucket men too saw female activities as important to the enterprise.[5]

The women's involvement in the industry extended beyond the material: their concerns, preferences and traditions reinforced the values that ensured the whalefishery's success. According to local legend, Nantucket girls spurned the advances of any youth who had not yet "struck his whale," and wives condemned the husband who returned without a sufficiently "greasy ship." One Nantucket wife whose husband's earnings from his last voyage had about disappeared, reputedly remarked as she served a meagre dinner, "Well, John, one or t'other of us has got to go round Cape Horn pretty soon, and I ain't goin."[6] These apocryphal stories, however suspect the specific details, underscore not only a flintiness of female spirit but also the degree of female adaptation to the fishery that more contemporary evidence bears out (such as the notable matter-of-factness with which one Elizabeth Chase Gardner, a Nantucket widow, mother, and mother-in-law of mariners, referred to the hazardous trip around Cape Horn as "a good voyage for the unstable youth").[7]

An anonymous diarist who visited Nantucket sometime in the early 1820s described how Nantucket "sons are taught to aspire to a harpoon and their daughters to a whaleman." He observed that "the young men generally go their first voyage at the age of from 15 to 17 ... they go round the cape, are gone from three to four years, come home, and stop a few months to marry their chosen, and off they go again for another three year trip ... the females bear a three year separation, with more patience and resignation than does our country girls on the main land, to part with their Johnathans even for three days."[8]

The visitor also observed (with some amusement) how the conversation of the "Nantucket beauties" he met "dwelt almost continually upon whales and whaling ... of the arrivals and clearances of port that day, of the hardships, miraculous escapes, fortunes and misfortunes, and everything else that appertains to a sailors life, which their fathers, brothers, friends, lovers, and husbands had experienced, in their several voyages to the Brazil Banks or round Cape Horn."[9] In his 1834 novel about eighteenth-century Nantucket, Joseph Hart similarly described the women's habit of "oddly mixing nautical phrasing with that which landsmen are accustomed to." He continued, "to the successful prosecution of their trade, the energies of all the inhabitants, both male and female, are constantly directed."[10] Nantucket women did not themselves put to sea or pursue the whale, but their familiarity with the process and their easy use of the specialized language reflected the level of their involvement in the industry *and* it marked them as different from other American women.

To anyone from off-island, Nantucket society appeared distinctive in its adaptation to the demands of whaling, its Quaker faith, and the island insularity which accentuated both. Observers from the eighteenth to the twentieth centuries have drawn a connection between the qualities encouraged by Quaker theology and Nantucket men's dominance in the early whaling industry.[11] Hart referred to Nantucketers as "that sort of half quaker-half sailor breed, to be found no where else on earth." I would argue as well that the elements of Quakerism enabling Nantucket women to develop the unusual independence noted by historians of early feminism, also enabled them to sustain their community through the peculiar rhythms and stresses as the whaling industry developed.[12]

The diary kept by Rhode Island Quaker wife Lydia Almy, while her husband Christopher shipped out on a whaler owned by the prominent Nantucket-New Bedford Rotch family in 1797, demonstrates both the activities and attitudes with which she supported their family during Christopher's absence. The female agency to which Crevecoeur referred is clearly evident in the range of Lydia's efforts. In an early diary entry, she lamented she was "in no way to due any thing towards earning my liveing which seems rather to distress my mind knowing that my dear husband must be exposed to wind and weather and many hardships to indure whilst I am provided for in the best manner."[13] So, in addition to the normal round of household tasks and childcare, Lydia also took in a boarder and tanned skins to earn cash.

While Lydia missed her husband, she generally subordinated her fears and wishes to her sense of obligation. "O that my Dear husband may be returned to me again in the Lords time missing his agreeable company very much," she recorded. But she observed that "I have everything to make me comfortable and happy and want for nothing of this worlds goods except the company my dear husband," and she reminded herself, "saith my soul be still there is a voice that the muffling waves must obey." She considered her separation from Christopher to have been mandated by God in order, she wrote, "to ween our affections from this world and fit us for his own servis." Though Lydia, in Rhode Island, was on the margin of the whaling community, for her as for her Nantucket contemporaries in the industry's centre, tradition and religious faith directed their response into resignation and acceptance.[14]

The movement of the whalefishery's centre of gravity, sometime around the 1830s, from the island of Nantucket to New Bedford on the mainland neatly symbolizes a major transformation in the ways in which the industry and its community were organized. At sea, the pursuit of whales remained a unique activity, the whalemen a breed apart. On land, however, the boundaries between the maritime and land-based communities began to blur as the business side of whaling expanded in scale and complexity.

As labour demand increased, the region from which the officer group was drawn broadened from Nantucket alone to all of southern New England, the men leaving behind female connections in villages and towns that, while nearby, did not revolve wholly around the industry. Nor were they predominantly Quaker; the connection between the sect and the industry receded. New Bedford itself, as it grew rapidly into a city, displayed an increasing heterogeneity and complexity, segments of which were only distantly responsive to the rhythms of whaling. Maritime reformers even found a need to remind the rest of New Bedford of the connections between the city's prosperity and growth and the efforts of the men in the fleet, distant in the Pacific, Indian and Arctic Oceans on voyages that now lasted from three to five years.

As Eric Sager has argued for the Canadian case,[15] the development of the maritime industries in the United States formed an important part of the sweeping economic and social transformations that made up nineteenth-century industrialization. Integral to this process was a polarization in gender roles. When work (or, more precisely, the kind of labor that was valued as "work") was removed from the home, men went with it into the marketplace. Women remained behind within an increasingly (conceptually) isolated domesticity, their labor no longer defined as "work," their most important tasks defined as the nurture and emotional support of their families.[16]

The gender polarization occurred within the whaling community as well, despite the fact that the sea remained what it had traditionally been, an overwhelmingly male workplace. The conceptual realignment that linked domesticity and seafaring, and sentimentalized both, was clearly not a local response to any new spatial or organizational differentiation of men's and women's work. Rather, it appears to have been a set of new ideas and values lifted, perhaps in part imposed, from the outside as the whaling community became less insular. The ideas were given special force by their correspondence to (and explanatory power for) the evident difference between land and sea: after all, blue water seamen and their families measured the separation between work and home not by hours or miles, but by years and thousands of miles.

The first place in which the sentimentalization of seafaring appears to have been explicitly articulated was in the early nineteenth-century religious reform movement aimed at sailors. Patterned on British example, the earliest American group specifically aimed at sailors' souls was (probably) the Boston Society for the Religious and Moral Improvement of Seamen, founded in 1812. By the mid-1820s, there were over 70 "port societies" up and down the eastern seaboard trying to convert, uplift, and control that "interesting" class of men, sailors.[17] The tracts, appeals, sermons, and other publications generated by the maritime reform movement display a significantly altered understanding of the relationship between land and sea. For the first time, the traditional vices to which seamen were prone (obscenity, promiscuity, drunkenness, instability, and antipathy to religion) were viewed as stemming not from sailors' innate depravity, nor from the unique conditions of their occupation. Rather, now the dangers the seamen encountered on land were held to outweigh by far the dangers they faced at sea. Sailors' problems were attributed to their lack of the "mutual guardianship and instruction" of church membership, "the restraint of public opinion," and, especially, "the sweet charities of the domestic circle."[18]

The Reverend John Weiss, speaking to a group of New Bedford whaleship owners in 1849, urged them each to "imagine yourself a member of that floating population in every city, who look from afar at your peace and comfort, who look in at the windows of your homes ... longing to be seated within the charmed circle of that firelight, where affection, refinement, decency, honor, expand like grain in the sun." Whalemen, Weiss said, "these heroes of a three years campaign return at last ... they come home to fall into the hands of harpies, to be stripped in grog-shops ... they land and are adrift." Therefore, he argued, "the first prerequisite for the moral improvement of seamen, for their improvement as a class, is a Seamen's Home."[19]

Of all the activities undertaken by the mid-century maritime reformers, only providing a place to worship took precedence over the movement to build sailors' homes.[20] The establishments actually built never provided housing for more than at most a couple of hundred seamen a year each, an insignificant number in ports like New York, Boston, and New Bedford, where tens of thousands of sailors came and went every year. The reformers appear to have met with monumental disinterest on the part of seamen themselves and active resistance from boarding-house keepers and other waterfront interests.[21] Yet the attempt was important, because the preoccupation with the Homes against such opposition demonstrated that the reformers understood sailors' problems as deriving not from the social relations of their work but rather from a perversion of their family life, and it betrayed the reformers' faith in the (newly) sanctified home as the appropriate arena for addressing those problems.

In one typical appeal, the editor of the *Sailor's Magazine* wrote: "Ye who taste the sweets of home, and enjoy the comforts of the domestic fireside — sheltered from the storm with your loved ones around you, think of the wandering, homeless sailor; think of his perils and dangers at sea, think of the snares and temptations that beset him on shore. Does he not need, does he not deserve at our hands an asylum — a *Home*; where he may enjoy some of the comforts from which he has been so long estranged!" Moreover, the editor continued, "the establishment of Sailors' Homes will cheer the heart of many a fond mother, whose son — perhaps an only son — is now a wanderer on the mighty deep; and whose prayers will arise for … all who are aiding in this benevolent work."[22] Here, in this shift of attention from the sailor to his mother, as in the Sailor's Home movement and reform efforts more generally, we can trace a shift in emphasis from sea to land, from maritime work to maritime home — in short, the sentimentalization of seafaring.

For maritime women, sentimentalization represented a *new* dramatization of their experiences, which downplayed or obscured their agency and activity. The distinctive Nantucket Quaker whale-woman, strong and independent, vitally involved in the whalefishery, was now disparaged in the popular imagination and diminished in her flesh-and-blood incarnations. In print, Crevecoeur's 1760 praise of Keziah Coffin, whose energy and financial acumen made her family one of the richest on colonial Nantucket, was replaced in Joseph Hart's 1834 novel by her vilification as a caricature of unwomanly ambition and unseemly meddling in men's affairs.[23] In real-life New Bedford, one Lucy Roberts, the fiancée of Captain Leonard Gifford, was denied agency (or even any humanity!) altogether when the shipowners referred to her as a "blooming Flower" who would be all the better if she remained unplucked for an additional year.[24] These were maritime women, then, who no longer seemed so distinctive —

indeed, they looked, talked, were viewed as, and apparently felt much like their non-maritime neighbors.

Somewhat ironically, the transformation is most clear in the women who remained closest to the industry, those few captain's wives who actually went to sea with their husbands. These women were pulled to sea, where most of them were acutely uncomfortable,[25] because they felt so strongly that their most important function was to be at their husbands' sides. Mary Brewster noted at sea in 1845, "I am with my Husband and by him will remain .... He can have no trouble ... but what I can know and share. When perplexed with the duties of the ship ... I can sooth his ruffled feelings .... If sick no hand like mine can sooth the sad heart." Yet the experience was often frustrating for the women (not to mention boring and lonely) because of their isolation and irrelevance to the main activity. "We are supernumaries; nothing for us to do but look on," remarked Mary Chipman Lawrence.[26]

Within the industrial community on shore, some of women's earlier functions were taken over by a whole host of service industries as the business expanded; the conceptual distance between work and home widened accordingly. When agents Thomas Knowles and Co. informed Captain Penniman's wife that they could purchase insurance for her husband's share of the cargo, she expressed no opinion but that the firm should "do what you think best."[27]

Within the home itself, the substance of women's labor was becoming obscured in the emphasis placed on its emotional associations. Samuel Braley, deep in the Indian Ocean in 1850, asked his wife Mary Ann to send him more of "Grandmother Douglas cotton stockings" because, he told her, "I cannot ware those that you knit, it seems sacrilege: how much I prize every thing that is the work of thy dear hands." And, when Samuel learned that Mary Ann had returned to their hometown to give birth to their first child, he wrote, "did your little Bosom heave one sigh for him that is far away? ... Oh that I could be with thee to comfort thee in thy coming tryals .... I never knew how much I loved thee till now when thou art about to suffer for me."[28]

With the sentimentalization of seafaring, the major role for maritime women like Mary Ann was to suffer for their men. Like their land-based sisters who were told to "suffer and be still," maritime women were told that "'men must work and women must weep."[29] In July 1838, the *Sailor's*

Magazine reprinted a piece out of the *Boston Recorder.* Under the title "Perils of the Sea," the report listed both the number of Cape Cod seamen lost during the year 1837 (78) and the number of seamen's widows then living on the Cape (914!). It continued by speculating in gruesome detail on the kinds of deaths men met with at sea (generally "violent and terrible") and meditating at length on the misery of the "bleeding heart" of "the mother, the wife, the sister" left at home.[30] The dangers men confronted on the ocean were causally linked to, and in part compensated for by, women's sufferings at home, while the notion of men's activity and women's passivity was stressed.[31]

Other evidence suggests, though, that the suffering by the women wasn't felt so much for the men as it was for themselves. Contrary to the new ideal, women did not retreat into passivity — many now (in contrast to the earlier Nantucket women) actively exerted pressure to keep their men at home. Young wives urged their husbands to forego seafaring on romantic grounds, as an expression of the depth of the women's feelings. Elizabeth Tabor wrote dramatically, "Dear Husband I hope that there will be a day that you will not have to plough the raging Ocion for your living, I will do all that I can to prevent it .... I do hope that we may never be sepperated agane in this World." She continued with some morbid speculation on whether he might at that very moment be sick or dying or even dead, and she added emphatically, "I do not want that you should follow the sea for your living."[32]

For women married longer, whose cares mounted with every additional child and year of their husbands' absence, the new emphasis on their deprivation and loss perhaps predictably shaded over into antagonism and even, on occasion, outright hostility.[33] On this topic, an anonymous piece from the *Sailor's Magazine* of 1838 is worth quoting at length.

> We can scarcely conceive a situation more wretched than that of the wife of an active sailor ... the anxiety which her husband subjects her to, will prey upon and finally destroy the finest constitution. Every wind that blows is a source of fear; every rain that falls causes sorrow; every cloud that rises is big with the fate of her nearest friend. These feelings, which tug at the heart-strings, are honourable to the nature of women, but noble and generous as they are, they are

poisonous to her existence, and sink too deeply into the breast to be eradicated."

In other words, the emotional experience of marriage to a sailor was physically injurious.

The author went on to assign blame: "Those who make long voyages pass but a small part of their time with their families; a few months at home, answer for years at sea, and they finally drop away, before they have hardly bestowed a thought upon death; or without, in many instances, leaving a competency for his family; and she who has borne up against trouble in her early life has to struggle with poverty in its decline."[34]

These are hostile words, and they seem to have expressed accurately a resentment felt by many maritime women. Myra Weeks, who noted that "I have to write with one hand and rock the cradle with the other," told her husband William, "I hope you will be blest with a short and prosperous voyage and then make up your mind to stay at home the remainder of your days .... I think it is rather lonesome to be shut up here day after day with three little children to take care of. I should be glad to know how you would like [it] .... I think that there may be some way to get a living without your always being away from your family and friends."[35]

Caroline Gifford, writing her whaler-husband Charles from the family farm in Dartmouth, Massachusetts, in 1866, exclaimed with obvious exasperation, "I call it a trial to bring up a family mostly without any Father to help manage .... I am in hopes if you live to perform this voyage that you will not have to go to sea again unless," she added pointedly, "you can enjoy yourself better on land." On one of Caroline's later letters, their daughter Eleanor penned an ambivalent postscript: "it seems a long time for a man to be away from his folks three or four years at a time. I send my love to you and hope you will prosper ... for it seems as though you ought to stay at home a while and not be on the water all your days."[36]

Rather than support and reinforcement for the enterprise, then, some women now demonstrated a rather subversive view of seafaring, or at least of seafarers. Libby Spooner wrote her whaler-husband, Caleb, "Nehemiah talks of moveing back to the farm I think he best wait till spring but he is a *sailor* and consequently very *uneasy*. I know something about it, they never stay set down in one place till they get so stiff and old they cannot get out of it."[37] Sarah Howland, who never criticized her husband directly, nonetheless remarked of their neighbour, "I doubt whether his attachment to his wife is much stronger than many that follow the seas for a livelihood."[38]

Captain William Loring Taber was stung when his wife Susan doubted his attachment to her. "You wrote you wish you could think that this was the last time we should be seperated," he recorded in one letter home, "you know that many have said so before, [but] that Agents give successful captains such inducements that they cannot resist them, and you will not insure one of my ambition against their temptation." But the captain insisted, "I think a married man's place is at home with his family, and if he can stay, he ought to." And his word was good; after his return a year later, he gave up commanding ships and managed them from shore instead.[39]

Many more mariners, though, continued to ply the sea as long as they were able, despite their sometimes fervent protests that *this* voyage would be their last. Captain Edward Ashley wrote home to his parents from the Pacific, "I do not think that I shall ever gow a whaleing again Caty [his young wife, then sailing with him] says she will not let me." Nonetheless, Ashley made at least two more whaling voyages — and simply left Caty behind.[40]

The attractions of the sea for men like Edward Ashley — and there were many like him — illustrate vividly that sentimentalization was not the only interpretation of seafaring current in the nineteenth century. Representing its flip side, the great sea fiction of Cooper, Melville, and Conrad rejected the land altogether. A whole sub-genre of travel literature and nautical reminiscences continued to foreground the ocean voyage and diminish its connection to land, often relegating any mention of the shore to the opening and closing paragraphs. Sea shanties and traditions displayed a deep ambivalence toward women and the land in general, expressing both desire and distrust. But, while rejecting the sentimental analysis of sailors' problems and maritime culture in general, these alternative interpretations actually reinforced the gender-marking by emphasizing women's symbolic roles over their substantive ones, and underscoring the association of masculinity with the sea and femininity with the land.

In this essay, I have tried to outline, primarily from the women's perspective, a polarization in gender roles as it occurred in the nineteenth-century whaling communities of southeastern New England. Unlike in other industrializing settings, this polarization did not occur as a direct result of the separation of work from home. Instead, the conceptual separation of spheres appears to have occurred as a part of the process by which the whaling industry was more fully integrated into the mainstream of American society: the sentimentalized interpretation of seafaring represented a convergence of maritime and non-maritime cultures. But, while it brought land and sea closer along conceptual shores, sentimentalization introduced new tensions and deepened divisions within the maritime community. Rather than bringing seamen home, it further isolated them, even from their own families. And, for the women, it only sharpened their unhappiness. Lizzie Howes of Cape Cod expressed the sense of a host of sea-wives when she wrote in frustration, "I think a seafaring man should *never* marry such is my opinion."[41]

NOTES

I would like to thank Judith Fingard, Valerie Burton, and Daniel Vickers for their perceptive criticisms of the version of this paper presented at the "Jack Tar in History" conference; I am especially indebted to Professor Burton, who correctly pointed out that the reconceptualization of seafaring I describe here is more appropriately understood as "sentimentalization" than "domestication." I am also indebted to Jeanne Boydston, Suzanne Lebsock, and Paul Clemens for helpful comments on an earlier version.

1. "The Sailor's Wife," *The Sailor's Magazine and Naval Journal* 33, no. 7 (March 1861).
2. The industry was anarchic in its inherent risk, its global dispersal in a context of severely limited communication, and in the heterogeneity and rapid turnover which characterized the foremast hands. On the issues of dependency within the industry and whaling community, see Lisa Norling, "Contrary Dependencies: Whaling Agents and Whalemen's Families, 1830-1870," *The Log of Mystic Seaport* 42, no. l, 3–12. Daniel Vickers has described how the labor force of the early whalefishery on Nantucket was divided into two segments: the positions of master and mate were "the exclusive preserve" of white, native-born Nantucketers, while the

crew was filled largely by local Indians in a state of informal debt peonage, plus a few white boys who were essentially officers-in-training. By the end of the colonial period, Vickers found, rapid growth in the industry coupled with shrinking opportunities on land pushed young white men as well as disadvantaged minorities, from throughout southern New England, onboard for temporary service as common laborers; the officers remained Nantucketers. See Daniel Vickers, "Nantucket Whalemen in the Deep-Sea Fishery: The Changing Anatomy of an Early American Labor Force," *Journal of American History* 72, no. 2, 277–96. Although a thorough quantitative study remains to be done, the evidence suggests that the two-tier pattern identified by Vickers persisted throughout the nineteenth century, though the scale shifted as the labor pool broadened in response to the industry's growing demand. It appears that the officer cadre (now increased in number, as vessels increased in number, size and complexity), was made up of men (still mainly native-born and white, though the number of Portuguese increased late in the century) drawn from throughout that southern New England region, while the forecastle was filled with a polyglot group of more easily exploited men drawn from underdeveloped regions around the world. See Elmo P. Hohman, *The American Whaleman* (New York, 1928), 48–70.

3. I discussed the industry's dependence upon this group of women in my unpublished paper, "Captain Ahab Had a Wife: Women and the Whaling Industry, 1820–1870," presented at the Organization of American Historians' Conference, Washington, D.C., Mar. 23, 1990.
4. J. Hector St. John de Crevecoeur, *Letters from an American Farmer* (1782; reprint New York, 1987), 157.
5. Crevecoeur, *Letters from An American Farmer* (see note 4), 157. He remarked on the early age at which Nantucket men married (pp. 141 and 146), an observation supported by Daniel Vickers ("Nantucket Whalemen in the Deep-Sea Fishery" [see note 2], 285), and Edward Byers in *The Nation of Nantucket* (Boston, 1987), 90–2, 181–2. Crevecoeur attributed this to their love of family life and Quaker patterns of sociability; Vickers and Byers to the opportunity afforded young men by whaling to acquire enough money to marry on at an early age. I would argue that an additional reason was the importance of wives' contributions, material, affective, and symbolic, to the enterprise.
6. Quote from William F. Macy, ed., *The Nantucket Scrap Basket,* 2nd ed., (1930; reprint Cambridge, Mass., 1984), 26. On Nantucket girls'

marriage preference for successful whalers, see p. 20. See also Joseph C. Hart, *Miriam Coffin or The Whale-Fisherman,* Vol. 1 (New York, 1834), 93-5.
7. Elizabeth Chase Gardner to Susan Gardner, fragment 10/23 ca. 1826, Mss. 87, Folder 33, Nantucket Historical Association, Nantucket, Mass. (hereafter NHA).
8. Anonymous diary, undated, circa 1821–32, Collection 28 (Unidentified Diaries), Folder 7, NHA (see note 7).
9. Ibid.
10. Hart, *Miriam Coffin* (see note 6), 1:32.
11. Elmo Hohman noted that "whaling demanded an unusual combination of qualities ... and the Quaker-Puritan-Yankee stock of southern New England, through training, temperament, and cultural environment, possessed these traits in rare degree .... Courage, hardihood, skill, thrift carried to the point of parsimony, shrewdness, stubborn perseverance, ingenuity, sturdy independence, a cold tack of squeamishness in driving bargains, and a righteous scorn for luxuries — these were characteristics ... inculcated by the philosophy of Quaker and Puritan forbears and modified by several generations of struggle with a niggardly and often hostile New World environment [which explain why] the leadership [of the industry] passed into the hands of Nantucket and New Bedford." Hohman, *The American Whaleman* (see note 2), 10. Edward Byers noted more generally, "in pre-revolutionary Nantucket an individualistic ethos dominated economic relations, providing a foundation for a culture of privatism that pervaded the religious and political life of the community .... In much the same manner as Philadelphia, Nantucket's privatism was validated by the competitive and individualized nature of commercial whaling, the widely shared prosperity, and the openness of the economy." He also remarked on the tribalism of Nantucket's leading (and Quaker) families. Byers, *The Nation of Nantucket* (see note 5), 155–8; quotation p. 158.
12. Historians of women have long speculated that the theological and institutional features of Quakerism accounted for the notable number of early Quaker women feminists; a few have drawn a connection between female activists and the Nantucket Quaker environment. Margaret Hope Bacon argued specifically that "Nantucket, with its isolation and frequent absence of husbands and fathers on whaling trips, became a training

ground for the development of strong Quaker women: Lucretia Coffin Mott, Martha Coffin Wright, Phebe Hanaford, Maria Mitchell, and many other pioneer feminists came from Nantucket." See Bacon, *Mothers of Feminism: The Story of Quaker Women in America* (San Francisco, 1986), 45–6. Elisabeth Anthony Dexter also noted the many active business women on Nantucket in her book, *Career Women of America, 1776–1840* (Francestown, N.H.,1950), 158–62.

13. Lydia Almy Diary, August 1797–June 1799, entry Dec. 21, 1797, typescript copy. Essex Institute, Salem, Mass. (hereafter EI). See also entries for Jan. 24, Feb. 28, Mar 7, 1798 and passim for examples of cash-producing activities.

14. Almy diary (see note 13), entries Sept. 16, 1798; ? 1797; May 9, 1798, EI.

15. Eric Sager, *Seafaring Labour: The Merchant Marine of Atlantic Canada, 1820-1914* (Kingston and Montreal, 1989).

16. The highlights of the most influential literature on the subject are usefully summarized in Francesca M. Cancian, *Love in America* (Cambridge and New York, 1987), 15–29. Though identified primarily as a white middle-class ideal, these new gender role definitions also affected families of other classes and races, even where women's material efforts remained crucial to family survival. See especially Jeanne Boydston, "To Earn Her Daily Bread: Housework and Antebellum Working-Class Subsistence," *Radical History Review* 35 (1986): 7–25.

17. The maritime evangelical reform movement resulted from the combination of two factors: first, the Second Great Awakening, which let loose a flood of religiously inspired reform energy throughout American society; and, second, expansion in the early national navy and maritime industries, with which came the increasingly disruptive presence of both seamen and the various kinds of "landsharks" who preyed upon them, in the burgeoning waterfront districts. The reformers' initial impetus was to distribute bibles and tracts on the waterfront, hire pastors to proselytize, and provide places for sailors to worship. Quickly, though, the reformers began to see a link between the sailors' moral, social, and physical well-being, and broadened their efforts accordingly. So, in a number of cities, they also began to establish seamen's savings banks, reading rooms, and hospitals (some still in operation today); with considerably less success, they tried to set up employment registry offices, to encourage maritime

boarding-house keepers to run orderly, temperate, and chaste facilities, and finally, to institute what they called Sailor's Homes. See especially Roald Kverndal's magisterial *Seamen's Missions: Their Origin and Early Growth* (Pasadena, c. 1986). Also useful are Harold Langley, *Social Reform in the United States Navy, 1798–1862* (Urbana, 1967), 47–67; Elmo Paul Hohman, *Seamen Ashore* (New Haven, 1952), 265–89; and Myra Glenn, "The Naval Reform Against Flogging: A Case Study in Changing Attitudes Toward Corporal Punishment, 1830-50," *American Quarterly* 35, no. 4 (Fall 1983): 408–25.

18. First Annual Report of the Board of Managers of the New Bedford Port Society for the Moral Improvement of Seamen (New Bedford, Mass., 1831). This analysis contrasts markedly with the view of seamen professed by earlier religious leaders such as Cotton Mather and John Flavel. See for example Mather's *The Religious Marriner* (Boston, 1700) and *The Sailours Companion and Counsellour* (Boston, 1709); and John Flavel, *Navigation Spiritualiz'd* (Boston, 1726).

19. John Weiss, "The Claims of Seamen" (Boston, 1849), Tract in the Port Society Collection, Special Collections, New Bedford Free Public Library, New Bedford, Mass.

20. The first was probably the Mariners' House in Boston, established about 1835 by the female Seamen's Aid Society (headed by none other than Sarah Josepha Hale, one of the primary architects of the ideology of domesticity, the influential editor of *Godey's Ladies Book*). Other cities up and down the eastern seaboard and Great Lakes followed suit; a home was instituted in New Bedford in 1851. See George Duncan Campbell, "The Sailor's Home," *American Neptune* 37, no. 3 (July 1977): 179–84; the reports on Sailors' Homes in various cities appearing frequently in the *Sailor's Magazine and Naval Journal* (e.g. on Portsmouth, Vol. 9, no. 10 [June 1837]: 306–7; on Newburyport, Vol. 15, no. 4 (December 1842): 107–8); and review the American Seamen's Friend Society records, Sailor's Home annual reports, 1838–62, Mss. coll. 158, G.W. Blunt White Library, Mystic Seaport Museum, Mystic, Conn. (hereafter MSM).

21. For an analogous case, see Judith Fingard, *Jack in Port: Sailortowns of Eastern Canada* (Toronto, 1982), 194–241, on the sailor's home movement as an attempted antidote for crimping abuses, and on waterfront resistance to the reform efforts, in the maritime provinces of Canada.

22. *Sailor's Magazine and Naval Journal* 14, no. 5 (January 1842): 161. The *Sailor's Magazine*, printed in New York and distributed internationally as kind of a maritime evangelical reform newsletter and clearinghouse by the American Seamen's Friend Society, was probably read more often by women than by the sailors it was ostensibly published for. Nathaniel Ames, who served in both the U.S. Navy and the merchant marine, belittled the magazine in his 1832 reminiscences, calling it "an exceedingly silly periodical" written "in a style too puerile, too silly for children of five years old." (Ames quoted in Langely, *Social Reform in the United States Navy* (see note 17), 57.) Judging by the lists of contributors to the reform groups reported in *Sailor's Magazine*, it seems more likely that the affecting vignettes and poems had their greatest impact on the "young ladies" of the Brooklyn Female Bethel Society, Vol. 9, no. 6 (February 1837), the "Female friend to seamen, Hartford," the "Old Mill Sewing Society, Bridgeport, Conn.," both Vol. 3, no. 3 (November 1830), and the like.
23. Crevecoeur, *Letters from An American Farmer* (see note 4), 159; Hart, *Miriam Coffin* (see note 6), 2:176, 194.
24. George Richmond to Leonard S. Gifford, June 19, 1854, Leonard S. and Lucy Gifford Papers, Mss. B 85-29 [sic], Old Dartmouth Historical Society Whaling Museum Library, New Bedford, Mass. (hereafter ODHS). The owners of Captain Gifford's ship were trying (successfully) to persuade him to stay in the Pacific an additional year; Lucy ended up waiting nearly six years before Leonard returned in 1857. They married two weeks after his arrival.
25. Joan Druet has studied every extant diary of a nineteenth-century whaling wife she could locate in archives and collections from New Zealand to New Bedford; her main impression is that most (but not all) of the wives were unhappy at sea. (Personal conversation, April 1989.) Druett has written that some of their journals "emanated contentment," whereas others "are depressing accounts of discomfort, loneliness, seasickness, and a deep grinding misery of pining for home." See Joan Druett, "Those Female Journals," *Log of Mystic Seaport* 40. no. 4 (winter 1989): 115–25.
26. Mary Brewster Diary kept onboard the ship Tiger, 1845–48, entry 12/26/1845, Log 38, MSM (see note 20); Mary Chipman Lawrence diary entry for 3/14/1857 in *The Captain's Best Mate: The Journal of Mary*

Chipman Lawrence on the Whaler ADDISON, 1856-60, ed. Stanton Garner, (Hanover, N.H., 1966), 19.
27. Exchange of letters between Thomas Knowles & Co. and Mrs. B.A. Penniman, ca. 1862–63, Knowles Family Business Records, Mss. 55, Subgroup 2, Series L, Sub-series 5. ODHS (see note 24).
28. Samuel Braley diary kept on board the ship *Arab* 1849–53, entries 12/21/1850 and 3/2/1850, Kendall Whaling Museum, Sharon, Mass. (hereafter KWM).
29. "Suffer and be still" was a Victorian prescription for ideal female behavior, quoted by Martha Vicinus in the title of her anthology, *Suffer and Be Still: Women in the Victorian Age*, ed. Martha Vicinus, (Bloomington, Ind., 1972). "Men must work and women must weep" is a line from a poem by Charles Kingsley, quoted in the Introduction, *To Work and to Weep: Women in Fishing Economies*, ed. Jane Nadel-Klein and Dona Lee Davis, (St. John's, Newfoundland, 1988), 7.
30. "Perils of the Sea," *Sailor's Magazine and Naval Journal* 10, no. 11, (July 1838); reprinted from the *Boston Recorder*.
31. For a significant parallel, see Dona L. Davis. "Woman the Worrier: Confronting Archetypes of Stress," *Women's Studies* 20. no. 2 (1983): 135–46.
32. Elisabeth Taber to John Taber, 5/1/1842, Alexander Hamilton Cory Papers, Mss. 80, Subgroup 3, Series K, Subseries 4, ODHS (see note 24).
33. A number of historians of nineteenth-century women have noted that the elaboration of a separate sphere for women brought with it an articulation of hostility toward men, especially in female reform movements. See, among others, Carroll Smith-Rosenberg, "Beauty, the Beast and the Militant Woman: A Case Study in Sex Roles and Social Stress in Jacksonian America," *Disorderly Conduct* (New York, 1985), 109–28.
34. "The Mariner's Wife," *Sailor's Magazine and Naval Journal* 10, no. 11 (July 1838); reprinted from the *New-Hampshire Telegraph*.
35. Myra E. Weeks to William Weeks, 7/10/1842, Alexander Hamilton Cory Papers, Mss. 80, Subgroup 3, Series K, Subseries 4, ODHS (see note 24).
36. Caroline Gifford to Charles Gifford, 6/7/1866: Eleanor Gifford postscript on letter from Caroline Gifford to Charles Gifford, 9/1/1867; Mss. 56, Series G, Subseries 7, ODHS (see note 24).

37. Libby Spooner to Caleb Spooner, 12/3/1858, Alexander Hamilton Cory Papers, Mss. 80, Subgroup 3, Series K, Subseries 4, ODHS (see note 24).
38. Sarah Howland to Philip Howland, 10/26/1845, Philip Howland Papers, KWM (see note 28).
39. William Loring Taber to Susan Taber, 11/20/1856, William Loring Taber Papers, Mattapoisett Historical Society, Mattapoisett, Mass. William Ashley concurred. He wrote his wife, Hannah, "it does very well for single men to be goin [whaling] a life time but I do not think it is healthy for the married." Shortly thereafter, William requested his discharge and left the voyage halfway through it; he returned to Hannah and the farm in Acushnet where he settled down permanently. (William Ashley to Hannah Ashley, 9/13/1863, privately owned collection, Acushnet, Mass.). Other mariners whose careers I traced, Philip Howland, Leonard Gifford and Abner Howes, took the less drastic measure of switching into other maritime industries that required shorter and more predictable absences from home.
40. Edward R. Ashley to parents, 12/1/1855, privately owned collection, Acushnet, Mass.
41. Lizzie Howes to Abner Howes, Jr., 10/1/1854, Hamer Family Papers, Schlesinger Library, Radcliffe College, Cambridge, Mass. Abner was a merchant seaman rather than a whaleman, but he and his family hailed from a part of Cape Cod which also supplied many men to the whaling industry.

Chapter Sixteen
'Better than Diamonds':
Sentimental Strategies and Middle-Class Culture in Canada West

Cecilia Morgan

The press in Canada West (mid-nineteenth-century Ontario) drew upon sentimental narratives and images to discuss themes and processes that were part of middle-class cultural and social formation in this period, particularly the development of the categories "private" and "public" and corresponding attempts to identify white, bourgeois womanhood with the former (the world of home and family) and middle-class masculinity with the latter (the world of the marketplace and political arena). Sentimental ideology also provided a means of writing about those deemed to be "others" in bourgeois and imperial discourses: working-class and plebeian men and women, Native men and women, black Canadians, men and women from non-British and Catholic countries, and sexual "deviants" involved in prostitution. The paper concludes with an exploration of how black Canadians, in the pages of Mary Ann Shadd's *Provincial Freeman*, attempted to both mobilize and counter the bourgeois languages found in the mainstream press. [...]

On a cold winter's day in a large city, so the story goes, a little girl had a chance encounter with a beautiful rich woman in front of a jeweller's store. The child was taking slippers for "spangling" back to her mother who did piecework in the garret where they lived; she had slipped on the ice in front of the store. She wore no shoes and her clothes were threadbare rags. Her father, she told the lady, was dead, her baby brother was ill, and her mother bound shoes. The pair she held in her hand had to be finished by tonight or there would be no more work and, moreover, her mother had no money to buy milk for the sick baby. Her listener, upon seeing the name stamped on the shoe, flushed and then turned pale; the child's story brought tears to her eyes but she went into the store without offering her any money and as she left the store the narrator tells us that the glitter of a diamond pin could be seen. The child, in the meantime, returned home to a "small, dark room" with only a candle, a scanty fire and a little piece of bread. After hearing her prayers and folding her "tenderly to her bosom," her mother told her that the angels would always take care of her and returned to her sewing. The child dreamt of "warm stockings, and new shoes." Did her mother dream of a "bright room, and gorgeous clothing, and a table loaded with all that was good and nice ... of a pleasant cottage, and of one who had dearly loved her, and whose strong arms had kept want and trouble from her and her babes, but who could never come back?" If she did entertain such fantasies, she also put her trust in God and asked for his forgiveness.

As the mother drifted off to sleep over the fine slipper, the door opened slowly and someone ("was it an angel?") entered, leaving behind soft, warm blankets draped over the girl, a blazing fire, a huge loaf, fresh milk, and, taking the unfinished slipper from the mother's hand, a bag of gold. In a "voice like music," the beneficent intruder said "Blessed thy God, who is the God of the fatherless and the widow," and departed, murmuring "Better than diamonds! Better than diamonds!" The mother awoke, saw the transformation and with "clasped hands and streaming eyes," blessed God for sending an angel. Leaving the garret, the narrator then takes the reader to a ballroom, with bright lights, music, flowers, dancing, happy faces, and beautiful women in rich dresses and jewels. But only one woman truly stood out from the crowd, wearing a simple white dress with only a rosebud on her bosom. Her voice, we are told, was "like the sweet sound of a silver lute"; she had no spangled slippers to wear but the "divine beauty of holiness had so glorified her face" that the narrator felt "she was indeed an angel of God."[1]

"Better than Diamonds" was by no means an unusual story in the canon of mid-Victorian sentimental fiction. The cast of characters (the pathetic yet brave widow and her family, especially the innocent child who was the catalyst for the beneficent anonymous donor's actions); the large, impersonal city, whose anonymity could allow it to be either London or New York; the themes of hard work, bad fortune (especially the absent father), maternal self-sacrifice, trust in providence, and virtue rewarded through the medium of feminine benevolence were all to be found in fiction published in newspapers, periodicals, and popular novels. As a number of historians of middle-class formation in Britain and America have pointed out, the tropes and rhetorical strategies of sentimental fiction were more than marketing devices deployed by middle-class writers eager to capture a reading audience. Sentimentality itself was a cultural tool that helped provide the middle classes with a framework for envisioning and regulating the relations of gender, class, and race within the British and American bourgeoisie. This framework helped to divorce the so-called public realm of political life from the private world of affections, masking and obscuring the relations of power and contestation that shaped and linked home, market, nation-state, and imperial power.[2]

Some Canadian historians have explored these issues, but middle-class cultural configurations in Ontario during the mid-nineteenth century have yet to receive the sustained attention given to developments in Britain and the United States.[3] Furthermore, with a few notable exceptions, historians of this period have not deployed gender as an analytical category and Canadian gender historians have not displayed much interest in mid-nineteenth-century Ontario. Yet by examining a selection of newspapers, including some that were well-known and politically influential, some from smaller centres, and one which represented the distinctive racial minority perspective of black Canadians, it is possible to explore this facet of middle-class cultural development and to examine how it was imbue with relations of gender and race. In the pages of the press members of the colonial middle class both were presented with — particularly through the medium of literature imported from Britain and America — and participated in their own moral self fashioning. [...] As in other national contexts during this period, the delineations of private and public were mapped out and usually (albeit not inevitably) coded as female and male, providing readers with a blueprint for the organization of colonial society.[4] [...]

By the early 1850s the British colony of Upper Canada (renamed Canada West in 1841 after its legislative union with Lower Canada/

Canada East) had undergone a number of significant shifts. Developments heralded by historians as shaping and signifying the emergence of the middle class included the attainment of responsible government, the expansion of the state in areas from banking and transportation to education, the growth of commercial and, on a smaller scale, manufacturing enterprises, an increase of immigration into urban centres, and the development of voluntary societies. The province's middle class was not as widespread as it would be later in the nineteenth century, and it was fragmented by regional, political, religious, and occupational differences.[5] But within the pages of the press, itself a bourgeois institution, dialogues were conducted between writers and readers on the nature of middle-class identities, moral virtues, and self-representation.[6]

The sentimental and, to a lesser extent, melodramatic, narratives and rhetorical devices of articles such as "Better than Diamonds" (printed in the *Niagara Mail* in 1853) permeated both fictional and factual writings in the press. They provided authors with convenient modes of explaining and justifying social, political, and economic changes. By valorizing the individual woman's or man's feelings and emotions, particularly humanitarian impulses; by evoking similar feelings in the spectator and reader; by placing sentiment upon a higher moral plain than unfeeling logic and rationality; by enacting sentimentality upon men's and, in particular, women's bodies through signs such as tears, sighs, groans, and sobs; by fetishizing innocence, particularly children's; and by linking these elements in familial relations, middle-class writers explained themselves and pronounced upon the character and activities of others. The rescue and redemption of workers, Native peoples, the sexually "deviant," and unbelievers whose presence was so often necessary to sentimental narratives were also crucial in the formation of middle-class identity; so too was a tendency to deny the power relations that framed encounters between them and Anglo-Canadian bourgeois men and women. Finally, gender relations were defined by middle-class commentators to elide or efface inequities of class or colonial expansion. A few authors, however, contested and provided alternative meanings of mid-century cultural and social developments; not all Upper Canadians believed in the power of "rescuing angels."

BOURGEOIS FAMILIES AND FASHIONABLE TEMPTATIONS

The strength of maternal love, considered to be an extremely powerful and entirely natural emotion, was a theme addressed in fictional pieces run by the Methodist newspaper, the *Christian Guardian*. "The Governor and the Mother," narrated by the president of Emory College, told of an encounter between the state's governor and the mother of a man condemned to death.[7] Set at the narrator's residence on the school's graduation day, the story reached its climax when she fell to her knees and begged the governor for pity, a sight that moved men (including the narrator) to tears. Lifting her, he repeated his refusal to pardon her son, whereupon a cross between a sigh and a groan came from her heart, "an indescribable out-breathing of all that is eloquent in grief and melting in sorrow." All fell silent, and the president's home, "so lately the scene of mirth, was like the court of death." In a passage evoking the prisoner's walk to the scaffold, she then rose, "tremblingly advanced," but on the last porch step "cast a melting look," made one last verbal appeal, and sank to the floor. This last entreaty had the desired effect, presumably, for upon rising and leaving she was followed by the governor.

Sentiment worked through and was enacted on the bodies of both women and men: the fainting, beseeching mother who, having walked sixty-five miles, prostrated herself before the masculine, upright body of the governor, and also the male spectators who were moved to tears as, it was hoped, would be the reader As well, the unnamed female protagonist was defined entirely by maternity; she had no other function or relationship to her audience. She was also the only woman in the otherwise masculine enclave of an institution of higher learning closed to women. The governor was presented in contrast as a dispassionate representative of the (masculine) public and the state, who was charged with the powers of life and death. He was not, however, impervious to the ties of affection and domesticity.[8]

Sentimental appeals based on selfless maternity evoked the highest moral values, possessing a rationality, logic, and sincerity superseding the supposedly logical reasoning of courtrooms and juries. In this context, a woman's body could be employed in ways that transgressed the boundaries of genteel femininity and that would be deemed disorderly in other contexts. A woman crying out, weeping copious tears, flinging herself on the floor, and displaying physical abandon in public were forms of physical expression that had earlier been decried by conservative commentators as symptoms of social and political anarchy. By the 1850s, they had also fallen into disfavour with many colonial evangelicals.[9] While sentimentality permitted certain physical displays of emotion for both women and men it also channelled these displays, demarcating and patrolling the boundaries between appropriate and inappropriate behaviours.

Relations between mothers and sons were a recurring theme in the fiction run by newspapers such as the *Guardian*. In "The Factory Boy," the nine-year-old hero has promised his dying mother that he would look after his younger siblings. He kept his promise and extended his care to his workmates' and neighbours' spiritual well-being. When he died prematurely in an industrial accident the streets were filled with mourners, his funeral was a sight rarely seen, and his dirge was "the uncontrollable groans of a heart-stricken multitude." Here the power of maternal affection and Christian piety were visibly intertwined. The dying body of the mother helped to trigger and set in motion true religion, realized at the story's climax in the damaged — yet redeeming — body of the son. His life and death also triggered emotional, physically manifested responses from the community.[10] Furthermore, as in "Better than Diamonds," gender was deployed to stabilize and contain class inequalities, effacing them by drawing the reader's attention to domesticity rather than to poverty or dangerous working conditions.[11]

While the beseeching bodies of mothers were enlisted in the struggle against immorality and irreligion, many religious writers emphasized the paternal authority of fathers and husbands. Men were urged to take an active role in religion, particularly in overseeing and guiding the religious practices of their households through family prayers. The lesson of didactic fiction such as "Family Prayers" was clear: "May heads of households consider well their responsibilities and train their children in the ways of duty of religion, and teach them a reverence for all the sacred ordinances of religious worship."[12] Those who did not fulfill these duties might see their wives and children enticed by the seduction of the ballroom, an ever-present danger in a society which, according to Egerton Ryerson, was undergoing a "too worldly, sensual, dancing epidemic at present." Balls were held to celebrate everything and anything, from the opening of lying-in hospitals to the arrival of a new governor.[13] Not only were such environments conducive to displays of physical abandonment — in themselves suggestive of sexual immorality — they also encouraged girls and young women to fritter away their time on frivolous accomplishments, rather than learning useful household skills that would win them sober and sensible husbands. In such writers' moral economy, a notable shift had occurred in the definition of "feminine" arts and crafts. The decorative and "modern" had replaced the long-standing utilitarian traditions of spinning, plain-sewing, knitting, straw plaiting, baking, brewing, and animal husbandry. The result did little to improve colonial social and economic conditions. Fashion, frivolity, urbanity, and possibly irreligion were signified by crochet hooks and embroidery, in contrast to the more useful tools of agrarian womanhood, the knitting needle and spinning wheel.[14]

Even writers who did not couch their critiques of bourgeois society in such nostalgic terms believed that overindulgence in fashion was contrary to women's well-being. Middle-class aspirations to fashionable respectability sacrificed a more natural environment and imposed restrictions of dress and movement on women and children.[15] The victimized wife, a favourite image of temperance literature, also appeared in such satires of middle-class pretensions as "Pipkin's Ideas of Family Retrenchment," in which Mr. Pipkin's fondness for expensive suits, horses, and wining and dining his male friends was conducted at the expense of his wife's and children's domestic comfort.[16]

Women could be victims in other ways, as the *Globe* told its readers in its 1855 tales of threats by sexual predators to the virtue of the city's young, single women. Such tales were not new: earlier in the century the Upper Canadian press had run cautionary stories of young women who had been betrayed and abandoned by duplicitous men.[17] Yet George Brown's revelations about the existence of Toronto brothels and their owners' need for young women's virginity elaborated upon earlier imagery, giving it specific local meanings and also pointing to a new sexual villain: the prostitute/madam. In its coverage of police raids on Toronto brothels, the paper constructed a world of "dissolute women," where male sexual desire might ultimately underpin the ruin of young girls, but women themselves were often the agents of their unhappy fates. "A Disorderly House" recounted the story of a fifteen-year-old girl enticed into a house of "ill fame" on Duchess street by a "set of dissolute women." Two officers were immediately dispatched to the address, where they found a number of women of all ages, a few of them drunk, lying on the floor and reclining on "bundles of rags."[18] In contrast to the scenes of middle-class domesticity that papers such as the *Globe* liked to describe, the house was sparsely furnished, with boxes for seats, an old bedstead, potatoes (possibly a hint that these women were Irish), a looking-glass, and whisky (symbolic of the vanity and moral weaknesses that had led to these women's downfall). Seven women were arrested and each given a month's hard labour.[19]

The problem did not end with their incarceration, however, for one month later the paper announced that the young daughter of a respectable tradesman had vanished. Private information led the police to a house on the west side of Victoria Street that had for some time been suspected of "harbouring disorderly females." The girl had apparently met a woman on the street who had lured her into the place "under the most specious promises"; she was now, the paper was happy to report, back at home with her parents.[20] To discuss the probable increase in prostitution during the mid-nineteenth-century growth, social commentary used melodramatic languages and narrative conventions encoded with images of women either as helpless innocents or as hardened madams who contributed to the innocents' social and moral ruin. Sexually predatory men might be understood to lurk behind the women who lay on bundles of rags, but the men who occupied centre stage in these tales were the Toronto police, the rescuers of young girls. These men represented the order of law and the state that was instrumental in restoring these girls to the safety of their families.

The Toronto police were not the only saviours in scripts of sexual danger. The city's Magdalen Asylum's *Report* of 1855 relied on many of the same rhetorical devices as the *Globe's* warnings, but it also deployed sentimental imagery in its tale of rescues and reformations. While the asylum's managing board consisted of eight men, including two ministers and men who were active in Toronto's voluntary societies, such as James Lesslie and G.W. Allan, the institution was also served by a thrity-one-member ladies' committee with surnames such as Baldwin, Dunlop, Robinson, and Lesslie. This group performed one of the asylum's most important activities: "the periodic visits of the ladies to Jail." From that institution the asylum gathered in its outcasts. Using the language of Christian love alongside the tropes of women's victimization and the lady who would uplift them, the report stated that the committee's members were "gratefully received" by those they visited, despite hearts hardened by licentiousness. When appeals were made to Christian love and the gospels were heeded, "many a weeping eye has given testimony that the springs of sensibility had not wholly been dried up in that moral descent." The asylum housed three women in a "hopeful condition" and had sent one to hospital, where she had recently died in hope of religion; six women had gone into service, four to their friends and three to the House of Industry. To be sure, these figures were small in comparison with rescue work in New York City but, nevertheless, the asylum performed a valuable service. The women in it were friendless and were "watched for by those monster criminals who keep houses of infamy and live by the ruin and death of women" (there were, the committee believed, at least ten such houses in Toronto). The "most wicked artifices are being constantly employed to supply them with victims": young, innocent girls, particularly those who were new to the city and looking for work, were enticed to these places and then ruined.[21] As we have seen, this story would be all too familiar to the paper's readers, although the villains of this piece — the monster criminals —were not given a gender-specific identity, unlike the hardened madams of the other articles. And, in the asylum's narrative of rescue and uplift, these unfortunates were saved by other women, by middle-class, respectable "ladies," not by representatives of the nineteenth-century state.

This choice of melodramatic narrative was not entirely new, nor was it confined to mid-nineteenth-century Ontario. These pieces were not just reflecting or describing a social evil in Toronto; instead, they were part of widespread Anglo-American discourses on commercialized sexuality.[22] Moreover, while the rescue and redemption of Toronto's fallen women by their moral sisters may have provided readers with the satisfaction of a morally uplifting ending to the narrative, sentimentality was never the only language used by the colonial press to represent gender relations and, in particular, womanhood. Other kinds of femininity and other kinds of women were delineated by writers' portraits that differed in many ways from the heroine of "Better than Diamonds," the Daughters of Temperance, or the virtuous rescuers of the Magdalen Asylum's penitent inhabitants. The records of convictions from the Lincoln and Welland county courts, for example, presented women as both plaintiffs and defendants: Harriet Allan prosecuted Jane Kirkland for assault and damage, Bridget Welsh charged Charles Blake for assault and battery, and Elizabeth Madden took Judy McNamara to court for a breach of a by-law.[23] Four years later, "Bloody Affray" recounted the story of two women of Hibbert Township who came to blows over a man whom both claimed as their husband. Ellen Doyle was arrested for attacking Mrs. Dougherty when the two met in the woods; Doyle cut her husband's first wife's throat with a razor, slashing her "sinews, veins, and windpipe." Although Mrs. Dougherty was not expected to live, she apparently had won the fight and received an apology from Doyle. The latter was a "fearful spectacle" upon her arrest, "being covered with wounds and her clothes saturated with blood."[24] The press treated this encounter with morbid fascination suggesting that such behaviour was not commonly found amongst women and that such women were decidedly not ladies.

Beyond even the maternal redemption offered by middle-class women of the Magdalen Asylum's voluntary committee, Ellen Doyle was deemed fit only for the punitive, paternalistic hand of the colonial state. For the readers of such pieces she served as a warning and reminder of the limits of sentimentality's power to regulate behaviour and character, but she also highlighted the need for such regulation in the first place, inspiring readers to re-examine and re-evaluate their character and, perhaps, to congratulate themselves on their moral distance from the Ellen Doyles of the colony.

Racial Redemption

Working-class prostitutes were one of many groups perceived by the colonial middle class to need rescue and salvation. For religious writers, the transformation of the potentially unruly bodies of Native peoples through Christianity was one of the triumphs of both revealed religion and the sentimental ethos. Children were particularly popular in sentimental writing and Native children delivered especially poignant messages in obituaries. For example the obituary of nine-year-old Ellen Hess, the daughter of Sampson, a Mohawk chief, told of her youthful piety and its effect on her family. Ellen, a student at the local mission school from the age of four, had woken her father with her praying a few nights before her death. Ellen "clapped her hands in seeming joyful emotion" in the "agonies of death," despite being "speechless."[25] Ellen's physical condition — the reasons for her death — is left unmentioned and is not important. Rather, the reader should be impressed, and presumably moved to tears by the power of religious faith, manifested upon her child's body, to transcend the "agonies of death" and become an instrument of her race's conversion.[26] The effect of the Gospel on her parents, both in family worship and in sustaining Ellen in her last days, raised the "writer's bowed head and drooping spirits" (many aspects of mission work at the Grand River were disheartening and discouraging) with '"results that may swell the celestial choir."

If Ellen Hess' death might be represented as a sentimental spectacle that transcended "race, class, and gender boundaries,"[27] the *Guardian*'s depiction of a camp meeting held at the Saugeen reserve near Lake Huron went even further in how reformed characters and morals might be written on Native bodies for the edification of a non-Native audience. The meeting was attended by Indians from Port Sarnia, Beausoeil, and Nawash, "A Lover of Camp Meetings" told the readers; some were pagans but most were "under the influence of Christianity." During the evening exercises, led by the Methodist missionary Conrad Van Dusen, "as the ground became illuminated by the surrounding fires the scene became truly impressive." A hymn of divine praise was "swelled forth by those whose manly voices in other years had joined to sing the song of war." Now, '"instead of brandished weapons and tomahawks reeking with the gore of human victims, whose bloody scalps of conquered foes lie scattered on the ground, or piled in heaps, or hung in show; we see the bended knee, we hear the humble prayer of supplication deep." This shift in Native masculinity was not lost on the writer, who went on in praise: "Christianity, most blessed, what changes hast thou wrought, yes what a trophy is here. Shall not heaven itself rejoice, and angels bright, their harps retune, of shining gold, to sing the praises of God and also to the Lamb."[28]

Clearly juxtaposed in this passage were elements that had previously signified Native manhood to many colonists — warchants, weapons, blood, and, especially, scalps — with those that now signalled Native men's identity: hymns, prayers, bent knees, and, above all, the subjugation of their bodies before a greater power. Instead of garnering the "trophies" of war, Native men now offered themselves as trophies to God, supposedly accepting both Christianity and white civilization. This passage was a particularly telling construction of the scene, because the Saugeen band had just been pressured to sign a treaty with the Canadian government surrendering their lands in the Bruce peninsula for non-Native settlement.[29] To be sure, four months earlier Van Dusen had protested the government's treatment of the Saugeen, pointing out to the *Guardian's* readers that they were still waiting for the fulfillment of "verbal promises" made at the signing of the treaty.[30] Yet evangelicals also hoped for the transformation of gender relations in Native communities, and the eradication of the warrior and hunter was a critical aspect of such changes.

Native men's bodies and morals — indeed, their entire culture — were thus seen as malleable, transmuted, and liberated of necessity for their own and their race's salvation. Colonial abolitionist rhetoric argued that the bodies of black men were not so much in need of an essential transformation as of a liberation that would restore the "innate" masculine dignity taken from them by slavery. In the pages of George Brown's *Globe* a number of rhetorical strategies were deployed to raise sympathy for the abolitionist cause, but a recurring figure was the black man whose masculine self-respect and honour had been affronted — although not erased — by the degradation of slavery. According to the *Globe,* the abolition of slavery would bring about a "glorious era" when all will be free and "the negro ... wakes to liberty" and "sleeps in peace." "Read the great charter on his brow/I am a man a brother now!"[31] It was not, as pro-slavery writers argued, any natural moral failing or character defect that had led slaves into their present condition. In "Beauties of Practical Republicanism," Brown castigated northern politicians who supported the 1850 Fugitive Slave Bill: "(should not) the heroism of these poor negros, who died rather than go back to life-bondage of mind and body, sink into utter bombast the shedding of blood in resistance of a tea-tax?"[32]

Brown felt obliged to spend a considerable amount of editorial ink defending both fugitives and free blacks from attacks on their characters and customs. A number of his readers agreed with his arguments.[33] "Pro-Slavery in a Church!" sent to the *Globe* by "An Observor [sic]" recounted an event that had recently occurred at a local Wesleyan church. A "fine, intelligent-looking, respectable and well-dressed lad" had been denied entry into a pew by his white companion's father; according to the writer the boy was "at least three-fifths to five-eights African." "The fine little fellow evidently felt this outrage upon his humanity, by retaining his hold of the door; and fixing his full, expressive eye, sparkling with indignation, which proved to be no other than a derisive look." He was pointed to a side seat but other members of the congregation, realizing what had just occurred, reacted with indignation and contempt. A gentleman "beckoned the little man" to his own seat and shared his scripture with him, inviting "his noble hand to press the same page with his own, thus sharing the sacred morsel together." The gentleman experienced happiness for having helped heal a "wounded spirit," the boy was made to feel welcome, and the congregation expressed its approval of the deed. "An Observor [sic]" suggested this incident might possibly have been motivated by class differences as well as racial prejudice, citing the growth of the invidious practice of using pews to classify congregations. The writer was indignant that the behaviour could occur in Canada; the colony's religious and philanthropic institutions, as well as its British constitution, should have guaranteed that Upper Canadians would not harbour "pro-slavery" sentiments.[34]

While the protagonist of this piece was a child and, like Ellen Hess, could be used to demonstrate the power of abolitionist sentiment, the foreshadowing of his manhood — "the little man," the "fine little fellow" — was meant to evoke not tears but righteous anger. Of course the image of the black child's and the white man's hands united in religious worship might bring forth a satisfied sigh directly from the reader's heart. In this tale, prejudice and bigotry were acknowledged, but they were personified as an immoral individual's aberration. The writer's point was that racist behaviour was not inherent in colonial structures and institutions. Instead, such conduct stemmed from one person's lack of enlightenment and humanitarian feeling. Racial prejudice thus could be countered by Upper Canadian political and social institutions and, even more importantly, by the moral suasion — expressed by the meeting of the hands — of those who took action to shame such individuals.

SELF-MADE MEN AND "NATIONAL" IDENTITIES

Anti-slavery rhetoric was deployed not only when the fates of Native peoples and blacks were at stake. Certainly it helped illuminate the plight of and raise sympathy for these particular groups; it suggested that their differences from those of European descent had been artificially imposed by cultural, socio-economic, and political forces. The trope of liberation from servitude was also deployed when distinctions needed to be drawn between Upper Canada and the United States or when the encroachments of the Catholic church were perceived as threatening the freedom of Upper Canadians. The language of anti-slavery was used to reinforce the colony's link to Britain and the imperial power's traditions of constitutional and religious freedoms (particularly those of Protestant churches). Much of this rhetoric was organized around the figure of the free, British, and Protestant man who had a history of combatting tyranny and absolutism. He would protect Upper Canadian liberties against slave-catchers, priests, and republican demagogues; he would also bring Native peoples under his protection and closer to his position. As an ideal to be worked towards (although never completely attained) by men of other races and a protector of the helpless and weak (especially women and children of all races and classes), in these discourses masculine integrity and morality was meant to complement the rescuing angels of sentimental fiction. Such a man was not, though, expected to emanate from a state of nature. His character was the product of years of careful maternal tutelage, followed by self regulation and control as he entered the workplace and became a responsible member of civil society.

[...]

The lessons in moral sagacity and self-control learned from pious mothers, writers on self-improvement, and temperance advocates were also used in the political realm, where a number of journalists and politicians held up the symbol of the "public man." The image developed during the 1840s political debates over the meanings of party in Canada West. The anxieties that surrounded the rise of political parties in the early 1840s may have dissipated by the early 1850s, but political figures were still identified as needing moral guidance — particularly those men who had succumbed to populist rhetoric.[35] While Brown's initial opposition to the Clear Grit movement would give way to an alliance with them in the mid-1850s, in the early years of the decade the *Globe's* editor not only "flatly rejected the Clear Grit program," he also charged its supporters with political immorality.[36] Many political figures, in Brown's opinion, did not measure up to the moral standards of the "public man" and sacrificed "manly independence" for sycophancy, falsehood, and manipulation of colonial politics for personal gain.[37] The *Globe* instructed its readers on how public men might identify and attain political morality: their private lives must be governed by the same moral standards as the public realm (particularly concerning sexual conduct); they must adhere to patriotic principles, the foundation of political principle and public service; they must be prepared to submit to the people's never-ending surveillance and judgment. The colony possessed many public men who could serve their country, "whose principles are sound, and motives pure."

[...]

The temptations of political life were particularly alluring because of the power that public men supposedly wielded, above all the power to dispense patronage, an essential element of nineteenth-century Ontario politics.[38] Brown's position was not held by all: as Paul Romney has argued, Brown and Hincks and their supporters represented differing perspectives on the meanings of political morality. Brown's beliefs reflected Lockean theories of representative government in which public officials were trustees empowered by the public to act for the social good, not their own. Other political figures, such as John Beverley Robinson, argued that public men's moral obligations did not preclude the use of political office to enrich their private life: public office was a piece of property bought by those of high rank, whose social and political standing entitled them to all of its fruits.[39]

Concerns over morality in public life were not limited to men who ran for office. Attacks on Catholics, many published by the *Globe*, often focused on the tyranny of ultramontanism (whereby a foreign, unelected power made decisions that affected the liberties of British subjects). They also suggested that men who obeyed the Catholic church had renounced their manly independence to bow to Rome's despotism, and were no better than slaves. With its suggestion that Catholic clerics (and their political supporters) were unmanly and effeminate, some of this rhetoric was redolent of 1820s and 1830s reform attacks on churchmen who took money from the state.[40] But attacks on bishops and priests in the previous decades had targeted them as parasites and sycophants because of their financial relationship to the state (whether Anglican or, after 1833,

Methodist); the articles of the 1850s were much more clearly focused on the Catholic Church and its effect on British manhood.[41] [...]

Sentiment and the *Provincial Freeman*

Black Upper Canadians' formations of race, gender, and class have received even less attention from historians than those of their white contemporaries.[42] The pages of the *Provincial Freeman* provide some hints for future research by historians. While not the first anti-slavery paper in the province, the *Freeman* was the first Upper Canadian paper to be co-founded and edited by a black woman, Mary Ann Shadd.[43] The *Freeman* emphasized "the elevation of the coloured people" through self-help. Some writers believed that elevation should create a black middle class. Moses argued that the African-Canadian community did not really need more labourers (although he hastened to assure his readers that all labour was inherently respectable). Instead, blacks in Canada should set their sights on becoming doctors, lawyers, schoolteachers, and merchants. They must educate themselves and their children, and with that end in mind, young men and women should form literary and debating societies. Such strategies may seem to replicate merely those of the white colonial middle class, particularly when coupled with the paper's emphasis on respectability through temperance. But we should also consider the differences that a history of slavery might make to narratives of racial and class uplift for, as Evelyn Brooks Higginbotham has argued, "racial meanings were never internalized by Blacks and whites in an identical way."[44] Shadd and other black writers supported black integration with whites, vehemently denounced those who opposed racial amalgamation as friends of slavery, and pointed to areas of the colony where blacks and whites coexisted happily. But they also insisted that blacks must take responsibility for their own fate. They hoped that whites (particularly white Upper Canadians whose connection to Britain would inspire them) would support their endeavours but, given the histories of racism and slavery in Anglo-American communities, many writers in the *Freeman* stressed that blacks must develop their own strengths as individuals and as a community. They could not rely solely on the goodwill of British men and women to perform their work for them.

Because of this insistence on self-sufficiency, and because the paper also appealed to a black audience, the language of the *Freeman* did not rely as heavily or exclusively on images of victimization as did anti-slavery rhetoric in the *Globe*. One writer insisted that not all blacks in Canada West came as fugitives who had to earn respectability in the eyes of whites. "Our Free Colored Emigrants" compared the position of this group to fugitive men and women who arrived in Upper Canada, "hunted" and destitute, and who therefore were given help and welcomed. Free blacks from the northern United States "who know the value of pounds, shillings and pence — who ha[ve] attended to [their] business without the anxious care' of a master" were not given the same reception, however, although they were progressive, enterprising and "go onward, planning, improving, accumulating and enlarging." While free blacks might feel less welcome than fugitives, they should play an essential role in the black community. As "a class of men not in service to any man, they must, by common consent, take a position in which they can cheer on the weaker brethren who have just emerged from oppression; and as the bone and sinew of a powerful and increasing class they will ... help to shape the destiny of this continent."[45]

The *Freeman*'s conception of gender relations also differed significantly from that of other papers. Instead of the ridicule and fear apparent in other Toronto papers when the American women's rights movement was discussed, Lucy Stone's Toronto lecture was described enthusiastically. Stone, Shadd informed her readers, had a reputation as a talented woman and orator; even in Toronto, with its "strong attachment to antiquated notions respecting woman and her sphere so prevalent," she was greeted with patience and much applause. The St. Lawrence Hall was packed and there were no shouts of brigadier or virago. Shadd was disappointed, however, that so few "coloured people seized upon the occasion to learn lessons of practical wisdom." Shadd's own support for women's suffrage influenced her treatment of Stone; the *Freeman* was one of the very few papers consulted here to accept women's right to speak *for* their rights in public. In its pages Lucy Stone thus appears as a very different figure than in other paper's published in the colony.[46]

Upon her resignation from the paper's editorship in 1855, Shadd wrote an "Adieu" to her readers that acknowledged the "difficulties, and ... obstacles such as we feel confident few, if any, females have had to contend against in the same business, except the sister who shared our labors [sic] for awhile." And "to colored women, we have a word — we have 'broken the editorial ice,' whether willingly or not, for your class in America; so go to Editing, as many of you as are willing, and able, and as soon as you may, if you think you are ready." Women who did not feel ready, Shadd wrote, should assist in other ways, by subscribing to the paper and encouraging their neighbours to do the same.[47] Shadd's comment about facing obstacles unknown to other women in journalism suggests that the configurations of race and gender might have very different meanings for African-Canadian women.[48]

While much work remains to be done on black women's and men's understandings of white womanhood in nineteenth-century Ontario, the *Freeman* suggests that they may have differed significantly from the image of the inherent beneficence and morel superiority of white women conveyed by evangelical writers. In the *Globe's* coverage of the address written by the Toronto Ladies' Association for Relief of Destitute Coloured Fugitives, the paper spoke of the usefulness of female influence, particularly within the family and in education.[49] The *Freeman* commended the appeal of white British women abolitionists who had called upon their American counterparts to work for the abolition of slavery.[50] But, as an article taken from "Lloyd's Newspaper" pointed out, American women had responded with an extraordinarily bad grace, so much so that their letter might have been written by a man. "We cannot mistake the masculine stride that distends the petticoats," wrote the author of "Mrs America answers Mrs England." Even if the response was the work of women, they "pucker their mouths, and with a prolonged, laborious, curtsey" beg English women to look to the behaviour of their own menfolk in India, Africa, China, and Ireland and towards the British working class. "With a truly feminine self-denial they swallow their indignation; put down the rising heart with a strong hand, and proceed with the catalogue. Sisters in America are so sisterly towards sisters of Stafford House!"[51] There was little here to suggest women's elevated morality or natural propensity to help the oppressed and down-trodden.

At times white women were directly implicated in the viciousness of slavery, as slaveholders themselves. Such was the lesson of "Slavery in Baltimore," which recounted the cruel treatment of slaves by rich owners. One particularly wealthy woman was notorious for her inhumanity. Her coachman died of frostbite after being kept outside on her carriage in bitter weathers; another slave, who escaped after similar treatment, was caught by the woman's son and made to run for sixteen miles; yet another woman was left crippled after falling from a third-storey window (she had fallen asleep while washing windows as the result of being deprived of rest as a punishment). "Such is the system as administered by the rich, the fashionable, and the aristocratic," concluded the writer.[52] The viciousness of this woman might be attributed to her class, for middle-class writers often targeted men and women of the aristocracy for their callousness towards the poor. This writer did not suggest that her womanly nature or maternal feeling might mitigate or soften her contempt for the human beings whom she owned and who served her.

Middle-class sentimentality was deployed to reify definitions of private and public and to exalt the middle-class family as the epitome of harmonious relations, yet at times the trajectory taken by sentimental rhetoric undermined apparently monolithic meanings and challenged the seeming confinement of middle-class white women to home and hearth. These women's voluntary efforts often deployed the kinds of rhetoric discussed above, shaping their work in temperance, religious fundraising and similar efforts within the public realm of Upper Canadian society.[53] None of this work, to be sure, enjoyed the same access to formal institutions and their prestige as the labours of men's organizations. Yet such women's willingness and ability to mobilize the languages of sympathy, sensibility, and domesticity begs further exploration from historians of Ontario's middle class, of colonialism, and of the women's movement of the late nineteenth century.[54]

At present it is difficult to determine, given the lack of research in this area, to what extent and in what ways these discourses shaped the subjectivities and identities of individual middle-class men and women; it also remains to be seen how these languages were contested and debated within the public realm of moral and social reform. As Bruce Curtis has pointed out, British and American school reformers vigorously opposed fiction because of its focus on experience and appeal to emotion. In their eyes, sentimental fiction also lacked rationality and self-discipline; readers constantly bombarded with pitiful tales would become hardened to real-life instances of suffering and would refuse to participate in philanthropic endeavours, thus precipitating working-class revolt.[55] Yet in the public pages of the colony's press, sentimental images of middle-class domesticity were a critical component of the language of bourgeois formation in nineteenth-century Ontario, justifying women's supposed confinement to the home because of their positions as wives and mothers; they also legitimated the individual woman's tears and the subjectivity that produced them. This language of feelings and affection reached beyond the individual to justify the mobilization of middle-class men and especially women, producing a consciousness that went beyond tears to the moral condition unpinning moral and social reform movements of the late nineteenth century. The contradictions that existed in mid-nineteenth-century, middle-class sentimental rhetoric may have supplied middle-class women later in the century with the scripts that allowed them to enact the roles of rescuing angels — with results that were contradictory for both themselves and for those deemed in need of salvation.

NOTES

I would like to thank Paul Deslandes, Steven Heathorn, and Tori Smith for their comments on an earlier version of this piece. I would also like to thank the *Journal of Canadian Studies* anonymous reviewers for their very helpful and perceptive comments and suggestions.

1. "Better than Diamonds," *Niagara Chronicle*, 11 March 1853.
2. For discussions of such literature and sentimental thought in general, see Ann Douglas, *The Feminization of American Culture* (New York: Knopf, 1977); Shirley Samuels, ed., *The Culture of Sentiment: Race, Gender, and Sentimentality in Nineteenth-Century America* (New York: Oxford University Press, 1992); G. J. Barker-Benfield, *The Culture of Sensibility: Sex and Society in Eighteenth-Century England* (Chicago: University of Chicago Press, 1992).
3. In the case of Canada West (present-day Ontario), work on the development of the middle class has focused on political and economic themes; see, for example, David G. Burley, *A Particular Condition in Life: Self-Employment and Social Mobility in Mid-Victorian Brantford, Ontario* (Montréal and Kingston: McGill-Queen's University Press, 1994). For examinations of social and cultural formation, see work in the history of education, particularly Bruce Curtis, *True Government by Choice Men? Inspection, Education, and State Formation in Canada West* (Toronto: University of Toronto Press, 1992); Bruce Curtis, *Building the*

Educational State: Canada West, 1836–1871 (London, Ont.: Althouse Press, 1988); Alison Prentice, "The Public Instructor: Ryerson and the Role of the Public School Administrator," in *Egerton Ryerson and His Times*, ed. N. McDonald and A. Chaiton (Toronto: Macmillan, 1978) 129–57; Robert Lanning, *The National Album: Collective Biography and the Formation of the Canadian Middle Class* (Ottawa: Carleton University Press, 1996).

4. See, for example, Leonore Davidoff and Catherine Hall, *Family Fortunes: Men and Women of the British Middle Class, 1780-1850* (Chicago: University of Chicago Press, 1987).

5. Many aspects of this process are discussed in Allan Greer and Ian Radforth, eds., *Colonial Leviathan: State Formation in Mid-Nineteenth-Century Canada* (Toronto: University of Toronto Press, 1992).

6. See Benedict Anderson, *Imagined Communities: Reflections on the Origins and Spread of Nationalism* (London: Verso, 1991) especially chapter three; also Jürgen Habermas, *The Structural Transformation of the Public Sphere. An Inquiry into a Category of Bourgeois Society*, trans. Thomas Burger and Frederick Lawrence (Cambridge Mass.: MIT Press, 1989), 59–67.

7. The press of both Upper Canada and Canada West often ran literature that originated in either the English and the American press. Our knowledge of circulation figures and readership of the colonial press is limited for this period, although W. H. Kesterton has argued that the number of newspapers grew from 1 in 1813 to 114 by 1853. The little that is known about subscription rates suggests that these publications were supported by a relatively small group, although the political impact of the press was far greater. Moreover, the number of subscribers also does not tell us much about total numbers of readers, since papers were likely passed around and read aloud. See W. H. Kesterton, *A History of Journalism in Canada* (Toronto: McClelland & Stewart, 1967), 11–44; Paul Rutherford, *The Making of the Canadian Media* (Toronto: McGraw-Hill Ryerson, 1978).

8. "The Governor and the Mother," *Christian Guardian*, 17 September 1851.

9. See Neil Semple, "The Quest for the Kingdom: Aspects of Protestant Revivalism in Nineteenth-Century Ontario," in *Old Ontario: Essays in Honour of J.M.S. Careless*, ed. David Keane and Colin Read (Toronto: Dundurn Press,1990), 95–117.

10. "The Factory Boy," *Christian Guardian*, 21 May 1851; see also "A Mother's Prayer," *Christian Guardian*, 13 June 1855.
11. Amy Schrager Lang, "Class and the Strategies of Sympathy," in *The Culture of Sentiment* (see note 2), 128–42.
12. Veritas, "Family Worship," *Christian Guardian*, 17 January 1855.
13. See the articles in the *Christian Guardian*: "The Dancing Season," "Dancing Among Professing Christians," 26 March 1851; "Dancing Among Professing Christians," 2 April 1851; "Dancing," 19 October 1853; "Revivals and Dancing Schools," 13 April 1853; "Shall Christians Dance?" 13 July 1853.
14. "The County Fair," *Niagara Mail*, 31 October 1855. See also "English Women in the Country," *Globe*, 3 April 1851; "A Word About the Plates in Books of Fashion," *Niagara Chronicle*, 21 August 1851.
15. Eliza Cook, "Best Rooms," *Canadian Son of Temperance*, 26 February 1851. This piece was also run by the *Globe*, 18 January 1851. See also "Woman Temperance," *Canadian Son of Temperance*, 8 February 1853; Fanny Fern, "Pipkin's Ideas of Family Retrenchment," *Canadian Son of Temperance*, 9 August 1953; Fanny Fern, "The Invalid Wife," *Provincial Freeman*, 27 May 1853. Similar pieces by anonymous authors were "Female Prudishness," *Provincial Freeman*, 20 January 1855, and "Miss Biffin the Limbless Lady," *Canadian Son of Temperance*, 15 November 1853. For Fanny Fern (Sarah Payson Willis), one of the most outspoken critics of antebellum domesticity, see Mary P. Ryan, *The Empire of the Mother: American Writing about Domesticity 1830–1860* (New York and London: Harrington Park Press, 1982), 118 and 123. Lauren Berlant, "The Female Woman: Fanny Fern and the Form of Sentiment," in *The Culture of Sentiment* (see note 2), 265–82.
16. Fanny Fern, "Pipkin's Ideas of Family Retrenchment," *Canadian Son of Temperance*, 9 August 1953.
17. See Cecilia Morgan, *Public Men and Virtuous Women: The Gendered Languages of Religion and Politics in Upper Canada, 1791–1850* (Toronto: University of Toronto Press, 1996), 143–5.
18. Precisely how they knew of the incident was not made clear, an absence of information that suggested the panoptic power of the force's surveillance and their knowledge of the city.
19. "A Disorderly House," *Globe*, 3 March 1855.
20. "Heartless Deception," *Globe*, 6 April 1855. See also "Society for the Protection of Young Females," *Globe*, 4 September 1853.

21. "The Magdalen Asylum — Annual Meeting," *Globe*, 28 May 1855.
22. See, for example, Anna Clark, "Queen Caroline and the Sexual Politics of Popular Culture in London, 1820," *Representations* 31(Summer 1990): 47–68; Judith R. Walkowitz, *City of Dreadful Delight: Narratives of Sexual Danger in Late-Victorian London* (Chicago: University of Chicago, 1992); Karen Dubinsky, *Improper Advances: Rape and Hetero-Sexual Conflict in Ontario, 1880–1920* (Chicago: University of Chicago, 1993). Although he does not focus on gender or sexuality, in "Law and Ideology: The Toronto Police Court 1850–80," Paul Craven notes the use of melodramatic language in police court reporting. See David Flaherty, ed., *Essays in the History of Canadian Law*, Volume II, (Toronto: University of Toronto Press, 1983), 248–307.
23. "Schedules of Convictions," *Niagara Chronicle*, 4 December 1851.
24. "Bloody Affray," *Niagara Mail*, 13 June 1855; see also "Frailty Thy Name is Woman," which was coverage of a similar clash (with less horrific results) between two women in Allegheny, New York (*Niagara Chronicle,* 26 August 1853).
25. A. W. Sickles, "Biographical," by *Christian Guardian*, 9 February 1853.
26. See Neil Semple, "The Nuture [sic] and Admonition of the Lord: Nineteenth-Century Canadian Methodist's Response to 'Childhood,'" *Histoire sociale/Social History* 27 (May 1981): 257–75.
27. Samuels, "Introduction," *The Culture of Sentiment* (see note 2), 3–8.
28. "Saugeen Camp Meeting," *Christian Guardian*, 4 October 1855. The "Lover" continued in this tone, describing the arrival of a party of white Christians from the nearby town of Southampton.
29. For a discussion of this treaty, see Donald B. Smith, *Sacred Feathers: The Reverend Peter Jones (Kahkewaquonaby) and the Mississauga Indians* (Toronto: University of Toronto Press, 1987) 225; also Peter S. Schmalz, *The Ojibwa of Southern Ontario* (Toronto: University of Toronto Press, 1991), 143–44.
30. C. Van Dusen, "The Saugeen Indian Affairs," *Christian Guardian*, 25 July 1855; also "Rama and Orillia Missions," 2 April 1851; "The Indian's Illustration," 23 March 1853.
31. "Slavery Not So Bad as People Think!" *Globe*, 11 March 1851. For a discussion of anti-slavery in Ontario, see Allan P. Stouffer, *The Light of Nature and the Law of God: Antislavery in Ontario 1833–1877* (Montreal and Kingston: McGill-Queen's University Press, 1992).

32. "Beauties of Practical Republicanism," *Globe*, 11 January 1851. This piece should also be read as a warning to those Clear Grits who admired American political culture of its moral consequences.
33. See, for example, "The Elgin Association," and "A Host of Negioes," 25 September 1851; "Anti-Slavery Society in Hamilton," *Globe*, 22 March 1853.
34. "Pro-Slavery in a Church!" *Globe*, 24 September 1853; see also "Slave Decoys at St. Catharines," *Globe*, 1 September 1855.
35. The emergence of the Clear Grit movement was an important part of this shift. Influenced by conceptions of American-style popular democracy, this group of men (many from the western area of the province) who challenged Robert Baldwin's liberal ministry have been described as left-wing: supporters of an elective constitution, the abolition of property qualifications for members of the legislature, fixed biennial parliaments, and representation by population. The Clear Grit platform also called for "free trade and direct taxation, the abolition of the Courts of Chancery and Common Pleas, the secularization of the reserves, and even Canadian control of external policy." For a discussion of the Clear Grits, see J. M. S. Careless, *The Union of the Canadas: The Growth of Canadian Institutions 1841–1857* (Toronto: McClelland & Stewart, 1967), 166–69; also his "Introduction" to *The Pre-Confederation Premiers: Ontario Government Leaders, 1841–1867* (Toronto: University of Toronto Press, 1980), 9–11. Careless, *The Union of the Canadas*, 169; see also *The Pre-Confederation Premiers*, 9–10.
36. Careless, *The Union of the Canadas* (see note 38), 169; see also *The Pre-Confederation Premiers* (see note 38), 9–10.
37. Brown's targets ranged from Malcolm Cameron, a wealthy lumber merchant from Sarnia who in 1850 had resigned his position as assistant commissioner of Public Works in Baldwin's cabinet in order to ally with the Clear Grits, to Francis Hincks, Baldwin's successor as western leader in the coalition government, and his supporters. See "The Sarnia Dinner," *Globe*, 16 July 1853; "Mr Vansittart," *Globe*, 9 August 1853.
38. S. J. R. Noel, "Canada West," *Patrons, Clients, Brokers: Ontario Society and Politics 1791–1896* (Toronto: University of Toronto Press, 1990).
39. Paul Romney, "'The Ten Thousand Pound Job': Political Corruption, Equitable Jurisdiction, and the Public Interest in Upper Canada, 1852–6," *Essays in the History of Canadian Law*, Volume II (see note 23),

143–99, especially 183; see also George A. Davison, "The Hincks-Brown Rivalry and the Politics of Scandal," *Ontario History* 81, no. 2 (June 1989): 129–51, especially 141–46.
40. See, for example "The Roman Organ," *Globe*, 1 July 1851; "William Lyon Mackenzie on Endowments," *Globe*, 30 April 1853.
41. J. R. Miller, "Anti-Catholicism in Canada: From the British Conquest to the Great War," in *Creed and Culture: The Place of English-Speaking Catholics in Canadian Society, 1750–1930*, ed. Terence Murphy and Gerald Stortz (Montréal and Kingston: McGill-Queen's University Press, 1993), 25–28. As Miller points out, not only was the church seen as intervening in the husband-wife relation, it was also perceived as a particularly misogynistic religion that denigrated marriage through its insistence on priestly celibacy and "destroyed the family by brutalizing and corrupting its heart, the wife and mother" (34–35). Later in the century, as J. R. Miller has argued, attacks on the church often focussed on the confessional and its potential to disrupt familial harmony by replacing a husband's authority with that of the priest.
42. Although see, for example, Robin Winks, *The Blacks in Canada* (New Haven: Yale University Press, 1971); C. Peter Ripley, *The Black Abolitionist Papers, Vol. 2, Canada, 1830–1865* (Chapel Hill: University of North Carolina Press, 1986); Peggy Bristow, Dionne Brand, Linda Carty, Afua P. Cooper, Sylvia Hamilton and Adrienne Shadd, *"We're Rooted Here and They Can't Pull Us Up": Essays in African Canadian Women's History* (Toronto: University of Toronto Press, 1994); Shirley J. Yee, "Gender Ideology and Black Women as Community-Builders in Ontario, 1850–70," *Canadian Historical Review* 75 (March 1994): 53–73.
43. Shadd, a member of a free black family from Delaware, had come to Canada in 1850, settling in Windsor and opening a school with money from the American Missionary Association. She quickly became involved in anti-slavery societies and in 1852 published *A Plea for Emigration*, which offered information on Canada West to African-Americans who wanted to move north. A year later Shadd founded the *Freeman*, inviting a prominent member of the African-Canadian community, Samuel Ringgold Ward, to serve as editor. But it appears that this was a task Ward performed in name only, for in 1854 when the paper moved to Toronto for one year Ward's name no longer appeared on the masthead.

Shadd continued to edit the paper with the help of her sister, Amelia, until 1855, just before she returned to southwestern Ontario to set up business in Chatham. The Reverend William Newman became the *Freeman's* editor, with Shadd devoting herself to the business of selling subscriptions and lecturing throughout the United States. She returned there in 1863 and, apart from visits to Canada in 1866 and 1881, spent the rest of her life in the United States. See Peggy Bristow, "Black Women in Buxton and Chatham, 1850–1865," *"We're Rooted Here"* (see note 57), 69–142, 105–122. See also Jim Bearden and Linda Jean Butler, *Shadd: The Life and Times of Mary Shadd Cary* (Toronto: NC Press, 1977). For Ward, the son of escaped slaves who had been a Congregational minister, teacher, temperance activist, and editor in New York state, and who was a fundraiser and lecturer for the Anti-Slavery Society of Canada, see Stouffer (note 32), 1201–29.

44. Evelyn Brooks Higginbotham, "African-American Women's History and the Metalanguage of Race," *Signs* 17, no. 2 (winter 1992): 251–74.
45. *Provincial Freeman*, 24 April 1853. See also the *Freeman's* editorial, "Introductory," 24 March 1853 and "Our Tour," 23 July 1854. At times the archetypal slave might be constructed as male. See "The Maroons," *Provincial Freeman*, 12 May 1855, for the story of Freme, the captive son of an African chief.
46. "Lectures," *Provincial Freeman*, 17 March 1855.
47. "Adieu," *Provincial Freeman*, 30 June 1855.
48. These differences are a theme addressed throughout Jacqueline Jones, *Labour of Love, Labour of Sorrow: Black Women, Work and the Family, From Slavery to the Present* (New York: Vintage Books, 1985).
49. "American Slavery," *Globe*, 11 January 1853. Brown also commended the ladies for not sweetening the truth, expressing it in plain speech.
50. This appeal was apparently sponsored by the Duchess of Sutherland; see Stouffer (note 32), 125–26.
51. "Mrs. America answers Mrs. England," *Provincial Freeman*, 24 March 1853.
52. "Slavery in Baltimore," *Provincial Freeman*, 30 June 1855.
53. "Knox Church Bazaar," *Globe*, 1 January 1851; "Soirees! Soirees! Soirees!" *Canadian Son of Temperance*, 19 April 1853; "The Women's Convention," *Canadian Son of Temperance*, 27 September 1853.
54. While work on women's participation in reform and suffrage has examined the relations of class and, to some extent, race to these movements, the

lack of an historiography for earlier decades of the nineteenth century makes it difficult to assess continuities and changes. See Linda Kealey, ed., *A Not Unreasonable Claim: Women and Reform in Canada, 1880s–1920s* (Toronto: The Women's Press, 1979); Mariana Valverde, *The Age of Light, Soap, and Water: Moral Reform in English Canada, 1885–1925* (Toronto: McClelland & Stewart, 1991).

55. Bruce Curtis, "'The Speller Expelled: Disciplining the Common Reader in Canada West," *Canadian Review of Sociology* and *Anthropology* 22, no. 3 (1985): 346–68, 357–58, 362.

Chapter Seventeen
The Case of the Missing Midwives: A History of Midwifery in Ontario from 1795–1900

C. Leslie Biggs

[...]

In recent years several histories of midwifery have been written.[1] While they vary both in time and place, each study reveals that the decline or elimination of the midwife can be attributed to the emergence of a male-dominated medical profession. Equally important, these studies demonstrate the role of patriarchal ideology which fostered male control over a uniquely female experience.[2]

This paper will analyze the relationship between the monopolization of medicine and the decline of female midwifery in Ontario. In order to do this, it will examine the major pieces of legislation governing medical practice from 1795 to 1900. Changes in the legislation reveal the medical profession's attempts to regulate its members, control education, and eradicate unwanted competition. In addition, because the issue of who should practise midwifery (i.e., female midwives or male physicians) became a heated one, an opportunity arises to examine the attitudes of both the medical profession and certain segments of the laity toward midwives. Finally, although the medical profession was successful in making midwifery illegal (except by a qualified practitioner), it does not automatically follow that attitudes would change. The last section of the paper examines the "meddlesome midwifery" debate which reveals that physicians were able to dominate childbirth by redefining it.

The Impact of The Institutionalization of Medicine Upon Midwifery

The first act to regulate the practice of physic and surgery in Upper Canada was passed on 6 July 1795.[3] This act made it illegal to practise medicine without a licence; only those who had university degrees or who were surgeons in the navy were exempt from licensing. But the act was found irrelevant to the conditions of the times. The absence of any record of an Examining Board being convened would seem to indicate that the act was not enforced.[4] Robert Gourlay stated that there were few men who were eligible to take the examination, and even those who held a university degree would not practise medicine since it was not profitable.[5] Furthermore, Gourley found the act particularily unfair to women since it prevented female midwives from practising:

> How absurd, how cruel, how meddling that a poor woman in labour could not have assistance from a handy, sagacious neighbour without this neighbour being liable to be informed upon and fined.[6]

However, despite its unfairness, the act was not repealed until 1806. The next act was similar to the statute of 1795 but it also provided:

> that nothing in this Act contained shall extend or be construed to extend to prevent any female from practising midwifery in any part of the Province, or to require such female to take out such license as aforesaid.[7]

This was the first piece of legislation to recognize female midwives as "legitimate healers."[8] It can be argued that by virtue of their femaleness (i.e., as both participants and observers in childbirth), female midwives' experience constituted acceptable and valuable knowledge in the eyes of the community. Hence, female midwives were exempt from licensing but male midwives were not. Even if this were not true, it was practical to exempt female midwives since there were approximately forty qualified medical practitioners to serve the needs of all of the Province in 1815.[9]

Despite the importance of female midwives, there was some opposition to the practice of female midwifery as this anonymous letter from "W" to the *Kingston Gazette* (1815) illustrates:

> An unfortunate female accoucheur from ignorance or trepidation, separated the funis [umbilical cord] from the placenta, leaving the latter within the patient causing her death .... The vigilance of the magistrates, the contempt of the public, the scorn of all good men must root out these pretenders and make them feel if they cannot see.[10]

This letter prompted a number of responses opposing W's position. One subscriber said that without female *accoucheurs* "those who live in the back settlements .... would be in a very distressing situation since the closest medical man was thirty or forty miles away."[11] Another letter from a "female accoucheur" expressed alarm that this critic "would shake the Province from one end to the other" and suggested that if it were not for midwives the writer may not have even been born.[12]

Female midwives continued to be exempt from licensing until 1865 when the provision in favour of midwives was dropped. However, this does not mean that their work had gone unnoticed by the medical profession. Several attempts, albeit unsuccessful ones, were made to regulate the practice of midwifery. In 1845, a bill was introduced which required that after one year from the passage of the act, every female candidate was "to be examined as to her qualification and ability to act as such Midwife."[13] In 1846 another bill was introduced requiring a similar measure, but it went into effect two years after the passing of the act.[14] Finally, in 1851, a bill was introduced to the legislature which excluded the licensing of midwives altogether; however, an amendment was later made to include such a provision.[15] All of these clauses were contained within acts which were aimed at creating a new College of Physicians and Surgeons and all were defeated.

An open letter to Dr. John Rolph (who founded the first medical school in Upper Canada in 1824 and later another in 1843) from the editors of the *Upper Canada Journal of Medical, Surgical and Physical Science*, "recommending that midwives should be obliged to gain a certain amount of practical and theoretical knowledge,"[16] and an editorial appearing in the *British American Journal of Medical and Physical Science* further indicates that the medical profession was concerned about this issue.[17] More importantly, the editorial illustrates the attitudes of the medical profession towards midwives and also how the licensing issue could have been used to eliminate female midwives from practice.

Taking a line of attack against midwives common to the emerging male medical profession, the editorial charged that female midwives were "very illiterate," thus confusing illiteracy with stupidity. It also invalidated experience as a legitimate source of knowledge. Consequently, if a midwife lost a life, her stupidity and ignorance were to be blamed; but if a medical man made a mistake, he was able to provide a "learned" explanation. Equally as important, midwives were characterized as dangerous, as this statement from *The British American Journal* strongly suggests:

> And when we consider the enormous errors which they [midwives] are continually perpetuating and the valuable lives which are frequently sacrificed to their ignorance, the more speedily some legislative interference is taken with respect to them, the better for the community at large.[18]

But despite these criticisms, the medical profession was very much aware of the effects of suddenly depriving women from "large tracts of country, scarcely or rarely visited by medical men" of the services of female midwives while they received formalized training. Therefore, the male doctors opted for "a more gradual manner" which entailed no specific course of study but required the women to submit to an examination (in this case, one year after the passing of the act). If we accept the medical profession's premise that midwives were illiterate, then this system of examination provided a politically expedient method of eliminating midwives. If it were a written examination, then they did not possess the skills to express themselves; if it were an oral examination, then they would probably lack the appropriate medical vocabulary. Furthermore, it would be difficult for midwives to submit to an examination since they were located in rural areas and the Board of Examiners tended to be located in major urban centers.

A brief review of the changes in the legislation between 1818 and 1865 reveals that the medical profession had made significant strides towards achieving dominance.[19] By 1865 the medical profession had established a system of licensing and registration, and medical education had gradually evolved from the old apprenticeship system to academic study in universities.

By 1869 the orthodox, eclectics and homeopaths had unified under one medical act. Prior to this time the eclectics, and homeopaths represented distinct schools of thought with their own Medical Acts, licensing boards and schools. The amalgamation of these schools represented steps towards a convergence of medical theory and practice. In addition, the act of 1869 provided for the establishment of a provincial College of Physicians and Surgeons which was empowered to administer licensing examinations and to set entrance standards and prescribed curriculum.

While it is quite clear that the medical profession had by no means consolidated its position of dominance, it is evident that it was rapidly moving towards self-regulated autonomy. At this point, the profession had some control over its members, and over the content of their work. Moreover, it appears that its status had considerably improved. Elizabeth McNab, in her study of the legal history of the health professions in Ontario, states that because the number of practitioners available had increased and the quality of services had improved, the passage of the Medical Act of 1865 became more acceptable and easier to enforce.[20] Finally, it is evident that each of the the divisions of medicine had been reasonably successful in obtaining the patronage of the social and political elite since all three groups had managed to get their own Medical Acts. After they amalgamated, this would prove even less difficult since they were no longer competing with one another.

Between 1869 and 1874, relations between the homeopaths, eclectics, and orthodox practitioners proved to be quite contentious, and a fierce debate developed around issues of examination, requirements for homeopaths and eclectics, and representation on the General Council (the governing body of the College). But by 1874, these internal difficulties would be resolved with the passage of yet another act.[21]

THE DEBATE OVER MIDWIFERY

After 1874, the College was able to turn its attention to the prosecution of unlicensed practitioners (frequently referred to as "quacks" and "irregulars"). From the minutes of the annual meeting in 1874, McNab reports that the Council had decided to appoint a prosecutor for each county. However, this proved to be too impractical, and in the following year it was agreed to appoint a public prosecutor for the province of Ontario.[22]

The actions of the Council did not go unnoticed. In fact, there seems to have been considerable opposition prompted by the prosecution of three individuals. An editorial in *The Globe,* entitled *Medicus on the War Path,* reveals the vehemence of the debate:

> The Medical Council has flung away the scabbard, it has opened the campaign against unlicensed knowledge; blood has been drawn; for the moment monopoly has triumphed; one fallen trespasser has bitten the dust....[23]

The debate turned on the medical monopoly of knowledge. The opponents of the "regular" practitioners argued that there should be no compulsory curriculum and advocated for "unrestricted" or "free trade" in the practice of medicine.[24] Some portion focused directly on midwifery. An editorial appearing in *The Globe* stated:

> In no way does the restriction imposed by the Medical Act operate more harshly and unreasonably than in imposing the terms of the law between women and the assistance they are accustomed to rely upon from members of their own sex ....[25]

Of major concern was the matter of "female delicacy." One writer regarded male practitioners attending women as the "quintessence of imposition" and that many women "shrink with horror from the interference of men at such times."[26] It was argued that because women did not protest the presence of male practitioners, they approved of them, but *The Globe* made the point that "it was easy to mistake quiet endurance for indifference!"[27] The newspaper also pointed out that women were less likely to confide in men and, therefore, more harm would result from the suppression of certain facts (due to modesty or fear for their reputation).

In the opposing camp, a country practitioner "sneered" at the concept of female delicacy. He asked:

> Are the women of Canada more refined in their feelings or more sensitive in their address than the Queen or the Princess of Wales and other ladies of the Royal family? They could have had the services of thoroughly experienced midwives ... yet they were all attended by professional men ....[28]

This statement is revealing because it suggests that one way male practitioners were able to gain control of midwifery was to align themselves with and serve the interests of the upper classes. When it became acceptable and even fashionable among "genteel" women to have male practitioners attend them during childbirth, these attitudes would eventually filter down and be accepted by the "lower" classes.

Furthermore, with regards to female delicacy, the country practitioner stated that:

> [He had] heard more vulgarity spiced with a considerable amount of obscenity in some lying-in chambers than [he had] heard in many a long day.[29]

This last statement has, of course, little to do with modesty but was a way of justifying the male practitioner's presence and, as *The Globe* most aptly pointed out, showed that the Medical Act did not "punish obscenity."[30]

Not surprisingly, a significant proportion of the debate centred on who should practise midwifery — female midwives or medical men. In a curious confession, a "Country Practitioner" suggested that the medical profession was not "enamoured with the midwifery branch of their business, as a rule, they cordially detest it." Yet in the next section of his letter, he berated midwives, calling them "Goody Two-Shoes" and suggesting that their only motives for participating in childbirth was "curiosity and the chance of a night's gossip." Furthermore, he undermined the value of their experience by citing their lack of knowledge in anatomy and, lastly, he strongly suggested that midwives were dangerous because of the "irremediable injury caused by their clumsiness."[31]

In support of midwives, *The Globe* observed that the medical profession was not indifferent to the practice of midwifery since the legislation distinctly identified midwifery as a branch of medicine which could only be practised by a "qualified practitioner." Then, *The Globe* suggested that although mistakes might have been made by midwives, it could also call to mind cases in which the "qualified practitioner (had) grossly blundered."[32] The paper added:

> The qualified practitioner can generally cover up his mistakes with some learned explanation and has no one to expose his error. But the uneducated woman who loses a patient has all the doctors at once to publish her misfortune.[33]

Lastly, while *The Globe* acknowledged that midwives were "extremely ignorant," they also recognized that this was easily remediable through education.[34] However, the paper conceded that the only alternative under the present act was to attend university and become a regular practitioner. In order to do this a woman would have to "endure the almost insupportable ordeal, opposition and persecution!" Therefore, they recommended circumvention of the law. If a midwife was hired as a nurse and gave her assistance when a crisis arose, she could not be prosecuted for *practising medicine*.[35]

The debate over midwifery was not only carried out in newspapers but also in the medical journals. An editorial in the *Canada Lancet* indicated that the medical profession followed the debate in *The Globe* and was aware of the paper's position:

> Much surprise and regret have been expressed by many intelligent people, both medical and lay, in this city and throughout Ontario, at the singular course of "*The Globe*" newspaper, in its support and advocacy of quacks and quackery in the medical profession.[36]

It is clear from the editorial that the medical profession was particularly concerned about female midwives and, in fact, appeared quite incensed at *The Globe's* suggestion that only female midwives should practise midwifery:

> We would like to know very much where *The Globe* gets its information regarding the desire of women to be attended by midwives .... The daily experience of medical men, however, is that women don't want midwives about them, as a rule they have no confidence in them.[37]

Lastly, a letter to the editor of the *Canada Lancet* written "on request of a number of physicians in the neighbourhood" reveals that regular doctors feared the economic competition of midwives.[38] However, the reason given by the doctor for the "dispensing of midwives" was that doctors were more competent and that midwives had "caused the death of many a woman."[39] Most of the letter, however, was devoted to lamenting the loss of income to midwives.

The letter stated that the licensing of midwives was "totally uncalled for in a country which is flooded with doctors" and later the writer observed:

> I do not know that I should object so much to the passage of the clause alluded to if doctors were as scarce and as difficult to obtain as they were years ago.[40]

These statements reinforce the view that doctors were tolerant of female midwives only while it was practical to be so. But by 1873 (when the above letter was written), the medical profession was growing rapidly and was well on its way to entrenching its monopoly. Clearly, the writer *believed* that there were enough doctors available to meet the needs of the community. Therefore, doctors were no longer dependent upon female midwives to provide these services. To the regular practitioners, then, female midwives represented a source of unwanted competition.

The writer felt that since doctors invested "the most valuable years of their lives as well as considerable money" in their education, then doctors should be "protected most stringently against the meddlesome interference on the part of old women."[41] In other words, one of the rewards of becoming a licensed practitioner was the right to maintain a monopoly over health care. Furthermore, the doctor writes that midwifery "is to many of us country doctors a very remunerative part of our business" and he expressed considerable irritation at the loss of income resulting from competition by midwives. According to the writer the amount of money lost to these "old bodies and a quack" would be a "decent living for (his) small family."[42] Female midwives were able to undercut the doctor's income because they charged two dollars for each case while the doctor charged five dollars.[43]

Almost twenty years later, in 1895, the issue of medical monopoly was raised by the Patrons of Industry, an opposition party in the Ontario Legislature. According to Elizabeth MacNab, the Patrons, who tentatively drew their support from the working class, were opposed to business and the professions because they exploited the working class. In particular, they were opposed to the professional colleges because the colleges "prevented poor men's sons from joining their ranks. The Patrons advocated the abolition of these colleges and 'free trade' in professional practice."[44] Having gained a presence in the legislature, the Patrons' first target was the medical profession. On 27 March 1895, the Patrons introduced what became known as the Haycock Bill, named after their leader.

One feature of the bill was to abolish the medical court and another was to license midwives. Midwives who attended ten cases of confinement would be eligible to practise midwifery upon paying a fee of one dollar for a licence. The reaction of the medical profession to the bill, in general, and to the clause regarding midwives in particular, was, as can be expected, overwhelmingly negative. An editorial appearing in the *Ontario Medical Journal* reflected this sentiment:

> The gist of the Bill was ridiculous in the extreme, both from the standpoint of benefit to the profession and benefit to the general public. All the good clauses in the Act were to be repealed, and many others, almost iniquitous ones, to be added, giving scope to any kind of quacks, fakirs and midwives.[45]

The fact that the bill was soundly defeated (71 to 15) indicates that the medical profession had strong support in the legislature. Furthermore, *The Globe*, which had been against the medical profession in 1875, had now reversed its position as the editorial below reveals:

> The Legislature did not go far wrong when considering Mr. Haycock's amendments to the Ontario Medical Act in making the public interest the final standard by which the proposed changes are to be judged. The Medical Act was passed for the protection of the public not for the purpose as some people suppose of creating medical practitioners of Ontario a closed corporation.[46]

So how successful was the medical profession in eliminating female midwives? We know from the Ontario *Sessional Papers* of 1899 that it was, in fact, making considerable headway against female midwives, although it had not yet eradicated the movement entirely.[47] Overall, 3% of all births in Ontario were attended by midwives. However, caution should be exercised in interpreting this figure since under the threat of prosecution, female midwives were not likely to report their presence. This figure, therefore, is probably an underestimate. Figures were given for the total number of births unattended by physicians in 1899 and this was 16% of all births. It seems unlikely that all of these women had their babies without any assistance. Thus, we can infer that some of these births were attended by midwives but, as suggested, this was not reported.

These statistics, however, also reveal a rural-urban dichotomy in the delivery of health care. For example, in the counties of Algoma and Renfrew, it was reported that midwives attended 10% and 12% of the births (respectively) while approximately 50% of the births in these counties were listed as unattended by physicians. Yet, in York, only 1% of the deliveries were attended by midwives and 3% were unattended by physicians. Thus, in the areas which were well established (such as York) and were densely populated, almost all of the births were attended by physicians and very few by midwives. In the urban areas we can conclude that the medical profession was most successful in eradicating the female midwife. However, in the newer, developing counties, there were few physicians available and therefore many births went unattended by physicians. It is difficult to imagine that 50% of the women had no assistance in their deliveries; more likely female midwives probably assisted with these births and did not report it. Thus, one can assume that midwives continued to practise in areas that were *unprofitable* for the medical practitioners.

The debate over midwifery as it was waged in the pages of *The Globe* and the medical journals reveals that in mid-nineteenth-century Ontario, it was a contentious issue. Medical practitioners' objections to female midwifery can be attributed in part to a desire to protect their own pecuniary interests. This is not surprising since in the mid-nineteenth century, physicians were barely able to eke out a decent living. It seems clear that a major tactic of the profession was to undermine the credibility of the midwives by characterizing them as dirty, ignorant, and dangerous.

On the other hand, those who supported midwives seem to have done so for two reasons. First, they wished to protect female modesty thereby reflecting the prudish Victorian values dominant at that time. (Values that the medical profession conveniently ignored when it came to the issue of midwives, yet indignantly espoused when the issue of female physicians came to the fore). Second, they did not seem to be convinced that medical monopoly of knowledge was beneficial to the community and therefore advocated free trade.

The opposition to medical monopoly tends to reinforce the view put forth earlier that while the profession was moving towards a position of dominance, it had by no means achieved it. However, the changes in the position of *The Globe* on medical monopoly and the sound defeat of the Haycock Bill strongly suggest that by the early 1900s the medical profession's monopoly was largely complete.

One reason for these changes in attitudes may have been that there had been improvements in medicine which convinced people of the medical profession's superior role in health care. Equally important, however, may be medicine's claims of being scientific in a period when the western world was enamoured with the rationality of science. It will become apparent that both of these developments would seem to have applied to changes in the "management of childbirth."

THE MEDDLESOME MIDWIFERY DEBATE

As discussed in the previous section, one method of changing attitudes was to undermine the credibility of midwives. A second, more subtle, method by which the medical profession came to dominate childbirth was by redefining it. The "meddlesome" midwifery debate is a reflection of this process.[48] Debate focused on whether childbirth practitioners should take a "laissez-faire" approach to labour and delivery and let nature take its course, or whether practitioners should take an aggressive, interventionist role in assisting labour and delivery (i.e. "meddlesome").

The change in nomenclature from midwifery to obstetrics reflects the success of the interventionist approach. As one practitioner phrased it:

> The art of midwifery belongs to prehistoric times; the science of obstetrics is the latest recognition of all ancient sciences. No branch of medicine demands more skill, presence of mind or justifiable daring than midwifery.[49]

Childbirth was "scientific!" Barbara Ehrenreich and Deirdre English argue in *For Her Own Good: 150 Years of the Experts' Advice to Women*, that since in the late nineteenth century "science was well on its way to becoming a sacred national value, any group which hoped to establish itself as 'experts' in a certain area would have to prove that they were rigorously scientific."[50] Furthermore, the authors suggest that "making something scientific became synonymous with reform."[51] The development of various procedures, techniques, and instruments (i.e., anaesthesia, antiseptics, forceps, and Ceasarean section) strengthened doctors' claims that childbirth was becoming "scientific." These developments were thought to be beneficial since they alleviated pain and lengthy labours. Moreover, only the experts were able to administer them. By taking an active role in the "management" of labour, the prestige of the doctor was further enhanced by his "justifiable daring."

The use of forceps provides a good example of the meddlesome midwifery debate. Forceps were first discovered by the Chamberlen family in England in the seventeenth century. Ann Oakley suggests that the mystique generated around the Chamberlens' use of the forceps "probably did a great deal to elevate the status of the male midwife."[52] In England by the 1720s, male midwifery became more fashionable among the upper classes and male midwives began to compete with female midwives for normal cases of labour. (Prior to this male midwives only attended complicated cases of labour.) Since female midwives were prohibited from using forceps "the use of surgical techniques even for normal labour was a means whereby male midwives were able to assert their superiority over the female practitioner."[53]

It is clear that even in the mid-nineteenth century, forceps were infrequently used. "The rule which guided obstetric teachers was that meddlesome midwifery was bad," and the use of forceps was considered to be a "dangerous operation"; therefore, they were to be used only as a last resort.[54] Physicians were not encouraged to take their forceps with them because:

> The impatience of the patient, the anxiety of the friends, and the doctor's wish to show that he was really doing something, would induce him to use the forceps before he ought....[55]

But, by the late nineteenth century, this maxim was being questioned. Many doctors claimed that this rule was "accountable for a great deal of suffering and a great many deaths."[56] One physician wrote that this convention was "to be utterly repudiated when applied to the skilful efforts of the educated accoucheur." He argued that once a doctor was satisfied that "Nature, unaided is unable to effect delivery within a safe period," then the forceps should be used. Furthermore, he denounced some of the guidelines taught in the 1850s (when he was in training) as no longer valid forty years later at the end of the nineteenth century.[57] As a result of this switch in attitude, there was a great change in the frequency of the use of forceps. Around 1855, one practitioner reported that over a 3-year period, there were 18 forceps cases for 6634 deliveries (1:360).[58] However, by 1868–1874 there were 639 forceps cases for 7027 deliveries (1:11).

At the same time, however, other doctors objected to the interventionist approach:

> It is felt that at the present rate of advance we shall soon overtake Nature and relegate her to a back place....[59]

These doctors suggested that forceps were often used too frequently and when they were uncalled for. Furthermore, one practitioner claimed that:

> The forceps are sometimes used to save time, sometimes to gain a little notoriety, sometimes for a double fee, and sometimes from ignorance....[60]

This particular doctor claimed that he had used forceps only a dozen times in twenty-five years of practice.[61] The success of the interventionist approach is perhaps best reflected in the statistics of modern-day obstetrical practice. In 1974, 21% of all deliveries in Ontario used forceps.[62]

The aim of this paper is to examine the relationship between the institutionalization and monopolization of medicine by male doctors, and the demise of the female midwife. Male physicians' desire to eradicate the female midwife stemmed, in part, from the belief that female midwives were dangerous; and, in part, from the desire to eliminate economic competition. Male doctors were able to gain control of childbirth by operating on a number of different levels. First, the doctors were able legally to prohibit female midwives from practising. Second, male doctors were able to undermine the credibility of midwives by characterizing them as dirty, ignorant, and dangerous. Finally, by claiming that childbirth was "scientific" and by using technology, the male doctors were able to "assert their superiority" over female midwives and in doing so redefined childbirth.

NOTES

The author wishes to thank Ruth Pierson, Wendy Mitchinson, and David Coburn for their comments and criticisms.

1. Suzann Buckley, "Ladies or Midwives? Efforts to Reduce Infant and Maternal Mortality," in *A Not Unreasonable Claim, Women and Reform in Canada 1880s–1920s*, ed. Linda Kealey (Toronto: Women's Press, 1979), 131–149; Jean Donnison, *Midwives and Medical Men: A History of Interprofessional Rivalries and Women's Rights* (London: Heinemann, 1977); Barbara Ehrenreich and Deirdre English, *Witches, Midwives and Nurses* (London: Writers and Readers Publishing Cooperative, 1973); Ann Oakley, "Wise Woman and Medicine Man: Changes in the Management of Childbirth," in *The Rights and Wrongs of Women*, ed. Juliet Mitchell and Ann Oakley (Harmondsworth, Middlesex: Penguin, 1976).
2. Nancy Schrom Dye, "History of Childbirth in America," *Signs* 6, no. 1 (1980): 98.

3. William Canniff, *History of the Medical Profession in Upper Canada, 1783–1850* (Toronto: W. Briggs, 1894), 19–21.
4. Ibid., 22.
5. Cited by Canniff (see note 3), 22.
6. Ibid.
7. Ibid., 30–32.
8. Elizabeth McNab, *A Legal History of Health Profession, in Ontario* (Toronto: Queen's Printer, 1979). McNab cites the act of 1795 as the first act to exempt midwives. The source of my information is Canniff (see note 3), who cited the entire act of 1795 which makes no mention of female midwives being exempted.
9. Canniff (see note 3), 31.
10. Letter by "W" to the *Kingston Gazette,* Nov. 18, 1815.
11. Letter by "a subscriber" to the *Kingston Gazette,* Dec. 2, 1815.
12. Letter by "a female accoucheur" to the *Kingston Gazette,* Dec. 2, 1815.
13. The proposed bill was cited in an editorial *The British American Journal of Medical and Physical Science* 1 (1845): 57.
14. The proposed bill was cited in an editorial in *ibid.* 2 (1846): 27.
15. The proposed bill was cited in an editorial in the *Upper Canada Journal of Medical, Surgical and Physical Science* 1 (1851): 71–115.
16. Letter appearing in *ibid.* 3 (1853–4): 271.
17. An editorial appearing in *The British American Journal of Medical and Physical Science* 1 (1845): 195.
18. Ibid.
19. See McNab (note 8), 4–19 for further details. Also see Charles M. Godfrey, *Medicine in Ontario* (Belleville, Ontario, Mika Publishing Company, 1979) for a detailed description of the changes in medicine and particularly in medical education.
20. MacNab (see note 8), 10.
21. Ibid., 16–19.
22. Ibid., 19.
23. Editorial, *The Globe,* Aug. 24, 1875.
24. Ibid.
25. Editorial, *The Globe,* Sept. 11, 1875.
26. Letter by "an observer" to *The Globe,* Sept. 6, 1875.
27. Editorial, *The Globe,* Sept. 11, 1875.
28. Letter by "a country practitioner," *The Globe,* Sept. 11, 1875.

29. Ibid.
30. Editorial, *The Globe*, Sept. 11, 1875.
31. Letter by "a country practitioner," *The Globe,* Sept. 11, 1875.
32. Editorial, *The Globe,* Sept. 11, 1875.
33. Ibid. See for example J. M. Penwarden, "Barbarous Treatment by a Midwife," *Canada Lancet* 4 (1872): 273–4.
34. Ibid.
35. Editorial, *The Globe,* Sept. 13, 1875.
36. Editorial, *Canada Lancet* 8 (1875): 40.
37. Ibid.: 60.
38. Letter to the *Canada Lancet* 4 (1873): 150.
39. Ibid.
40. Ibid.
41. Ibid.
42. Ibid.
43. *The Globe,* Mar. 28, 1875.
44. McNab (see note 8), 29.
45. *Ontario Medical Journal* 3 (1893): 251–2.
46. *The Globe,* Apr. 11, 1895.
47. Statistics are from Ontario, Report of the Registrar General, in *Sessional Papers* (no. 32), 1899.
48. See Wendy Mitchinson, "Historical Attitudes toward Women and Childbirth," *Atlantis* 4, no. 2, part 2 (1979): 13–34.
49. W. Symington, "Forty Years' Experience in Midwifery," *Canada Lancet* 17 (1885): 262.
50. B. Ehrenreich and D. English, *For Her Own Good: 150 Years of the Experts' Advice to Women* (New York, Anchor Press, 1979).
51. Ibid.
52. Oakley (see note 1), 36.
53. Ibid.
54. L. Athill, "Changes in Midwifery Practice and in the Treatment of Uterine Diseases During the Last Twenty Years," *Canada Lancet* 8 (1876): 171.
55. Dr. Harrison, "Operative Midwifery as It was Taught to Me and as I Practise it," *Ontario Medical Journal* 1 (1892): 154.
56. Athill (see note 54), 171.
57. Ibid.
58. Ibid.

59. "Meddlesome Midwifery," *Canada Lancet* 17 (1885): 25.
60. Letter to the Editor: Dr. Clark "The Use of Forceps," *Canada Lancet* 18 (1885): 73.
61. Ibid.
62. Statistics were calculated from Statistics Canada, *Surgical Procedures and Treatments* (Ottawa, 1974). Forceps delivery includes use of outlet forceps, low forceps, mid forceps and high forceps (used both with and without an episiotomy).

Chapter Eighteen
What if Mama is an Indian?

Sylvia M. Van Kirk

Recent historical studies of the mixed blood people of western Canada have concluded that within this broad category, there were specific groups that can be differentiated on the basis of ethnicity, religion, and class. In the period before 1870, there was a discernible Anglophone mixed blood group, sometimes known as the "country-born."[1] These people exhibited a cultural orientation quite distinct from that of the larger Francophone mixed blood group or Metis. There is considerable truth to Frits Pannekoek's assertion that the principal aspiration of this "country-born" element was assimilation into the British, Protestant world of their forefathers.[2] As Jennifer Brown has emphasized, this was due in large measure to an active and pervasive paternal influence within many of these British-Indian families.[3] Much work remains to be done, however, in analyzing the actual impact of this process of enculturation on the children of these families. In a useful article about the children of Chief Factor Roderick McKenzie and his Ojibwa wife Angèlique, Elizabeth Arthur has suggested that the pressures to succeed in their father's world imposed severe psychological distress upon them, especially the sons.[4]

This paper provides a case study of another prominent British-Indian family, the Alexander Ross family of Red River. In determining the success of the program of enculturation that British fathers, aided by church and school, mapped out for their children, it is useful to focus on the elite, for these fathers (usually retired Hudson's Bay Company officers) had the desire, along with sufficient rank, wealth, and education to secure the enculturation of their children as members of the British Protestant community in spite of their birth in a distant and isolated part of the Empire. The Alexander Ross family appears to have been one of the most successfully enculturated British-Indian families in Red River. Yet, ultimately, an outstanding younger son, James, suffered an "identity crisis" so profound that it destroyed him. The tragedy of his life is representative of the Anglophone mixed blood group as a whole. Owing to the irreconcilable conflicts of enculturation they experienced, they lacked the Metis sense of a cultural identity based on an acceptance of their dual racial heritage.

When the young Scots Presbyterian Alexander Ross first emigrated to the Canadas in 1804, he earned his livelihood as a schoolteacher. After several years, this profession yielded so few monetary and social benefits that he decided to try his fortune instead in the fur trade. As a clerk with the Pacific Fur Company, he helped to establish trade with the Okanagan Indians of the Upper Columbia River. Shortly after, around 1813, he wed *à la façon du pays* an Okanagan chief's young daughter whom he called Sally. Their first child, Alexander, was born in 1815, followed by three girls, Margaret (b. 1819), Isabella (b. 1820), and Mary (b. 1823). Although Ross had a high regard for the Okanagan people, as his family grew, he felt it best to remove them from the world of fur trade post and Indian camp. In 1825, he retired from the trade and settled his wife and children on an extensive land grant in the Red River colony. There he hoped they would be able to receive "the Christian education" he considered the best portion in life that he could give them.[5]

In time, the Ross family numbered twelve children in all — four boys and eight girls. For the eight youngest children, Red River was the only home they had ever known; they never had any contact with their mother's kin across the Rocky Mountains. We don't know what Sally Ross felt on taking leave of her father's people for the last time, but there is certainly evidence that her loving maternal presence considerably strengthened the Ross children's sense of family. Yet, as a Christianized Indian, the extent to which she transmitted her native heritage to her children appears to have been limited. That some Indian expressions were used in the family circle is evidenced by the little endearments James penned to his mother in later years, and the older girls were proficient in Indian crafts such as making moccasins.[6] But such attributes were almost completely overshadowed by the Scots Presbyterian influence of the father.

As the patriarch of "Colony Gardens," Alexander Ross shaped the upbringing of his half-Indian children. It was he who determined their religious and secular education, and who later gave land to his sons to establish their own households or provided succour for widowed daughters.[7] Ross' most ardent desire was that his family be imbued with the precepts of Christianity. Although disappointed that there was as yet no Presbyterian minister in the settlement, Ross had his wife and children baptized in the Anglican church. He and his wife were also formally married by the Reverend William Cockran in 1828. But while religious observances had to be made at the Anglican church, Ross kept his staunch Presbyterianism alive through regular family gatherings for Bible reading and prayers. All the while he campaigned to bring a Presbyterian minister to Red River, which was at last achieved in the person of the Reverend John Black, who arrived in 1851. Religion emerged as one of the most formative influences in the lives of the Ross children. Their sincere religious conviction gave them a sense of purpose — they subscribed to the Presbyterian view that God had put them on this earth to be instruments of His purpose and that He would reward those who diligently applied their talents.[8]

The application of the benefits of secular education seems to have been somewhat more uneven. With the exception of two of the younger ones, little formal education was bestowed upon the girls, most of whom married in their teens. But the sons, who were to carry on the family name, received the best education that Red River had to offer. William (b. 1825) was a very creditable graduate of the Red River Academy, while his younger brother James (b. 1835) was such an outstanding pupil of Bishop Anderson's that he was sent to further his education at the University of Toronto in 1853. The education of the youngest Ross children was taken over by the Presbyterian minister John Black. Sandy Ross (who was named in memory of his eldest brother who had died in 1835) was one of a class of six young scholars. Privately, Black tutored Henrietta (b. 1830), who later became his wife, and undertook to improve upon the superficial girls' school education that her younger sister Jemima (b. 1837) had received.

For the girls, marriage to a man of consequence in their father's opinion was practically the only route to assimilation. Significantly, four out of the six Ross daughters to reach adulthood married white men. In 1838, Margaret Ross married Hugh Matheson of Kildonan, and she was eventually listed in the Red River census as white. Henrietta's marriage to the Reverend John Black, while it helped to seal the family's identification with the Scots Kildonan community, also emphasized the family's orientation toward newcomers, for Black had but recently come from Canada. Isabella Ross' second husband was James Stewart Green, an American free trader who arrived in the settlement in the 1840s. Finally in 1860, the Canadian connection was further extended when the youngest Ross girl, Jemima, married William Coldwell, who had arrived the year before to start the colony's first newspaper.

These marriages to white men not only underscore the Ross family's desire to be viewed as "British," but they symbolize the way in which the family identified with the forces of "progress" in Red River. It was a measure of the family's success that its sons were equipped and ready to play a leadership role in the colony, to bring about a new order based on the benefits of civilization. Old Alexander Ross had every reason to be proud of his son William. By the early 1850s, William had succeeded to all his father's public offices, which included Councillor of Assiniboia, Sheriff, and Keeper of the Jail. "Is it not very pleasing to see a son step into the shoes of his father and do ample justice to all of these offices?" the old patriarch enthused.[9] William, who could not have been unaware that his station in the colony depended in large measure on the good will of the old Company establishment, did not publicly criticize the rule of the Hudson's Bay Company; yet, like many of his peers, he chafed under the old regime. He wrote to his brother James in 1856:

> You know the fact that Red River is half a century behind the age — no stirring events to give life and vigour to our debilitated political life — The incubus of the Company's monopoly — the peculiar government under which we *vegetate* ... all hang like a nightmare on our political and social existence .... Such a state of things cannot last forever,

sooner or later the whole fabric must be swept away .... We ought to have a flood of immigration to infuse new life, new ideas, and destroy all our old associations with the past, i.e. in so far as it hinders our progress for the future — a regular transformation will sharpen our intellects, fill our minds with new projects and give life and vigour to our thoughts, words, and action — when that day comes along you may rest assured that there will be no complaint.[10]

Just what role William Ross would have played in the turbulent years that followed must remain a matter of speculation, for a few months after he wrote these words he was dead, cut down at the age of thirty-one.

James Ross, however, emerged as an ardent champion of the cause of Canada in Rupert's Land. It is scarcely surprising that from young James' point of view, Canada was the land of opportunity. He performed brilliantly at Knox College, winning an impressive array of scholarships and prizes. His father, highly gratified, exclaimed, "What will they say of the Brûlés now?"[11] Socially, James' acceptance also seemed to be complete, for in 1858 he married Margaret Smith, the daughter of a respected Scots Presbyterian family in Toronto. To marry a white woman represented a considerable achievement for a British-Indian man, and was almost unheard of in Red River. Both of James' brothers, for example, had married well-connected British-Indian women.[12]

On the surface, the children of Alexander Ross were extremely successful in terms of criteria derived from their father's world; yet they were not immune to social gossip that was essentially racist in nature. Instances of racial prejudice were evident in the community's reaction to Henrietta's marriage to the Reverend John Black. It was intimated that his marriage to a native would prove detrimental to his ministry.[13] Indeed, at least some members of the predominantly white congregation resented the prominent position of this "halfbreed" family — they occupied three out of the six prestigious square pews. The ears of young Jemima Ross were stung by remarks that Mr. Black must feel rather ashamed to see all his "black" relations when he stepped into the pulpit.[14] Although she tried to make light of the situation, it is evident that Jemima was wounded and began to feel ambivalent about having an Indian mother. Although privately she might have been quite devoted to her mother, she became increasingly embarrassed to be seen in public with her. Ambivalence toward their native mothers, which was in essence an ambivalence toward their own Indian blood and heritage, was evidently not uncommon among British-Indian children. James Ross himself lamented that "halfbreed" children often did not show enough respect to their Indian mothers. He feared that some of his brothers and sisters might succumb to this temptation, especially after the death of their father, which prompted his anguished admonition, "What if Mama is an Indian?"[15] While James loved his mother, it is difficult to interpret this statement as a positive defence of his mother's Indianness. What the statement does signify is that, *even* if their mother was an Indian, she was a most exemplary mother and for that reason was entitled to the love and respect of her children. Her simple Christian virtue, he argued, was far more worthy of esteem than the superficial accomplishments of some white ladies held in such high regard in Red River. But the fact that he felt moved to make such a comparison indicates the social strains to which the younger members of the family in particular were exposed.

James' own response to racial prejudice, to which he appears to have been quite sensitive, was to work diligently to prove that one could rise above the derogatory stereotypes of mixed blood people perpetrated in non-native circles in nineteenth-century Red River.[16] Indeed, these stereotypes were uncomfortably close to home. On reading his father's book, *The Fur Hunters of the Far West*, James was disconcerted to find that his own father made unflattering generalizations about halfbreeds, characterizing them as "fickle" and "destitute of steady purpose." "I think some of your statements about Halfbreeds unnecessarily harsh," James could not help telling him, and he vowed that his father would never be able to accuse him of being guilty of such behavior.[17]

In fact, James Ross seems to have been almost obsessed with the desire to make his father proud of him. He could not fail. The pressure on him increased unexpectedly when in 1856 not only his elder brother but his father died. Within a few short months, the Ross family had suffered a double blow — not only had they lost their guiding head, but also the one who had been groomed to take his place. In a British-Indian family where the family's welfare and status was so dependent upon the father, his demise could be catastrophic. Again James Ross acknowledged that "halfbreed" families generally dwindled into insignificance after the patriarchs died.[18] He fervently believed that the same must not happen to the Ross family. In a moving letter to his siblings, he exhorted them to a standard of conduct that would ensure the family's standing and respectability within the community.

After completing his B.A., James Ross returned to Red River with his Canadian bride in the summer of 1858. In assuming the mantle of family leadership, he was considerably proud to be chosen to follow in the footsteps of his father and brother by being appointed Sheriff and Postmaster. Unlike his brother, however, James Ross felt compelled to speak out against the Company. In the late 1850s, agitation for a Canadian takeover was growing and it found widespread support in the Anglophone mixed blood community. In 1857, for example, the mixed blood sons of the late Chief Factor Alexander Kennedy had obtained hundreds of signatures to a petition appealing to the Legislature of the Province of Canada.[19] James Ross was ideally placed to continue this campaign and he found his vehicle for expression in *The Nor'Wester,* of which he became co-editor in 1860. But Ross was to learn that although the Company might be weakened, it had not yet lost all power. In 1862, after publishing a petition that ran counter to the one being promoted by the Hudson's Bay Company on the question of defence for Red River, Ross found himself summarily divested of his appointed offices. Shortly afterward, he became heavily involved in the sordid Corbett case; along with a significant sector of the British-Indian community, he seemed to feel that the unhappy minister was being persecuted because of his anti-Company stance.[20] By 1864, with his prospects tarnished, Ross, perhaps at his wife's urging, decided to return to Canada.

So promising did Canada seem that James urged other members of the family to emigrate. William and Jemima Coldwell and young Sandy Ross with his mixed blood wife Catherine Murray arrived in Toronto the following year. It was not a happy interlude. Although he had previously spent some years at Knox College, Sandy was so homesick that he and Catherine returned to Red River within twelve months. Jemima Coldwell also did not adapt well to her new surroundings. Although she had a fine house, she may have shared her sister Henrietta's apprehension that a "dark halfbreed" like herself would never really be acceptable in Canadian society.[21] In any event, Jemima grew increasingly melancholy, especially after the death of her eldest daughter, and she herself died in Toronto in 1867.

Only James seemed to thrive — his list of accomplishments was increasingly impressive. He completed his M.A. degree and articled at law, coming first in the class when he was admitted to the bar. He quickly attracted the attention of George Brown, and later became a lead writer and reporter for *The Globe*. As Jennifer Brown has pointed out, Canada could absorb a few talented native sons, isolated as they were from their fellows.[22] Doubtless, James Ross would have prospered had he stayed in Canada. Instead he returned to Red River on the eve of momentous change. He had been encouraged by the lieutenant-governor-to-be, William McDougall, who advised him that the new Canadian possession would need leaders like himself. Indeed, few could match his credentials. A man of striking mien and persuasive speech, he was fluent in both English and French, devoted to Red River, but with influential and sympathetic ties to Canada. Ross had always felt that his destiny was somehow bound up with the colony. Here was the golden opportunity — the longed-for time that his brother had not lived to see. The Anglophone mixed blood community was apparently ready to secure the promise of their British Protestant heritage through union with Canada, and Ross intended to lead them to it.

For James Ross, however, the Red River Resistance proved to be not only a political but a personal crisis of great magnitude. It essentially destroyed him. Instead of providing consistent leadership, Ross vacillated. At first the ardent champion of the Canadian cause, he ended up as Chief Justice of Riel's provisional government. Ross was won over by Riel's appeal to racial unity — the Metis were not fighting solely for their rights, but for the rights of all the indigenous people of Red River. As anglicized as he might be, Ross could not ignore the Indian dimension of his heritage; indeed, he was far more Indian by blood than was Riel. The bond of their native ancestry made Ross anxious to avoid taking up arms against the Metis. Nothing was worth a civil war against "brothers and kindred."[23] As a result, Ross' course throughout the resistance was to try desperately to maintain peace and prevent the clash that he feared might result in the massacre of the English sector of the community.[24] Yet his course was a tortured one; as a darling of the Canadian cause, it was not easy to be allied with Riel. Friends and relatives in Canada suspected

Ross of treasonous conduct and British-Indian countrymen who remained opposed to Riel accused him of being a self-seeking rogue.[25] In turmoil, Ross was driven to drink. His feelings of ambivalence and guilt must have been profound. Hopelessly torn between the Canadians and the Metis, he was quite unable to deal with this polarization of his heritage. All his life he had believed that he could transcend the limitations of his origins; but one suspects that the events in Red River had made him begin to doubt McDougall's assurances that native rights would be respected. It must have hurt him deeply when even his beloved *Globe* printed disparaging remarks about renegade halfbreeds, tarring the entire mixed blood community with the same brush. Ross and others were horrified at the violence of the Canadian troops. The Anglophone mixed blood community experienced a real sense of disillusionment with the Canadians when they actually arrived, realizing that they, too, could fall victim to racist attacks.[26]

In the summer of 1870, James Ross took a trip to Toronto to settle some business affairs. It was in some sense a pilgrimage, a reaffirmation of his ties with Canada. He was able to pull himself together and returned to Red River with renewed purpose. He hoped to escape the stigma of his association with Riel and be called upon to serve in the new administration of Governor Archibald. Instead, he suffered the mortification of seeing himself passed over in favour of Canadian newcomers.[27] Whether he would ever have been able to fulfil his outstanding promise remains conjecture; he died in September 1871.

After James' death, the youngest son, Sandy, did not take over as head of the Ross family. Although not much is known about him, he was the most insecure of all the sons and never found his niche. Death claimed him early, too, at the age of thirty-one. The leadership of the Ross family passed to the white sons-in-law, the Reverend John Black, who remained concerned for the family's welfare even after the death of Henrietta in 1873, and especially William Coldwell, who married Jemima Ross (née McKenzie), William Ross' widow, in 1875.

In spite of their great promise, an air of tragedy hung over the children of Alexander Ross. By 1874, they were all dead (except one daughter), most having died in their thirties. Like other mixed blood families, they were susceptible to lung diseases, but one wonders to what extent psychological stress contributed to their poor health. It seems that the degree of psychological dislocation was proportional to the degree to which they attempted to imitate the ways of the newcomers.

The ones who fared best were the daughters, perhaps partly because there was less pressure on them to succeed. Yet even here the most well-adjusted seem to have been those who were not forced to completely suppress their Indian heritage. Mary Ross, for example, who married the mixed blood Orkneyman George Flett, eventually helped her husband establish a Presbyterian mission among the Riding Mountain "Chippewas" or Saulteaux. There her familiarity with the Indian language and customs was an advantage, not a detriment.[28] Her younger sisters who married prominent whites had to confront prejudice more directly. Henrietta was able to weather the racial jibes of the Kildonan community, being greatly assisted by a loving and supportive husband, but Jemima, who was the youngest and most upwardly mobile, had a great deal of trouble coping with her situation.

The sons suffered most. Their fate is important, for in the 1850s and '60s, talented young Anglophone mixed bloods like themselves were emerging as important leaders in Red River.[29] In 1861, according to fellow countryman A. K. Isbister, British Indians occupied nearly all the important and intellectual offices in the colony. Most prominent among them was James Ross.[30]

Indeed, the pressure on Ross must have been enormous, for he was held up as an example to all. Yet James Ross' crisis in 1869–70 is really symbolic of an inherent flaw in the enculturation process to which Anglophone mixed blood children were subjected. The Red River Resistance polarized the settlement into two elements — white and Metis. British-Indian leaders such as James Ross, discovering that they were really neither, were essentially paralyzed by their own ambivalence. Ultimately, the cultural biases of the newcomers, often racist in nature, denied to this group the successful integration into white society that they desired.[31] Significantly, the new elite of Winnipeg soon bore little resemblance to the old Red River elite that had given Isbister so much satisfaction. Yet, leaders such as James Ross could not be Metis, even though they might have felt a bond of kinship with the French-Indian community. Unlike the Metis, the Anglophone mixed bloods lacked a distinct cultural identity based on the duality of their heritage, and this made it difficult for them to build upon their uniqueness as a people of mixed racial ancestry. In 1869–70, the Metis were secure enough in their own identity to champion the cause of native rights and would henceforth emerge as the strongest of the mixed blood community. The particular tragedy of the "British-Indian" people of Rupert's Land was that, in the end, they were neither white nor Metis.

NOTES

1. The phrase "country-born" was first brought into use by John Foster in his Ph.D. thesis, "The Country-born in the Red River Settlement, 1820–50"(University of Alberta, 1972). Other terms include "Hudson's Bay English" and "Red River Halfbreed." I am grateful to Irene Spry for suggesting the designations Anglophone and Francophone in reference to mixed bloods.
2. See Frits Pannekoek, "The Churches and the Social Structure in the Red River Area 1818–1870" (Ph.D. thesis, Queen's University, 1973).
3. Jennifer Brown, *Strangers in Blood: Fur Trade Families in Indian Country* (Vancouver: University of British Columbia Press, 1980), 216–20.
4. Elizabeth Archer, "Angelique and her Children," *Thunder Bay Historical Museum Society, Papers and Records* 5:30–40.
5. Alexander Ross, *The Fur Hunters of the Far West* (London: Smith, Elder and Co., 1855), 2:233.
6. Public Archives of Manitoba (hereafter P.A.M.), Alexander Ross Family Papers, James to his father, Dec. 31, 1853; Alexander to James, June 11, 1854; James to his father, July 1, 1854.
7. The Ross family seems to have conformed to the patriarchal household described by Frits Pannekoek in his article, "The Demographic Structure of Nineteenth Century Red River," in *Essays on Western History*, ed. L. H. Thomas, (Edmonton: University of Alberta Press, 1976), 83–95.
8. P.A.M. (see note 6), Ross Family Papers, James to his father, July 1, 1854.
9. Ibid., Alexander to James, Aug. 25, 1854.
10. Ibid., William to James, Feb. 9, 1856.
11. Ibid., John Black to James, Feb. 9, 1854. *Bois Brûlés* was a term used originally to apply to the Metis. It could be translated as "mixed blood" or "halfbreed."

12. William Ross married Jemima McKenzie, a daughter of former Hudson's Bay Company officer Roderick McKenzie, and a grand-daughter of Chief Factor James Sutherland. The youngest son, Sandy Ross, married Catherine, the daughter of prosperous Kildonan settler Donald Murray and his mixed blood wife Catherine Swain.
13. Hudson's Bay Company Archives, D. 5/38, Jas. Sinclair to Simpson, Dec. 11, 1853, f. 342 and Jn. Bunn to Simpson, Dec. 16, 1853, f. 372d–373.
14. P.A.M. (see note 6), Ross Family Papers, Jemima to James, Nov. 9, 1854.
15. Ibid., Jas. Ross to siblings, Dec. 25, 1865.
16. For a discussion of the growth of these stereotypes, see Brown, *Strangers in Blood* (note 3).
17. P.A.M. (see note 6), Ross Family Papers, James to his father Oct. 1856. James may well have thought that his father was ashamed of his half-Indian family. Significantly, their existence is never mentioned in Alexander Ross' later volume, *The Red River Settlement*.
18. Ibid., James Ross to siblings, Dec. 25, 1856.
19. "Petition of Inhabitants" in L. G. Thomas, ed., *The Prairie West to 1905* (Toronto: Oxford University Press, 1975), 59–61.
20. For a discussion of this episode, see Frits Pannekoek, "The Rev. Griffiths Owen Corbett and the Red River Civil War of 1869–70." *Canadian Historical Review* 57, no. 2: 133–49.
21. P.A.M. (see note 6), Ross Family Papers, Henrietta to James, early 1854.
22. Jennifer Brown, "Ultimate Respectability: Fur Trade Children in the 'Civilized World'," *The Beaver* (Spring 1978): 48–55.
23. W. L. Morton, ed., *Alexander Begg's Red River Journal* (Toronto: Champlain Society, 1956), 422.
24. P.A.M. (see note 6), Ross Family Papers, James to his wife, Sept. 24, 1870.
25. Morton, *Begg's Journal* (see note 23), 351; P.A.M. (see note 6), Ross Family Papers, Jas. Smith to Maggy, Nov. 30, 1869; Rev. John Laing to Ross, Feb. 1870.
26. P.A.M. (see note 6), Ross Family Papers, James to his wife, Sept. 29, 1870; Matthew Cook to Jas. Ross, Nov. 22, 1870.
27. Ibid., James to Governor Archibald, Mar. 11, 1871.
28. P.A.M. (see note 6), William Coldwell Papers, Draft notes about Mary Ross Flett.

29. Frits Pannekoek has suggested in his thesis that the "country-born" or Anglo-Indian community was not able to produce its own leaders. The evidence does not seem to support this. Men such as William Hallett, James Sinclair, and the Kennedy brothers, in addition to the Ross brothers, were leaders and more attention needs to be given to their role.
30. W. L. Morton, *Manitoba, A History* (Toronto: University of Toronto Press, 1967), 90.
31. Consider the fate of William Hallett, for example. An ambitious man, he was to suffer racial prejudice in his attempt to succeed in white society. He committed suicide after the failure of the "Canadian party" to overthrow Riel.

Appendix A
Thayendanegea

Barbara Graymont

Thayendanegea (he also signed Thayendanegen, Thayeadanege, Joseph Thayendanegea, and Joseph Brant), Mohawk interpreter, translator, war chief, and statesman; Indian Department officer; member of the wolf clan; his Mohawk name means he sets or places together two bets; probably born *circa* March 1742/43 in Cayahoga (near Akron, Ohio), son of Tehowaghwengaraghkwin; died 24 November 1807 in what is now Burlington, Ont.

According to testimony Joseph Brant gave to John Norton, he was "descended from Wyandot prisoners adopted by the Mohawks on both the father and mother's side"; his grandmother had been captured when the Wyandots were living in the vicinity of the Bay of Quinte (Ontario). The tradition that the Mohawk chief Hendrick [Theyanoguin] was an ancestor of Brant has been affirmed by historian Lyman Copeland Draper. In 1879, an elderly Mohawk woman named Katy Moses, who was a distant relative of Brant's third wife, told Draper that Brant's mother was descended from Hendrick. Charlotte Smith, *née* Brant, a granddaughter of Joseph, said that Brant's mother was Hendrick's granddaughter. When Brant visited England in 1775–76, he was interviewed at length by James Boswell, who wrote an account for the *London Magazine* of July 1776. In it Brant is called the grandson of the chief who visited England in the time of Queen Anne. But Mohawks use the term grandfather to refer also to great- and great-great-grandfathers and to great-uncles, and a chief named Brant (Sa Ga Yeath Qua Pieth Tow) who was also in the 1710 delegation may have been related to Joseph in some way.

Joseph was probably born in March 1742 of the Julian calendar. Estimates of his year of birth made by subtracting his age at death as given by his biographer William Leete Stone produce a date of 1743, but this purely arithmetical calculation ignores the change from Julian to Gregorian calendar which took place in his lifetime. Joseph's father, Tehowaghwengaraghkwin, who was reputed to have been a prominent warrior, died while his son was an infant. A few years before the outbreak of the Seven Years' War, Joseph's mother took him and his sister Mary [Koñwatsi?tsiaiéñni] to the Mohawk valley, settling at Canajoharie (near Little Falls, New York), which had been her home before the family's emigration to the Ohio country. She married again, her new husband being a man named Carrihogo, or News Carrier, who was known to the whites as Barnet or Bernard, and by contraction, Brant. Young Joseph was called Brant's Joseph and finally Joseph Brant. Author William Allen, who knew Joseph Brant's son Joseph and possibly obtained the information from him, says that the stepfather, a chief, "was denominated an Onondaga Indian." Stone, who interviewed various descendants, says that the stepfather was a Mohawk.

Brant's first military service with the British came when he was about fifteen, during the Seven Years' War. He took part in James Abercromby's campaign to invade Canada by way of Lake George (Lac Saint-Sacrement) in 1758, and he was with the warriors who accompanied Sir William Johnson, superintendent of northern Indians, in the 1759 expedition against Fort Niagara (near Youngstown, New York). The next year he was a member of the force led by Jeffery Amherst that descended the St. Lawrence to besiege Montréal.

Brant's stepfather died about 1760. Testimony that Draper received from Brant's godson, John "Smoke" Johnson, indicates that a warrior known as Old Crooked Neck "took charge" of young Brant and brought him to Sir William Johnson. Impressed by his abilities, Johnson decided to send him to school. In the summer of 1761, Joseph was dispatched along with two other Mohawk boys to the Reverend Eleazar Wheelock in Lebanon (Columbia), Connecticut, to be enrolled in Moor's Indian Charity School.

Wheelock referred to him as "being of a Family of Distinction ..., was considerably cloathed, *Indian*-fashion, and could speak a few Words of English." His mental capacities and demeanour commended him highly to Wheelock. Brant was soon employed in teaching the Mohawk language to a fellow scholar, Samuel Kirkland, who planned to be a missionary to the Iroquois. On 4 November 1761, Brant and Kirkland went to Iroquois country to secure six more boys for the school. They returned a few weeks later with two Mohawk boys and a promise from Johnson that he would send more when families had returned from the fall hunt.

So promising a student was Brant that Wheelock had planned to let him accompany Kirkland when he went on to the College of New Jersey (Princeton University); there Brant could continue tutoring the aspiring missionary in the Mohawk language while he himself studied in the local grammar school, perfecting his English and "pursuing other parts of Useful Learning perhaps fitting for College." The plan did not materialize, and in 1762, Kirkland went to the college alone.

Wheelock described Brant in February 1763 as being "of a Sprightly Genius, a manly and genteel Deportment, and of a Modest and benevolent Temper, I have Reason to think began truly to love our Lord Jesus Christ Several Months ago; and his religious Affections Seem Still agreeably increasing." At this time Brant's tutor, Charles Jeffry Smith, was making arrangements to take him with him to Mohawk country, where the two could continue to teach each other their respective languages and where Smith could serve as a missionary to the Mohawks. In May 1763, however, a letter came for Joseph from his sister Mary calling him home, since the Indians were displeased with his being at the school, "don't like the People &c." Wheelock begged Johnson's indulgence for a few more months until Smith could be ready for his mission tour, and until Wheelock had had an opportunity to take Brant on a trip to Boston and Portsmouth, New Hampshire, on school business.

Brant and Smith left for Mohawk country in the summer of 1763, and though both Smith and Wheelock looked forward to Brant's return to the school, it was not to be. Johnson in fact was contemplating sending him to New York City where he could be prepared for entrance into King's College (Columbia University). However, upon advice that prejudice against Indians was running high in the city as a result of Pontiac's uprising, Johnson sent him and three other Mohawk youths to missionary Cornelius Bennet in the Mohawk valley to further their education.

Along with other Iroquois allies of the British, Brant participated in the 1764 campaign against the Delaware Indian settlements on the Susquehanna River, and he was one of the volunteers on John Bradstreet's expedition against the western Indians that same year. His activities gave rise to the false rumour in New England that he had put himself at the head of a large party of Indians to attack the British. Though Wheelock's confidence in Brant remained unshaken, the tale hurt his school financially. Wheelock later wrote that Brant had been "useful in the War; in which he behaved so much like the Christian and the Soldier, that he gained great Esteem."

On 25 July 1765, Brant married an Oneida woman, Neggen Aoghyatonghsera, whose English name was Margaret, daughter of Isaac of Onoquaga. The ceremony was conducted at Canajoharie by missionary Theophilus Chamberlain, who described the bride as "a handsome, sober, discreet & a religious young woman." The Brants had two children, Isaac and Christiana, and lived in a comfortable house at Canajoharie where missionaries labouring among the Iroquois were always welcomed. Neggen contracted consumption and died, probably in mid-March 1771. Brant then went to live with John Stuart, Anglican missionary at Fort Hunter, New York. He soon applied to Stuart to marry him to Neggen's half-sister, Susanna. Stuart declined since the Church of England forbade such close kinship marriages, and Brant thereupon approached a German minister, who performed the ceremony. Susanna died after a brief time, leaving no issue. About 1779, Brant married Catharine [Ohtowaʔkéhson], reputedly the daughter of former Indian agent George Croghan. She was from a prominent family and later became clan matron of the Mohawk turtle clan; her brother Henry [Tekarihó:ken] was the tribe's leading sachem. Seven children were born of this marriage: Joseph, Jacob, Margaret, Catharine, Mary, John [Ahyouwaeghs], and Elizabeth. Brant sent Joseph and Jacob to the Wheelock family at Hanover, New Hampshire, in 1800. Both Dartmouth College and Moor's Indian Charity School were located there by this date, and the boys were entered in the school. It was John, however, who became prominent in Mohawk tribal affairs and in Upper Canadian politics.

During the time Brant spent with John Stuart, he had assisted the missionary in translating the Gospel of St. Mark, a concise history of the Bible, and an exposition of the catechism into the Mohawk language. In Stuart's estimation Brant was "perhaps ... the only Person in America equal to such an undertaking." Brant's services and talents were also valued by Johnson, who used him as an interpreter and a translator of speeches into the languages of the Six Nations. Brant spoke at least three of these languages fluently. Norton states in his *Journal* that shortly before dying in 1774 Johnson used his influence with the Mohawks to have Brant chosen a chief, presumably a war chief, but that Brant accepted the honour with some hesitation. Brant also served Sir William's successor, Guy Johnson. In 1775, he received the appointment of "Interpreter for the Six Nations Language" at an annual salary of £85 3s. 4d., American army currency.

After the outbreak of hostilities in the Thirteen Colonies in 1775, Brant remained loyal to the king. He went to Montreal with Guy Johnson in the summer and in November embarked for England with Johnson, Christian Daniel Claus, and a few associates to present their position on Indian affairs to the British government. Brant was generally lionized, introduced to some of the leading men in the arts, letters, and government, inducted into the Falcon Lodge of freemasons, and had his portrait painted. According to Boswell, he "was struck with the appearance of England in general; but he said he chiefly admired the ladies and the horses." He did not, however, neglect the serious side of his mission. He and his Mohawk companion, Oteroughyanento (Ohrante), presented Iroquois grievances about encroachments on their lands to Lord George Germain, secretary of state for the American Colonies. "It is very hard when we have let the Kings subjects have so much of our lands for so little value, they should want to cheat us ... of the small spots we have left for our women and children to live on," Brant said. Germain fully agreed that the Indians had been wronged by the Americans but stated that the government could not attend to redressing these grievances until the dispute with the king's rebellious subjects had been settled. He hoped that the Six Nations would remain loyal and could, as a consequence, be assured "of every Support England could render Them." The promise satisfied Brant and he later repeated it in a speech to the Six Nations. Indeed, as a result of discussions with numerous English leaders of varying political persuasions, he became more firmly convinced than ever that the welfare of the Indian nations lay in a continuing alliance with the king.

Brant and his companions returned to North America in time to participate in the battle of Long Island in the summer of 1776. Then he and his loyalist friend Gilbert Tice went in disguise through the American-held countryside to Iroquois territory, where Brant urged the Indians to abandon their treaty of neutrality with the Continental Congress and actively support British arms. After persistent effort he eventually raised a force of about three hundred Indian warriors and one hundred white loyalists. For nearly a year, he remained in the Susquehanna River region. Operating out of Onoquaga (near Binghamton, New York), he made several excursions with his Indian-loyalist band to encourage white resistance, rouse the Indians, and confiscate food. In July 1777, he arrived at Oswego, followed by about three hundred warriors, to join Barrimore Matthew St. Leger's campaign. He participated in both the siege of Fort Stanwix (Rome) and the nearby battle of Oriskany that summer.

In January 1778, Brant left Fort Niagara with a party of warriors to reconnoitre in Indian country and be on the lookout for any American invasion attempt. In May and June his forces attacked Cobleskill and Durlach (Sharon). Again quartered at Onoquaga, he continued to send out foraging and scouting parties. Accompanied by a ranger detachment under Captain William Caldwell, Brant and his warriors attacked and destroyed German Flats (near the mouth of West Canada Creek) in September. During October, he and his men continued their raiding operations, mostly in Ulster County. He then joined forces with Captain Walter Butler's rangers and some Senecas for an attack on Cherry Valley early in November. During the course of events, the Senecas detached themselves from Butler's command and killed indiscriminately, friend and foe alike, throughout the settlement. Brant and his followers tried desperately, and with some success, to save numbers of white non-combatants from the fury of the Seneca warriors. According to every report, wrote Mason Bolton, commandant at Niagara, Brant "behaved with great humanity to all those who fell into his hands at Cherry Valley."

During July 1779, Brant and his Indian-loyalist band attacked the settlement of Minisink (Port Jervis) and cut to pieces the militia sent in pursuit of them. On 29 August at the battle of Newtown (near Elmira), which was the major engagement of the Sullivan-Clinton expedition into Iroquois country, the Indians were less fortunate. A force of Indians, rangers, and a few regulars, commanded by Major John Butler, Brant, Kaieñ?kwaahtoñ and Kaiūtwah?kū (Cornplanter), was defeated and obliged to retreat under the onslaught of the American army. The sheer number of the Americans and their superiority in weapons and supplies prevented any further full-scale confrontation for the remainder of the expedition, and the American invaders totally devastated the Indian country as far as the Genesee River before turning back. The Indian refugees were forced en masse into the area around Fort Niagara, straining British resources to the utmost.

Far from crushing the Six Nations, the invasion only increased their determination for revenge. Numerous raiding parties spread terror through the American frontier settlements during 1780. In the spring, Brant and his band were raiding near Harpersfield, New York, In July they laid waste the villages of pro-American Oneidas and Tuscaroras. Brant was also with the Indians and loyalists who devastated the Mohawk valley settlements and the Schoharie region later that year.

Brant had been serving as a captain in the Indian Department at least since early 1779, although he did not have a commission. On 16 April 1779, Germain sent Governor Haldimand a commission signed by George III for Joseph Brant as colonel of Indians in appreciation of his "astonishing activity and success" in the king's service. Haldimand suppressed the document, courteously explaining to Germain that Brant, despite his meritorious activity, was relatively young compared to the other Indian war leaders, "has been very lately known in the War Path," and although distinguishing himself was as yet far from being recognized by the senior war chiefs as having an equal footing with the most experienced warriors of the confederacy. Such a mark of distinction, if it were presented to Brant, Haldimand warned, would therefore "be productive of very dangerous consequences" in stirring up jealousy and animosity towards him among the leading Iroquois warriors. Consequently Brant did not receive an official commission until 13 July 1780 when, on the recommendation of Guy Johnson, Haldimand made him a captain "of the Northern Confederate Indians."

Despite his captaincy, Brant preferred to fight as a war chief. He later explained to Sir John Johnson that that rank gave him command of more men in battle than was customary with a captain. The British officers who served with Brant and the commanding officers who received reports of his military behaviour always had the highest praise for him. He emerges in the official dispatches as the perfect soldier, possessed of remarkable physical stamina, courage under fire, and dedication to the cause, as an able and inspiring leader, and as a complete gentleman. White volunteers are known to have requested transfer from the rangers so that they could join Brant, "a person they had confidence in & had volunteerly served under with much satisfaction."

In early 1781, Brant and John Deserontyon were planning to attack the Oneidas once more. Because of a rumoured invasion of the Ohio country by George Rogers Clark, however, Guy Johnson diverted Brant's activities to that quarter. Brant and seventeen warriors left Fort Niagara on 8 April 1781 for the Ohio Indian villages, where they remained several months encouraging the inhabitants. On 26 August, Brant, with a hundred whites and Indians, utterly defeated an equal number of men from Clark's army, killing or capturing all of them.

Brant's final military service during the revolution came in 1782, when he and his warriors assisted Major John Ross' men in repairing Fort Oswego. Then, in July, he set out with a large party of warriors and a company of light infantry from the fort to harry the American settlements; he was summoned back, however, by Haldimand's announcement of peace negotiations and the consequent recall of all war parties. Hostilities were drawing to a close, but Brant's great career as a statesman was just beginning.

In the peace negotiations between Great Britain and the United States, Britain completely ignored its Indian allies and transferred sovereignty over all British-claimed land as far west as the Mississippi River to the Americans, even though almost the entire territory was occupied by Indians, who believed they had never relinquished it to the whites. When Brant learned of the treaty's terms, he angrily exclaimed that England had "sold the Indians to Congress." The indignation of the Six Nations at their betrayal led the British administrators in Québec to attempt to mollify them by various means. Sir John Johnson, superintendent general of Indian affairs, told them that "the right of Soil belongs to and is in yourselves as sole proprietors" beyond the boundary established by the 1768 Treaty of Fort Stanwix — a line running southwest from that fort to the Ohio River and thence to the Mississippi. Such statements about land title were bound to mislead Indians by obscuring the distinction between ownership of land and sovereignty over it. The British also maintained control of forts Oswegatchie (Ogdensburg, New York), Oswego, Niagara, Detroit, and Michilimackinac (Mackinac Island, Michigan), all in ceded territory, and urged the formation of a confederacy by the Iroquois and the Indians to the west. In addition, colonial officials appealed to the home government to secure a land grant within the province for the faithful Iroquois. Haldimand made arrangements for a tract on the Bay of Quinte to be provided for the Mohawks, who had lost all their land as a result of the war, and for other Six Nations Indians and their allies who cared to immigrate. The Senecas, however, objected to the location. They were the westernmost Iroquois tribe and their lands were not immediately threatened by the Americans. Most of them planned to stay where they were, and in their view a settlement on the Bay of Quinte would endanger the Six Nations by dispersing them over too great a distance. They offered the refugees instead a gift of land in the Genesee valley. Though the Mohawks refused the offer, Brant was persuaded that the Seneca reasoning had merit. Through him the Mohawks therefore requested of Haldimand a new grant closer to the traditional Six Nations homeland. In the autumn of 1784 they received a huge tract along the Grand River (Ontario), which the Mississauga Ojibwas had relinquished in May, and, with the exception of the Fort Hunter Mohawks under John Deserontyon who preferred to settle at the Bay of Quinte, they established themselves on this land. A census made in 1785 shows more than four hundred Mohawks, several hundred Cayugas and Onondagas, and smaller groups of Senecas, Tuscaroras, Delawares, Nanticokes, Tutelos, Creeks, and Cherokees to a total of 1,843.

Brant played a major role in attempts to forge the Six Nations and the western Indians into a confederacy to oppose American expansion. In August and September 1783, he was present at unity meetings in the Detroit area and on 7 September at Lower Sandusky (Ohio) was a principal speaker at an Indian council attended by Wyandots, Delawares, Shawnees, Cherokees, Ojibwas, Ottawas, and Mingos. There he feelingly presented his grand vision: "We the Chief Warriors of the Six Nations with this Belt bind your Hearts and Minds with ours, that there may be never hereafter a Separation between us, let there be Peace or War, it shall never disunite us, for our Interests are alike, nor should anything ever be done but by the united Voice of us all, as we make but one with you." The confederacy forged at these meetings would continue to be a principal concern of Brant's for a number of years.

From 31 August to 10 September 1784, Brant was at Fort Stanwix for peace negotiations between the Six Nations and New York State officials, but he did not attend the treaty held at the same place with the commissioners of the Continental Congress in October. He did, however, express extreme indignation on learning that the commissioners had detained as hostages several prominent Six Nations leaders, including his friend Kanonraron (Aaron Hill). Brant delayed an intended trip to England attempting to secure their release.

In late 1785, Brant set sail to present Mohawk claims for war losses to the government, to petition for a half-pay pension, to request publication of religious literature in the Mohawk language, and to receive assurance that Indian land had not been given to the United States. Most important, he wished to ascertain whether the faithful Indian allies of the king might expect support from the British government should war break out between the Americans and the confederated Indians over American encroachment on Indian lands. He made the trip over the strong opposition of Sir John Johnson, who urged him to stay at home and attend to the affairs of the confederacy.

In England Brant succeeded in securing his pension and a compensation of about £15,000 for the Mohawks. As for his query whether the Indians would "be considered as His Majesty's faithful allies, and have that support and countenance such as old and true friends expect" should "serious consequences" develop over American encroachments on Indian land, Brant received an assurance from Home Secretary Lord Sydney of the king's continual concern for Indian welfare and a recommendation from the king that the Indians conduct their affairs "with temper and moderation" and a "peaceable demeanor," all of which would "most likely ... secure to themselves the possession of those rights and privileges which their ancestors have heretofore enjoyed." It was obviously a polite refusal to become militarily involved in the Indians' problems.

The Indian confederacy was not functioning as Brant had planned. The Americans had ignored it and had insisted on making treaties with smaller groups of Indians. The resulting treaties of Fort Stanwix (1784), Fort McIntosh (1785), and Fort Finney (1786), with their extortion of huge land grants, caused deep resentment, growing factionalism, and a disintegration of the unity Brant had sought to establish. He made trips to the Ohio-Detroit region in 1786, 1787, and 1788 to strengthen the confederacy and urge peace with the United States. He also tried hard to secure the Muskingum River (Ohio) as the boundary between the Indian nations and the United States, but such a settlement was not then acceptable to the American government.

The achievement of unanimity among the diverse Indian nations was one of the most difficult tasks undertaken by Brant and was never fully accomplished. His attempts to halt the treaties held by Major-General Arthur St. Clair with the Indians at Fort Harmar (Marietta, Ohio) in 1789 were not successful; the American general conducted one with the Iroquois, exclusive of the Mohawks, and another with the Potawatomis, Sauks, Ottawas, Ojibwas, Wyandots, and Delawares. Predictably — St. Clair's policy was to divide and conquer — there was not a full representation even of the nations who were present. The policy led to Indian resentment and reprisals against white settlers and resulted in three full-scale American retaliatory invasions.

Brigadier-General Josiah Harmar's punitive expedition against the Shawnee and Miami villages along the Miamis (Maumee) River in October 1790 was defeated and turned back. Both Governor General Lord Dorchester [Guy Carleton] and Sir John Johnson told Brant that they wished to effect a peace between the western Indians and the United States, but both men also persisted in deliberately deceiving him concerning the boundaries established by Great Britain and the United States in 1783. They assured him once again that the king had not really given away the Indian lands in the west to the Americans and that the boundary set at the Treaty of Fort Stanwix in 1768 was still in effect. The deception helped provide the British in Canada with an Indian buffer on their frontier and laid the blame for white expansion into the west solely on the Americans.

Brant went into the Indian country south of the Great Lakes in the spring of 1791 to continue his consultation with the western nations. In a council held at Detroit and attended by deputy Indian agent Alexander McKee and representatives of the confederacy, the Indians agreed that the Muskingum River should be their eastern boundary and sent Brant and twelve other deputies to Québec to inform the government of their decision. Brant wanted to learn if the British would back the Indians in obtaining recognition of their boundary. Dorchester assured the deputies that the king had not transferred their country to the Americans, but he also emphasized that the government could not involve itself in any hostilities. The reluctance of Dorchester to commit the government militarily was a disappointment to Brant. The Americans in 1791 had held a treaty with that portion of the Six Nations living south of the Great Lakes and successfully neutralized them. A treaty with the powerful Cherokees farther to the south had also been concluded. These American diplomatic successes further undercut the strength of the western confederacy.

In November 1791, however, St. Clair's army was defeated by western Indian forces under Little Turtle [Michikinakoua] near the Miamis Towns (Fort Wayne, Indiana). Because of Brant's prestige and great influence with the Indian nations, President George Washington and Secretary of War Henry Knox invited him to the seat of government at Philadelphia in 1792 to seek his good offices in effecting peace in the west. It was the first of several trips Brant would make to confer with American government officials on Indian business. Though he was firm during the visit in protecting the Indian interests and though he rejected the American offer to him of a large land grant and a pension, which he considered a bribe, he believed that a compromise could be worked out on the boundary question and he prepared to travel to the western confederacy in search of a peaceful solution. Because of a sudden sickness, he arrived too late for the confederacy council held at the Glaize (Defiance, Ohio) from 30 September until early in October 1792, but he did have several unsuccessful consultations with the various Indian nations, who he now found had hardened their demands and were insisting on the Ohio River as a boundary. At a council between American commissioners and the confederacy Indians at Lower Sandusky in the summer of 1793, Brant had no more success in securing a compromise. Although the American commissioners were authorized to make some concessions so long as their existing settlements in the region could be maintained, the western Indians were adamant that the Ohio River should be the border and that all white settlements should be withdrawn. The failure of the negotiations made war inevitable and led in 1794 to the battle of Fallen Timbers (near Waterville, Ohio), where the western Indians were resoundingly defeated by Major-General Anthony Wayne's army.

After Wayne's victory, Brant and Lieutenant Governor John Graves Simcoe both went west in order to encourage the Indians to remain united. Brant promised them warriors from the Six Nations. These attempts to bolster the confederacy proved futile. The Treaty of Greenville conducted by Wayne in 1795 effectively spelled the end of the grand plan of Indian unity. Moreover, the onset of the French revolutionary wars in Europe had made Britain anxious for peace at any cost in North America. By Jay's Treaty of 1794, she had agreed to surrender the border forts to the United States, and in 1796 these symbols of British support for the Indian cause were turned over to the Americans.

With the change in British policy, Brant's persistence in encouraging Indian unity and in maintaining contacts with the other Indian nations became a source of annoyance and suspicion to the British government and to administrators such as Dorchester in the Canadas, who tried to keep the Indians divided, dependent, and subservient. Whereas they had once fostered an Indian confederacy and had encouraged Brant's leadership, they now tried to discourage his diplomacy, undercut his influence, and redirect his activities to his own settlement. Brant was not one to be easily deterred, and the resulting controversy caused tension for many years.

At the Grand River, Brant was the main spokesman. Though only a war chief, he served in the capacity of a sachem. He always worked closely with Tekarihó:ken, the leading Mohawk sachem, but it was to Brant that the chiefs entrusted their diplomacy and land negotiations because of his education, his fluency in English, his many contacts with government officials in England and Canada, and "his knowledge of the laws and customs of the white people." His long association with the Johnson family and his familiarity with the upper classes in Great Britain and North America led him to adopt their manners. He lived in a genteel English style, had about twenty white and black servants, kept a well-stocked table, was waited on by black servants in full livery, and entertained graciously. In 1795, he secured a large tract of land from the Mississauga Indians in the vicinity of Burlington Bay (Hamilton Harbour), which purchase the government confirmed, and he subsequently moved into a fine house he built there. Whites who knew him socially expressed admiration for his intellect, his civility and amiable temperament, his dignity, and his ready wit. Physically impressive, he was 5 feet 11 inches tall, erect, powerful, and well formed, though tending to stoutness in his later years.

Brant had a continuing concern for the intellectual and spiritual advancement of his people. During the Revolutionary War he had obtained a schoolmaster for the Mohawk settlement near Fort Niagara and had a little log chapel built near present-day Lewiston, New York. After the immigration to the Grand River, he helped secure a school, a schoolmaster, and a church, and by 1789 he had also translated a primer and the liturgy of the Church of England into the Mohawk language. He was planning to write a history for the Six Nations, but evidently, from the press of business, never began the project. He also attempted for a number of years to obtain a resident Anglican clergyman for the settlement and in 1797 turned his attention to Davenport Phelps, a son-in-law of Eleazar Wheelock, who was living in Upper Canada and practising law. He urged Phelps to apply for ordination so that he could serve the Grand River community. Both Peter Russell, administrator of Upper Canada, and Bishop Jacob Mountain objected to Phelps because of his American military service and his alleged political views and activities. Brant carried on a lengthy correspondence with British officials on his behalf, but to no avail. Finally, through Brant's urging, Phelps obtained his ordination in New York. He preached for a while near Burlington Bay but did not settle at the Grand River and soon returned to the United States. Brant's considerable efforts to secure a resident minister for his people thus came to naught.

A tragic incident occurred in Brant's family in 1795 during the annual distribution of government presents at Burlington Bay. Isaac Brant, who had a violent temper, attacked his father with a knife, wounding him in the hand as his father warded off the blow. Brant drew his dirk in self-defence and in the struggle inflicted a scalp wound on his son. Isaac refused medical attention, and in a few days the wound became badly infected and proved fatal. Brant turned himself in to the authorities but was exonerated. His role in his son's death was a sorrow he bore for the remainder of his days.

A dispute that was to last for several years developed between the Mohawks of the Grand River and the Caughnawaga and St. Regis Mohawks during the late 1790s. The latter, by the treaty of 31 May 1796 with the state of New York, abandoned their claim to an extensive area of land in the northern part of the state, the St. Regis Indians agreeing to confine themselves to the boundaries of their present reservation along the St. Lawrence River. The chiefs, including Atiatoharongwen, who negotiated the treaty later blamed Brant for the sale of their lands. The charge was completely unfounded and unjust. It arose out of a misunderstanding, a desire to shift the blame to another, or deliberate misrepresentation to the Caughnawaga and St. Regis Indians on the part of Egbert Benson, the chief New York negotiator. It took Brant four years to secure the complete details of the negotiation from the Caughnawaga and St. Regis Indians and from Albany officials, all of whom were reluctant to release information. Through painstaking search and interviews with most of the principals except Benson, who refused to cooperate, Brant was able to clear himself and the Grand River Mohawks.

Scarcely any problem was more enduring or more vexing to Brant than the controversy over the nature of the Six Nations' title to the Grand River lands and the extent of the grant. According to the original Haldimand grant, a tract of approximately two million acres, from the source to the mouth of the river and six miles deep on each side, had been given to the loyalist Six Nations Indians. Later the government claimed that a mistake had been made in the original grant in that the northern portion had never been bought from the Mississaugas and the king accordingly could not grant what he had not bought. Despite repeated urgings by Brant and the other chiefs, the government never made the additional purchase. Brant also believed that the area along the Grand River was too large for the Indian population to farm and too small for hunting. With whites moving into the region in increasing numbers and more land being cleared, game was becoming scarce. He therefore wanted the community to realize a continuing income from the land by sales and leases to whites. Brant also strongly believed that whites living among them and intermarrying with them would bring and transmit skills needed by the Indians in a changing environment. Though Brant was firmly convinced that the land was, or should have been, granted to the Indians on the same basis as to the white loyalists, in fee simple, to do with as they wished, both Lord Dorchester and Lieutenant Governor Simcoe advanced the curious argument that the king's allies could not have the king's subjects as tenants. The Royal Proclamation of 1763, which had prohibited individual whites from purchasing Indians' land in order to guard the Indians against fraud, was cited. Simcoe further emphasized that the Grand River grant was meant solely for Indians and was never to be alienated. Brant refused a title deed from Simcoe that forbade alienation. By 1796, Dorchester and Simcoe had finally relented to the extent of agreeing that Grand River lands might be leased, although the government would have the right of pre-emption; Brant continued to oppose any restriction of Indian sovereignty.

Brant's leadership did not go unquestioned. Fort Hunter Mohawk Aaron Hill and his brother Isaac (Anoghsoktea) had complained to Lord Dorchester in 1788 about Brant's policy of bringing whites among them. They also resented his growing political influence. Moreover, the land sales resulted in tangled finances because several of the purchasers were unable to keep up with their payments. Some Indians began to blame Brant for the financial mess and the lack of income from the sales. A few even believed he was pocketing the money. Indeed the tensions at the Grand River may have prompted Brant's decision to move to Burlington Bay.

In order to secure for the Six Nations the right of complete control over their Grand River lands, Brant contemplated another trip to England to lay their grievances before the government. Lacking the funds for such an enterprise, he went instead in early 1797 to Philadelphia to relay his complaints to the British minister, Robert Liston. Brant's strategy there was to talk openly about concluding an alliance with the French if his people were not better treated and to let the rumours drift back to Liston. In conference with Liston, he then rehearsed the whole history of the Six Nations' troubles with the government and accused the authorities in the Canadas of refusing to sanction land sales by the Indians because they had personal designs on those same lands.

Brant deliberately associated with the pro-French party in the American capital and studiously avoided mixing with anyone from the administration, even ignoring the repeated invitations of Secretary of War James McHenry to call upon him. McHenry had arranged an appointment for him with Washington, but Brant departed Philadelphia without meeting the president and left behind many complaints that he had not been treated well by the American government officials. Liston's description of Brant as "so determined, so able, and so artful" was apt.

Brant's behaviour was alarming to both Liston and the British authorities in Canada. Rumours were rife of a Franco-Spanish attack on British possessions by way of the Mississippi, and it was feared that discontent among the Indians might lead them to join such an invasion. Thus in 1797, Brant, through extreme pressure on Peter Russell, received approval for the land dispositions already made. This was only a temporary respite, for the government continued in subsequent years to hold a totally negative attitude toward any Indian right to sell or lease lands to individuals.

Also in 1797, the Mohawks were successful in negotiating a settlement with New York State for the woodlands surrounding their former villages at Fort Hunter and Canajoharie. Brant and John Deserontyon held a treaty at Albany with New York State on 29 March 1797 by which the state awarded the Mohawks a modest compensation of $1,000 and $600 for expenses.

Brant was still determined to secure full Indian sovereignty over the Grand River lands, and he sent his associate John Norton to England in 1804 to present the Indian case and to get the original Haldimand grant confirmed. William Claus, deputy superintendent general of Indian affairs in Upper Canada, reacted by attempting to manipulate Brant's ouster as chief. Claus sent an Indian emissary, a Cayuga chief named Tsinonwanhonte, to the Grand River to undermine Brant and also wrote to officials in England in an effort to sabotage Norton's mission. Not being able to persuade the great majority of Grand River Indians that Brant and Norton were corrupt and working against their interests, Claus sowed distrust among the Six Nations on the American side of the border. They called a Six Nations council at Buffalo Creek, despite the fact that the grand council fire of the Six Nations Confederacy had been moved several years before to the Onondaga village at the Grand River. This rump council, composed mostly of Senecas, disavowed Norton's mission and deposed Brant as chief. Only a few people from the Grand River attended the meeting. A delegation from the Buffalo Creek council then went to Fort George (Niagara-on-the-Lake), Upper Canada, and held a similar council with Claus, who sent a copy of the proceedings to England and thereby effectively destroyed Norton's mission. Brant later complained that Claus had dictated this document and that a number of the common folk had signed as chiefs to give the pronouncement more weight.

Brant fought back vigorously, berating in council those from the Grand River whom he charged with being Claus's dupes. Then he went to Fort George and held a council on 28 July 1806 to accuse Claus of duplicity, reminding him that the Indians who chose to remain with the Americans had no equity in the Grand River lands and no say in their governance. The Grand River chiefs backed Brant fully and continued him in his chiefly office. He also received support from an anti-government faction that included William Weekes, judge Robert Thorpe, and missionary Robert Addison. He was planning another trip to England to plead the Indians' cause and repair the damage Claus had done, but death claimed him.

Joseph Brant had been impressed by much in white culture. He admired the technology of the whites, their style of living, and their industry. He saw that in the changing circumstances in which Indians then lived, the traditional social structure of women farmers and men hunters would not suffice, for game was growing scarce and hunting accordingly declining. As a consequence, there soon would be more likelihood of hunger and only a reduced role in life for the Indian men. For Indians to survive, they would have to adopt white methods of agriculture, raising domestic animals and encouraging the men to become farmers. He invited white families to come and live by his people at Grand River "for the purposes of making roads, raising provisions and teaching us the benefits of agriculture." Brant was furthermore convinced that one of the best means of helping his people through the transition was intermarriage with the whites. There were other features of white culture that Brant valued highly. He was a conscientious Anglican, translating portions of the Bible and helping to found churches for his people. He also saw the necessity of Indians becoming literate in their own language as well as in English and he diligently promoted education.

But there were aspects of white culture that Brant shunned, comparing them unfavourably with the less competitive, more egalitarian ways of the Iroquois. He was repelled by the deep-seated class divisions in white society, the harshness of its laws, the inequitable dispensing of justice, the suppression of the weak by the strong, the horror of the prisons, and the particularly shocking practice of imprisonment for debt. "The palaces and prisons among you form a most dreadful contrast," he reminded a white correspondent. "Go to the former places, and you will see perhaps a *deformed piece of earth* assuming airs that become none but the Great Spirit above. Go to one of your prisons; here description utterly fails!" He was well aware that among whites the laws could often be manipulated or bypassed by the powerful and that "estates of widows and orphans" could be "devoured by enterprising sharpers" — a thing that never happened among Indians. These aspects of white culture Brant considered totally inconsistent with the teachings of Christianity. "Cease, then, to call yourselves Christians, lest you publish to the world your hypocrisy," he admonished the same correspondent. And then he turned back upon the whites a favourite epithet of theirs that had always incensed the Indians: "Cease, too, to call other nations savage, when you are tenfold more the children of cruelty than they."

The moral deficiencies in white society were not only an offence to Brant's idealism. He saw them as practical obstacles that hindered his people from adopting the features of white civilization necessary for their survival. Writing to Samuel Kirkland in 1791, he explained: "A chain of corroborating circumstances, and events, seems to evince to them that the white people, under whatever pretence, aim at their destruction — possess'd with such Idea's their prejudices naturally encrease and seeing the sword in one hand, supported by injustice and corruption, is it any wonder that they suspect the sincerity of any proposals made on the other hand for so great a change as civilization must make ...."

Brant was a noble figure who dedicated his whole life to the advancement of his people and who struggled to maintain their freedom and sovereignty. His major failure was his inability to understand the nature of British imperialism and to comprehend the fact that the British would not permit two sovereignties to exist in Upper Canada. The Indians were manipulated and exploited by the British government to serve the purposes of the empire: they were encouraged to cede their land in time of peace, pressured to become military allies in time of war, ignored in the treaty of peace, urged to form an enlarged confederacy as a barrier between the British and the Americans, and coerced to abandon the confederacy when the British had composed their differences with their enemy and growing Indian power threatened to rival their own. British colonial agents were then urged to foster jealousies and divisions among the Indian nations in order to keep them in a state of continual dependency upon the British government. Nor did Brant really understand how dependent the Indians had become in their new environment close to their white neighbours. Even land sales by the Six Nations, which Brant supported for immediately practical reasons, would eventually attach them irreparably to the surrounding white economy as Indian land holdings diminished. Only Brant's larger vision of Indian unity, had it been achieved, would have succeeded in maintaining Indian sovereignty for a longer period and slowing white expansion. In this plan he was defeated by jealousies and divisiveness among the confederated Indian nations, and by American and then British successes in undermining the general confederacy. When Tecumseh revived the concept of a confederacy in the next generation, it was already too late.

Additional Information and Sources

There are several portraits of Brant. At least two were made of him during his first visit to England in 1776. Of these, the well-known one by George Romney is in the National Gallery of Canada, Ottawa. Another was the work of an unknown artist commissioned by James Boswell and was reproduced in the *London Magazine* for July 1776. The Benjamin West study of Guy Johnson, painted in England in 1776, shows in the background an Indian often thought to be Brant. From the features, this supposition would seem unlikely. He may be either an idealized Indian or Oteroughyanento. During Brant's second trip to England, in 1786, his portrait was painted twice by Gilbert Stuart. One work was commissioned by the Duke of Northumberland, an acquaintance from the American Revolutionary War, and is still in the private possession of the family at their home in Guildford. The second Stuart portrait, which has become as famous as the earlier Romney one, was commissioned by Francis Rawdon, another wartime acquaintance, and is now at the New York State Historical Association, Cooperstown. A copy is in the British Library. A miniature of this portrait was in the possession of the Brant family in the nineteenth century. Also during his 1786 visit, a portrait of him wearing the uniform of an officer of the Indian Department and Indian headdress was painted by John Francis Rigaud. After Brant's return to North America, the portrait was sent to him through the courtesy of Haldimand, who was living in England. The original seems to have disappeared, but a copy is in the New York State Education Department at Albany. There are four studies of Brant by William Berczy. The earliest, a watercolour bust portrait, was painted some time after 1794 and is in the Musée du Séminaire de Québec. Berczy made what seem to be two copies in oil of this watercolour, but slightly modified, being head to waist portraits, with the right hand resting on a tomahawk. Both are in private collections, in Montréal and Baltimore. Another Berczy, *circa* 1800, is a full-length portrait depicting Brant at the Grand River, and is in the National Gallery of Canada. While on a trip to Philadelphia in 1797, Brant sat for Charles Willson Peale. This painting is now in Independence Hall, Philadelphia. What was probably the last portrait of Brant was painted in Albany in 1805 or 1806 by Ezra Ames. A copy of it was made by George Catlin, and an engraving from the latter by A. Dick was printed as the frontispiece for the second volume of William Leete Stone's biography of Brant. The Catlin copy, which hung in the New York State Library in Albany, was destroyed by fire in 1911. The original Ames portrait is now in Fenimore House, New York State Historical Association.

Brant's house in Burlington was demolished in 1932. Construction of the present Joseph Brant Museum was begun in 1937 on land once owned by Brant. It contains the staircase and some other pieces of the original building.

In the nineteenth century, Brant's papers were in the possession of his youngest daughter, Elizabeth Brant Kerr, and subsequently of her descendants. These papers were borrowed and many of them copied by Stone and Lyman Copeland Draper. Almost all the known Brant manuscripts, either published or unpublished, have been cited by M. J. Smith, "Joseph Brant, Mohawk statesman" (Ph.D. thesis, University of Wisconsin, Madison, 1946). A large amount of Brant correspondence is in BL, Add. MSS 21661–892; PAC, MG 11, [CO 42] Q; MG 19, F1 and F6; and RG 10. The most extensive Brant collection in the United States is Draper MSS, ser. F, held by the State Historical Society of Wisconsin. A number of Brant letters and speeches, some of them in Mohawk, are in the Burke Library, Hamilton and Kirkland Colleges (Clinton, New York), Kirkland MSS; NYPL, Philip Schuyler papers; New York Historical Society (New York), Henry O'Reilly coll. of docs. relating to the Five Nations and other Indians; and the Historical Society of Pennsylvania (Philadelphia), Indian records coll.

Additional sources used in the preparation of this article include: Dartmouth College Library (Hanover, N.H.), MS 001329, Account of Wheelock scholars, 1743–61, comp. Frederick Chase; MS 765429.1, Theophilus Chamberlain to Eleazar Wheelock, 29 July 1765. New York Historical Society, Jelles Fonda papers, "Journal kept on the expedition of Sir William Johnson and Gen. Jeffrey Amherst against Montreal, June–October 1760." USPG, B, 2 (mfm. at PAC). *Anthony Wayne ... the Wayne-Knox-Pickering-McHenry correspondence*, ed. R. C. Knopf

(Pittsburgh, Pa., 1960; repr. Westport, Conn., 1975). [James Boswell], "An account of the chief of the 'Mohock Indians' who lately visited 'England' (with an exact likeness)," *London Magazine: or, Gentleman's Monthly Intelligencer* (London), 45 (1776): 339. *A brief narrative of the Indian charity-school, in Lebanon in Connecticut, New England; founded and carried on by that faithful servant of God, the Rev. Mr. Eleazar Wheelock,* [ed. Nathaniel Whitaker] (London, 1766; repr. [Rochester, N.Y., 1909?]). P. Campbell, *Travels in North America* (Langton and Ganong). "Census of Niagara, 1783," *Ontario Reg.* ([Madison; N.J.]), 1 (1968): 197–214. *Corr. of Hon. Peter Russell* (Cruikshank and Hunter). *Corr. of Lieut. Governor Simcoe* (Cruikshank). *The documentary history of the state of New-York ...*, ed. E. B. O'Callaghan (4v., Albany, 1849–51), 4. [Frederick Haldimand], "Private diary of Gen. Haldimand," *PAC Report,* 1889: 127, 129, 131, 135, 139, 145, 151, 157–59, 161, 167, 273. *Johnson papers* (Sullivan et al.). *The letters of Eleazar Wheelock's Indians,* ed. J. D. McCallum (Hanover, 1932). *Loyalist narratives from Upper Canada,* ed. J. J. Talman (Toronto, 1946). *Mich. Pioneer Coll.*, 12 (1887); 20 (1892). Norton, *Journal* (Klinck and Talman). *NYCD* (O'Callaghan and Fernow), vol. 8. "Petitions for grants of land" (Cruikshank), *OH,* 24: 30. *The private papers of James Boswell from Malahide Castle; in the collection of Lt.-Colonel Ralph Heyward Isham,* ed. Geoffrey Scott and F. A. Pottle (18v., [Mount Vernon, N.Y., 1928–34]), 11. "The probated wills of men prominent in the public affairs of early Upper Canada," ed. A. F. Hunter, *OH,* 23 (1926): 341–44. U.S., Congress, *American state papers* (Lowrie et al.), class II, vol. [1]. *Valley of Six Nations* (Johnston). Eleazar Wheelock, *A plain and faithful narrative of the original design, rise, progress, and present state of the Indian charity-school at Lebanon, in Connecticut* (Boston, 1763).

William Allen, *The American biographical dictionary ...* (3rd ed., Boston, 1857). "Calendar of state papers," *PAC Report,* 1933: 87–88, 100. *Handbook of American Indians* (Hodge), 2: 741–42. Barbara Graymont, *The Iroquois in the American revolution* (Syracuse, N.Y., 1972). R. H. Kohn, *Eagle and sword: the federalists and the creation of the military establishment in America, 1783–1802* (New York and London, 1975). W. H. Mohr, *Federal Indian relations, 1774–1788* (Philadelphia, 1933). W. L. Stone, *Life of Joseph Brant -Thayendanegea ...* (2v., New York, 1838). M. W. Hamilton, "Joseph Brant painted by

Rigaud," *New York Hist.* (Cooperstown, N.Y.), 40 (1959): 247–54; "Joseph Brant: 'the most painted Indian.'" *New York Hist.,* 39 (1958): 119–32. F. W. Hodge, "Some portraits of Thayendanegea," *Indian Notes* (New York), 5 (1928): 207–17. C. M. Johnston, "Joseph Brant, the Grand River lands and the northwest crisis," *OH,* 55 (1963): 267–82. E. H. Phillips, "Timothy Pickering at his best: Indian commissioner, 1790–1794," Essex Institute, *Hist. Coll.* (Salem, Mass.), 102 (1966): 163–202. L. B. Richardson, "The Dartmouth Indians, 1800–1893," *Dartmouth Alumni Magazine* (Hanover), 22 (1929–30): 524–27. G. J. Smith, "Capt. Joseph Brant's status as a chief, and some of his descendants," OH, 12 (1914): 89–101.

Appendix B
Koñwatsiʔtsiañni

Barbara Graymont

Koñwatsiʔtsiaiéñni (Gonwatsijayenni, meaning someone lends her a flower, Mary Brant), Mohawk, head of the Six Nations matrons; born *circa* 1736; d. 16 April 1796 at Kingston (Ontario).

Details of Mary Brant's birth, parentage, and early years are obscure. She may have been born at the upper Mohawk castle of Canajoharie (near Little Falls, New York), her family's home; or, like her younger brother Joseph [Thayendanegea], she may have been born while her parents were living in the Ohio region. John Norton in his *Journal* states that Joseph was born at Cayahoga (near Akron, Ohio) and was "descended from Wyandot prisoners adopted by the Mohawks on both the father and the mother's side." William Allen, who had interviewed Joseph Brant's son Joseph, stated, perhaps on the son's authority, that Brant's father was an Onondaga chief. This assertion would not negate Norton's claim that the Brants were of Wyandot ancestry and Mohawk nationality since, in the matrilineal Iroquois society, children took the nationality of their mother. Some authorities claim that the father of Mary and Joseph was a respected sachem. According to Norton, he was "a great Warrior" who died when the children were young. The mother then took Mary and Joseph with her to Canajoharie shortly before the outbreak of the Seven Years' War. Eleazar Wheelock, at whose mission school in Connecticut

Joseph Brant once studied, said that the Brants were "a Family of Distinction" among the Mohawks.

There was a persistent tradition in the Mohawk valley among both whites and Indians that Mary and Joseph Brant were descended from King Hendrick [Theyanoguin]. The nineteenth-century historian and archivist Lyman Copeland Draper, who did painstaking research on the Brant genealogy, found confirmation of such a relationship. A Mohawk woman named Katy Moses, aged seventy-seven in 1879 and "distantly related to Brant's last wife," stated that "she learned many years ago from aged Mohawks, that Brant's mother was a daughter of Old King Hendrick." Joseph Brant's granddaughter Charlotte told Draper that Joseph's mother was a granddaughter of Hendrick.

Mary, or Molly as she was generally known, possibly attended one of the Church of England mission schools in the Mohawk valley. Her later letters, if authentically from her own hand, show that she was mistress of a fine penmanship and a proper English style. There is some evidence, however, that she was only semi-literate and that the letters were dictated to an amanuensis.

She evidently accompanied the delegation of twelve Mohawk principal men who, under the leadership of Hendrick, went to Philadelphia in the winter of 1754–55 to discuss with Pennsylvania officials the fraudulent sale of lands in the Wyoming valley to a group of Connecticut speculators. Christian Daniel Claus, who had accompanied the delegation, stated that at Albany on the return trip an English captain "fell in Love wth. Ms. Mary Brant who was then pretty likely not havg. had the small pox."

According to a Mohawk valley tradition, Molly first attracted Sir William Johnson's attention at a militia muster, when she leaped upon the back of a horse behind an officer and hung on to him as the horse dashed about the field, much to the amusement of the spectators. Their first child, Peter Warren Johnson, was born in 1759, the same year that Johnson's wife Catherine Weissenberg died. Molly and Sir William had seven more children who survived infancy. Although Johnson referred to her in his will as his "prudent & faithfull Housekeeper" and to the children as his natural children, there is a persistent tradition that they were married according to Indian ceremony, which was not recognized as legal for members of the white community. Johnson treated her with every respect, furnished her and the children with every comfort and luxury befitting an upper-class family, and provided generously for them in his will. He also permitted the children to bear his surname. The eldest, named in honour of Johnson's uncle, Sir Peter Warren, probably received his early education in the Mohawk valley but in 1772 was sent to Montréal for further schooling. In 1773 Johnson sent him to Philadelphia, where he was apprenticed to a dry-goods merchant. Indicative of his genteel upbringing were his requests to his father for a watch so that he might be on time for dinner appointments and for work, some French and English books to read at leisure, a Mohawk book so that he would not forget his Indian tongue, and help in securing a violin. Of his mother, he requested some Indian curiosities to show his Philadelphia friends. His letters indicate a close and affectionate relationship between Johnson, his Mohawk consort, and their children.

Mary Brant presided over Johnson's household with intelligence, ability, grace, and charm, and she effectively managed the estate during Johnson's many and prolonged absences. A contemporary author described her as a "daughter to a sachem, who possessed an uncommonly agreeable person, and good understanding." Because of her important family connections among the Iroquois, she was also of inestimable value to Sir William during his negotiations with the Indians.

After Sir William's death in 1774, she and her children moved to Canajoharie, for the Johnson Hall estate had passed into the hands of John Johnson, Sir William's white son. At Canajoharie she was highly respected both as the relict of Sir William and as a woman of quality in her own right. She maintained a comfortable existence in a well-furnished house and dressed in Indian style, but in the finest cloth. In his will Sir William had left her a lot in the Kingsland Patent (in present-day Herkimer County), a black female slave, and £200, New York currency. With her legacy she opened a store among the Indians, where she traded chiefly in rum.

Upon the outbreak of hostilities between Great Britain and the colonies, the Brants became staunch loyalists. Early in the conflict Mary Brant did all in her power to feed and assist those loyalists who had taken refuge in the woods, and she also sent ammunition to supporters of the king. In August 1777 she performed one of her most noteworthy achievements when she dispatched Indian runners to inform Barrimore Matthew St. Leger's forces, then besieging Fort Stanwix (Rome, N.Y.), of the approach of a large body of American militia. This timely warning resulted in the successful ambush of the Americans by the Indians and loyalists at nearby Oriskany.

After the battle the Oriska Indians, a part of the Oneida nation who had supported the Americans in the campaign, revenged themselves upon the Mohawks, and particularly upon Mary Brant, by attacking and despoiling both Canajoharie and Fort Hunter, New York, the lower Mohawk castle. Mary Brant and her family, who had lost most of their possessions in the attack, took refuge at Onondaga (near Syracuse), the capital of the Six Nations Confederacy, where she submitted her grievances to the confederacy council and was promised satisfaction.

She then moved to Cayuga (south of present Cayuga, New York), where she had distant relatives; and during the months of discouragement after the Stanwix campaign, when the Indians pondered their losses and wavered in their support of the king, she rendered invaluable service by encouraging and steadying them in their alliance. In one important council she even publicly rebuked the venerable Kaiñ?kwaahtoñ leading war chief of the confederacy, for counselling peace with the Americans. Her entreaties won over the whole council. Daniel Claus correctly assessed her influence with the Iroquois: "one word from her goes farther with them than a thousand from any white Man without Exception who in general must purchase their Interest at a high rate."

Soon afterwards Major John Butler prevailed upon Mary Brant to come to live at Niagara (near Youngstown, New York), a major military base where she could be of much use to the British by advising and interceding with the Indians. As head of a society of Six Nations matrons which was particularly influential among the young warriors, she was highly esteemed in the confederacy. She arrived at Fort Niagara in the late fall of 1777 and for the next several months was of inestimable assistance there as a diplomat and stateswoman. She was consulted by the Indians on all issues of importance and often cautioned them against making unwise proposals to the commander of the fort.

In July 1779, at the suggestion of the commander, who found his facilities at the fort strained, she reluctantly left her elderly mother behind and went with her family to Montréal, where she placed two of her daughters in a boarding school. In the autumn of 1779, when she heard of the destruction being wrought in Iroquois country by the forces of the Sullivan-Clinton expedition she hastened to return to Niagara to be of what assistance she could. But she never reached Niagara, for she agreed instead to remain at Carleton Island, New York, where there was a large Six Nations settlement and where she was able to assuage the disgruntled and resentful Indians during the discouraging winter of 1779–80. The commander, Alexander Fraser, highly praised her leadership during those months, affirming that the Indians' "uncommon good behaviour is in a great Measure to be ascribed to Miss Molly Brants Influence over them, which is far superior to that of all their Chiefs put together." A woman of spirit and sometimes of temper, she remained fiercely loyal to her family and to the memory of Sir William and bitter towards the American rebels, who had driven her and her people from their homeland.

In 1783, at the end of the war, she moved to Cataraqui (Kingston, Ontario), where Haldimand ordered a house to be built for her. She lived the remainder of her life at Kingston, highly respected by her neighbours. In 1783 also, Haldimand set her pension at £100 annually, the highest paid to an Indian. In addition she received compensation from the British government for her losses during the war. She made a trip back to the Mohawk valley in 1785 and visited Schenectady, where the Americans attempted to persuade her to return with her family. Several years later she was offered financial compensation by the Americans for her confiscated lands if she and her children would return and settle, which offer she "rejected with the utmost contempt."

Little is known of her later years, though reports of travellers afford the occasional glimpse. On 13 September 1794 Mrs. John Graves Simcoe [Elizabeth Posthuma Gwillim] permitted Mary Brant, who was ill, to travel with her aboard the *Mississauga* from Niagara to Kingston. "She speaks English well," noted Mrs. Simcoe in her *Diary*, "and is a civil and very sensible old woman." In April of the following year Mary Brant successfully prescribed a favourite Indian remedy, the root of sweet flag (*acorus calamus*), for Governor Simcoe, who had been extremely ill with a persistent cough. The medicine relieved his malady "in a very short time."

Mary Brant remained a devout Anglican, regularly attending services at St. George's in Kingston, where she "sat in an honourable place among the English." She died on 16 April 1796 and was buried in the cemetery (now St. Paul's churchyard) in a ceremony conducted by the pastor John Stuart, who had once been missionary to the Mohawks at Fort Hunter. All her daughters, save one who remained single, married white men of distinction in Upper Canada. Her son George Johnson, known among the Indians as Big George, farmed and taught a day school not far from Brantford for many years. Peter died in 1777 in Philadelphia while serving with the 26th Foot.

A woman of high intelligence and remarkable ability who was at ease in two cultures, Mary Brant personified the dignity and influence accorded to respected mothers among the Iroquois people. In a society in which the mothers chose the sachems and influenced the warriors, Mary Brant played a unique role. Her descent from a high-ranking Indian family, her liaison with Sir William Johnson, and her own talents enabled her to wield great power at a critical moment. This power she exerted at much personal cost in a cause which she believed just. Her loyalty to her own family, to her people, and to the traditional Iroquois alliance with the crown was steadfast and enduring. The military officials who had most to do with Indian affairs during the American Revolution recognized how essential her leadership was in maintaining the morale and loyalty of the Iroquois. History has subsequently been less than kind to her in often overlooking her achievements. Unquestionably she was one of the most devoted United Empire Loyalists.

Notes

BL, Add. MSS 21661–892 (transcripts at PAC). Clements Library, Sydney papers, secret service payments, 1782–91, Nepean papers, compensation for Joseph and Mary Brant, 31 March 1786. N.Y. Hist. Soc. (New York), Misc. MSS Haldimand, Haldimand to John Johnson, 27 May 1783. New York Public Library, Manuscripts and Archives Division, American loyalist transcripts, XXI, p.331; XLIV, pp. 107, 118; Schuyler papers, Indian boxes, box 14. PAC, MG 19, F1; RG 1, L3, 186. PRO, CO 42 (mfm. at PAC). Wis., State Hist. Soc. (Madison), Draper MSS, ser. F.

Can., Dept. of Militia and Defence, General Staff, *A history of the organization, development and services of the military and naval forces of Canada from the peace of Paris in 1763, to the present time* ... (3v., [Ottawa, 1919–20]), II. [C D. Claus], *Daniel Claus' narrative of his relations with Sir William Johnson and experiences in the Lake George fight*, [ed. A. S. Walcott] ([New York], 1904). [A. MacV. Grant], *Memoirs of an american lady* ... (2v., London, 1808). [E.P. Gwillim (Simcoe)], *The Diary of Mrs. John Graves Simcoe* ..., ed. J. R. Robertson (Toronto, 1911; reprint 1973). [S. A. Harrison], *Memoir of Lieut. Col. Tench Tilghman* ... (Albany, N.Y., 1876; repr. New York, 1971). *Johnson papers* (Sullivan et al.). *Kingston before War of 1812* (Preston). [John Norton], *The journal of Major John Norton, 1816*, ed. C. F. Klinck and J. J. Talman (Toronto, 1970). *NYCD* (O'Callaghan and Fernow), VIII. *The Susquehannah Company papers*, ed. J. P. Boyd (4 vols., Ithaca, N.Y., 1962), I. Eleazar Wheelock, *A plain and faithful narrative of the original design, rise, progress, and present state of the Indian charity-school at Lebanon, in Connecticut* (Boston, Mass., 1763).

William Allen, *The American biographical dictionary* ... (3rd ed., Boston, Mass., 1857), 131–32. *Notable American women, 1607–1950: a biographical dictionary*, ed. E. T. James et al. (3 vols., Cambridge, Mass., 1971), I, 229–30. Graymon, *Iroquois*. W. L. [and W. L.] Stone, *The life and times of Sir William Johnson, bart.* (2 vols., Albany, N.Y., 1865). H. P. Gundy, "Molly Brant — loyalist," *OH*, XLV (1953), 97–108. M. W. Hamilton, "Sir William Johnson's wives," *New York History* (Cooperstown), XXXVIII (1957), 18–28. Jean Johsnton, "Ancestry and descendants of Molly Brant," *OH*, LXIII (1971), 86–92.

Appendix C
Distribution of the Black Population of Canada West by Place of Residence, 1861

Michael Wayne

ALGOMA DISTRICT	12
BRANT COUNTY (465)	
Brantford	58
Town of Brantford	284
Burford	73
Onondaga	3
Paris	18
South Dumfries	15
Tuscarora	14
BRUCE COUNTY (10)	
Arran	2
Brant	2
Kincardine	1
Village of Kincardine	5
CARLETON COUNTY (3)	
Fitzroy	1
March	1
Nepean	1

DUNDAS COUNTY (20)	
Matilda	1
Morrisburgh	6
Williamsburgh	12
Winchester	1
DURHAM COUNTY (48)	
Bowmanville	10
Cavan	2
Clarke	6
Hope	4
Newcastle	7
Port Hope	19
ELGIN COUNTY (85)	
Bayham	8
Malahide	23
Southwold	11
St. Thomas	40
Yarmouth	3

ESSEX COUNTY (3,508)		Collingwood	2
Amherstburg	373	Derby	1
Anderdon	456	Egremont	4
Colchester	937	Euphrasia	13
East Sandwich	442	Glenelg	35
Gosfield	101	Holland	16
Maidstone	234	Melancthon	7
Malden	275	Normanby	45
Malden Asylum	9	Osprey	7
Rochester	6	Owen Sound	86
Town of Sandwich	95	St. Vincent	6
West Sandwich	47	Sullivan	16
Windsor	533	Sydenham	5

FRONTENAC COUNTY (169)		HALDIMAND COUNTY (253)	
Bedford	2	Canboro	6
Hinchinbrooke	2	Dunn	5
Kingston	21	Dunnville	62
Penitentiary	78	Mouton	10
Pittsburgh	14	North Cayuga	118
Portland	9	Oneida	23
Portsmouth	10	Seneca	27
Storrington	9	Walpole	2
Wolfe Island	24		

		HALTON COUNTY (233)	
GLENGARRY COUNTY (43)		Esquesing	11
Charlottenburgh	13	Georgetown	3
Lancaster	30	Nassagaweya	51
		Nelson	22
GRENVILLE COUNTY (18)		Oakville	37
Edwardsburg	5	Trafalgar	109
Kemptville	1		
Prescott	12	HASTINGS COUNTY (87)	
		Belleville	33
GREY COUNTY (379)		Hastings Road	5
Artemesia	105	Huntingdon	4
Bentinck	31	Madoc	1

Marmora	1	Sarnia	4
Rawdon	7	Town of Sarnia	45
Sidney	13	Warwick	5
Thurlow	4		
Trenton	8	**LANARK COUNTY (12)**	
Tyendinaga	11	Burgess	6
		Perth	4
HURON COUNTY (92)		Ramsey	2
Ashfield	6		
Biddulph	59	**LEEDS COUNTY (64)**	
Colborne	1	Bastard	20
Grey	12	Brockville	9
Howick	1	Elizabethtown	27
Hullet	1	Leeds	8
McGillivray	1		
McKillop	1	**LENNOX COUNTY (29)**	
Stephen	8	Adolphustown	1
Usborne	1	Camden	4
Wawanosh	1	Ernestown	8
		Fredericksburgh	2
KENT COUNTY (4,736)		Napanee	6
Camden and Gore	669	Richmond	7
Chatham	1,252	Sheffield	1
Chatham and Gore	737		
Dover	209	**LINCOLN COUNTY (911)**	
East Tilbury	43	Caistor	8
Harwich	457	Gainsborough	1
Howard	51	Grantham	96
Orford	8	Grimsby	33
Raleigh	1,310	Louth	17
		Niagara	60
LAMBTON COUNTY (133)		Town of Niagara	87
Brooke	2	St. Catharines	609
Dawn	55		
Euphemia	15	**MIDDLESEX COUNTY (319)**	
Moore	4	Caradoc	7
Plympton	3	Delaware	6

East Williams	6	West Whitby	2
Ekfrid	15	Town of Whitby	8
Lobo	13		
London	192	**OXFORD COUNTY (552)**	
Metcalfe	8	Blandford	7
Mosa	29	Blenheim	19
North Dorchester	24	Dereham	51
Strathroy	8	East Nissouri	1
West Nissouri	11	East Oxford	20
		East Zorra	25
NORFOLK COUNTY (149)		Ingersoll	149
Carlotteville	6	North Norwich	17
Town of Simcoe	48	North Oxford	17
Townsend	8	South Norwich	148
Walsingham	3	West Oxford	31
Windham	31	West Zorra	11
Woodhouse	53	Woodstock	56
NORTHUMBERLAND		**PEEL COUNTY (73)**	
COUNTY (129)		Albion	1
Alnwick	1	Brampton	12
Village of Brighton	4	Caledon	6
Cobourg	61	Chinguacousy	17
Colborne	3	Toronto	37
Cramahe	3		
Haldimand	23	**PERTH COUNTY (105)**	
Hamilton	24	Blanchard	11
Murray	9	Downie	1
Seymour	1	Easthope	3
		Ellice	6
ONTARIO COUNTY (42)		Elma	7
East Whitby	8	Hibbert	2
Mara	1	Logan	1
Oshawa	8	Mitchell	3
Pickering	12	Mornington	13
Reach	1	South Easthope	5
Scott	2	St. Mary's	14

Stratford	38	Flos	15
Wallace	1	Innisfil	7
		Mono	9
PETERBOROUGH		Mulmur	1
COUNTY (67)		Nottawasaga	2
Ashburnham	7	Orillia	9
Asphodel	1	Oro	97
Ennismore	4	Reformatory	7
Minden	8	Sunnidale	14
Monaghan	10	Tecumseth	2
Otonabee	3	Vespra	1
Peterborough	23	West Gwillimbury	7
Smith	11		
		STORMONT COUNTY (35)	
PRESCOTT COUNTY (2)		Cornwall	17
Longueuil	1	Town of Cornwall	14
South Plantagenet	1	Osnabruck	4
PRINCE EDWARD		**VICTORIA COUNTY (3)**	
COUNTY (12)		Lutterworth	1
Ameliasburgh	5	Mariposa	2
Hallowell	3		
Picton	3	**WATERLOO COUNTY (123)**	
Sophiasburgh	1	Berlin	9
		Galt	31
RENFREW COUNTY (3)		North Dumfries	7
Westneath	3	Preston	2
		South Waterloo	5
RUSSELL COUNTY (9)		Waterloo	1
Clarence	9	Wellesley	41
		Wilmot	7
SIMCOE COUNTY (300)		Woolwich	20
Adjala	2		
Barrie	54	**WELLAND COUNTY (535)**	
Bradford	1	Bertie	78
Collingwood	70	Chippawa	32
Essa	2	Clifton	26

Crowland	1	**YORK COUNTY (482)**	
Fort Erie	35	East Gwillimbury	40
Humberstone	18	Etobicoke	83
Jail	4	Holland Landing	5
Pelham	13	King	41
Stamford	190	Markham	10
Thorold	61	North Gwillimbury	5
Village of Thorold	39	Scarborough	5
Wainfleet	7	Vaughan	30
Willoughby	31	Whitchurch	1
		York	224
WELLINGTON COUNTY (410)		Yorkville	38
Amaranth	4		
Arthur	1	**CITY OF HAMILTON (476)**	
Elora	9	St. Andrew Ward	111
Eramosa	8	St. George's Ward	86
Garafraxa	7	St. Lawrence Ward	171
Guelph	7	St. Mary's Ward	53
Town of Guelph	39	St. Patrick's Ward	55
Maryborough	14		
Minto	1	**CITY OF KINGSTON (162)**	
Nichol	3	Cataraqui Ward	23
Peel	296	Frontenac Ward	18
Pilkington	14	General Hospital	1
Puslinch	7	Ontario Ward	11
		Rideau Ward	32
WENTWORTH COUNTY (364)		St. Lawrence Ward	25
Ancaster	51	Sydenham Ward	12
Barton	140	Victoria Ward	40
Beverley	13		
Binbrook	4	**CITY OF LONDON (370)**	
Dundas	19	Ward 1[a]	370
East Flamboro	31		
Glanford	16	**CITY OF OTTAWA (34)**	
Saltfleet	27	By Ward	19
West Flamboro	63	Victoria Ward	2
		Wellington Ward	13

CITY OF TORONTO (987)		St. James' Ward	86
St. Andrew's Ward	116	St. John's Ward	539
St. David's Ward	22	St. Lawrence Ward	48
St. George's Ward	21	St. Patrick's Ward	155

a) The blacks of London were actually dispersed throughout the seven wards of the city, but confusion in the way in which the enumerators entered the data makes it appear as if they all lived in a single ward.
Source: Canada West Manuscript Census Schedules, 1861.

AGMV Marquis

MEMBER OF THE SCABRINI GROUP

Quebec, Canada
2001